TESOL Interfaces

TESOL Interfaces

Compendium

Volumes 1-6

Edited by
David Kent

Pedagogy Press

Copyright © 2017.
All rights reserved.

The copyright of individual articles remains with each author(s). Articles reprinted, with light editing, and author permission.

No part of this publication may be reproduced, distributed, or transmitted in any form or by any means, including photocopying, recording, or other electronic or mechanical methods, without prior written permission, except in the case of brief quotations embodied in critical reviews and certain other noncommercial uses permitted by copyright law.

Disclaimer: While efforts were taken to ensure that the articles included herein present accurate data, the views expressed by the authors are their own, and do not necessarily reflect those of the editor or of the publisher.

Trademark Notice: Product or corporate names may be trademarks or registered trademarks, and are used only for identification and explanation without intent to infringe.

Although every precaution has been taken to verify the accuracy of the information contained herein, the author and publisher assume no responsibility for any errors or omissions. No liability is assumed for damages that may result from the use of information contained within.

A catalogue record for this book is available from the National Library of Australia

ISBN: 9781925555196 (paperback)

Pedagogy Press
www.pedagogypress.com
Sydney, Australia.

Special Edition

DEDICATION

*For students and alumni of the
Graduate School of TESOL-MALL.*

CONTENTS

Acknowledgments — xi
Contributors — xii
Preface — xiii

Part One – TESOL Interfaces 1(1) – 2007 — 1

1. There is a place for learning experiences — 2
   Darryl Daniel Bautista
2. Consensus in professional development schools: A discourse approach to conflict — 5
   Rodney W. Pederson
3. Effective multimedia-based learning in EFL: Comparing two comprehension models — 30
   David Kent
4. Negotiating diversity through an arts-based method: Using dramatic monologue to explore responsible teacher conversations — 43
   Darryl Daniel Bautista & Julian Kitchen

Part Two – TESOL Interfaces 2(1) – 2008 — 71

5. Solidifying academic tradition — 72
   David Kent
6. Multimedia and language learning websites and their place in English education: Evaluation strategies for EFL teachers — 75
   Ezekiel Mentillo
7. The social construction of literacy – A case study of literacy practices in the UK — 101
   Kolawade Waziri Olagboyega

8. A documents analysis of the English textbooks currently used in Korean elementary schools with some comments on problems inherent to the system: A practical approach to teaching English mostly in English (TEE, TEmE)   125
Mark C. Love

9. The new 21st century literacy: Problems and challenges for the digital age   145
Thomas D. Clark

Part Three – TESOL Interfaces 3(1) & Interfaces 3(2) – 2009   149

10. Language is used   150
Mark C. Love

11. Responding to behaviors of resistance in Japanese university EFL classrooms   153
John Burrell

12. Realizing benefits of CALL (Computer Assisted Language Learning) in English language learning classrooms   168
Chris J. Brennan

13. Culture in English language Teaching   200
JiaJia Ren

14. The need for a comprehensive SLA theory: What place does that theory have in TEFL?   207
Eric D. Reynolds

15. Special issue: 1st Woosong mini-conference   239

16. Research Skills   240
Mark C. Love

17. Digital storytelling: Making meaning from experiences   242
David Kent

18. Online-English activities for the classroom and at home   243
Michael Peacock

19. Task-based blogging: An invaluable asset to the EFL/ESL teacher — 246
Adam Parsons

20. Evaluating and selecting internet-based instructional tools for the EFL classroom: Where to go and how to get there — 252
Ezekiel Mentillo

Part Four – TESOL Interfaces 4(1) & Interfaces 4(2) – 2010 — 263

21. A petition for practical pedagogical projects — 264
Mark C. Love

22. Sacred, scared, scarred: An autoethnographic portrait of teaching as unbecoming amidst the ambiguities of life — 267
Paul Badenhorst

23. The JungChul cyber English learning program — 296
MiSug Gu & David Kent

24. English quest – A large scale, task-based activity — 308
Joel Hopkinson

25. Making students critical readers in a Korean middle school reading class — 319
Yoojin Sohn

26. Special issue: 2nd Woosong mini-conference — 333

27. Getting started with your research project — 334
Eric D. Reynolds & Josephine Mirador

28. Getting online with Moodle in the EFL context — 335
Michael Peacock

29. Digital storytelling for your Classroom! — 336
Justin McKibben

30. Webquests as a task-based, inquiry-oriented, computer assisted, language learning exercise — 337
Joel Hopkinson

31. Replacing the workbook with blog homework — 338
Adam Parsons

32. Science and English integrated learning based on topics — 339
ChanMi Park

Part Five – TESOL Interfaces 5(1) – 2011   340
    33. Particularity, practicality, and possibility in TESOL   341
        Josephine Mirador
    34. Adoption of famous characters in an RPG setting   344
        Michael Armstrong
    35. Composition of the Modern Family   355
        Gerald Von Bourdeau
    36. Is conformity really the answer? On Simpson's East-West classroom culture conflicts   367
        Neil Briggs
    37. Issues with academic vocabulary acquisition suggest low level learners need ESAP not EGAP   378
        Mat Terret

Part Six – TESOL Interfaces 6(1) – 2012   400
    38. Eclecticism in TESOL   401
        Eric D. Reynolds
    39. Intrinsic and extrinsic motivation (and discipline) in the EFL environment   403
        Tory S. Thorkelson
    40. Giving creative control to EFL students through short film-making   420
        Sarah Elizabeth Seitzinger
    41. Getting started with TESOL research: Searching the literature   453
        Eric D. Reynolds

ACKNOWLEDGEMENTS

The hard work, and dedication, behind producing each of the journal issues found in this compendium is attributable to:

Editor(s) in chief
Eric Reynolds (2012-)
David Kent (2007-2011)

Senior Editors
David Kent (2012-)
Eric Reynolds (2007-2011)
Myeonghee Kim
Mark Love
Sunyoung Park
Rodney Pederson

Editorial Board
Darryl Bautista
Candace MacDonald
Josephine F. Mirador
Kolawole Waziri Olagboyega
Richard Sjoquist

Consulting Editor
Matthew Hathaway

CONTRIBUTORS

Michael Armstrong

Paul Badenhorst

Darryl Daniel Bautista

Chris J. Brennan

Neil Briggs

John Burrell

Thomas D. Clark

MiSug Gu

Joel Hopkinson

David Kent

Julian Kitchen

Mark C. Love

Justin McKibben

Josephine Mirador

Ezekiel Mentillo

Kolawole Waziri Olagboyega

ChanMi Park

Adam Parsons

Michael Peacock

Rodney Pederson

JiaJia Ren

Eric D. Reynolds

Sarah Elizabeth Seitzinger

YooJin Sohn

Mat Terret

Tory S. Thorkelson

Gerald Von Bourdeau

PREFACE

The *TESOL Interfaces Compendium* is a collection of the first six volumes of the faculty journal of the Graduate School of TESOL-MALL at Woosong University in the Republic of Korea. The journal was initially established with the intent of providing alumni, current students, members of the public, and the wider academic community an avenue for publishing their works while going through the peer-review process. As such, *TESOL Interfaces* was envisioned as an interdisciplinary publication exploring interfaces between TESOL, critical perspectives, and multimedia through mixed, quantitative, and qualitative research methodologies. To date, the journal has served as a venue for new and experienced researchers to disseminate their work to a wider audience.

Each section of the *TESOL Interfaces Compendium* represents an annual volume of the *TESOL Interfaces* online journal. It is hoped that this book, marking the decennial of the first journal issue, will provide education and something new for all teachers and students of TESOL. Current students of the Graduate School of TESOL-MALL will find much knowledge from their peers, and hopefully, alumni will recall fond memories of their time spent earning their master's degree. Other interested parties may enjoy reading this book and come to understand the passion, dedication, and hard work that goes into becoming a proficient teacher of English to speakers of other languages.

David Kent.

Part One
TESOL Interfaces 1(1)

2007

1. There is a Place for Learning Experiences
Darryl Daniel Bautista

Rather than compose an editorial, it would be best to begin, perhaps, along the lines of a salutation, a celebratory remark for Woosong TESOL-MALL and its latest stride. Beginning an online journal has turned out to be quite a learning experience. Like many new experiences, there is much pre-planning and negotiating. But without our initial steps then we take no steps at all. There is simply a sense of stagnancy. For the teacher researcher desiring change and senses of newness, Diamond and Mullen (1999) offer an advisory detail: "Rather than merely waiting/holding on, May we always seek to grow ..." (460).

And so, welcome to *Interfaces*/인터페이스.

With this first issue, we attempt to cross into the foray of online academic journals. Our site is still being worked and reworked and reworked some more, so bear with us as we, too, learn from what Dewey (1938) terms an educative experience.

As you journey around the site you will discover that there are five faculty members in Woosong University TESOL-MALL. We represent a diverse mix of theoretical approaches when it comes to conceptualizing classroom research. We have come from our past classroom teaching experiences, moved onwards to graduate teaching and currently, our separate career steps have converged here under the banner of TESOL-MALL. With *Interfaces*/인터페이스, we extend our interconnections—our meeting places of research philosophy or the boundaries at which our conceptualizations meet face to face—to those both interested and involved in TESOL-MALL environments.

Our online journal brings to you a diversity of articles relative to issues in TESOL-MALL through research grounded in both quantitative and qualitative design. In this issue, you will note three articles introducing the research frameworks that the authors ascribe to within their particular inquiries. We believe the articles example the scope of topics that future issues of *Interfaces/인터페이스* will offer.

Rod Pederson, TESOL-MALL Academic Director, offers his *Consensus in Professional Development Schools: A Discourse Approach to Conflict*. The article investigates the role of consensus in school/university partnerships by exploring the affect of communication and discourse theories on the literacy practices of English education.

David Kent, TESOL-MALL Assistant Professor, offers his article entitled *Effective Multimedia-based Learning in EFL: Comparing Two Comprehension Models* exploring multimedia-based resources in EFL classrooms. The article discusses concepts of instructor awareness when constructing learning content and when evaluating media resources.

Darryl Bautista, TESOL-MALL Assistant Professor and Julian Kitchen, Assistant Professor from Brock University Canada, offer a collaborative paper titled *Negotiating Diversity through an Arts-Based Method: Using Dramatic Monolog to explore Responsible Teacher Conversations*. The article explores an arts-based method for preservice teachers who negotiate policies of diversity for their future classrooms.

As time passes, we hope to offer more articles relevant to TESOL-MALL research inquiry. For now, we build upon this learning experience in the hopes of seeing *Interfaces/인터페이스* continually change and grow. Connelly and Clandinin (2000) advise that the process of learning "is always changing and it is always going somewhere" (2).

With this in mind, we wish *Interfaces*/ 인터페이스 steady progress along its way.

References
Clandinin, D. J., & Connelly, F. M. (2000). *Narrative inquiry*. San Francisco: John Wiley.
Dewey, J. (1938). *Experience and education*. New York: Touchstone Book, Simon and Schuster.
Diamond, C. T. P., & Mullen, C. A. (1999). The *postmodern educator*. New York: Peter Lang Publishing.

2. Consensus in Professional Development Schools: A Discourse Approach to Conflict
Rodney W. Pederson

This paper reports on the establishment of the Pennsylvania State University-State College Area School District Professional Collaboration Project. While the goal of the project was to create a community of inquiry regarding the literacy practices of State College High School's English program and a better vehicle for teacher education, the interactions between school and university participants focused on issues of trust and consensus. The conflicts arising from these issues not only hindered the goals of the Professional Development School (PDS), but also created a barrier between university and school participants which, in turn, effectively silenced the intern teachers. The project included five university associates (One professor and four Ph.D. students, four mentor teachers, and four intern teachers. Triumvirate groups were formed for the purpose of inquiry. All whole and individual group meetings were recorded and transcribed. This paper investigates the conception of consensus as being necessary to school/university partnerships by examining how the application of communication and discourse theories work to hinder or facilitate inquiry into the literacy practices of English education. This paper found that consensus served to hinder inquiry and that the discourse perspective of 'dissensus' (Trimbor, 1998) allowed a free exchange of ideas necessary for successful inquiry.

> *I look at it as if I am in a tug of war and I am right in the middle of it. I can relate to both parties and I want to stay in both parties. That is basically why I am so quiet at those meetings. Because it is set against both the university as well as the high school. They are set against each other for*

some reason. I don't know where this conflict came from. It is as if we take one side, then the other will get mad at us. It shouldn't be about taking sides, you should freely express what you are thinking about, but you can't do that (Intern Denise Savini, 11/23/98).

So we have established that there are several discourse communities going on out there. There is yours that is somewhat uninitiated, ours that is trench warfare talk, and yours that is always big words (Mentor Sandra Wyngaard, 9/30/98).

Introduction

While participating as a teacher researcher in the Pennsylvania State University-State College Area school District Professional Collaboration Project, I became a member of a group that was dedicated to the establishment of a Professional Development School (PDS) for the purpose of reforming traditional models of teacher education. PDS's, and the various other names associated with them, such as School/University collaborations, communities of inquiry/practice, and magnet schools have become increasingly common in teacher education in American universities (Beach & Myers, 2001). The central organizing concept of the program was to be the reflective and scholarly inquiry of practice in English Education. The PDS was comprised of four intern teachers (two undergraduate and two Masters level students), five mentor teachers, and five university associates (four doctoral students and one professor). Although participants' expectations upon entering this program were those of engaging in collaborative teaching and research, conflicts between and within the three groups involved in the program were to frame the experiences of the PDS's inaugural year. In my capacity as a university associate it might be assumed that my perspectives on the PDS were vastly different from those of participants from the other groups. While this was true in some instances, I found that I shared Denise and Sandra's concerns that the three groups within the PDS were positioned as adversaries rather than collaborators.

In looking at the three groups that formed the PDS, one can question what differences underlie each group that would explain the adversarial relationships. As members of each group were products of public schools and institutions of higher learning, it might be assumed that a such shared discourse communities would foster collaborative relations. However, as discourse theorist's (Foucault, 1984; Gee, 1993; Bourdieu, 1991; Lankshear, 1997) point out, each individual is a member of multiple discourse communities, which overlap and agree or conflict with those of others. Mentor teachers shared the discourse of the university, albeit at an undergraduate or Masters level, but spent the majority of their professional lives within the discourse community of the public school. Intern teachers shared the discourse of both the public school and university as students, not as teachers. As teachers, university associates shared the discourse of the public schools, but not the discourse of the individual school, and shared the discourse of the university, but at a higher academic level than either the mentor or intern teachers. These similarities and differences in educational and professional experiences constituted what Gee (1993) calls an 'identity kit' which served as the basis for individual and group social interactions. Despite the good intentions of all, conflict marked the experiences of all in the public spaces of group meetings.

Literature regarding the formation of PDS's commonly report that conflicts between individuals and participant groups are not only common, but inevitable (Clift et al., 1997; Osguthorpe, 1998). In relevant literature causes for conflicts vary from singular to schematic interpretations. Often these interpretations report problems in communication as a general cause while listing individual, discrete causes under the heading of communication. Schverak (1998) reports that communication problems among university members and teachers, university members and interns, and between teachers manifest themselves in conflict over the negotiation of roles, goals,

and structure of a program. However, there may be a simpler (more elegant) way to explain these conflicts. Discourse theory not only allows a singular explanation for the causes of conflict in a professional collaboration, but also defines conflict as being a necessary aspect of collaborative partnerships. From a discursive perspective, then, conflicts may be viewed as extant to the realm of judgment as a necessary step in the creation of a collaborative partnership. More important, communication theory does not interrogate how the ideologies of different groups, as manifested through perceptions of differing pedagogies, become the primary site of conflict. In viewing ideology as subservient to communication, communication theory allows the entrenchment of we-they dichotomies instead of the negotiated construction of new subjectivities for the purpose of educational reform.

Communication Theory

Literature reporting communication as a general cause of conflicts within professional development schools often display commonalties in analytic approaches that are presented as specific schema that may be used to identify individual problems in communication. Trubowitz & Long (1997) report that a lack of communication in the negotiation of roles and program structures within a PDS often result in increased conflicts. Kersch & Masztal (1998) report that problems in communication may be more clearly seen as arising from participant's differing conceptions of individual roles within the program, the goals of the program, and dissatisfaction with the structural elements of the program (meeting times, teacher release time, and decision making apparatus). Schverak (1999) also report conflicts as being embedded in differing perceptions of roles, goals, and program structures.

Here, the fundamental causes of conflict are seen as arising from ambiguities in program structure that must negotiated by the participants, which agrees with NCATE's PDS Standards Project's assertion that although clear structural guidelines serve to reduce conflict, ongoing negotiation of program design is necessary (Osguthorpe, 1998). These types of analytic frameworks focus on individual elements of communication, for example the negotiation of roles, to reach a consensus. In this way, it is the process of communication through negotiation that is the means of obtaining something of value to the program, namely, consensus. This problem solving orientation views consensus as a possible and necessary outcome of a successful PDS.

Other studies seek to extend the concept of conflict resolution through negotiation by focusing on how the ideologies of individual participants impede communication. Friend & Cook (1996) report that analyses of the interactions between participants reveals communication problems as arising from conflict within individuals, between individuals with different goals, and individuals with the same goals. Similarly, Clift (1997) reports that communication problems are based within the limitations imposed by the definition of roles, conceptions of what it means to work as a professional within a given institution, conceptions of professional learning, and competition among educators for attention and career advancement. While these studies shift the analytical focus of ineffective communication to differing ideologies among participants, the purpose of conflict resolution remains as the impetus for analysis.

Friend & Cook (1996) state that conflict is neither good nor bad, but is labeled one way or the other through negotiation. "Often, professionals who successfully manage conflict develop more open, trusting relationships with one another. This facilitates their subsequent interactions" (200). Clift (1997) takes a similar approach by acknowledging that participants belong to different discourse communities, but report that the attainment of a common language, through negotiation, is the primary goal of communication analysis.

The applications of communication theory to professional development schools that view consensus as a desirable goal attainable through processes of conflict resolution are insufficient as they do not conceptualize ideology as the primary basis for conflict. This view of conflict has three deleterious implications. First, the belief that conflict is a negative consequence of interpersonal communication, or at best, neutral. While approaching conflict as something to be solved facilitates the construction and maintenance of a collegial atmosphere, it overlooks how interpersonal relationships serve as a site of ideological struggle. If conflicts are not considered to be necessary, interrogation of the values and beliefs underlying pedagogy become problematic. Second, defining consensus as a valuable goal also defines pedagogy as a static product that may be agreed upon. Although achieving consensus may promote closer working relationships between collaborators, it may also silence voices offering differing ideologies that are an important resource for the vitality of pedagogical innovation. Third, approaching conflicts as a manifestation of communicative deficiencies focuses the attention of PDS participants on their methods of communication, not the messages they are trying to communicate. By focusing on communication as a means for conflict resolution, Denise and Sandra spend their energies attempting to achieve consensus. This strategy may achieve a more emotionally satisfying and less stressful environment, but it will neither change the power dynamics that give voice to some and silence others, nor allow conflicting ideas to be debated in the public space.

Discourse Theory

Discourses, or forms of life, involve agreed-upon combinations of linguistic and non-linguistic behaviors, values, goals, beliefs, assumptions, and the like, which social groups have evolved and which their members share. The important point here is that the language component is inseparable from the other elements in these 'combinations'. Language is interwoven with them to make up each particular Discourse or form of life (Lankshear, 1997, 25).

Discourse theorists commonly name ideology as the central organizing factor of a discourse, or discourse community. Implicit in this conception is that ideology is the driving force behind the relations of power and the distribution of goods and services in a community (Gee, 1993; Bourdieu, 1991; Lankshear, 1997). While applications of communication theory to collaborative partnerships also make reference to ideology as being one basis for conflict, as in Clift (1997) rendering of implicit and explicit conceptions of working and learning in a PDS, ideology does not hold a central position in theory. This conception is problematic as communication theory primarily serves as a vehicle for negotiating tensions for the purpose of creating a collegial atmosphere in which collaboration can occur, not for the creation of a public space that serves to raise ideological questions that may promote innovative literacy practices.

Discourse theory provides a way of viewing social interactions within a PDS without instilling a we-they dichotomy that hinders the successful establishment of a community of practice between the school and the university. Sandra's observation draws a we-they line of conflict that can, then, only be negotiated in terms of language. Denise displays the end-result of this perception by detailing the reasons for the silencing of the interns. In attributing the causes of conflict to differences in language use, the underlying differences in ideology hinted at by Sandra may never be fruitfully discussed. By approaching conflict not as a problem initiated under schemata of communication, but as an inevitable outcome of contact between different groups, discourse theory allows for an analysis of social interactions in which communication is but one part of an integrated and interrelated system of relationships.

By linking the concept of discourse as an interactive system of language and social factors to the functions of a discourse, it is possible to assess conflicts between disparate discourses, as in a PDS, as an inevitable phenomenon. According to Gee (1993) discourses, or discourse communities, are inherently ideological, resistant to internal criticism, defined in opposition to other (competing) discourses, and control the distribution of social power and hierarchy. In this way, discourse theory allows for an analysis of data that not only conceptualizes conflicts in a PDS as a natural consequence of the collaboration between competing discourses, refuting the notion of specific schematic causality, but as a site of ideologically contested, multi-layered, and interrelated linguistic and social relationships. Conflict, then, as an ideological struggle within a community, may be productive as change can only come to a discourse from the inside

(Foucault, 1984: Bourdieu, 1991). Thus, contesting differing educational ideologies in a public space invites participants to engage in a reflexivity of theory and practice that can change the way we think about teaching.

Other theoretical concepts within discourse theory are also instructive regarding the establishment of new discourse communities (PDS's) within a larger discursive structure (public schools); namely, the theories of social reproduction (Bourdieu, 1977; Giroux, 1997; Apple, 1998) and disciplines (Bourdieu, 1988; Foucault, 2002). Social reproduction is a well known phenomenon that is a normal function within a discursive structure. Specifically, since discourses control the values, beliefs, ideas, and nature of criticism of a discourse community, these world views tend to be taught, and re-taught, to succeeding generations within the discourse (Bourdieu, 1991; Gee, 1993). Foucault (2002) refers to this discursive reproduction of education as the disciplining of the (academic) disciplines. The rationale for emphasizing these theoretical constructs is to illuminate how common discursive structures within a larger discourse actually serve to stifle dissent, creativity, and change in ways that lead to the ultimate stagnation of the discourse itself. As such, these theories serve as a warning beacon to complacency, conformity, and maintenance of the status quo within any discourse community. Specifically, they serve to warn educators to be skeptical about so-called "best practices" and be aware of how the voices of their peers may be being silenced.

Discourse theory also allows for contradictions in data between language and the negotiation of roles to be explained as a natural consequence of a reciprocal relationship. This analytical approach is helpful as enables the observations of both Sandra and Denise to be interrogated in terms of how the underlying ideology of their words drives the conflicts that they perceive. Discourse theorists commonly conceive of language and the establishment and maintenance of hierarchies as mutually constitutive (Bourdieu & Wacquant, 1992; Gee, 1993; Lankshear, 1997). This means language is used to wield power (as in how Denise felt silenced), define and uphold positions of power, and gain access to power. What this means for the researcher, or an individual within the contested arena of a burgeoning discourse, as in a PDS, is that conflicts are necessary components of construction and may be targeted as areas of inquiry, not problems to be solved. John Trimbor's (1998) view of consensus as a utopian ideal that restricts ideological discussion through unequal relations of power supports this discourse perspective. According to Trimbor, 'dissensus' is a necessary and natural component of intersubjective relationships. Ideological struggle is seen as innate to human social interaction. In short, discourse theory views ideological struggle not only as a fundamental component of the construction and function of discourse communities, and disparate discourse communities, but as the primary vehicle for innovation and change.

The PDS

Discussions into the desirability and feasibility of the Pennsylvania State University- State College Area School District Professional Collaboration Project began in 1996. Following discussions between university and school representatives it was agreed that the program would be an alternative teacher certification process in English education in which intern teachers would engage in a full year of first hand teaching experience, under the guidance of a mentor teacher, in lieu of 33 credit hours of university instruction. The establishment of a PDS at State College High School was to center around an apprenticeship model based on theories of a community of practice (Reason, 1998). Fundamental to this design was an inquiry into practice in which the members of the community share an equal access to literature, ideologies, materials, and community structures. Implicit to the process was an emphasis on the praxis of theory and practice, critical reflection, and critical inquiry within a community of practice for the purpose of educational reform for social justice (Dr. Myers, Sept. 13, 1998).

Following negotiations between district administrators, school faculty, and university program director Dr. Jamie Myers, the project was implemented at the commencement of the 1998 school year. The program structure included four individual inquiry groups comprised of one intern teacher, mentor teacher, and doctoral student. The role of the intern was to observe the practice of the mentor teacher, discuss the pedagogical and theoretical implications of the observed practice in relation to readings given by the mentor or associate, and to become progressively involved in the day-to-day operations within the classroom. The role of the mentor teacher was to facilitate the professional development of the intern teacher through direct example, instruction, and collaboration. The role of the associate was to document the progress of the project, to be a theoretical and pedagogical resource to the intern teacher and mentor teacher, and to act as a sounding board/emotional outlet for the intern teacher. Program director Dr. Myers had administrative, supervisory, and pedagogical duties. In addition to being a liaison between the school district and the program, he served as a supervisor over program structure, the nuclear groups, and was a theoretical and pedagogical resource for all of the members. Central to this triadic relationship was the underlying inquiry into the application of theory to practice for the purposes of the professional development of all members of the project. The working program structure was to be decided through the negotiation of project participants.

It was decided to hold tri-weekly meetings to discuss the status, evolution, and problems of the project. A central component of the tri-weekly meetings was to be the discussion of relevant scholarly articles that group members submitted. Although it was clear that the discussion of scholarly research was central to the project's design and goals, the mentor teachers dropped this aspect of the meetings within a month due to a stated lack of available time. Initially, at least one of the tri-weekly meetings was to be held on the university campus so that the intern teachers would feel connected to the university. However, this proposal was rebuffed by the mentor teachers along with limiting the number of weekly meetings to two. Scheduling conflicts and a paucity of time were the reasons given for this structural change. In addition to the bi-weekly meetings to be held in the school, one all-day meeting to be held off of the school campus was scheduled to occur each month. The agendas of these meetings were to be divided between the three groups, with the intern teachers having the majority of time allotted. This meeting was insisted upon by the university project head as necessary to keep the connection between the interns and the university, so that they wouldn't feel 'cut off'. The university associates were also supposed to have weekly de-briefings at the university. However, as the schedules of the university participants were rife with time conflicts, few meetings were held. It was for this reason that the doctoral students were only mandated to attend one meeting per week and the monthly meeting. Therefore, any discussion of problems, concerns, or ideas by the university participants occurred through impromptu meetings and electronic correspondence.

The data reported in this paper was taken from weekly audio recordings made and transcribed by the associates of full PDS and nuclear group meetings. Field-notes were added to the data corpus as chance meetings in passing during the school day were common. Field-notes were also used as a less intrusive method of data collection. Other forms of data included unit plan materials, intern-mentor journals, and electric correspondence. Although the structural form of the Penn State University-State College Area School District Professional Collaboration Project differed from other studies, both Schverak (1998) and Clift (1998) used similar methods of data gathering.

PDS and Discourse

In the PDS, the relationship between ideology and relations of power were evident prior to its establishment. In a meeting of university associates Dr. Myers explicates how ideology and its attendant relations of power were involved in discussions about the feasibility of establishing a PDS:

Dr. Myers: *We did a lot of stuff with the study group about internships and inquiry, and we began to formulate the proposals to run through the various administrative channels, with the overall theme being that of inquiry. The teachers and interns would be involved in inquiry into classroom experiences and pedagogy. I had to present the "program" to the ninth grade group of teachers to see if they would be interested in doing that and the first meeting did not go well at all. They really thought that it would just be too much for them to be interested in, and I was satisfied at that time to say that this internship program wasn't possible. But the district insisted that we continue to talk, and Sandra pushed this into being, and so I was asked to come back and talk to the ninth grade teachers again, and I got word that the teachers agreed to do it* (9/23/1998).

Here, communication theory might posit that differences in ideology (inquiry and pedagogy) and concerns over structural aspects of time (added duties for the teachers) were successfully negotiated so that the program could be established. A discourse perspective, however, might view the 'negotiation' of teacher resistance to ideological and structural intrusion as being a manifestation of administrative power wielded through the office of the State College Area School District's Secondary English Department Head Sandra Wyngaard. Dr. Myers' observation points at issues of work and time on the surface, but also clearly implies differing ideologies, as manifested through conceptions of inquiry and pedagogy, as being of central significance. As such, the participation of the teachers was not wholly willing. The implication in the exercise of district power is the silencing of some teachers and the reduction of university goals for the program. By approaching the differences through communication theory, a type of consensus was reached that allowed the program to begin, but limited the possibilities for a free exchange of ideas.

In a PDS full group meeting Dr. Myers illustrated the relationship between institutional structure and ideology in terms of how it affected teachers within the PDS:

Dr. Myers: *One of the reasons why we felt a PDS year long internship was an advantage over the typical model of student teaching was that one of the complaints that we always had from student teachers was that the requirements of teaching took them away from their work in the classroom. We didn't want that to happen. We don't want projects that take away from your work in the classroom. It's very clear to me that conceptualizing the work of a teacher differently is very difficult to do in the current structure of school and teaching. It's almost impossible to re-conceptualize the work of a teacher to include this engagement in*

Consensus in Professional Development Schools | 19

scholarship that engages in thoughts and experiences beyond your classroom (2/4/1999).

Communication theory might point out that the negotiation of structure (time) within the program could allow mentor teachers to engage in scholarly activity. This, however, would overlook fundamental ideological differences in the program regarding what being a teacher should mean. As exemplified by Sandra's statement at the beginning of this paper, teachers often do not conceptualize their work as involving the intellectual praxis of theory and practice. Differentiating between 'trench warfare talk' and 'big words' implies a resistance to scholarship, and thereby, praxis. In an associate's meeting Dr. Myers supports this assertion by illustrating how the mentor teachers viewed differing ideologies in the program, as expressed through the concept of inquiry, as a difference in roles between participants.

Dr. Myers: *The way they conceptualize their participation did not grow out of any conversations about inquiry, pedagogy, and curriculum that were part of the study groups, or graduate course work. Just their definition of what it is that they are supposed to be doing and what interns and university people should be doing. From my viewpoint, they are not thinking about their work as inquiry and, therefore, they don't think about your interaction with them as part of an inquiry* (9/23/1998).

While negotiation of the differing roles in the program to reach a consensus allowed the program to run more smoothly, the concurrent silencing of individual's with less power would pushed aside the ideological differences manifested through theoretical and pedagogical approaches that had the potential to positively affect the literacy practices of all involved.

The conflicts in the PDS that emerged in the public spaces of group meetings were most often talked about in terms of differences between the discourse of the school and the university. At a full group meeting mentor Carol Paul linked the idea of separate discourse communities to the negotiation of roles in the program and the necessity of building trust between groups.

Carol: *I think I liked Rod's (associate) statement when he defined it as a different discourse community. Therein lay the problem that the languages we speak are different and those results are the connotations and denotations of language. I think that's what has caused our problems when we start talking about the ramifications, for example, of bringing new text into the classroom, and that sort of thing. There's a certain kind of intimidation that occurs, the trust is not yet there. We need to work on that trust (9/30/98).*

Carol's reading of tensions in the PDS parallels a communication theory perspective as she sees the primary problem as based in language and the desirable solution being a clearer definition of roles. By conceiving of conflict as a problem to be solved through communication, Carol diminishes the space for ideological discussion implied by her recognition of contested ideas of textuality. The following excerpt from a small group discussion between associate Jim Albright and mentor Sandra Wyngaard more clearly illustrates how an emphasis on communication served to polarize the program into ideas of 'we' and 'they'.

Jim: *I think there is a kind of discourse about the difference between the 'ivory tower' and the real world of school that's been picked out and played out between the State*

	College High versus Penn State in this that has caused a barrier with education.
Sandra:	*I think there are two different discourse communities and I think that, yes, when I'm at those meetings, I don't feel as though I'm a member of both. I don't feel that there's one discourse community being played out there. I feel there are two of them. There's a tension that I feel between, yes, the university, and perhaps the agenda that we have at the high school. I think that if we had worked to build trust that these things would be okay. And I think that, yes, there is a sort of Ivory Towerness that pervades our meetings. Jamie typically goes into this discussion of language and literacy and my eyes glaze over.*
Jim:	*That's an interesting ... if I could just defend that for a minute...only in a culture with a historical party called the 'know nothings' would a comment like that be based ... Now I've insulted everybody. Only in the profession which I've been part of for three decades, that has such an anti-intellectual ...*
Sandra:	*That's precisely the problem that we've had all along. If you recall, in the initial document that Jamie drew up, we were called technicians, and you guys were called intellectuals. Need I say more? I will maintain that I am just as intellectual as you, Jim. And perhaps just as contemplative and reflective as you.*
Jim:	*But then we hear the discourse that when he mentions language and literacy, my eyes glaze over (9/30/1998).*

Here Jim's attempt to situate conflict in the arena of contested ideologies is rebuffed in favor of a belief in oppositional roles. Negotiation of these perceived oppositional roles might lead to a consensus for civility in communication, but would not interrogate the differing beliefs about language and literacy; as evidenced by Dr. Myers' observation that teachers did not view their work as inquiry. Furthermore, it overlooks how issues of power, as manifested through perceptions of hierarchies, also play a major role in ideological conflict.

The 'we-they' dichotomy of power relations was not secluded to conflict between school and university. Conflicts of hierarchy were also to be found in each separate group. In the cases of mentors and interns, the hierarchies within each group, and their relation to the hierarchy of the PDS, were viewed as obstacles to communication, not something that needed to be contested in a public space. A discussion between associates Dr. Myers and Larry Ferguson and intern Denise Savini illustrates how a communication perspective may exclude those with less power from public conversation.

Dr. Myers: *Do you think that the kind of cultural roles that people represent superseded their interpersonal relationships and that's what led to the "talking down"? Rather than having somebody who's in a similar role disagree with you?*

Denise: *Perhaps. We were all peers at one point. Then the categories started flying. Who was who? I think that was wrong.*

Larry: *Things fell back into certain cultural hierarchy roles. There's a myth that people at the university talk down to people in school. I call it a myth because I don't*

> *know if it's intentional. It's a different theoretical conversation about school. As the meeting went on pretty soon, some of the interns didn't talk.*

Denise: *I didn't feel like I was part of the discourse anymore. I didn't have anything to contribute.*

Larry: *It got to the point where this huge debate was going on, and you were the audience.*

Denise: *It got to the point where certain people were authority figures. You felt like, I'm not going to say anything because I'll be wrong (9/23/98).*

This silencing of the interns was not the only way in which hierarchies were perceived to be barriers to communication. In a full PDS Meeting mentor Ellen Campbell related her concerns regarding the dysfunctional communication existing in the PDS by stating:

Ellen: *My big concern, from an educator's standpoint, is that I have felt a huge power struggle in this group. I have felt it go on between the university and teachers. I've felt it among the teachers and amongst the university group (2/10/99).*

Again, calls for conflict resolution through increased communication overlook the ideological basis of hierarchy within a community. Thus, conflict resolution through negotiation for consensus silences individuals lacking power, thereby silencing open debate.

Conflicts of hierarchy within the associate group were not expressed in terms of the roles between professor and student.

Dr. Myers' dual role as graduate assistant supervisor and program director was not a matter of debate in the group. Dr. Myers' belief in the social construction of knowledge gave the associates a measure of intellectual autonomy within the program. However, differences in ideologies were, nonetheless, apparent. And, although associates were working in nuclear groups with mentors and interns, these differences affected the ideological struggles of the PDS as a whole. During an associate meeting associate Jim Albright's analysis of associate's final role highlights how ideology and power work together to stratify communities.

Jim: *Our role, no matter how nice we present ourselves, is always going to be interpreters of the stories they (mentor teachers and interns) tell or enact, so that gives us the incentive to do that (9/16/98).*

Although I believed that social perceptions of hierarchy placed us in a more prestigious position in terms of the production and analysis of knowledge, I also believed that this statement displayed a belief in the intellectual primacy of our position. I believed that this viewpoint diluted the social aspects of the construction of knowledge and marginalized the voice of the mentors and interns. However, the social perceptions of hierarchy embedded in Jim's statement illustrated how issues of ideology and power relations were overshadowed by issues of communication.

When ideological issues were voiced during PDS meetings they were inevitably cloaked in references to the building of trust through communication. The contested ideologies of teaching language and literacy were always secondary to the desire for the development of trust through a negotiated consensus, as the following statement by mentor Sandra Wyngaard makes clear:

Sandra: *There's never any full circle discussion of what he (Jamie) means There is some tossing out of words, some wonderful words, and yes I get inspired, but you know something, the relevance of all that, beyond the fact that I understand that yes, the position I'm in, what I do, is a social interaction. Teaching language and literacy comes as a result of social interaction. Primarily it's a communication problem, a trust problem. We (mentor teachers) talked about getting the agenda of the university, which I'm not really sure about, the concept of pedagogy, and what is the pedagogy of the university? What is my pedagogy? We feel that the university has a pedagogy that we don't understand, and at the same time we have a pedagogy, that the university doesn't understand (9/30/1998).*

Sandra's call for a negotiated pedagogy seems to relate an understanding of ideology as the central issue contributing to the conflict. However, stating the problem as one of communication and trust, the possibilities for contesting disparate ideologies in the public space are obviated. A discussion between associate Jim Albright and mentor Sandra Wyngaard illustrates the teachers' unwillingness to confront ideological issues.

Sandra: *There is an article that paints a fairly bleak picture of our school and calls for the readjusting of our English Department. It totally shocked me. The difficulty is that I see this and I think how is this going to go over with the interns? I asked a graduate student if I could see the article and I was never given the chance to see the article, and then I read the results of the thesis. And the final sentence calls for a complete revamping of the English department and I'm thinking why is this*

> being given to the interns, and what chance do we have of reaching interns in a positive way given this kind of stuff?

Jim: *You are fearful that it could undermine.*

Sandra: *That is exactly what I am talking about. Believe me, I've worked in other districts; I've been in other English departments. We have the most merit scholars in the state this year, primarily because we have such a fine school. And contributing to that is an extraordinary English department. And it really hurt (9/30/1998).*

Here, the agreement that "it could undermine" presents a belief in the merits of ideological and institutional reproduction that speaks in terms of being "hurt". Sandra's fear of having conflicting ideologies freely discussed in the public space serves to limit the voice of associates and limit the access to knowledge of the interns. Communication theory might contend that this conflict could be solved through a negotiation of goals for the program. A discourse perspective, on the other hand, would situate the conflicting ideologies on a field of community struggle. This 'dissensus' is necessary as change within a discourse can only occur from within (Foucault, 1984: Bourdieu, 1991; Gee, 1993).

Conclusion

Developing a collaborative partnership between a school and university is a difficult task. Problems of communication frequently occur in the negotiation of roles, goals, and structure of a program. Emphasizing the resolution of conflicts through negotiation to reach consensus has several positive aspects: the creation of a collegial atmosphere, closer collaborative relationships, and emotional equanimity. There is little doubt that the application of communication theory to the conflicts within a PDS facilitates the development of a smooth running program with a majority of happy members. However, is continuity and equanimity what innovations in teacher education are designed to produce? Communication theory may have applications to a wide range of conflicts within a PDS, but it may also be self-defeating in terms of what a PDS is supposed to be.

The concept of consensus implies an agreement by all parties involved to a specific operational ideological position. This conception of consensus as a stated value of a PDS overlooks how power relations within socially constructed hierarchies validate the voices of some and silences others. In this way the resolution of conflicts through negotiated consensus obviates a free discussion of ideologies in the public space. By restricting the discourse[s] of the PDS, the possibilities for the voicing and application of new ideas are diminished. If the purpose of a PDS is to foster a working praxis through a reflective and reflexive synthesis of scholarship, inquiry, and practice within a community of practice, then, consensus serves only as an impediment to development. Social relationships in a PDS need to be seen for what they are: relationships between people who come from multiple, overlapping, conflicting, and agreeing discourse communities that have differing ideological conceptions about pedagogy, relationships, and the social world. Discourse theory offers a way of understanding the complex relationships in a PDS without drawing combative lines. It allows participants to understand that this is how we get along; that conflicting ideas are not only natural consequences of interaction, but productive ones as well.

References

Apple, M. (1998). *The curriculum: problems, politics, and possibilities.* Albany, New York: SUNY Press.

Beach, R., & Myers, J. (2001). *Inquiry-based English education: engaging students in life and literature.* New York: Teachers College Press.

Bourdieu, P. (1991). *Language and symbolic power.* Cambridge, MA: Harvard. University Press.

Bourdieu, P. (1977). *Reproduction in education, society and culture.* New York: Sage Publications.

Bourdieu, P. (1988). *Homo Academicus.* San Francisco: Stanford University Press.

Bourdieu, P., & Wacquant, L. (1992). *An invitation to reflexive sociology.* Chicago: The University of Chicago Press.

Clift, R. et al. (2001). Collaborative leadership and shared decision making. *Journal of Teacher Education (52),* 27-42.

Foucault, M. (1984). *The Foucault reader.* New York: Random House.

Foucault, M. (2002). *The archaeology of knowledge.* New York: Routledge.

Friend, M., & Cook, L. (1992). *Interactions: collaboration skills for professionals.* White Plains, NY: Longman.

Gee, J. (1993). Orality and Literacy: From the Savage Mind to Ways With Words. In L. Cleary & L. Michael (Eds.), *Linguistics for teachers.* New York: R.R. Donnelly & Sons.

Giroux, H. (1997). *Pedagogy and the politics of hope: theory, culture, and schooling: a critical reader.* New York: Westview Press.

Lankshear, C. (1997). *Changing literacies.* Philadelphia: Open University Press.

Kersh, M. & Masztal, N. (1998). An analysis of studies of collaboration between universities and K-12 schools. *Educational Forum, 62*(3), 218-225.

Osguthorpe, R. (1998). *Balancing the tensions of change: Eight keys to collaborative educational renewal.* Thousand Oaks, CA: Corwin Press.

Reason, P. (1998). Three approaches to participative inquiry. In N. Denzin & Y. Lincoln (Eds.), *Strategies of Qualitative Inquiry.* Thousand Oaks, CA: Sage Publications.

Schverak, A. et al. (1998). Using content analysis to evaluate the success of a professional development school. *The Educational Forum, 62,* 27-52.

Trimbor, J. (1998). Consensus and difference in collaborative learning. In P. Shannon (Ed.), *Becoming political: reading and writings in the politics of literacy education.* Portsmouth, NH: Heinemann.

Trubowitz, S., & Long, P. (1997). *How it works: Inside a school-college collaboration.* New York: New York Teachers College.

3. Effective Multimedia-Based Learning in EFL: Comparing Two Comprehension Models

David Kent

Multimedia comprehension models can be essential in helping determine the effective use of various media types in learning and teaching contexts. Keeping this in mind two models are compared, and the major implications for designing multimedia-based learning content for adult EFL students stemming from these models is presented. Ultimately, three distinct notions emerge that prove central to any development of multimedia for use in the adult EFL context. It is also viewed as important that media use within classes is employed for the purposes of leading to student knowledge gains, and therefore emphasizes learner-centered design. As a result, instructors need to be aware of paths to follow when constructing learning content, and when evaluating the media resources they apply with students on a day-to-day basis.

Background

The essence of multimedia instruction is reliance on very different types of sign systems, and it is recognized that these differences have fundamental implications for comprehension and learning (See Holzinger, 2001; Mayer, 2001, 2003; Schnotz and Bannert, 2003; Someren, Reimann, Boshuizen, & de Jong, 1998). Yet, central to any form of multimedia is communication, and it is the need to communicate data in multiple ways, in various mediums, that has led to the continual evolution of multimedia development.

Yet, as Owston (1997) remarks, in and of itself no medium can likely improve learning in significant ways when used to deliver instruction. Instead, the key to promoting learning is grounded in how effectively the medium of instruction in the teaching and learning context is exploited (Davies & Carbonaro, 2000). In this regard, several researchers such as Mayer (2003) and Schnotz and Bannert (2003) have developed multimedia comprehension models. Such models can provide educators with clear paths to follow when developing materials for use with students, but perhaps more importantly, they can better serve our understanding of the pathways of student learning. That is, how students understand learning content when presented through various media types, and how knowledge gained from such presentation is retained.

The Promise of Multimedia

The promise of learning from multimedia, as Mayer (2003) highlights, is promoting learner understanding resulting from instructors tapping the power of verbal and visual formats of expression. The use of graphics in this manner can allow for the multimedia effect, described by Mayer (2001, 2003) and Moreno (2003), along with a coherence effect (Mayer, 2003), to arise. In these cases, words and graphics placed close to each other are better able to prime the cognitive processes required for active learning over word only presentations. This combined with the spatial- contiguity effect (Mayer, 2003), seeing items placed near each other, allows learners to hold corresponding items in working memory at the same time and results in simultaneous mapping. Further, with irrelevant data removed deeper learning can occur as extraneous material is not interfering with cognitive processing. So too, as Moreno (2003) presents, the temporal contiguity principal sees students learn better when on-screen text and visual materials are integrated rather than separated; the modality principle sees students learn better when verbal information is presented as speech rather than visually on-screen; and, the split-attention principle sees students learn better when the instructional material does not require them to split their attention between varying sources of mutually referring information.

As Brinton (2001) notes, use of media materials can introduce an 'authenticity' to language classes, and come to establish relevance between in-class learning material and the world outside, thereby a more meaningful learning process can result.

Nonetheless, teacher created media materials consume more production-time over the generation of standard lesson plans, and as a result, many instructors are unwilling or unable to commit to such an endeavor. For those teachers that do however, selection of visual and textual material for use with EFL classes should be considered just as important as something such as the vocabulary selection process. Given that different teaching situations dictate the type of vocabulary that needs selecting, and the four major reasons for selecting vocabulary lay with expediency (appropriate classroom terminology), cultural factors (terms suitable for the learning group), frequency (common word usage), and needs and levels (terms that are learner useable in real life situations) (Gairns & Redman, 1986).

Visuals for use with language learners as Canning-Wilson (2001) explains, should be colorful, contain a story line, be relative to previous learner experience, and associable to places, objects, people, events, or animals of which learners are familiar. Visuals therefore, like vocabulary, need to be selected based on the learner and language practice desired, and as a result be relative to the lesson, as opposed to visuals selected simply because they are perhaps meaningful to the teacher. Canning- Wilson also stresses that to use visuals in language teaching contexts involves believing that visuals facilitate learning; visuals (combined with text) are more likely to lead learners to more in-depth thinking and processing of language; and that, in some contexts and uses, like Schnotz and Bannert (2003) indicate, visuals may inhibit the learning process. That is to say, inappropriate forms of visualization can obstruct mental model construction - just by adding graphics to words does not always result in automatically fostering learning (Mayer, 2003).

Visual use with EFL learners needs to promote higher-order thinking, and assist learners with comprehension from oral as well as textual data. In addition, for text- based material, as researchers like Clark and Clark (1977) have long recognized, even though the reading process is tied to other elements of language processing, such as extracting meaning from speech, it is much more than simply printed speech. Visual components used in the representation of text are markedly different from those received by auditory means, and as such make different demands on the recipient, including that involving processing skills of the information provided. As a result, meaning from text cannot be passively obtained. For language learners the reading process also carries with it vocabulary acquisition and, especially for beginners, first language reading strategies and behavior may come to inhibit second language acquisition from printed text.

Today, the shift of language teaching from teacher-centered grammatical emphasis to learner-centered communicative teaching has accompanied another shift in education. That is, as Froehlich (1999, 150-151) indicates, the learning process once "required patience, concentration and the ability to internalize information and transform it into knowledge", but now, it is "characterized by being informed and entertained simultaneously through a combination of complementary, easily absorbable signals to our senses ... Foreign Language education nowadays has to be fun". It is therefore even more important that the development of language learning material, which employs various media types, must be based on principles associated with learner-centered design.

Learner-centered designs, by applying knowledge about how people learn and think, are the focus of incorporating aspects of cognitive science into the design of multimedia content (Quinn & Wild, 1998). In this sense, Eklund and Woo (1998) draw attention to a number of cognitive theories useful for application in multimedia development, including Activity Theory and Cognitive Flexibility Theory. Activity Theory is viewed as an 'object-oriented' approach in which interactions are mediated between subjects and objects, and Cognitive Flexibility Theory is interpreted as allowing increased comprehension and domain transfer of a concept when it is viewed from multiple perspectives or from a "variety of forms". Although people can construct mental representations of information from various single media such as illustrations, audio, or text, Borsook, Higginbotham, and Wheat (in Canning-Wilson, 2001) state that it is more likely learners will remember information when there are more sensory nodes where mental representation can be stored.

Yet, combinations of various learning methods, like using text and graphics together, may not always lead to effective learning, as Canning-Wilson (2001), Mayer (2003), and Schnotz and Bannert (2003) have highlighted, and therefore models are required.

Models are required not only to determine better paths for student learning, but, more importantly, better paths for educators to follow when constructing learning content.

Comparison of two Multimedia Comprehension Models

The models compared here are that of Mayer (2003) as well as Schnotz and Bannert (2003). The differences and similarities of each are illustrated below (see Table 1, and Table 2 respectively), and are then discussed. As part of this discussion, implications for designing effective multimedia for use with adult EFL students arising from these models are put forth.

Importantly, each of the models below can apply to the means of representing multiple media types in both interactive and non-hands-on activities. Yet, of special note, the Mayer model is focused on problem-based instruction, and it is this kind of instruction that is often required in ESP (English for Specific Purposes), such as when teaching business English, engineering English, medical English, and so on; whereas the Schnotz and Bannert model focusing on task-based instruction lends itself more to the general EFL conversation class where learners must use English for communication. Although each model can equally apply to all EFL settings as the teaching of language, no matter what the context, essentially involves aspects of both problem-solving transfer and task-based instruction.

Table 1.

Comparison of Two Multimedia Learning Models: Differences

Mayer Perspective	Schnotz and Bannert Perspective
(a). Draws on dual coding, separate channels for visual/pictorial and auditory/textual processing where each can be encoded into long-term memory integrated by a one-to-one mapping process.	(a). Propositional representations and mental models are based on different sign systems, and different principles of representation, which complement one another. There is no one-to-one relationship between external and internal representations.

(b). Material to be learnt must be meaningful (i.e. for problem-solving), multimedia instructional messages would not include arbitrary lists of facts or procedures.

(c). Students can learn more deeply from multimedia than words alone. The human mind works in a prescribed manner, and information must be molded to fit the constraints of this system before active processing can occur. As such, both visual and verbal representations need to be held in working memory at the same time before deep learning or problem solving skills can become evident.

(d). A dichotomous view: separate processing of auditory/verbal and visual/pictorial information, processing ability within each channel is limited. Therefore, meaningful learning occurs when learners engage in active cognitive processing.

(b). Learning from verbal and pictorial representation considered a task-oriented process of constructing multiple mental representations.

(c). Inclusion of graphics is not always better for learning acquisition, task-appropriate graphics support learning while task-inappropriate graphics interfere. That is, the structure of graphics, or form of visualization, can affect the structure of the mental model derived from the material. Processing of information is based on top-down and bottom-up activation of cognitive schemata, which can have both an organizing and selective function.

(d). An integrative view: text (external descriptive) leads to internal descriptive and internal depictive mental representation, pictures (external depictive) lead to internal depictive and internal descriptive mental representation, therefore mental models are not bound to specific sensory modalities and can interact with prior knowledge.

(e). Involves learner selection (of sounds and images for further processing), organization (forming a coherent mental representation of visual and verbal material), and integrating (building connections between verbal and pictorial models with prior learning) in an iterative fashion as the means to produce a learning outcome that can be stored in long-term memory.	(e). Involves information selection, information organization, parsing of symbol structures (descriptive/textual representation), mapping of analog structures (depictive/pictorial representation), model construction (from propositional representation to a mental model), and model inspection (from a mental model to propositional representation) as the means to produce a learning outcome that can be stored in long-term memory.

Table 2.

Comparison of Two Multimedia Learning Models: Similarities

Mayer, and Schnotz and Bannert Perspectives
(a). Both models are based on cognitive theory, viewing multimedia use taking into account the ways consistent with how people learn.
(b). Both models distinguish between verbal and visual information flows, but give different emphasis to the forms of information involved in the way they are processed.
(c). The theory behind each model applies to interactive (e.g., computer-based) and non hands-on activities (e.g., printed text and graphics or book-based content).
(d). The essence of both models is the development of coherent mental representations.
(e). Structurally both models are similar; the Schnotz model can be seen as an elaboration and recasting of what Mayer proposed quite some years earlier.

Essentially, the major implications emerging from both the Mayer and Schnotz and Bannert multimedia comprehension models, that are particularly influential for developing EFL media-based learning content for adult students, are:
- ways consistent with how people learn must be taken into account when developing media for use with learners;
- selection, organization, and internalization of the material under study needs to occur in students before it can lead to any knowledge gains, although Mayer compared to Schnotz and Bannert hold different views on how this occurs; and,
- graphics and text combined can lead to better understanding of learning material, but as Schnotz and Bannert highlight they must be appropriate, and as Mayer states, effectively combined.

Both models, being based on cognitive theory, present the importance of developing learning content based on the ways people learn and think. However, the perspectives taken by each model in this regard are somewhat different. Schnotz and Bannert take an integrative view where mental models are not bound to specific sensory modalities, and can interact with prior knowledge. On the other hand, Mayer essentially relies on aspects of dual-coding (separate and limited channels of processing), and where meaningful learning occurs when students engage in active cognitive processing. In addition, the two models show that the processes of selection, organization, and internalization of both the visual and textual information presented to learners is necessary before it can lead to any successful knowledge gain by students. That is, according to Mayer, selection involves the learner taking aspects of the material presented for further processing; organization includes processing the selected aspects into a mental representation;

while integrating is establishing connections between the visual and textual data with existing knowledge. However, the Schnotz and Bannert view of how this occurs sees both top-down and bottom-up activation of cognitive schemata occur in the selection and organization process; while internalization occurs through the construction of a mental model through a schema- driven mapping process as internal depictive representations that interact with existing knowledge.

Further, each model shows that the inclusion of both text and graphics within learning material promotes better understanding that can lead to the construction of knowledge. Adding graphics to text, and simplifying the text presented, would also prove useful for EFL resources utilized with adult students. In fact, this has long been done with children and the use of such resources as picture dictionaries, but not always taking into account learner-centered designs as presented in each of the models compared here.

Importantly however, analysis of these two multimedia comprehension models demonstrates that any graphic for use as an EFL resource should be learner-centered, focused on providing education to the learner, and not applied as is often the case, whether intentionally or unintentionally by publishers or teachers, for simply aesthetic reasons. That is, employed to make resources more colorful and attractive to learners, rather than taking into consideration the effectiveness or appropriateness of the inclusion of such content within learning material.

While there is nothing wrong with attracting the learner with pleasing depictions, educators need to be more sophisticated in their approach to the roles that pictures can serve. 'Fun' is not the only aspect of language education. We should also be concerned with what learning opportunities pictures provide once the learner engages with them. For Example, if illustrations also assist the learner to process verbal material more effectively, then the educational value is greatly increased.

Further, it is important for instructors to be aware of the various multimedia comprehension models that exist, so that in light of recent research and theories they can successfully evaluate any instructional resources they must use within class, as well as be able to practically apply such constructs in the design and development of their own learning content.

Conclusion

In the EFL teaching environment, texts and visual materials are usually school dictated rather than teacher selected or developed. It is therefore increasingly important that educators in such environments are able to assess the effectiveness, particularly in light of recent theories and research, of both the instructional material they must use, and that they can adapt or develop themselves, to determine resource suitability for use with students in class.

In the current era, it is increasingly important to understand how learning from multiple media sources and the combination of multiple media types occurs, and to develop appropriate teaching methods with such resources, so that material generated by either instructors themselves, or publishing houses, can provide the most effective learning gains for students. To this end, several multimedia comprehension models have been developed, and two of the most notable have been compared. Although each model presents different views for how multimedia materials are processed by the learner, central to each model as well as the development of multimedia for adult EFL students are three distinct notions. These are 1) content development needs to stem from learner-centered designs well-grounded in concepts of cognitive theory; 2) selection, organization and internalization of the information being studied must occur, and be internalized by students, before learning can result; and, 3) the effective combination of appropriate visual and textual data can allow for better understanding of learning content presented to students.

References

Brinton, D. M. (2001). The Use of media in language teaching. In Celce-Muria, M. (Ed.), *Teaching English as a Second or Foreign Language* (459-476). Boston, MA: Heinle and Heinle.

Canning-Wilson, C. (2001). Visuals and language learning: Is there a connection? *The Weekly Column, 48. ELT Newsletter*. Retrieved from http://www.eltnewsletter.com/back/Feb2001/art482001.htm

Clark, H. H., & Clark, E. V. (1977). *Psychology and language: An introduction to psycholinguistics*. New York: Hardcourt and Brace.

Davies, J., & Carbonaro, M. (2000). Developing web-mediated instruction for teaching multimedia tools in a constructionist paradigm. *International Journal of Telecommunications, 6*(3), 243-265.

Eklund, J., & Woo, R. (1998). *A cognitive perspective for designing multimedia learning environments*. Paper presented at the 1998 National Conference of the Australasian Society for Computers in Learning in Tertiary Education, Wollongong, Australia.

Froehlich, J. (1999). Language lab – multimedia lab – future lab. In G., Hogan-Brun, & U. O. H., Jung. (Eds.), *Media, multimedia, omninmedia* (149-155). Frankfurt, Germany: Peter Language Publishers.

Gairns, R., & Redman, S. (1986). *Working with words*. Cambridge, England: Cambridge University Press.

Holzinger, A. (2001). *Definition of multimedia.* Retrieved from http://www-ang.kfunigraz.ac.at/~holzinge/mml/mml-multimedia-definition.html

Mayer, R. E. (2001). *Multimedia learning.* Cambridge, England: Cambridge University Press.

Mayer, R. E. (2003). The promise of multimedia learning: Using the same instructional design methods across different media. *Learning and Instruction, 13,* 125-139.

Owston, R. D., (1997). The world wide web: A technology to enhance teaching and learning. *Educational Researcher, 26*(2) 27-33.

Quinn, C., & Wild, M. (1998). Supporting cognitive design: Lessons from human- computer interaction and computer-mediated learning. *Education and Information Technologies, 3*(3), 175-185.

Schnotz, W., & Bannert, M. (2003). Construction and interference in learning from multiple representation. *Learning and Instruction, 13,* 141-156.

van Someren, M. W., Reimann, P., Boshuizen, H. P. A., & de Jong, T. (Eds.), (1998). *Learning with multiple representations.* Oxford, England: Elsevier.

4. Negotiating Diversity through an Arts-Based Method: Using Dramatic Monologue to explore Responsible Teacher Conversations

Darryl Bautista
Julian kitchen

Teacher conversations and the manner in which teachers interact play an important role in establishing Canadian school atmosphere. In our study, we conduct a workshop with preservice teachers to consider the role of teacher talk. We developed an arts- based dramatic monologue, presented it to a preservice teacher education class and began discussions on the idea of responsible teacher conversations. Our monologue explored a staffroom teacher conversation caught up in the cultural realities of one's perception of another's spoken words. We asked future teachers about the nature of conversations when the parties involved clash over spoken intention and understood meaning. We further challenged them to seek out ways to assuage tensions associated with these conflictive moments. In this article[1], we outline our objectives, detail the content of the workshop[2] and conclude with an exploration of the responses from the preservice group.

Introduction

To begin our arts-based inquiry, Julian and I look to Alter's (1993) understanding of teachers and their classrooms of diversity:

> *Insights from the analysis of ourselves, our classrooms or communities, and our world can result in more authentic teaching, learning and living* (4).

We both firmly believe in the future role of teachers in terms of diversity education and advocacy of acceptance for all who enter the school community. The initial goal of our collaborative endeavor was to seek out new ways to engage future teachers regarding issues of diversity and equity. Although, these issues are addressed in depth by many teacher education programs and more new teachers recognize that their classes are diverse, the teaching and learning of diversity, in our opinion, can never be considered a completed task. With the changing Canadian cultural landscape, we believe that teacher educators must continually visit and revisit why and how acceptance of others is taught to future teachers.

While preservice teachers are presented with much valuable information about a range of equity issues and there is much dialogue about the implications for students and classrooms, their "knowledge as attribute" is often not evident in their "knowledge as expressed in practice" (Clandinin & Connelly, 1998, 157). Teacher educators need to explore ways in which to address this gap between the theoretical acceptance and the encouragement and incorporation of these concepts into teachers' practice. Since Julian and I believe that "artistic and social forms of expression can create the conditions for promoting self-acceptance, self-esteem, resilience, and synergy within and between human beings" (Diamond & Mullen, 1999, 25), we decided to develop an experiential, arts-based approach to diversity and equity education in a preservice classroom.

The aim of this paper is to examine the responses of preservice teachers to our workshop that included a performed monologue and follow-up activities. We consider ourselves to be teachers in the classroom so we, too, are not removed from the teachers that we discuss. Julian, a Canadian teacher educator, commits himself to helping preservice teachers understand issues of diversity and equity. Darryl, a Canadian and Filipino sketch comedy performer, and an art-based teacher/researcher has written previously about intercultural negotiations and (re)conceptualizations of diversity for Canadian teachers. Our research here presents the dramatic monologue in promotion of our own teacher awareness as well as the awareness we tried to generate with the pre-service class. In particular, we focus our discussion on whether the workshop informed their (re)conceptualizations of equity and diversity issues.

Objectives of Our Inquiry

Julian and I believe equity and diversity issues are central to teacher education and development in an increasingly diverse society. While education systems embrace diversity in theory, there are questions regarding the practice of equity by classroom teachers and within the cultures of schools. Wayne (2003) stresses the need to create within teacher education classes "a space where we can engage in dialogue that challenges our opinions, attitudes, values and beliefs; a space where we feel safe to talk about issues of power relations and interlocking systems of oppression" (6). Creating such a space is not easy; some preservice teachers are unaware of the degree of inequity faced by members of minority groups and some accept the need for equity intellectually without being aware of the ways in which they may support inequity "by virtue of their silence" (Mark, 2003, 20). All teachers, whether preservice or in- service, need to reflect upon and examine how our own biases and stereotypes influence the ways in which we interact with others (Conle et. al., 2000) if we are to address equity and diversity issues in our future/current professional lives.

We believe that teachers need to situate their understandings within their "personal practical knowledge" (Connelly and Clandinin, 1988) that is, teacher knowledge steeped in reflecting on past, personal and practical experiences to inform a teacher's current and future perspectives on teaching. Teaching, then, is a process that is constructed and continuously re-constructed, as a teacher frames new experiences into their personal practical knowledge. We also draw upon the ideas of Dewey's (1938) continuity of experience "that every experience both takes up something from those which have gone before and modifies in some way the quality of those which come after" (35). Also, we recognize that teacher's sensitivity to diversity and equity issues is informed by the "professional knowledge landscapes" (Clandinin and Connelly, 1995), which includes places within the school but outside of the classroom such as the staffroom. As teacher conversation plays an important role in establishing the school atmosphere, we want prospective teachers to consider how they can re-script staffroom conversations of prejudice in order to promote equity and diversity.

Our scripted monologue concerns a teacher conversation, a conversation which reveals that "cover stories" (Clandinin & Connelly, 1995) of inclusion often disguise "secret stories" (Crites, 1971) of prejudice. Its purpose was to prompt an examination of equity and diversity issues as embodied in teacher personal practical knowledge and the professional knowledge landscapes on which they work. Julian's impression was that didactic approaches often change intellectual understandings without effecting deeper changes in "personal practical knowledge" (Connelly & Clandinin, 1988) or classroom practice. Julian approached Darryl about working together to develop an arts-based resource for teaching diversity and equity. Darryl identified the dramatic monologue, an arts-based form, as a means of, perhaps, widening the lens of intercultural discussion among preservice teachers.

In conceptualizing our monologue, we began by establishing setting and developing the content. The staffroom, the main setting, is the place of conflict while the second setting, a teacher's classroom, is where the monologue is actually spoken. The staffroom was selected as the primary setting because though a 'safe' space, sometimes outside of the classroom, teachers let down their guard because they assume that their peers are culturally aware. They expect peers to engage in conversation without racial or discriminatory slurs. Most teachers educate students about acceptance of others in the classroom and so, amongst peers in the staffroom, the feeling is that teachers can 'let down their guard' so to speak. Julian and I argue that diversity is not absent from the staffroom and that discriminatory comments ensue.

Many teachers learn to deal with students who voice prejudicial comments, but our particular puzzle within this paper deals with teacher-to-teacher relations. We both recalled incidents of teachers making remarks that could be regarded as insensitive. As we further deliberated our monologue, key questions came to mind. What happens when teacher colleagues are the culprits of prejudice? How can teachers cope with a colleague's voiced prejudice? Who decides what acceptable 'teacher talk' sounds like? How should a teacher respond to unacceptable teacher talk? Do teachers really need to be held accountable for everything they do and say even amongst colleagues? Do teachers need to educate each other? Through the dramatic monologue, we attempted to seek out possibilities amongst these research puzzles.

As Julian and I talked more, we agreed that the term diversity extends beyond ethnicity. The students within classrooms come from a multiplicity of difference in relation to others. Diversity in today's Canadian society is no longer about the visible cultural markers of our classrooms. Discussions of diversity need to reflect 'hidden' identities (sexual orientation, religious beliefs, personal lifestyle choices, and families of divorce, poverty, and others) that are not so easily identifiable. Although our script recounts racial prejudice, we concede that this is just one of many forms of discrimination. If teachers are to build principles of tolerance, they should reflect on their own behaviors and identities in relation to the lived diversities both inside and outside the classroom.

Miller (1994) writes of the "surprise of a recognizable person" (505), a self created through language and other forms of social organization. Julian and I agree that a teacher educates within a complex network of human interactions and that teacher self-awareness in relation to others helps a teacher realize his/her affect within this interconnected web. We feel that teachers must be conscious and conscientious of their spoken words because toxic or not, teacher talk can have a great effect whether it is within the staffroom, in the classroom or the school itself.

We understand teacher-to-teacher conversation as rooted in personal life philosophy, and it comes with great responsibility since "we know we are, in our lives, caught up in a story, already involved in a drama of some sort" (Kerby, 1991, 7). When teachers, share their lives, their opinions, they also share glimpses of their personal philosophy that may or may not agree with others. They may say things they don't mean, they may judge others, or they might show latent prejudices. Whether complimentary or judgmental, when a teacher talks, many ears are listening. We believe teachers are accountable when their comments are misconstrued or understood as prejudice.

This is not to say that all teacher-speak is problematic. But when it is, it needs to be addressed. Giroux (1996) writes, "The central challenge for educators ... is rethinking and rewriting difference in relation to wider questions of membership, community and social responsibility" (91-92). Our collaborative work explores the notions of membership, community and social responsibility when it comes to Canadian teachers in support of diversity and equity for all.

Our Methods

After developing the dramatic monologue and planning the activities, we presented to a preservice teacher education course of 36 students. The ethno-cultural background of the students (self-identified by the students during a pre-workshop exercise) included 24 white students, 3 of which were Jewish; also, 5 Asian, 3 South Asian, 3 Chinese students and 1 Black student participated in the study. The course entitled *Teacher Education Seminar* led by Julian, introduced pre-service students to an array of classroom themes including assessment, classroom management, and special education. In one of the classes devoted to issues of equity and diversity, Julian and I conducted our 3-hour workshop.

Our methodology stems from qualitative designs as defined by Punch (1998); it involves audio and video recording, the collection of classroom artifacts, personal reflections by the participants and open-ended survey questions, interviews, focus group discussions, and semi-open observation and document collection.

Our data consists of the following:
1. Audio and video recordings of the students in the workshop
    (a). We reviewed the tapes in order to observe classroom dynamics and individual responses to the activities

2. Artifacts created by workshop students during the activities (e.g., drawings, chart paper)
    (a). We reviewed the artifacts generated by students in order to examine how the activities contributed to learning in the classroom setting
3. Personal reflections by the teacher researchers of this paper
    (a). To examine our responses to the activities and how the students responded
4. Student responses to 'Survey: Responding to Scaffolding Questions'
    (a). The survey results were compiled and analyzed to discover the personal responses of individual students and to determine their overall impressions at the conclusion of the activities
    (b). Eighteen of the 36 students completed the survey

For this paper, we focus primarily on the survey results in order to consider the impact the classroom activities had on student teacher perceptions concerning equity and diversity. The other data sources recount student teacher perceptions as expressed in the survey, and inform our analysis of the responses to the scaffolding questions.

Our Scripted Monologue

Our scripted monologue examples the idea of negative teacher talk and its affect on other teachers since "the effectiveness of arts-based postmodern activity depends upon the degree to which it arouses (rather than 'transmits') particular feelings and images and the degree to which it momentarily captures and provokes experiential learning" (Diamond & Mullen, 1999, 24). We attempt to broaden the pre-service instruction experience examining the interpersonal relationship that takes place among teachers. The dramatic piece (after both researchers dialogued its potency) forms the basis from which our inquiry begins.

Abrams (1993) describes a dramatic monologue as being a "type of lyric poem" (48) through which the speaker expresses a process of perception of *self* and/or *other*. The voice of the monologue (herein identified as the speaker) expresses his experience as it affects his understandings of self and other. Our speaker is "a single person, who is patently not the poet, utter[ing] the entire poem in a specific situation at a critical moment. ... This person addresses and interacts with one or more other people ... to reveal to the reader, in a way that enhances interest, the speaker's temperament and character" (48). The speaker of our monologue works through notions of isolation. He is a visible minority teacher aware that conversations he hears are sometimes rooted in discrimination, both intentional and unintentional.[3] As Kerby (1991) writes, "Questions of identity and self-understanding arise primarily in crisis situations and at certain turning points in our routine behavior. Such events often call for self-appraisal" (7). Our speaker copes with a situation involving a teacher colleague making a stereotypical remark construed by the speaker as offensive. The speaker explores the comment's resonance with his past and present lived experiences. The speaker also contemplates voicing his concerns to fellow teachers and the positive and negative repercussions that may or may not ensue.

When Darryl composed the monologue, he remembered both personal and professional experiences of negotiating his cultural self-identity. Like Paley (1979), he felt that "coming to terms with my difference, prepares a person for all kinds of differences" (29). His visible minority status continuously informs his teacher identity and so, he believes that personal and professional experiences (Connelly & Clandinin, 1988) meld into his understandings of teacher selves since "their [teachers] past profoundly affects their present actions" (Knowles, 1998, 703). As a school student, he experienced moments of discrimination and these same moments of discrimination carried over into his pre-service program. As a teacher researcher, they sometimes co-exist in his daily practice continually transforming his current understandings of diversity and equity issues. These moments propel his writing since "the culturally marginalized writer will engineer approaches to language and form that enable a particular residue (genetic, cultural, biographical) to become kinetic and valorized" (Wah, 2000, 51).

Darryl's perceptions are not the only basis for this scripted monologue. It is also informed by Julian's negotiation of his personal and professional identity, his experiences as a teacher, and his present work as a teacher educator. As we began the process of discussing the script and the workshop to follow, we shared our experiences in the hopes of finding ways through the labyrinth of discrimination.

In the following section, we offer our monologue entitled *'Who Speaks for Whom?'* in its entirety. After placing it here, we then begin to explore its thematic connections to equity and diversity policy as well as share responses from students in the preservice class.

Who Speaks for Whom?

{A single chair behind a desk, single spotlight on the set. The audience sees a teacher marking steadily, and then stopping. He fidgets, he takes a sip from his coffee mug, and he rises from his chair. He begins to speak}.

Teacher: *(smilingly) This may be clichéd but Monday, I know you exist, and Monday, you trouble me so. Yes, that's right, Monday — I don't like you.*

On Saturday I try to catch up on my marking and Sunday I try to catch up on my life, but by nightfall, I start to fret about you, Monday. (change of tone) But that is okay.

Blah! I shouldn't be so angry with myself.

It's lunchtime on a Monday and here I am in my classroom keeping myself occupied. Some days, I just can't go into the staffroom. Some days, it troubles me to be around other teachers.

(pensive and to the audience) I ask you to do me a favor. Listen to the voices around the staffroom one day. Just listen. Find that Zen place inside your head, close your eyes and wait ... 2 ... 3 ... 4 ... There! Did you hear that?

When you stop and survey, you can hear a colleague, consciously or unconsciously, make, what the research calls, a harsh uninformed stereotypical generalization. I call it a racist commit. Plain and simple.

Most of the time, you can brush off the stupid comment, but what about on the days when you can't? What about when someone goes way too far? And why the hell should I ignore the comment? What do you do?

Well, logic reminds you that they are people and all people make mistakes.

And so, there is the dilemma. Because they are people, they are not perfect. I know this. I get it. But I think we, teachers, should be conscious of our words and heck, even each other.

Why? Well, why not? If we ask students to show respect to others then shouldn't we set the example and show respect to each other? If we are teachers then what do we teach? Just subjects?

Let me tell you a story.

Last Friday, I was having lunch in the staffroom with other teachers and we were engaged in a conversation about student interest in certain subjects and someone said, "Well, you know those Asians, it is typical for them to behave that way. That's the way they are. They are good students but not good at expressing themselves".

I couldn't believe my ears. As both an Asian and a Canadian, I felt insulted and betrayed.

This teacher made her comment and walked away from the staffroom table. And then the bell rang. I had no time to react and other colleagues left before I could even talk with anyone.

The conversation moved on for everyone else, but it did not move on for me, dammit. Yeah, maybe I should let it go but then what happens when a similar thing takes place in my classroom. Do I tell the students involved to just 'let it go'? Do I tell them not to stand up for themselves?

I could have, should have, and would have shared my concerns. Could have, should have, would have, but I did not. (regretfully)

What the hell? Why do I feel such anger? I will tell you why.

As a child, I experienced a great deal of labeling — social categorizations, stereotypical notions, preconceived opinions — whatever the experts want to call it. I grew up drowning in so many labels.

One time, my 'labeler' was my elementary teacher. He said, "Good job Bruce Lee!" which for him was a compliment, but for me, it kinda hurt. I wasn't Chinese. I wasn't an immigrant. In my mind, I was just a Canadian 10-year-old kid. At that moment, though, I understood that I was different.

So, I grew up suspecting all teachers because of that unjust comment. I was looking for my teachers to screw up and pigeonhole me into the Asian stereotype you know, the "good at math, very passive, likes to eat with sticks, can't stop bowing" thing ... I would look for it all so that I could label them back as an "ignorant dumb ass teacher".

And here it is again ... I feel like that angry kid trying to make sense of another teacher's words ... I feel like lashing out ... I am the teacher who fights because I was the child who couldn't.

(angrily) Here's my advice to the ignorant teacher. Don't label me behind my back or to my face. Don't mark me with what I am not. Or if you do, accept the consequences. Maybe, I am the student who will not co-operate in your class. Maybe I will suck up to you because I think you don't like me. Maybe I will tell my parents you are racist or maybe I will tell students about how you treated me and that you hate Asians—

(enraged) What about that!?

(pause) You know, I hope I have become a good teacher ... one who tries not to label students because the hurt is too real for me, too personal. I would never forgive myself if I found out I hurt a student like that.

Okay ... We all have the right to say whatever we want but we should choose to voice certain things with caution.

(Calming down) When I think about it now, if I say something to my colleague, there will be consequences. If I say nothing, I teach her that it is okay to freely make uninformed comments. I can't keep waiting—

> *(sits down) I am here, at my desk, pretending to be "preoccupied" and feeling isolated and so much emotion, yeah, emotion.*
>
> *And I have no idea what am I going to do.*
>
> (Edited June 2007, originally written June 2004).

Our Findings
Student Responses to the Dramatic Monologue

In this section, we summarize student responses to the questions asked in a response sheet handed out during the workshop. The survey was entitled 'Responding to Scaffolding Questions' and can be found at the end of this article in Appendix B. Each student who completed the survey answered all five questions.

Scaffolding Question 1
Discuss the effectiveness of the dramatic monologue as an instructional technique.
Eighteen respondents stated that the dramatic monologue was an effective instructional technique. Student comments include: *very effective, better than lecturing* and *makes the issue real, personal, concrete.*

Some students felt the monologue was *quite illuminating because of the stress certain readers or the performer can place on certain aspects* and *well-suited to stimulate discussion of the issue of stereotypes because it lacked details which would have made the discussions too specific.* One student responded: *I think it is important for teachers to show students that they too prepare for pre-service presentations—so that students do not feel like they are the only ones put in vulnerable situations.*

There were also some concerns expressed about the dramatic monologue format. One student expressed concern that the monologue *leaves little room for subtlety/complexity because it unintentionally creates a stereotype of its own.*

Scaffolding Question 2
Discuss the effectiveness of the dramatic monologue 'Who Speaks for Whom? in regards to addressing issues of Equity and Diversity in Education.

Seventeen respondents indicated that they thought *'Who Speaks for Whom?'* was effective in addressing issues of equity and diversity. The other response was ambiguous in that it agreed and yet the respondent felt the monologue provided insufficient information; all in all, while clearly positive, most students wanted more information.

Some representative comments include:
- *It got me thinking of how even positive stereotypes can be seen as offensive by some.*
- *I can really feel how difficult the choices are that the narrative forces.*
- *[The monologue] made me wonder if I ever said a racially unacceptable comment which may have offended people around me.*

Scaffolding Question 3
Discuss the effectiveness of the follow-up activities in prompting examination of the issues raised in the dramatic monologue.

Responses to the follow-up activities were more ambiguous. Ten students responded positively to the activities on a whole, while the other eight focused on one or two activities.

We developed five response activities and summarize them here. The detailed text of the activities can be found in Appendix A at the end of this article.

Activity 1
Individual Arts-Based Response
Students were given a copy of the monologue and after reading the text, they were asked to highlight and/or 'doodle' in the margins of the script. This activity encouraged students to individually respond to keywords of phrases in the text.

Activity 2
In pairs-Dialoguing the Monologue
In pairs, students were asked to dialogue their responses to the presentation of the monologue. They could share their marked passages and/or notes from Activity 1 or they could comment on the performance of the monologue.

Activity 3
Group Activity-Describing the Other
In groups, students were asked to form larger groups and dialogue the female teacher within the monologue. Students were asked to give life to the role of the 'offensive' teacher, her words and whether or not her intentions were positive, negative or neutral. Using chart paper, they were asked to note keywords from their discussions.

Activity 4
Group Activity-Possibilities through (Re) Enactment

In groups, students chose between acting out two scenarios. The first scenario was the students could assume the role of another teacher in the staffroom at the time of the exchange or of the principal after the speaker visits his/her office or of a student offering their take on the situation. The students who chose this option performed their choice for the entire class.

The alternative scenario choice asked students to create the dialogue of a future meeting between the speaker and the 'offending' teacher from the monologue. After scripting, the students who chose this option performed their dialogue for the entire class.

Activity 5
Individual Activity-Personal Written Response

At the end of the presentation, students were asked to complete our survey entitled 'Responding to Scaffolding Questions'.

Activity 1 generated a number of strong responses; one student said it *stressed me out to have to draw'*, while another felt it was biased in favor of artistic students. The role-play activity, in which groups adopted roles such as the offending teacher, the person she spoke to, the principal and others, was received well. While most responses indicated approval of these roles, some were not comfortable in their roles. One non-white student, much to her surprise, discovered that *it's important to look at the motives of the perpetrator ... in order to come up with effective solutions to equity issues.*

Scaffolding Question 4
How has today's workshop informed your personal understanding of Equity and Diversity issues?
The responses to this question were quite varied. Overall, we identified 13 responses as largely positive, 3 as negative and 2 as neither.

Some of the positive comments were:
- *[The monologue] helped enlighten me on the reasons other people have for disagreeing.*
- *I am more cautious with the choice of words I use.*
- *[The monologue] did really increase my awareness of my own behavior.*
- *It shows how difficult it is to put theory into practice ... demonstrates how complex a racial situation can be.*

Some concerned students stated:
- Too many students *interested in platitudes* regarding an extremely, extremely complicated situation.
- *Most of the discussion was at a fairly unchallenging level.*
- *The format was well-intentioned, but ultimately I would have liked a more thorough approach.*

Scaffolding Question 5
Any additional comments ...
This section was primarily used to amplify comments similar to the ones listed in Question 4. There were suggestions about how to change aspects of the monologue. Most students wanted more explicit details about the speaker and the offending teacher.

Discussion of the Inquiry

From our inquiry, we begin to understand "the stories that these new teachers tell of their lives as student teachers and beginning teachers [are] ... acts of meaning (Bruner, 1990) through which they are making sense of the work of teaching" (Rust, 1994, 9). Many of these future teachers describe the monologue as indicative of ideas they would like to know more about in terms of handling tension filled situations between colleagues.

Interpreting and reflecting upon the workshop and the responses of preservice teachers, we further identified several interesting themes that inform our future use of arts-based methods and instruction in teacher education programs.

The overwhelming positive responses to the first survey question suggest that the dramatic monologue format has a place in the instructional repertoire, although changes need to be made. In re-writing this monologue, we will consider including additional information without compromising our commitment to raising questions rather than locating answers. For example, the speaker of the monologue could offer more detail about the heated exchange including the tone of voice, the nature of the conversation topic prior to the offending teacher's remark and also, the reason why the speaker feels the remark to be intended as negative or insulting. Perhaps, more detail about the offending teacher could be included as in whether this is a one time comment or a repeated behavioral pattern.

The responses to the second question were consistent with our goals in creating this monologue. We wanted students to consider what their own actions would be and how they would grapple with this complex issue if they were the speaker, the offending teacher or another member of the school community. The responses also indicated that the audience responded emotionally and experientially to the monologue, rather than just intellectually. Intellectual responses generally emerged later, as the students further interpreted the monologue's meaning and attempted to explore the speaker's dilemma through role play.

The responses to the third question were interesting. Some students were less comfortable with arts-based methods than with traditional approaches. For example, the student, a drama graduate was "stressed out" by doodling though s/he loved the role-playing activities. If teachers desire to create classrooms that celebrate both artistic ways of knowing and forms of expression, then Julian and I believe that preservice teachers need to become more acclimatized to arts-based forms.

While the activities were largely effective, less attention was given to each activity than to the larger framework of the three-hour class. Also, we tried several different strategies in order to discover how students would respond. The role-playing activities were very informative, though groups may have benefited from more time and structure. On a side note, though the Follow-up Activity 1 asking students to 'highlight' or 'doodle' was helpful for some, we will have to reconsider how we might employ this tactic in the future.

Ultimately, in terms of assessing the value of this dramatic monologue as a tool for teaching about equity and diversity, the most important responses came from the fourth survey question. The 13 positive responses reinforce our interpretations of the answers to the second question. The preservice students increased awareness of their personal conduct in schools suggests that this approach was effective in prompting reflection. Statements regarding the 'multilayered' nature of the situation helped raise awareness of the contextual and interpersonal aspects of this issue. At the same time, requests for more information about the case and more articles on the equity and diversity remind us that this lesson was somewhat decontextualized from other elements of the course that dealt with these issues. In future, we would frame the monologue within a larger unit of study. One possibility would be to follow-up over several days, with the monologue stimulating reflection and related suitable resource materials enhancing their interpretation.

For us, the dramatic monologue becomes an example of an artistic research form to promote teacher development. Barone writes, "artistic researchers seek language uses that are evocative, metaphorical, figurative, connotative, poetic and playful" in order to spark learning (in Diamond & Mullen, 1999, 43). We think that this non-traditional method is useful in helping teachers and students alike contemplate and construct notions of responsibility when we speak of diversity. We took an artistic risk in order "to take up the task of developing analytic practices that cross irregular, unexplored terrain rather than to reproduce arguments within the geometries of recognizable intellectual space" (Jipson & Paley, 1997, 6).

By engaging the feelings and experiences that underlie their personal practical knowledge as teachers, a monologue such as 'Who Speaks for Whom?' has the potential to reach teachers who do not internalize more didactic lessons regarding equity and diversity.

We have come to understand that dialoging issues of diversity is the responsibility of all involved in current and future classrooms. Slattery (1995) asserts, "The knower cannot be separated from the known and meaning cannot be separated from the context that gives rise to the meaningful experience. Educators must (re)envision their relationships with students and with each other and begin to find ways to affirm and validate every voice in the school community" (264). From policymakers to administration, from teachers to students, we create a school space negotiating multitudes of understandings when it comes to unconditional acceptance of each others' differences.

Inclusion within our schools amongst all participants is essential. Before teachers can model inclusiveness and build acceptance within their classrooms, they can look to each other in order to understand how personal experiences inform professional practice. They can learn to be aware of their own transgressions.

Our dramatic monologue, *'Who Speaks for Whom?'* was designed to prompt meaningful reflection and discussion. It would be interesting to see whether or not and to what degree these discussions have become part of these future teachers' classroom practices. Perhaps, in time, re-gathering these individuals and having them share experiences would provide data for a future article. For now, in this piece, we choose to focus on our work's short term effects.

Extrapolating from our experiences in this research project, we think the dramatic monologue combined with experiential follow-up activities can transform practice by attempting to connect with the experiences of preservice teachers. We also think that the dramatic monologue as explorative teacher educator tool is transferable to in-service teacher development. We invite teacher educators to explore arts-based inquiry as in our research on dramatic monologue and for that matter, in all of its forms as another approach to promoting equity, celebrating diversity, and building hopeful schools for all.

End Notes

[1] Amendments have been made to this article since its original drafting in 2004. The amendments include changes to specific writing elements as in the article's unity, coherence and structure. There have been no changes made to the student data collected. The editing of the article was undertaken by Darryl Bautista (primary author) with the permission of Julian Kitchen for the inclusion in this journal November 2007.

[2] The draft of this paper entitled "Let's talk diversity: a dramatic monologue as a tool for responsible teacher conversations" was presented at the *American Educational Research Association* conference San Diego, California in April 2004.

[3] For the purposes of our study, we name the speaker as "he" because Darryl, an ethnic minority, performed the piece. The monologue speaker could be reworked for other cultural markers – gender, religion, sexuality and so on.

References

Alter, G. (1993). Empowerment through narrative: Considerations for teaching, learning and life. *Thresholds in Education, 19*(4), 3-5.

Clandinin, D. J., & Connelly, F. M. (1995). Teachers' professional knowledge landscapes: teacher stories – stories of teachers – school stories – stories of schools. *Educational Researcher, 25*(3), 24-30.

Clandinin, D.J., & Connelly, F. M. (1998). Stories to live by, narrative understandings of school reform. *Curriculum Inquiry, 28*(2), 149-164.

Conle, C., Blanchard, D., Burton, K., Higgins, A., Kelly, M., Sullivan, L., & Tan, J. (2000). The asset of cultural pluralism: An account of cross-cultural learning in pre-service teacher education. In *Teaching and Teacher Education, 16,* 365-387.

Connelly, F.M., & Clandinin, D. J. (1988). Studying teachers' knowledge of classrooms: Collaborative research, ethics and the negotiation of narrative. *The Journal of Educational Thought, 22(2A),* 269-282.

Connelly, F.M., & Clandinin, D. J. (1988). *Teachers as curriculum planners: Narratives of experience.* Toronto: OISE Press.

Crites, S. (1971). The narrative quality of experience. *American Academy of Religion Journal, 39(3),* 291-311.

Diamond, C. T. P., & Mullen, C. A. (1999). *The postmodern educator.* New York: Peter Lang Publishing, Inc.

Dewey, J. (1938). *Experience and education.* New York: Touchstone Book, Simon and Schuster.

Giroux, H. A. (1993). *Living dangerously: Multiculturalism and the politics of difference.* New York: Peter Lang Publishing.

Jipson, J.A., & Paley, N. (Eds). (1997). *Daredevil Research: Re-creating Analytic Practice.* (6-8). New York: Peter Lang Publishing.

Kerby, A. P. (1991). *Narrative and the self.* Indianapolis: Indiana University Press.

Knowles, J. G. (1988). A beginning teacher's experience: Reflections on becoming a teacher. *Language Arts, 65(7),* 702-711.

Mark, K. (2003). An argument for anti-racism education for school personnel. *Orbit, 33(3),* 20-22.

Miller, J. L. (1994). 'The surprise of the recognizable person' as a troubling presence in educational research and writing. *Curriculum Inquiry, 24(4),* 503-512. Cambridge, MA: Blackwell Publishers.

Paley, V. G. (1979). *White teacher.* Massachusetts: Harvard University Press.

Punch, K. (1998). *Introduction to social research: Quantitative and qualitative approaches.* London: Sage.

Rust, F. (1994) Professional conversations: New teachers explore teaching through conversation, story and narrative. *Teaching and Teacher Education, 15*(4), 367-380.

Rynor, M. (2001, Fall). Labels That Stick. *The University of Toronto Bulletin,* 5(5).

Slattery, P. (1995). *Curriculum Development in the Postmodern Era.* New York & London: Garland Publishing, Inc.

Wah, F. (2000). *Faking It Poetics & Hybridity Critical Writing 1984-1999,* (51). Edmonton, Alberta: NeWest Press.

Wayne, N. (2003). Anti-racism in teacher education: Rethinking our practice. *Orbit, 33*(3), 6-8.

Appendix A
Follow-up Activities to Monologue Workshop

Activity 1
Individual Arts – Based Response

If you have an affinity for doodling, you will enjoy this activity. You will be given a copy of the monologue and preferably with a different colored pen write or draw around the text. Perhaps, there are parts of the text that you connect with, perhaps there are words that trouble you or perhaps, you associate an image with a certain line or passage from the text. Perhaps, you have a similar story connected to the monologue. Feel free to scribble or illustrate your thoughts around the margins, and in the blank spaces. This activity connects both your written and visual responses to the text by allocating them in and around the actual monologue.

Activity 2
In pairs – Dialoguing the Monologue

With a Partner, share your arts-based responses and discuss the images, ideas, words et al that you designed and/or composed.

Activity 3
Group Activity – Describing the Other
Assume the role of the *other teacher* in this Dramatic Monologue and recreate her voice. Perhaps create a rejoinder to this monologue presenting the situation from her point of view. What is her perception of the incident? What emotions, if any, does she feel? How would she respond to this monologue? What if you were the *other teacher* in this piece? What would your reaction, if any, be? On the paper provided, jot down keywords that arise during your discussion. Be prepared to share your discoveries.

Activity 4
Group Activity – Possibilities through (Re) Enactment
Discuss possible methods of handling the situation or your attempts at appeasing both sides involved. What would you say to the speaker about this dilemma if you were sitting in front of him? What would you say to the other teacher involved if she was sitting in front of you? Role play, if you wish, changing the person giving advice. What would another teacher say? What would the principal say? What would a student say? You can construct a short skit (5 minutes). Be prepared to share your discoveries.

In your group select two people, one as the speaker in the monologue and the other as the *other teacher* in the monologue. Now, put your acting "masks" on and recreate the scene where these two meet after this incident in the staffroom. Create the dialogue that could possibly ensue. You decide how the situation plays out— positively or negatively. Other group members could become other teachers in the staffroom witnessing the exchange and they could interject their thoughts at any time. You can construct a short skit (5 minutes). Be prepared to share your discoveries.

Activity 5
Individual Activity – Personal Written Response

Now that you have had a chance to hear numerous perspectives, respond to the scaffolding questions on the sheet provided offering your personal and professional response. The sheet details: sharing your responses to the class discussions of the day, offering your questions or puzzles that need to be addressed and also, sharing your thoughts on the dramatic monologue as an instructive teaching tool within the classroom landscape. There is also an area designated for your written permission to use your comments (anonymously) for our collaborative endeavor.

Appendix B
Responding to Scaffolding Questions

1. Discuss the effectiveness of the dramatic monologue as an instructional technique.
2. Discuss the effectiveness of the dramatic monologue *'Who Speaks for Whom?'* in regards to addressing issues of Equity and Diversity in Education.
3. Discuss the effectiveness of the follow-up activities in prompting an examination of the issues raised in the dramatic monologue, *'Who Speaks for Whom?'*
4. How has today's workshop informed your personal understanding of Equity and Diversity issues?
5. Any additional comments ...

Name (please print): _____

I grant permission to use my (anonymous) written response for research publication purposes for the project entitled **'LET'S TALK DIVERSITY: A DRAMATIC MONOLOGUE AS A TOOL FOR RESPONSIBLE TEACHER CONVERSATIONS'** by Julian Kitchen and Darryl Bautista. (Please sign, if interested only).
SIGNATURE: _____

Part Two
TESOL Interfaces 2(1)

2008

5. Solidifying Academic Tradition
David Kent

The Graduate School of TESOL-MALL is proud to have established an academic and publishing service for new academics, and students of MA TESOL programs in Korea and around the world (see Bautista, 2007). This continues with the second issue of our online journal *Interfaces*, and solidifies for Woosong University a link to a research agenda that is an entrenched aspect of the higher education community (Brew & Baud, 1995).

Master and doctoral degree students, or recent graduates, are encouraged to submit articles for publication after working with their current supervisors to prepare an article for submission. However, Woosong students are especially encouraged to submit research articles as these will count as a pass for one Comprehensive Examination Paper. Student research articles will also be in the running for an annual 'Best Student Paper Award' in the form, for example, of department store gift certificates. (Note: forum articles are acceptable for Woosong masters students seeking a pass towards candidacy, but these are not in the running for the comprehensive examination pass or the student paper award).

It is hoped that through the process and experience of publication the continuously changing relationship between knowledge, teaching and research (see Brew, 1999) can be further explored and contextualized by future graduates and budding scholars. It is only through such an endeavor that graduate students, particularly those in Korea, can come to understand the importance of conducting research, and the impact of globalization and changing roles in the setting of higher education in Asia (refer to Altbach, 2004; and, Coaldrake & Stedman, 1999).

For the current issue we have collated two research articles, and two forum articles:

Multimedia and Language Learning Websites and their Place in English Education: Evaluation Strategies for EFL Teachers by Ezekiel Mentillo reviews existing research and strategies for evaluating multimedia software and internet-based materials for use in the EFL context. The article then comes to offer a new and more refined instrument for such evaluation.

The Social Construction of Literacy – A Case Study of Literacy Practices in the UK by Kolawole Waziri Olagboyega seeks to contribute to a continued exploration of third space or 'in between' literacy. Ultimately, the article explores the conceptual tools necessary to enable practitioners to characterize the space between literacy as expressed in the new adult core curriculum and literacy as expressed by the individual seeking to be confident with his/her reading and writing ability.

A Documents Analysis of the English Textbooks currently used in Korean Elementary Schools with some Comments on Problems Inherent to the System: A Practical Approach to Teaching English Mostly in English by Mark C. Love reviews existing materials used in Korean elementary schools to provide English teaching, and provides a document analysis. Factors that need considering, and various implementation techniques are also introduced along with practical methods to overcome shortcomings of the material.

The New 21st Century Literacy: Problems and Challenges for the Digital Age by Thomas D. Clarke explores the challenges and problems revolving around digital literacy. In this regard, the article recognizes various aspects that need addressing in order for the 'literate' to stay proficient and the 'illiterate' to acquire skills

We hope our readers will be able to enjoy a well-earned break over the next few months, enjoy reading this issue of *Interfaces*, and recharge for the forthcoming academic year. The next issue of *Interfaces* will be published mid-June of 2009, and we look forward to all future submissions.

References

Altbach, P. G. (2004). Globalization and the university: Myths and realities in an unequal world. *Tertiary Education and Management, 10*(1), 3-25.

Bautista, D. D. (2007). Editorial: There is a Place for Learning Experiences. *Interfaces, 1(1)*. Retrieved, November 27, 2008, from http://interfaces.tesolmall.net/jarticles/one-one/editorial1-1.pdf

Brew, A. (1999). Research and teaching: Changing relationships in a changing context. *Studies in Higher Education, 24*(3), 291-301.

Brew, A., & Baud, D. (1995). Teaching and research: Establishing the vital link with learning. *Higher Education, 29*(3), 261-273.

Coaldrake, P., & Stedman, L. (1999). *Academic Work in the Twenty-First Century: Changing roles and policies*. Occasional Papers Series. Canberra, Australia: Department of Education, Training and Youth Affairs.

6. Multimedia and Language Learning Websites and their Place in English Education: Evaluation Strategies for EFL Teachers

Ezekiel Mentillo

When considering the incorporation of multimedia learning systems into the language classroom many educators find themselves confronted with a lot more questions and choices than answers. Not all teachers are multimedia or computer experts and with the plethora of choices out there it can be very easy to make quick or rash choices based on the wrong details (Park, 2006). This article will examine some existing evaluation strategies' strengths and weaknesses. It will employ some of these strategies in the evaluation of several different language learning websites. A new set of evaluation criterion will be put fourth, based on existing models, theories, methods, and approaches, and utilized in a website review framework. A reflection and analysis will then be presented which will evaluate the effectiveness of the instrument. Ultimately, this article strives to provide an evaluation model that language teachers can easily use and interpret when confronted with the difficulties of selecting technological learning websites that are effective for themselves and their students.

Introduction

Why do educators, particularly language educators, need evaluation criteria for language learning, multimedia, and technology oriented education? What should these criteria consist of? These are the fundamental questions pertinent to this article. Education, both formal and informal, has inspired academic research for generations. From Dewey (1897) to Freire (1970), education as a social phenomenon instils an almost intrinsic sense of curiosity to those involved in it. Why is this? Is it because, deep down, we all want to be the best educators we can be? Is it because it is expected in the field of academia in order to garner some measure of fame or recognition? Whatever the motives, one need only do a search on EFL or ESL education, sift through vast number of articles in the TESOL Quarterly, or visit the language acquisition and TESOL (Teaching English to Speakers of Other Languages) sections of a library to see the concern that has been placed on language education over the years and generations. However, the current and next generation of education has become increasingly complicated. These complications stem from a new social force that has emerged and grown at a phenomenal rate in the last 40 years to embed and intertwine itself in almost every major function of human activity; technology, computers, and the internet (Sims, 2004).

Multimedia, language learning software, and language learning websites have begun to appear at incredible rates all over the world (Mayer, 2003; Park, 2006; Prensky, 2007; Sims, 2004). In fact, "there are now over 19,000 educational software programs from preschool through college from over 1,300 different publishers, and 316 software programs under the category of ESL (English as a Second Language)" (Park, 2006). With these kinds of numbers the need for evaluation standards and guidelines for software and web provided language learning material is of crucial importance, particularly to those who lack an expertise in the area of CALL (Computer Assisted Language Learning). This article will examine some of the evaluation tools available to educators and researchers in the area of CALL.

Another concern involved in the evaluation of CALL systems surrounds the criteria employed and the theoretical lens, if one is present at all, through which these criteria are derived (Mayer, 2003; Prensky, 2007; Thomas, 1997). It has been a concern of many in the field of multimedia education, and education as well, as to whether or not educational theory can or should be transferred from the classroom to the computer or even used at all (Burston, 2003; Kent, 2007; Mayer, 2003, 2007; Park, 2006; Prensky, 2007; Thomas, 1997). In order for evaluation techniques and criteria to be effective in evaluating language learning software and websites said criteria should be based, at least in part, on existing theory and research that have proven, through various forms of data, their triumphs and tribulations in the area of language acquisition (see Mayer; and, Burston). On the other hand, these criteria need to be creative and flexible enough to be able to discover new and often unexpected things (Prensky).

Theories can sometimes act as blinders to researchers (Thomas, 1997). This can narrow the research by shaping inquiries, imposing delimitations, anticipating outcomes, or simply disregarding data because it contradicts canonized theories within the field (Thomas, 1997; Prensky, 2007). It is also possible that computers and technology have created an entirely new area of education that cannot be defined or codified by existing research or data (Prensky). Further, Prensky suggests that along with this new field of study there are in fact two emerging classes of people. Those who were raised in a pre- technology era and were thrust into the computer age (Digital Immigrants). And those who were born into the computer age and thus more acclimated to its concordant environment (Digital Natives). One thing is certain, this age that sees technology rapidly growing and changing is yet still connected to the pre-technology generation, and we need to create new tools (Morgan, 2008; Sims, 2004). We, as educators, need to develop a means for "Digital Natives" and "Digital Immigrants" to collaborate and create tools, methods, and approaches for integrating technology into language education (Prensky, 2008; Park, 2006).

Some Evaluation Strategies

The purpose of this article is to investigate language learning website and software evaluation models and provide a model that is easier to use and less time consuming. These existent models, through investigation, use, analysis, and reflection contributed greatly to the development of an evaluation instrument that will provide teachers and educators a tool by which they can more easily evaluate language learning websites. The model proposed in this article entitled PWELT (Practical Website Evaluation for Language Teachers) is designed to be informative, pragmatic, time effective, and easy to interpret. This article is the first step in developing a set of evaluation models, akin to those of Son and Park, which will be designed to fit those involved in the educational process (teachers, students, administrators, parents, researchers, technicians, and publishers). However, for this process to be efficient some specific approaches were employed.

"In order to develop a Web evaluation system, it is important to undertake a research-based investigation of current Web sites, develop a prototype system, and then evaluate and adjust the prototype accordingly" (Son, 2005, 216). It also proved essential to not only look at criteria employed for evaluation, but also those used in the development of language learning websites. The first step, as Son suggests, is to take a research-based approach to investigation. There are a wide variety of criteria available to researchers evaluating language learning websites. Son provides a very good outline of some of these criteria as represented in Table 1.

Table 1.
Son's Outline of Existing Web site evaluation criteria

Researcher	Criteria
Alexander & Tate (1996)	Authority
	Accuracy
	Objectivity
	Currency
	Coverage
Davis (2000)	Authority and credibility
	Citation and accuracy
	Content
	Design
	Timeliness or Currency
Joseph (1999)	Speed
	First impression – general appearance
	Ease of site navigation
	Use of graphics/sounds/videos
	Content/Information
	Currency
	Availability of further information
McKenzie (1997)	Reliability
	Accuracy
	Authority
	Currency
	Fairness
	Adequacy
	Efficiency
	Organization
Nelson (1998)	Purpose
	Pedagogy
	Design/Construction
Schrock (1996)	Technical and visual aspects of the Web page
	Content
	Authority

Sequin (1999)	Origin
	Design
	Content
	Accessibility
	Currency

The criteria presented in Table 1 have many things in common, but the most prominent similarity between the systems is the inclusion of content. It is impossible to evaluate language learning sites, or any other learning website, without evaluating the content presented therein. However, with language learning websites numbering in the thousands evaluating content of every website is extraordinarily time consuming. So, putting content aside, there are among these criteria and terms, a great deal of broad and ambiguous terms and concepts that could be open to a great deal of interpretation by different academics and researchers. Understanding terminology can greatly affect understanding which can, in turn, affect evaluation criteria selection. Thomas (1997) provides an excellent example of how terminological interpretations can affect research and understanding:

'Theory' as a word must be one thing or another. It cannot — if it is to be used seriously to describe a particular kind of intellectual construction in education — have two or more meanings, unless the context in which it is used can universally and unequivocally distinguish those meanings. If we are to understand what "pipe" means, the word must refer only to that class of objects normally thought of as pipes; it must not also refer to dogs, vacuum cleaners, and trees. And if "pipe" does happen to be inconvenient enough to refer, as my dictionary tells me it does, to a musical wind instrument, to a tube, or to the note of a bird, I can be confident that the context — sentence, paragraph, or longer passage — will finish the job and furnish the right meaning. I cannot be so sure with "theory." For it is my contention that the context cannot distinguish the strong colors of meaning that alter with various uses of "theory," since the users themselves are rarely aware of the meaning they intend. (4).

The authors and researchers, as represented in Table 1, contextualize their intentions when defining each of their criteria. However, Thomas (1997) illustrates that some terms have with them a great number of epistemological and ideological strings attached that are often difficult to sever. With so many interpretations and implied meanings, it is even more difficult for teachers, who may or may not be educational research experts, to select language learning websites from the evaluation tools available to them at present. While current evaluation strategies, techniques, and criteria may be extremely thorough and specific, they seem to cater to a unique audience and assume terminological and theoretical understanding is present. More adaptation and refinement could produce a more egalitarian evaluation instrument.

Table 1 provides a general understanding of criteria to be considered in the evaluation of language learning websites and software; however through looking at CALICO (Computer Assisted Language Instruction Consortium) (CALICO, 2005) four evaluation criteria categories emerged as most commonly used. They are (1) Technical features, (2) Activities (procedure), (3) Teacher fit (approach), and (4) Leaner fit (design) (CALICO, 2005; Park, 2006). These four, along with many of the others provided in Table 1, seem most available to individuals who are versed in educational research and literature. While the function of these four criteria is apparent, they are so broad that they are open to a great deal of interpretation and involve a great deal of explanation (Park). It seems a daunting task to undertake when a teacher might have over 100 different sites to choose from and the resources available are either too expensive or difficult to interpret (Park, 2006; Son, 2005). Evaluation criteria could be more effective if they were situated in the context of the reviewer (Son). Evaluation instruments that cater to all stakeholders involved in the learning process from teachers, students, parents, publishers, administers, to researchers could provide a clearer and more informative evaluation (Son). This demands criteria that are available and intelligible to people outside the areas of educational research, TESOL, and applied linguistics.

Evaluation Instrument

In developing an evaluation strategy it is important to look at the rationale behind the initial creation/development of such tools as well as existing evaluation criteria, as mentioned above, along with others such as usability (Shield & Kukulska-Hulme, 2006). In this regard, Bell (1998) and Kelly (2000) provide a good framework when designing language learning websites (see Table 2). These frameworks, in addition to existing evaluation criteria can help to form the basis of an evaluation instrument. In simple terms it provides a very good way to see if web and software designers are practicing what they are preaching. The eight aspects asserted in Bell's framework and the nine proposed by Kelly are much more obvious and could prove to be more informative to teachers without an extensive theoretical background than some of the other criteria mentioned previously. They focus on aspects of websites that are pragmatic, fairly free of academic jargon, and thus more approachable to stakeholders like parents, students, and teachers with either limited or outdated theoretical and technical understanding (Prensky, 2007).

Table 2.

Bell and Kelly Frameworks for Designing Language Learning Websites

Bell Framework (1998)
1. Know your goals
2. Keep it simple
3. Borrow with honor
4. Provide context
5. Don't assume knowledge on the user's part
6. Don't assume technology on the user's part
7. Test your pages
8. Keep your pages up to date
Kelly Framework (2000)
1. Make your site usable by everyone if possible
2. Make your site as fast as possible
3. Make your site easy to use
4. Make your site useful
5. Maintain Integrity. Be professional
6. Make your site friendly and fun to use
7. Use 'cutting edge technology' wisely and effectively
8. Remember that what you think is true may not be true
9. Worry about the minority who use less powerful computers, use older browsers and have slow Internet access

Based, in part, on the scope of these aspects of website development, Son (2005) designed 15 areas by which websites could be evaluated. These 15 areas were rated on a 5-point Likert type scale ranging from "Very satisfactory", "Satisfactory", "Uncertain", "Unsatisfactory", to "Very Unsatisfactory." Park (2006) argues that the subjectivity of using a Likert type scale leaves the data open to criticism but, this scale, similar to questionnaires, leaves the reviewer at least some minimal degree of autonomy when performing evaluations (Park). While the subjective aspects might leave the results open to criticism, it also allows the reviewer the chance to maintain and assert his/her point of view. If a collaborative approach, using multiple stakeholders and their points of view, were employed then perhaps those subjective viewpoints might be seen as points of insight into the educational process and the participants involved therein.

The Likert type scale also includes "uncertain" as a way for reviewers to exclude elements of websites that they don't understand without negatively or positively affecting the overall rating of the site. Along with the 15 areas of evaluation presented in Table 3, Son (2005) also included a cover page with space for a Title, URL, target audience, language activities, and a brief site description. The cover page or "at a glance" description is also present in other evaluation frameworks (CALICO, 2005).

Table 3.
Son's 15 Website Evaluation Criteria

	Website Evaluation Criteria
1. Purpose	Is the purpose clear?
	Is the content in line with the purpose?
	Is the website appropriate for its targeted learner?
2. Accuracy	Is the content accurate?
	Are spelling and grammar accurate?
3. Currency	Is the Website current?
	Is the Website updated regularly?
4. Authority	Is there information on the author?
	Is the author well-recognized for his or her work?
5. Loading Speed	Does the Website download fast?
	Do the content pages download efficiently?
6. Usefulness	Does the Website provide useful information?
	Are the language activities or tasks useful?

7. Organization	Is the Website well organized and presented? Is the Website interesting to look at and explore? Are screen displays effective?
8. Navigation	Is the Website easy to navigate? Are on-screen instructions easy to follow? Is it easy to retrieve information? Are hyperlinks given properly?
9. Reliability	Is the Website free of bugs and breaks? Is the Website free of dead links?
10. Authenticity	Are the learning materials authentic? Are authentic materials provided in appropriate contexts?
11. Interactivity	Is the Website interactive? Are methods for user input effectively employed?
12. Feedback	Is feedback on learner responses encouraging? Is error handling meaningful and helpful?
13. Multimedia	Does the Website make effective use of graphics, sound and color? Is the level of audio quality, the scale of graphics or video display appropriate for language learning?
14. Communication	Can the user communicate with real people on-line through the Website? Is on-line help available?
15. Integration	Can the learning materials be integrated into a curriculum? Does the content fit with curricular goals?

Based on the work, research, and insights from Bell (1998), CALICO, Kelly (2000), Park (2006), and Son (2005) a more accessible and pragmatic website evaluation framework has been constructed and is presented in Table 4 below as PWELT (Practical Web Evaluation for Language Teachers). The framework developed retains effective aspects while including others with changes and adaptations. The use of a title page that provides at a glance information (as present in CALICO evaluations as well as Park's criteria) was both informative and easily accessible. Core technical features such as integration, multimedia, organization, navigation, reliability, and currency are both effective and informative, and thus they were incorporated into the PWELT model.

Several of these features were combined into one evaluation criteria or augmented with other factors appropriate for consideration. For example, 'navigation' was supplemented with 'accessibility' in order to incorporate the use of labels and links as well as ease of access to different activities.

The framework has a title page that shows the title, URL, target language, activity types, system requirements, and a brief site description. This 'title page' is provided so that teachers can get a broad outline of what the site consists of so that they can gain a basic understanding of the site at a glance. The instrument consists of 18 different areas of investigation divided into two separate orientations. The first, 'technological orientation' includes 10 aspects of the website that have to do with the various technological aspects of the site such as, organization, first impression, navigation, and usability. The second, 'educational orientation' includes eight aspects of the site that have to do with educational efficiency such as purpose, scaffolding, feedback, and validity.

The 18 criteria employed in the PWELT model were chosen to cater to the needs and expertise of language teachers. The criteria focused on 'educational orientation' are ones that incorporate theoretical and pedagogical areas of investigation such as validity, purpose, and scaffolding along with more contextually based evaluation tools like authenticity, entertainment, and integration. Scaffolding is included as a means to evaluate if important tools are given to the learner in order to succeed in the activities presented and as a way for teachers to ascertain what, if anything needs to be provided prior to students working with the web site. Purpose and validity are criteria aimed more towards insuring sound educational foundations are present within the site.

The criteria for the 'technical orientation' section of PWELT provide a means by which the technical aspects of a web site can be evaluated as well as interpretational feedback based on things like first impression, usability, and appeal. This kind of feedback brings a qualitative edge to the evaluation that allows teachers to offer their experience and feedback using different language learning web sites. Appeal/first impression was chosen as a way to recognize the importance a 'first impression' can have in web site selection (Park, 2006).

Table 4.
PWELT Criteria

Technological orientation	
1. Appeal/First Impression	Does the website hook your interest? Are you interested in looking further?
2. Accessibility/Navigation	Are activities easy to access? Is the site easy to navigate? Are instructions clearly labeled and easy to read?
3. Organization	Is the site organized? Are links easy to access and conveniently placed? Are activities logically organized?
4. System Requirements	Are system requirements clearly defined? Does the site specify exactly what software/hardware is needed?

5. Reliability	Is the site free of bugs or breaks? Is loading speed reasonable?
6. Currency	Is the website current? How often is the site updated? Is the site free of dead links?
7. Commercialism	Is the site obscured by advertisements?
8. Interactivity	Does the site utilize Web 2.0 technology? Are there interactive aspects to the site? (Chats, forums, etc.)
9. Multimedia	Does the sight effectively use a variety of different graphics, sounds, colors, videos, etc? Is the level of audio, video, or graphic quality appropriate for language learning?
10. Usability	Is the sight easy to use for both native and non-native English speakers, both teachers and students?
11. Purpose	Is the purpose clear? Is the content in line with the purpose?
12. Scaffolding	Are activities properly scaffolded? Are learners provided with warm up activities, vocabulary, and/or other materials to prepare them for the activity?
13. Authenticity	Is material authentic? Are voices, dialogues, topics, graphics, videos, etc. authentically represented contextually?
14. Integration/Application	Are materials and lessons easily integrated into an existing curriculum or educational system? Does content reflect curricular goals and objectives?

15. Feedback	Is feedback provided to the learner? Is feedback meaningful and supportive?
16. Validity	Do tasks and activities reflect a pedagogical or theoretical underpinning? Is content in line with a specific approach or approaches?
17. Accuracy	Is content correct? Are grammar, vocabulary, reading, and writing accurate?
18. Entertainment	Is the site interesting or entertaining? Is the site going to encourage further and extended use?

These 18 criteria are each employed for specific reasons. The specificity of the criteria primarily applies to *teacher* evaluations of different websites. When devising methods for evaluation it is important to ascertain 'Who evaluates language learning software/websites?' (Park, 2006). Determining who is going to do the evaluating is one of the first steps in devising and or proposing a model for evaluation (Son, 2005; Park, 2006). One must also ask the question 'Why are we doing the evaluation?' (Park, 2006). The PWELT evaluation model is proposed for its pragmatism. The application of evaluations should be of the utmost importance. Choosing to employ technology in the language classroom for technologies sake alone can have a negative impact on the language learning process (Morgan, 2008). For evaluations to be most effective not only do they need to be informative, but they should also be accessible to those who may not have technical or educational expertise. Assumptions should not be made about language teachers understanding of technical and/or pedagogical jargon just as websites should not be designed for those with the most sophisticated computer systems (Kelly, 2000). Evaluations should not necessarily cater to the lowest common denominator, but should at least be accessible to all those involved in the process (Kelly).

Implementation

With an evaluation model in place several websites were evaluated to test the efficiency the PWELT model. First, the model proposed by Son (2005) was used to evaluate several different language learning websites. After the evaluations a critical analysis of the evaluations and the instrument was conducted. Subsequent to the analysis some areas emerged in which the model could be improved. First, some additional information could be provided on the 'title page.' This could lead to the title page to be more informative, particularly with regard to system requirements. In this way language teachers could immediately identify exactly what types of requirements their systems would need to have in order to effectively implement them into their classrooms. This is a very simple way in which teachers could narrow down the scope of their search based on the systems available to them. It should be noted that further research and refinement of the PWELT model needs to be done to in order to assess if the evaluation model is truly effective.

The PWELT model also provides a list of the different activities available on the website. This is yet another way in which teachers can quickly and efficiently narrow their search based on the types of activities they are looking for. This is important as the sheer volume of language learning websites demands a quick way for teachers to narrow their search without having to actually visit and navigate each and every site themselves, a task that most teachers and researchers can tell is very time consuming. By leafing through evaluation 'title pages' teachers can determine which sites might be effective for their classrooms without even having to go online. PWELT is not intended as a model by which language teachers should base web site selection on, but a tool to inform and alleviate some of the time management issues that language teachers may face.

The next change that was applied was to separate the 18 evaluation criteria into two separate sections. These different sections made it easier to evaluate the sites and their component parts. By compartmentalizing the criteria, evaluators may be able to focus more on the technical aspects of the site during the primary visit. Subsequent visits could then focus on the pedagogy, content, integration and other educational aspects of the sight. The compartmentalizing of evaluation foci may also help for teachers or researchers to put more attention on aspects of web sites more suited to their areas of expertise. For instance, a teacher with a rich technical background may choose to spend more time evaluating the technical aspects of the site. Thus, the first section focuses on technological features of the site. If the technical features do not meet expectations then the evaluation can be shortened without expending serious amounts of time or energy. The first technical evaluation criterion is 'first impression.' This has the potential to be one of the most valuable, and often most misused evaluation criteria. Teachers who are stretched for time or lack technical expertise might find themselves lured by the 'wow factor' a website possesses and overlook other more crucial aspects of the site (Park, 2006).

If the site meets the technical standards of the evaluator then the educational features can be evaluated. For a teacher with more of a pedagogical expertise this is one of the most integral and time consuming processes. By the point of educational evaluation the scope of the search could have become more significantly focused due to the technical evaluation 'weeding out' those sites that are not compatible with their systems. Teachers can then spend their time sifting through educational content (according to Son (2005) in Table 1, one of the most important features) of sites that they know they can use.

This model was designed to save time and be useful for teachers. It was proposed as a way in which teachers can quickly ascertain the importance and applicability of a language learning web site without having to read sometimes long-winded, jargon laden academic and/or technical reviews.

Reflection and Conclusions

Retrospective analysis can be one of the most useful tools in a teacher's critical arsenal. Keeping this in mind, the PWELT model proposed in this article builds on and extends existing models. Although the model still needs to undergo further trialing, its development is a change toward increasing the ease and effectiveness of language learning web site evaluations for teachers. However, the model does not take into account the opinions of other important stakeholders in the educational process and a later iteration will need to focus more on this aspect.

As mentioned earlier, collaboration is one of the greatest tools at the language instructor's disposal. It is only through getting all parties involved that more effective evaluation tools and thus more effective language learning websites can be reviewed and developed. Park (2006) developed a conceptual map for "A New Consortium of Educational (Language Learning) Software Evaluation" (see Table 5). This conceptual map concisely identifies some major stakeholders in the educational process and what their roles need to focus on in the design and evaluation of language learning software and websites.

Table 5.
Park's Conceptual Map of a New Consortium of Educational (Language Learning) Software Evaluation

Teacher's Roles (including parents and administrators)	1. Checking necessity of software use 2. Considering contexts and environments 3. Evaluating software programs with updated tools 4. Classroom teaching or field trials 5. Reflection on interaction and effects 6. Professional development
Researchers Roles (teacher educators')	1. Preparing methodological guidelines 2. Evaluating the outcomes of educational software 3. Providing psychometric standards and content information 4. Collecting data from field tests 5. Providing updated comprehensive guidelines 6. Providing the opportunities of professional development
Publisher's Roles (including software designers)	1. Collecting the information of teaching methodology from researchers 2. Collecting evaluation tools and research results 3. Collecting all the content components of the software 4. Frequent update and revision 5. Searching for other supporting ways (e.g., Internet) 6. Collecting feedback from teachers and researchers before and after publishing

This conceptual map encapsulates the steps necessary to develop more effective language learning websites and software as well as more efficient evaluation models and techniques. However, this model fails to take into account other stakeholders in the educational process; teachers and parents.

The 'Consortium for Evaluation' provided above could be extended to include students' and parents' specific roles in the development and evaluation of language learning software and websites. Since many teachers and researchers may occupy multiple roles, in that they may also be parents and/or students, in the consortium it is important that we understand our roles and do our best to fulfill them in order to continue to improve language education as it continues to evolve (Sims, 2004). As technology tends to evolve more rapidly than educational research, it is of vital importance that educators have effective evaluation tools at their disposal (Prensky, 2007; Mayer, 2003). It is only through collaborating with parents, publishers, researchers, technical experts, teachers, and students that we can hope to keep pace with the steady surge of technology.

Technology is here to stay. Technology alone, however, can introduce some difficulties into the learning process (Morgan, 2008). Teachers are present to provide educational guidance and identify some of the difficulties that can arise when incorporating technology into the language classroom (Mayer, 2003; Morgan, 2008). Education is and always will be dependent on the human parties involved. The evaluation model proposed in this article emphasized the need for evaluation tools to be easy to use and easy to interpret. The next step will be to embrace an educational consortium and develop evaluation models and frameworks, for all parties involved, which cater to their individual expertise. The PWELT model proposed in this article is but one step in the creation of evaluation tools that can help determine the value and effectiveness of language learning websites. Education is a social phenomenon and thus will often include the social parties involved. While technology continues to play bigger and bigger parts of human life it is important to remember that more technology is not always better, particularly in the field of education. Technology developed on the fly and haphazardly applied to educational programs could be more harmful than helpful (Morgan, 2008). As Burston 2003 states, "pedagogy must drive technology and not vice versa".

References

Burston, J. (2003). Software selection: A primer on sources and evaluation. *CALICO Journal, 21*(1), 29-40.

Dewey, J. (1897). My Pedagogic Creed. *Wikisource,* Retrieved from http://en.wikisource.org/wiki/My_Pedagogic_Creed

Fetaji, B. (2007). E-Learning Literature Review to Investigate Reasons of E-Learning Failures to Meet the Expectancies. In G. Richards (Ed.), *Proceedings of World Conference on E-Learning in Corporate, Government, Healthcare, and Higher Education 2007* (266-275).

Freire, P. (1970). *Pedagogy of the Oppressed.* New York, NY: Continuum.

Jeong, B.S. (2005). Exploring and evaluating language learning Web sites. In Son, Jeong- Bae and O'Neill, Shirley, (Eds.) *Enhancing learning and teaching: pedagogy, technology and language* (215-228). Australia: Post Pressed.

Kelly, C. (2000). Guidelines for Designing a Good Web Site for EFL Students. *The Internet TESL Journal, 6*(3). Retrieved http://iteslj.org/Articles/Kelly-Guidelines.html

Kent, D.B. (2007). Effective Multi-Media Based Learning in EFL: Comparing Two Comprehension Models. *Interfaces, Vol. 1*(1).

Morgan, M. (2008). More Productive Use of Technology in the ESL/EFL Classroom. *The Internet TESL Journal, 14*(7).

Park, J.S. (2006). Language Learning Software Evaluation: Top-down or Bottom-up? *Asian EFL Journal, 13*(2).

Shield, L. & Kukulska-Hulme, A. (2006). Are Language Learning Websites Special? Towards a Research Agenda for Discipline-Specific Usability. *Journal of Educational Multimedia and Hypermedia, 15*(3), 349-369.

Sims, R. (2004). Trends, Fads and Futures: 21 Years of Educational Multimedia - Where Have We Got To, and Where Should We Go? In L. Cantoni & C. McLoughlin (Eds.), *Proceedings of World Conference on Educational Multimedia, Hypermedia and Telecommunications 2004* (3755-3766).

Appendix

Practical Web Evaluation for Language Teachers (PWELT) Language Learning Website Evaluation Form		
Site Information		
Title		
URL		
Target Audience		
Language Skills/ Language Focus Area	☐ Reading ☐ Speaking ☐ Listening ☐ Writing	☐ Grammar ☐ Vocabulary ☐ Pronunciation
	Other _____	
Activity Types		
System Requirements	☐ Flash player ☐ QuickTime ☐ Media Player ☐ Writing	☐ Speakers ☐ Web cam ☐ MP3 player ☐ Java script
	Browser type _____ Other _____	
Site Description		

Site Evaluation: Technological Orientation	
1. Appeal/First Impression Does the website hook your interest? Are you interested in looking further?	☐ Very satisfactory ☐ Satisfactory ☐ Uncertain ☐ Unsatisfactory ☐ Very Unsatisfactory
2. Accessibility/Navigation Are activities easy to access? Is the site easy to navigate? Are instructions clearly labeled and easy to read?	☐ Very satisfactory ☐ Satisfactory ☐ Uncertain ☐ Unsatisfactory ☐ Very Unsatisfactory
3. Organization Is the site organized? Are links easy to access and conveniently placed? Are activities logically organized?	☐ Very satisfactory ☐ Satisfactory ☐ Uncertain ☐ Unsatisfactory ☐ Very Unsatisfactory
4. System Requirements Are system requirements clearly defined? Does the site specify exactly what software/hardware?	☐ Very satisfactory ☐ Satisfactory ☐ Uncertain ☐ Unsatisfactory ☐ Very Unsatisfactory
5. Reliability Is the site free of bugs or breaks? Is loading speed reasonable?	☐ Very satisfactory ☐ Satisfactory ☐ Uncertain ☐ Unsatisfactory ☐ Very Unsatisfactory
6. Currency Is the website current? How often is the site updated? Is the site free of dead links?	☐ Very satisfactory ☐ Satisfactory ☐ Uncertain ☐ Unsatisfactory ☐ Very Unsatisfactory

7. <u>Commercialism</u> Is the site obscured by advertisements?	☐ Very satisfactory ☐ Satisfactory ☐ Uncertain ☐ Unsatisfactory ☐ Very Unsatisfactory
8. <u>Interactivity</u> Does the site utilize Web 2.0 technology? Are there interactive aspects to the site? (chats, forums, etc)	☐ Very satisfactory ☐ Satisfactory ☐ Uncertain ☐ Unsatisfactory ☐ Very Unsatisfactory
9. <u>Multimedia</u> Does the sight effectively use a variety of different graphics, sounds, colors, videos, etc? Is the level of audio, video, or graphic quality appropriate for language learning?	☐ Very satisfactory ☐ Satisfactory ☐ Uncertain ☐ Unsatisfactory ☐ Very Unsatisfactory
10. <u>Usability</u> Is the sight easy to use for both native and non-native English speakers, both teachers and students?	☐ Very satisfactory ☐ Satisfactory ☐ Uncertain ☐ Unsatisfactory ☐ Very Unsatisfactory
11. <u>Purpose</u> Is the purpose clear? Is the content in line with the purpose?	☐ Very satisfactory ☐ Satisfactory ☐ Uncertain ☐ Unsatisfactory ☐ Very Unsatisfactory
12. <u>Scaffolding</u> Are activities properly scaffolded? Are learners provided with warm up activities, vocabulary, and/or other materials to prepare them for the activity?	☐ Very satisfactory ☐ Satisfactory ☐ Uncertain ☐ Unsatisfactory ☐ Very Unsatisfactory

13. <u>Authenticity</u> Is material authentic? Are voices, dialogues, topics, graphics, videos, etc. authentically represented contextually?	☐ Very satisfactory ☐ Satisfactory ☐ Uncertain ☐ Unsatisfactory ☐ Very Unsatisfactory
14. <u>Integration/Application</u> Are materials and lessons easily integrated into an existing curriculum or educational system? Does content reflect curricular goals and objectives?	☐ Very satisfactory ☐ Satisfactory ☐ Uncertain ☐ Unsatisfactory ☐ Very Unsatisfactory
15. <u>Feedback</u> Is feedback provided to the learner? Is feedback meaningful and supportive?	☐ Very satisfactory ☐ Satisfactory ☐ Uncertain ☐ Unsatisfactory ☐ Very Unsatisfactory
16. <u>Validity</u> Do tasks and activities reflect a pedagogical or theoretical underpinning? Is content in line with a specific approach or approaches?	☐ Very satisfactory ☐ Satisfactory ☐ Uncertain ☐ Unsatisfactory ☐ Very Unsatisfactory
17. <u>Accuracy</u> Is content correct? Are grammar, vocabulary, reading, and writing accurate?	☐ Very satisfactory ☐ Satisfactory ☐ Uncertain ☐ Unsatisfactory ☐ Very Unsatisfactory
18. <u>Entertainment</u> Is the site interesting or entertaining? Is the site going to encourage further and extended use?	☐ Very satisfactory ☐ Satisfactory ☐ Uncertain ☐ Unsatisfactory ☐ Very Unsatisfactory

Overall Rating	☐ Very satisfactory
	☐ Satisfactory
	☐ Uncertain
	☐ Unsatisfactory
	☐ Very Unsatisfactory
Comments	
Reviewer	**Date**

7. The Social Construction of Literacy – A Case Study of Literacy Practices in the UK

Kolawole Waziri Olagboyega

This article is a contribution, or at least signposts a contribution, to a continued exploration of third space or 'in between' literacy. This third space 'in between' literacy is a hybrid literacy discourse, apart from the autonomous vs. multiplicity polarity. It is a discursive exploration that acknowledges Literacy practices as fluid, migratory and continuously mutating, with emergent literacies simultaneously embodying and transcending the practices and ideologies from which they are formed. My intention is to imagine what a developmental framework, enabling a full analysis of this hybridity, this constant re-negotiation between the local and distant (Brandt & Clinton, 2002), between the local and global, between Literacy and literacy, may consist of. What conceptual tools are necessary to enable practitioners to characterize the space between literacy as expressed in the new adult literacy core-curriculum and literacy as expressed by an individual who wants nothing more than 'to feel more confident about her reading and writing'.

Introduction

This research project represents my ongoing attempt to explore the varying spaces surrounding adult literacy that have come to define my experience within academic and practitioner networks. It is an exploration that occurs within the context of a particular organization's attempt to interpret and implement New Labor's Skills for Life agenda.

This agenda is, in part, an articulation of the status awarded literacy by various late-capitalist governments struggling to assert/retain ascendancy within an increasingly competitive globalized economy. Contemporary policy makers, in their drive to improve the nation's basic skills, herald and cherish a belief in literacy as possessing breathtaking qualities.

> *Our success in the world, and the cohesion of the communities in which we live, depend on how well we utilize the skills and abilities of all our people. A prosperous and decent society ... [cannot be achieved] ... while large numbers of people lack basic literacy and numeracy skills (Blunkett, 2001, 2).*

Literacy is offered as an uneasy combination of superhero and deity - economic savior, healer of marginalized communities. It has the capacity to stimulate functional, intelligent, work-dedicated families, communities and individuals. Without literacy the country is doomed to economic oblivion, a mythology reified by continual shock: horror newspaper headlines, saturated with moral panic, invoking the illiterate as folk devil and economic saboteur (Barton 2000, 14). The thinly disguised quantophrenics, revealed in the Big Magic numbers of international surveys of adult literacy showing Britain as lagging behind our European counterparts, rationalize this mysticism.

The Skills for Life agenda has a localized expression that alters the institutional life of everyone involved in the delivery of adult basic skills. Providers of adult learning are persuaded through funding incentives into implementing the Basic Skills Quality Initiative.

This initiative focuses on the delivery of four key objectives:
1. improvement in the quality of basic skills provision
2. improved experience for learners
3. increase in the number of learners participating in basic skills provision

4. improvements in the retention and achievement rates on basic skills programs

Skills for Life at a London College

At Ealing, Hammersmith and West London College Literacy Centre (henceforth EHWLC Lit) the re-articulation of the national agenda has taken the form of firstly a vision:

Recognizing that basic skills is an important barrier to learning, the EHWLC Lit aims to remove these barriers for all those with basic skills needs and support their continued learning through:

Discrete basic skills program with clear progression routes and appropriate accreditation where relevant;

- *Specialist provision for students with learning difficulties and disabilities through its SLDD provision and for deaf people through its Centre for Deaf People;*
- *Engagement programs for specific targeted groups using a range of curriculum 'hooks';*
- *Additional learning support and open access study skills center.*

A vision that is further reduced to concrete activities with quantifiable outcomes:

Over the next three years the EHWLC Lit aims to build on this provision and develop further opportunities through:

- *Partnership Basic Skills provision in the community;*
- *Short course program of integrated basic skills and vocational/academic subjects with clear progression routes;*
- *Increased awareness by all staff of the impact of basic skills needs on the teaching and learning process and a staff development program for teaching staff across all areas* (EHWLC Lit., 2000).

Rationale: Professional Pragmatism

If the Basic Skills Quality Initiative represents a figurative backdrop to this study, in the foreground are various contradictions and inconsistencies that continually unfold in the process of its implementation. I discuss these discrepancies using the geographic metaphor of distance and space.

This is a metaphor inspired by the work of Edwards (1997) who offers an understanding of education as shifting from what was – prior to the operationalization of learning society – a neatly bounded, clearly defined field of work into a de-differentiated ambiguous moor land. In using this metaphor I am suggesting that while 'literacy' may be viewed as a single terrain, a distinct country, its boundaries, its defining features, its shape and climate are far from unified.

As a literacy practitioner, I am inexorably drawn into a consideration of spaces:
- between literacy as policy construction and literacy as lived experience;
- between perceptions of what adults with poor literacy can do and what those adults so defined describe themselves as doing;
- between what policy and pedagogy determine that adults with poor literacy need and what those same adults describe as their needs

This research project represents my attempt to further define and map these spaces: to establish boundary points, contours, agreements, arguments and contestations by gathering and analyzing the words and images invoked by my counterparts when asked about their views, experiences, perceptions, values, beliefs, practices and knowledge of literacy.

This study has the potential for immediate and direct professional gain. An exploration of, literacy as defined at the

EHWLC Lit would provide a clearer and more sustainable framework for the delivery of the Skills for Life agenda. The introduction of a sustainable adult literacy program to the EHWLC Lit implies an enormous cultural shift, a radically altered organizational ethos. EHWLC Lit, a center in a large general further education college in West London, has not traditionally worked with communities who fall outside the ABC1[1] category. Colleagues retell, with pride, stories of their success in resisting the utilitarian vocationalizm that dominates much post- compulsory education, provocatively holding onto its commitment to adult learning as a leisurely pursuit, the 'Liberal Arts'. It has in many respects the feel of a would-be university for adults. The staff newsletter boasts that staff members are not experts in their field, but 'the' experts in their field. An often-pointed out response to the possibility of identifying and supporting students with literacy difficulties is that 'we don't get such students here'. I describe the above based on my experiences of the organization in which I work. It is and can only be a particular partisan view - an interpretation of the significance of selected utterances woven together to form an image: a fabrication. Yet EHWLC Lit's Basic Skills Quality Initiative Vision, the removal of poor basic skills as a barrier to learning, has potency because of the context from which it emerges - a context that has not traditionally prioritized the needs of marginalized communities.

The drive to ensure this organization becomes more sensitive to the needs of students with literacy difficulties inevitably furthers the interests of those of us working primarily with the C2Des[2]. Indeed, I would suggest, the nature of policy change is such that if the professional interests of particular groups are furthered, the interests of other groups are potentially undermined, compromised or in some way redefined. Inherent in the process of cultural change is the possibility of conflict.

My struggle to understand literacy at EHWLC Lit does not emerge from a desire to produce consensus, to neutralize conflict. My approach is one of wanting to establish how a program of adult literacy can be developed in the organization, embedded within the pedagogic practices of colleagues, in ways that cohere with their perception of literacy and its significance. At an organizational level the study furthers the sustainable and successful implantation of the Basic Skills Quality Intuitive, and thus New Labor's Skills for Life agenda.

Beyond the Pragmatic: Theoretical

The literacy of policy makers is unproblematically defined by the Basic Skills Agency as:

"The ability to read, write, and speak in English (or Welsh), and to use mathematics at a level necessary to function at work and in society in general" (Basic Skills Agency, 2003). This stands in diametric opposition to literacy as conceptualized by the ethnographers of the New Literacy Studies: *'Literacy may be defined as the space between thought and text'* (Barton and Hamilton, 1998).

There has in recent years - since the development of the New Literacy Studies - been a paradigm shift in how literacy is studied. This has resulted in a shift from a psychological or cognitive model of literacy as a set of pre-defined skills, a series of absolute behaviors to one that incorporates a view of literacy as essentially relational, a historically situated social and communicative practice. The ecology of literacy in everyday life repositions literacy and definitions of literacy as ideological. It is no longer an autonomous gift bestowed on certain individuals, but is contingent and therefore implicated in institutional purposes and power relationships.

This undermines the notion of understanding literacy in terms of lack or deficit; contemporary policy has institutionalized this view of deficit in the abstraction of literacy as level. The literacy of policy construction exists on a vertical line from Entry Level 3 to Level 2; this metaphor implies that individuals have this or that amount of literacy that can be measured using uni-dimensional scale. This abstraction co-exists with the caveat that students invariably present with a spiky profile - that is they portray characteristics and behaviors belonging to varying levels simultaneously. It is, however, possible to view the caveat 'spiky profile' as the defining feature of literacy rather than an anomaly. This is the stance of the ethnographers from the New Literacy Studies; literacy is a series of practices - literacies - in which people engage with texts in diverse ways as part of discourse communities. Literacy practices represent ways of being in the world and exist alongside other culturally defined ways of being, including ways of talking, acting, thinking, believing, valuing and interpreting (Hamilton 2000).

These representations of Literacy (with a capital 'L' to suggest the uni-dimensional construct of policy makers) and literacies (with a small 'l' to suggest the multiple literacies of ethnographers) are for the moment presented dichotomously (Gee 1996). This is not literacy as a continuum, one inexorably metamorphosing into the other, existing at a point where for an ephemeral moment at least they each become indecipherably the other. The autonomous Literacy of the policy makers, emerging from what Hamilton (2001) describes as enactive research - research which justifies particular short term policy interventions to solve a perceived problem quickly; versus the ecological literacy of ethnographic research, with its pronounced ethical stance, that offers an in-depth portrayal of literacies and values, beliefs, practices that explain how and why people behave the way they do with text. The two notions co- exist as if they inhabited mutually exclusive zones.

The difficulty with this mutual exclusion is that autonomous models of literacy overlap continually with vernacular literacies within a single entity – an organization, person, classroom or text. They can only be viewed as theoretical polarities - a discourse dichotomy. The interaction of literacy as lived experience, and literacy as policy construct experienced by literacy practitioners and recipients of the Skills for Life agenda – is a remarkably unexplored, untheorized space. Anita Wilson, in attempting to unravel this intricacy, has described the juxtaposition as 'third space' literacy (Wilson 2000).

This study is a contribution, or at least signposts a contribution, to a continued exploration of third space or 'in between' literacies. This third space 'in between' literacy is a hybrid literacy discourse, apart from the autonomous vs. multiplicitous polarity. It is a discursive exploration that acknowledges literacy practices as fluid, migratory and continuously mutating, with emergent literacies simultaneously embodying and transcending the practices and ideologies from which they are formed.

My intention is to imagine what a developmental framework, enabling a full analysis of this hybridity, this constant re-negotiation between the local and distant (Brandt & Clinton 2002), between the local and global, between Literacy and literacy, may consist of. What conceptual tools are necessary to enable practitioners to characterize the space between literacy as expressed in the new adult literacy core- curriculum and literacy as expressed by an individual who wants nothing more than 'to feel more confident about her reading and writing'.

As the new Head of Skills for Life and Adult Development at the College, my desire is to come to an understanding of how my colleagues accommodate apparent contradictions, within the center: the organization, the manager, the management team, the teacher, the student or the text - each of my colleagues has to reconcile or hybridize contradictions in these domains, (or find some other mechanism that enables them to co-exist). In wanting to find out the possibilities for this mix, I need to uncover how agreement and contestation coalesce around my subject, literacy.

I work towards the creation of the possibility of dialogue between the two positions, inviting the autonomous view of literacy in policy construction to become alert to the insights of literacy as socio-cultural practice, and the proponents of a socio-cultural view to offer an account of how and why they continually assert themselves to destabilize or further the autonomous literacy that dominates public life. In adding a dimension to an understanding of literacy, the study has a potential impact beyond the EHWLC Lit. It highlights some of the possible issues and constraints experienced by colleagues working in other similar situations.

To gain entrance to this territory, I ask a single question:
"Do students, tutors and managers at the EHWLC Lit share a common conception of what literacy is, how literacy is learnt and who literacy students are?"
In suggesting the study is about space, I have potentially already answered the question. And yet, my hunch that these differences exist is only a hunch. I may find more agreement than contestation. There is after all a popularized and publicly available definition of literacy.
My earlier discussion may have implied that an understanding of competing theorizations of literacy as a polarity is an accepted framework. I want to deviate from this position and suggest greater diversity and fragmentation than the polarity sketched above admits.

The Irish National Adult Literacy Agency (2003), offers a far more expansive view of literacy than one widely accepted and used by the Basic Skills Agency in England.

> ... *the integration of listening, speaking, reading, writing and numeracy. It also encompasses aspects of personal development, social, economic, Emotional, and is concerned with improving self-esteem and building confidence. It goes far beyond the mere technical skills of communication. The underlying aim of good literacy practice is to enable people to understand and reflect on their life circumstances with a view to exploring new possibilities and initiating constructive change.*

Yet the contrast between the two organizations is by no means definitive. A quick visit to the National Literacy Trust (2003) website offers greater alternatives:

> *Literacy can be defined on a number of levels. It is obviously concerned with the ability to read and write but a fuller definition might be the capacity to recognize, reproduce and manipulate the conventions of text shared by a given community* (Hertrich, 2003, 5),

or

> *Using printed and written information to function in society in order to achieve one's goals, and to develop one's knowledge and potential* (OECD, 1996),

again,

> *To acquire literacy is more than to psychologically and mechanically dominate reading and writing techniques. It is to dominate those techniques in terms of consciousness; to understand what one reads and to write what one understands: it is to communicate graphically. Acquiring literacy does not involve memorizing sentences, words or syllables – lifeless objects unconnected to an existential universe - but rather an attitude of creation and*

The Social Construction of Literacy | 111

> *re-creation, a self-transformation producing a stance of intervention in one's context* (Freire, 1973, 24).

The above conceptualizations occupy ground wider and deeper than implied by an either/or binary.

My preferred consideration, a self-referential quote and chanced upon truth that emerged from my attempt retell a misread and misremembered quote, somehow manages to be of analytical value:

> *An individual or a community may be understood as literate once they have learnt to mimic the conventions surrounding the linguistic and textual practices of those groups who hold authoritative positions within a given community.*

Or

> *Literacy is part of our class system ... the great divide in literacy is not between those who can read and write and those who have not yet learned how to. It is between those who have discovered what kinds of literacy, society values and how to demonstrate their competencies in ways that earn recognition.* (Margaret Meek, Emeritus Professor of Education at the Institute of Education, *'On Being Literate'*- a lecture delivered in 2004*)*.

An exploration of this rupture is not necessary in this context. I refer to it here in an attempt to establish lateral boundary points within which literacy as policy construction and literacy as lived experience locate themselves. I hope also to make it clear that these boundary points are not adequately conceptualized as existing along a continuum of - say - technical to social definitions of literacy. A continuum or binary does not provide a complex enough metaphor for codifying these distinctions.

I stop well short of suggesting literacy can only be understood as a fragmented and individualized construct within which each practice unfolds its particularity; what I move towards is a construct based on a multi dimensional matrix incorporating an understanding of literacy of, for and where; this may be transformed into literacy metaphors that include: literacy as skills, tasks, practices or critical reflection.

This is my attempt to explore Wilson's 'third space' or 'in between' literacy; a literacy of the twilight zone; a literacy that exists beyond, outside, within, parallel to, that is surrounded by/contained within literacy as autonomous singularity or social multiplicity. It attempts to challenge the binary these two positions insists upon and rather views the tension between the two as a creative composite. Within any organization where literacy is part of the curriculum -implicitly or explicitly - within in fact almost any learning exchange that involves the use of text - spoken or written - there is on a daily basis a juxtaposition between the officially sanctioned and admitted literacy that managers are compelled to implement and the living literacy that participants bring with them to the encounter. This meeting creates a culturally specific hybrid a twilight literacy that within a multi-dimensional matrix has its own distinct features.

The outcome then, of this study that carefully collects and attentively arranges the words of my colleagues - is the creation of a conceptual hybrid; a discursive construction made up of competing, contradictory in/coherent fragments into a fluctuating whole.

Research as an Analytical Daydream

My epistemology, sense-making preferences are firmly located within a qualitative paradigm. In 'Understanding Social Research', Usher (1997) offers two allegorical and cautionary tales about research. In one tale protagonists search for order amidst a series of computer generated random associates. Driven by the determined belief in the existence of a unitary plan all involved - the generators of the random script and those seeking to uncover its truth - die in horrible and bizarre circumstances. The second tale offered by Usher is the story of a detective setting out to discover the identity of a murderer; the crime scene is that of a library with a single book - the identity of which remains unknown - sought as providing a unitary answer. Searching for an unknown truth, the discovery of which will explain everything, has parallels with the researcher's quest for social scientific authoritative knowledge. Yet, in Usher's quoted tale, the 'truth' is discovered by chance - a dream, an accident, a misreading, misremembering or misinterpretation.

I accept the challenge presented by Usher (1997) and resist the desire for a single unitary truth to emerge through this study. There is perhaps no single third space or 'in between' literacy that possesses the cohesion I strive to attain. Literacy as a shape-shifting, polymorphous fluctuating fragmentation that refuses definition - may be the nature of things. My search for a reconciliation of competing and contested literacies may compel me to acknowledge that contradictions co-exist within a single entity, with apparent ease.

My role as researcher may be to offer an interpretation of that contradictory co-existence. To define a social meaning that emerges from and is shaped by human thought and existence.

My preferred research approach to data gathering is the interview. With Usher's caution in mind, I am compelled to consider carefully the ontological nature of the phenomenon I am exploring during the interview process. Foddy (1993) reminds me in unambiguous terms that any claims based on interview data are extremely tenuous. According to Foddy, during interviews people do not always tell the truth - they misremember, or lie, or mis-present themselves or they speak from *egos* for one moment and *id* the next. There is a gap between what people say and what people do. Their attitudes and beliefs are extraordinarily unstable – whimsical. How questions are worded, the interaction between interviewee and interviewer influences the nature of responses. People misinterpret questions and answers. They subvert, divert or simply misread; they respond to data external to the interview process, or internal but not immediately or apparently relevant to the question at hand; they respond to the way a question is asked rather than the question itself - assuming it is possible to identify a ' question' itself that exists apart from the way a question is asked. They answer questions about which they have no real basis for an answer. They uni/bi-laterally de/co-construct truths at will. I lean towards an understanding of research as an auto/biographical science that wilfully churns values, politics, subjective affectation and knowledge.

I would suggest that the data gathered during the interview process is the randomly generated script of Usher's first tale. Any truth I discover within it rests on my willingness to draw on my subjectivity - to daydream as well as to analyse.

Discourse

Discussion *"Stories are the secret reservoir of values; change the stories individuals or nations live by and tell themselves, and you change the individuals and nations". (Okri, 1996).*

In working with marginalized communities and moving them from 'dysfunctional' literacy to 'functional' literacy, those of us involved in the Skills for Life agenda are insistent that what we are doing is offering adults a good thing. The imperative to develop the nation's basic skills is considered - without doubt - a benign enterprise. This is a questionable conviction. Tremendous amount of energy goes into persuading people back into education; within months of the publication of the Kennedy Report discourses surrounding post-compulsory education were saturated by the phrase 'widening participation'; the mere use of which signified awareness of, belonging to a particular community within the College. It is now *de rigueur* to find entire college departments - or sections within departments, certainly a senior manager, devoted to recruiting 'hard-to-reach' adult learners. There is an implicit institutional recognition that a significant portion of the communities we are called upon to 'help' - 'do not care or do not know' that they have a problem (Moser Report 1999).

There are counter discourses to this narrative. I would suggest that there may be times when becoming literate has ambivalent consequences; an intricately balanced relationship within a community or household may be thrown into disarray by one member acquiring autonomous literacy independence and the beliefs, values, ways of behaving, ways of being that go along with it. If literacy is viewed as a social practice, ignoring dysfunctional literacy could be theorized as ignoring an accepted 'self that causes contradictory strains in other aspects of an individual's life.

Having sketched a dominant and counter literacy narrative, I want to place this discourse within an institutional setting and consider the varying ways it shapes not the explicit construction of polices but the implicit interpretation and implementation of those policies. How does the pathologization of the illiterate express itself within an organization? How are the discourses surrounding literacy taken-up, used and/or resisted? What are its local and material effects?

What I aim at understanding is how individuals, in the context of an organization, in the context of a life-world, in the context of a unique trajectory hear and interpret literacy discourses. How do they draw upon and actively assemble the varying discourses that affect their working lives – managerial, economic, pedagogic, exclusion, and the quality of work. How do these discourses impact upon and shape localized literacy discourses. My emphasis is less upon what my colleagues actually do – it is rather more focused on what they say about what they do: a discourse about practice rather than a discourse of practice.

Discourse is here understood as a way of organizing meaning, which finds partial though not exclusive, expression in language. I am referring to something that cannot be reduced to a detailed textual analysis, although lexicalizations, patterns of transitivity, use of active - passive voice are part of the approach. In this study my aim is to understand how literacy, literacy learning and literacy learners are produced, not by a single unitary individual, not as a figurative object of a linguistic system, nor as a socio-economic by product but rather how power - knowledge constructions cohere through various texts, to create the conditions of possibility for different language acts that becomes embedded in the organization. How do the discourses surrounding literacy map onto what can be said, thought and done at the EHWLC Lit?

An immediate and localized illustration of the power of discourse relates to a concept of 'acquired learning difficulty'. Through a series of discussions, I became aware of a student who had no designated medicalized cognitive deficiency but had simply been born in a country that did not have compulsory / accessible primary schooling, and in any case had travelled extensively (as an international footballer) in his mid-40's came to the EHWLC Lit wanting to learn how to read. His independent ability to access text was limited to completing his name and address on a form, understanding the stations on the underground, struggling with the headline in a newspaper. Joining a class would have been difficult for him because of his approach to reading. It is assumed in most literacy classes that individuals can read independently, unaided. This particular individual was unable to. In order for him to gain one-to-one support - the organization created a linguistic category: 'acquired learning difficulty'. Once discursively constructed as having an 'acquired learning difficulty', he became entitled to one-to- one support. A student who relates to text and those around him in a similar way, but without the sobriquet 'acquired learning difficulty' does not receive any additional funding from the government for one-to-one support.

This is in many ways similar to the discourse surrounding dyslexia. Students designated - or to use the medical term most commonly used in colleges, 'diagnosed' as having dyslexia are allocated a considerable degree of financial resources. The way in which this individual interacts with text by being labelled 'dyslexic' is considered special, in any case by nature different to the way a student who is defined as having low levels of literacy even if when assessed using a similar process they may be 'measured' as at a similar level, and may be enrolled on the same program of study. The dyslexic student is defined as 'intelligent' but with a disability that prohibits development of literacy skills; the literacy student's intelligence is not considered as relevant. This echoes the Victorian Parish Councils charitable giving and the distinction made between the deserving and undeserving poor - the dyslexic, as the deserving poor with a medical disability, is morally entitled to support. The person with low levels of literacy, who probably wagged school for years as the undeserving poor, is given no such attention.

I quote these as instances where discourse, where knowledge - power determine how the organization behaves towards a particular individual, how it defines and then responds to their perceived needs. It constructs categories that exist simply because those calling them have determined their existence. They then act as if they were real.

My attempt is to understand the stories that my colleagues tell when they talk about literacy at the EHWLC Lit.

Research Methods
Data Generating and Gathering

My main source of data will be interviews, but the intention is to ask both direct and indirect questions - to focus not on the implementation of the BSQI but to share with the readers and participants of this research, some personal and professional experiences of literacy. At some point these ideas may be used to sketch a hybrid literacy composite with some suggestions regarding how these features may impact upon the delivery of the organization's agenda.

Interviews will be undertaken with the following people:
- Assistant Principal responsible for implementing the Basic Skills Quality Initiative
- Senior Head of Program - Essential Skills & Learner Services
- Members of the Basic Skills Strategy Group
- Tutors working on discrete Basic Skills Program; an integrated course – usually non-basics kills specialists who are providing student support
- Students who have joined Basic Skills classes
- Students who have joined other courses and who make use of learning support.

For the first, experimental, phase of the project, a research project into the practicalities of doing research at my place of work, I intend to interview four colleagues. The more detailed research project to follow will involve much nearer to twenty participants and may involve a revisitation of the original interviewees.

The intention is to transcribe these interviews and treat the transcription as text to be analyzed. Alongside these interviews, I would like to interrogate government policy by analysing in detail defining policy publications such as *Delivering Skills for Life*, *Core- Curriculum,* and *Success in Literacy and Numeracy.*

I aim at devising a series of questions that would enable me to interrogate the policy text and dialogue derived text in a very similar way. The interviews will be semi- structured and timed. The practical consideration of colleagues with intense workloads suggests this as the most likely way to encourage agreement to be interviewed.

Data Analysis
Stephen Ball (2001) describes discourse as about not only what can be said and thought, but also about who can speak, when, where & with what authority. His view highlights not only the power of discourse, but also the power to make discourse. This is a power that derives not from language itself – language may describe or obscure it – but from institutional positioning.

In examining the words of my colleagues, how they are uttered, what reception they are given, and by whom, with what influence, and with what references they draw, I occupy an uneasy position. My dilemma is one faced by anyone who explores the hidden territories of pre - con - sub - text. I am implicated within the very discourses I critique, co-conspirator in discourses I describe as appearing common sensically benign. Yet, by invoking the notion of reflexivity, I recognise my role within while placing myself outside, perhaps slightly above the discourses I systematically analyse. Is this possible? I have no vocabulary within which to think outside the discourse I not only inhabit but actively *construct* as a literacy worker. In analysing discourse and their relationship to power / knowledge constructions, I award myself the role of saviour, liberator, detective, one who has managed to rise above it all – including my colleagues. I position them as guilty, ill-informed, used by politicians to implement an oppressive agenda that marginalizes the very communities it pretends to empower.

At this point I can see no way out of this dilemma. A reversion to playful, anything goes, mine as one-story among many with no special status amounts to little more than superficial nihilistic cynicism. The insistence on validity as little more than a paradigmatic bifurcation (Scheurich, 1997), an anachronistic hang-over from positivism, a subterranean fear of an essentialized other, may resolve my dilemma, but render the entire exercise of questionable value. In offering the study as research into literacy at EHWLC Lit, I also suggest a secondary project, as research into the process of research. I hope to further explore this dilemma and identify a less fidgety position.

For the moment, I reserve the right to accept the words offered to me by colleagues as gifts; gifts that I have a responsibility to creatively work with to co- construct a mutually recognizable, even if not completely shared narrative around literacy learning and learners.

Interrupted Silences

If the discussion so far has concentrated on defining the research trajectory as technical (- what I intend to do, how I intend to do it), and epistemological (- what I hope to learn from the experience), the notion of publicly disseminating the research findings insists on a personal and transforming discussion; it compels a confrontation with issues of voice, representation, solitude, solidarity and place within a knowledge generating community.

I may choose to historicize and name my location in terms which both foreground and obscure considerations of race, gender, sexuality, dis-ability and other indices of oppression. But my marginalized status is undermined by my role as researcher: active and complicit in an anthropological project which scientifically validates voyeurism by placing the colonized other under the ethnographer's gaze.

The ambiguous safety of silence – here positioned as strategic resistance, a refusal to be known, a face-saving rejection of the invitation to participate in a genderized and racialized epistemological language game, is shattered by the notion of sharing research. Once the research is finalized and 'approved' it signifies the possibility of my gaining access to institutionalized discourses of power, and a requirement that I argue for, in defense of, not only my own academic interest, but the interests of those who have participated in the project, or the interests of those who with or without participating, are none-the-less leading protagonists within the project: namely C2Des[2] who have tentatively begun to 'opt-into 'New Labor's Skills for Life agenda.

In disseminating research findings my silent sanctuary is, if not completely shattered, at least interrupted: yet another invasion on my peace and quiet!

The opportunities for this interruption are plenty:
- Distribution of the full research project to colleagues at EHWLC Lit.
- Re-presentation of key considerations to emerge from interviews as a series of recommendations about the best way to implement the Basic Skills Quality Initiative to Basic Skills Strategy group - or Senior Management Team at the College
- Submission of an appropriately slanted version to relevant academic journals;
- Participation in a doctoral students' poster conference
- Leading a discussion group at a relevant conference hosted by Research and Practice in Adult Literacy - a lose gathering of practitioners and researchers sympathetic to the New Literacy Studies
- The re-presentation of central issues as teaching and learning materials for student teachers interested in understanding the relevance of the New Literacy Studies
  The re-presentation of central issues as teaching and learning materials for literacy students interested in exploring the connections between how they use and learn literacy in and out of institutionalized settings.

End Notes

[1] ABC1 is a social demographic classification used in the United Kingdom and the Republic of Ireland. It refers to those in the **middle class**. (A = Upper Middle Class, B = Middle Class, C1 = Lower Middle Class).

[2] C2DE is also a social demographic classification used in the United Kingdom to equate to the **working class**. (C2= Skilled Working class, D = Working Class, E = Underclass).

References

Blunkett, D. (2001). *Skills for Life: The national strategy for improving adult literacy and numeracy skills.* United Kingdom: Department for Education and Employment

Ball, S. (2001). Performativities and fabrications in the education economy in Gleeson & Husbands: *The Performing School.* London: Rutledge Falmer.

Barton, D. (2000). Moral Panics about Literacy. In *Lancaster University, CLS Working Paper Series.* Retrieved from http://www.lancs.ac.uk/unpubs/cls/wpapers.htm

Barton, D. & Hamilton, M. (1998). *Local Literacies: Reading & Writing in one Community.* London: Routledge.

Basic Skills Agency (2003). Basic Skills Agency. Retrieved from http://www.basic-skills.org.uk

Edwards, R. (1997). *Changing places? Flexibility, Lifelong learning and a learning society.* London: Routledge.

EHWLC (2001). *EHWLC Lit Vision for Basic Skills.* Internal document from the Basic Skills Strategy Group at EHWLC Lit.

Foddy, W. (1993). *Constructing Interviews for Interviews and Questionnaires.* Cambridge: Cambridge University Press.

Freire, P. (2003). *National Literacy Trust.* Retrieved from http://www.nationalliteracytrust.org.uk

Gee, J. P. (1996). *Social Linguistics and Literacies: Ideology & Discourse.* London: Routledge, Falmer Taylor & Francis Group.

Hamilton, M. (2001). Privileged Literacies: Policy, Institutional Process and the Life of the ILS. In *Language & Education,* 15(2 & 3).

Hertrich, J. (2003). *National Literacy Trust.* Retrieved from http:www.nationalliteracytrust.org.uk

Moser, C. (1999). *A Fresh Start.* United Kingdom: Department for Education and Employment.

Okri, B. (1996). *Birds of Heaven.* London: Phoenix.

Scheurich, J. (1997). *The masks of validity: Research methods on the post-modern*, London: Routledge, Falmer Taylor & Francis Group.

Usher, R. (1997). Challenging the power of rationality in McKenzie et al, *Understanding Social Research*. The Falmer Press.

Wilson, A. (2000). There is no escape from the Third Space. In Barton, Hamilton & Ivanic (Eds.) *Situated Literacies*. London: Routledge, Falmer Taylor & Francis Group.

8. A Documents Analysis of the English Textbooks Currently used in Korean Elementary Schools with some Comments on Problems inherent to the System: A Practical Approach to Teaching English 'Mostly' in English (TEE, TEmE)[1]

Mark C. Love

This paper looks at the current materials being used in Korean elementary schools to teach English. After a very brief look at teaching methods and factors such as semantic ranges that should be considered when teaching and integrated into teaching, the author lists a few techniques he regularly uses in classes. Love then performs a documents analysis of the materials used in the elementary school system and goes on to list some problems inherent in the current school system. He proceeds to offer practical ways for teachers in the school system, both non-native speaker and native speaker, to overcome the shortcomings of the materials. Some suggestions for supplementing these materials with multi-level classes, now endemic to Korea, are made at the end of the paper. As Love has spent the vast majority of his time in Korea teaching at the university level, he mentions mistakes he regularly sees students make at the university level that he hopes can be corrected at a lower level.

Introduction

It was kind of you to invite me to talk to you today about the topic of teaching English in English. From last September to December, I had the opportunity to spend three months teaching at a high school in South Chungcheon Province. I'm just telling you this to let you know that I understand a bit about the teaching situation in the schools right now. I was told to make this talk very practical rather than theoretical and to try and give you some suggestions about what you can do to teach in English. I thought about this, and thought, "What is more practical than what I do in the classroom every time I teach conversation?" So, I have based this talk around how I plan and conduct my own conversation classes. I have a feeling that the more senior teachers among you will already know most of what I'm about to say. If you already know everything I tell you, I apologize in advance. However, I have been in Korea since 1996, and have taught in most of the venues - from the Hogwan level to graduate school classes. So, I hope to offer at least one or two tips from my experience. I'm looking forward to hearing your teaching tips in the sessions after this.

Teaching English in English (TEE)

For the record, I, too, do not agree 100% with an English ONLY policy in a mostly monolingual classroom, which is what the Korean classroom situation is (see E. Auerbach, 1993, for a criticism of the English only in the classroom position). I do not understand the new TEE (Teaching English in English) program of the government to mean that. To be honest, I do not use only English in my classroom. When I encounter a phrase that I think my students might not know, I think it is perfectly legitimate, and can also be much more efficient, to give them definitions in Korean rather than only in English, which can leave students with only a vague conception of what a word or expression means. We just need to be cautious about language interference, which we can try to counter by teaching students things such as denotations, connotations, collocations, synonyms, antonyms and semantic ranges. One thing to note is that collocations, especially prepositions, are not focused on much in the current textbooks. I would also note that it is important to try and teach the semantic range, that is, the range of meaning a word has, for words that have different ranges than their common translations in Korean or English. A perfect example of this is the Korean word 약속, whose range encompasses the English words *appointment, plans,* and *promise*. I would also teach the difference in meaning of the English word promise, which is a bit more serious, and the Korean word 약속, which is generally less serious (see fig. 1).

Semantic Ranges
약속 has a very wide semantic range
Compared with these English words that have narrower semantic ranges

Promise	Appointment	Plans (note plural)
I *promised* my mother that I would never come home late again. One could also teach that *I have a promise tonight* is a common mistake.	I have a doctor's *appointment* at 3 today.	Do you have any *plans* this weekend? One could also teach that *I have a plan this weekend* sounds strange.

Figure 1.
Semantic range of the word 약속

When giving explanations of terms, I would recommend a three tier approach, with an additional optional step.

1. Give a rough meaning
    A watermelon is a big fruit that is green on the outside and red on the inside. It has lots of seeds.
2. Provide a dictionary meaning in English
3. Ask students for the Korean for this term/expression
    수박
4. *Optional:* use a website such as Wikipedia (2008).

The first stage would be to give a definition in English. I usually give the simplest definition that I can think of, which is sometimes terribly inadequate. I then give a formal dictionary definition. Finally, I ask my students for a Korean translation of the word or expression, which I've already looked up so that I will know if they're correct or not. Often students confer with each other in their own languages to make sure that they have indeed provided the correct translation. I let them look up words in their dictionaries, too, rather than hastily giving them the translation because I believe the process of negotiating meaning helps them to remember the vocabulary. I know some native speakers who absolutely refuse to allow any conversation in the classroom that is not in English (See Auerbach [1993] for a summary of oppressive techniques English teachers employ/have employed in the classroom). I, however, view this conversation as a positive activity and never stop students when they do this. Those teachers who absolutely refuse any language other than English to be spoken in the classroom are practicing a form of of what Robert Phillipson labels linguistic imperialism (specifically, 'the monolingual fallacy'; 1992). In addition, letting students converse in their own language creates a safe house; Pratt defined safe houses as "social and intellectual spaces where groups can constitute themselves as horizontal, homogenous, sovereign communities with high degrees of trust, shared understandings, and temporary protection from legacies of oppression" (1991, 40). These safe houses are 'zones' where students "negotiate the discursive and ideological challenges of the academic contact zone" (Canagarajah, 2004, 176). In a sense, these are places where students feel comfortable and can express their true feelings free from the teacher's control. Finally, if students can't provide a translation, I give one to them. If they do provide one, I echo their response: I repeat what they said (with corrections), so that they get some more reinforcement. Through this method, the students are certainly hearing the term asked about three more times, and thus are getting some passive and active vocabulary reinforcement.

I sometimes use a fourth step and visit an internet site, especially when I'm explaining nouns. Wikipedia has pictures of just about everything, so when my explanations seem to flounder, Wikipedia often provides a picture that clarifies everything.

Dynamic Equivalence Versus Literal Translation

Now, it is in teaching idioms and slang where translation theory comes in. The most useful theory I have encountered among translation theories is that of literal translation (문자 그대고) versus dynamic equivalence (Eugene A. Nida, 1964). Now, a literal translation (what Nida calls *formal equivalence*, a term that I don't use because I believe the expression 'literal translation' is more readily understood by a reader) is a non- figurative, straightforward translation - what the words literally mean. An example of this can be shown by an analysis of the expression 호랑이도 제 말하면 온다더니 양반은 못된다. If one were to translate this literally, one could translate it as, "If a tiger comes when you talk about it, then it won't become Yangban" or "it will not become upper-class". However, if one were to use dynamic equivalence, the translation would be ... "Speak of the devil". Now, this is actually an abbreviated form of the expression, "Speak of the devil and he will appear." A second example is the Korean expression 개꿈. Literally translated, this would be "A dream about a dog," or so I'm told. But using the theory of dynamic equivalence, we would translate it as "a pipe dream." Both have the dynamic meaning of a very unrealistic goal or dream. Now, teaching both the literal meaning(s) and the dynamically equivalent meaning(s) reinforces the term, as students hear the expression a number of times and come to understand its literal meaning, its dynamically equivalent meaning, and when to use it.

English Corpora

I know that many here worry about what language and terms to use in the 'English only" classroom. Well, the internet is a wonderful source of sentences if you want to look up examples. Wikipedia is a good site for general definitions, as is Merriam-Webster Online (2008). Another good source is Collins-Cobuild's *The Bank of English* (2008). I liked the days when it was free on the internet, but now it can be bought with a Collins-Cobuild dictionary for about 30,000 won, the last time I checked. It is also available as a subscription on-line. That will provide you with full sentence examples. A free resource which is similar to *The Bank of English* is *The Corpus of Contemporary American English* (COCA; See G. Fox, 1998, for a good description of how to use concordances in the classroom). Also, Yahoo Korea's and Naver's dictionaries provide many examples for you. You could also use *The Bank of English* or *COCA* to do some corpus linguistics work, but that's another story. (Another site that one can use to do corpus linguistics work is MICASE: Michigan Corpus of Academic Spoken English [2008], but that's really limited to more advanced English.)

Less is More

Many people also wonder about filling the whole class time with English. My personal English conversation classroom philosophy is *less is more*. The term *less is more* originally comes from Robert Browning's "Andrea del Sarto". While in Browning's poem the narrator is considering painting, I find it easier to understand the expression *less is more* if I think of decorating. A room with only a few objects in it can look much nicer than a room cluttered with objects. (If I were teaching, I would draw students' attention to the fact that *with* is the preposition that accompanies *cluttered*.) In a similar way, I feel that when I'm teaching conversation classes, the *less* I speak in my classroom the better. The *more* I speak, the *less* time my students have to practice. As such, I try to limit what I say to providing very brief explanations and modeling activities. This is contrary to many television shows one watches on EBS that are supposed to be teaching English, but in which only five minutes of a thirty-minute show is actually conducted in English. I think it is this kind of approach that the government policy of teaching only in English is attempting to correct. To return to the topic of how I manage my classroom, I think that a very successful class for me is one in which I speak to the entire class as a group for less than ten minutes, on average. Of course, this will vary by what topic I am teaching. Now, the target language I use, that which I model, is usually found at the top of most supplementary materials, or in the explanation of the activity provided for the teacher. So, if you were doing this, you wouldn't even have to come up with a full ten minutes of English. I regularly just use the language modeled by the activity and provide explanations, which I've already talked about today. If you really want to find some sample sentences, you could use any of the sources mentioned above. I find that if I try to introduce too many concepts into a lesson, it becomes too confusing for students to follow, and then students get confused when they try to produce the target language. So, I try to keep it simple. After I've explained an activity and modeled it, usually having two students model the first example for the class, and perhaps drawing students' attention to some of the matters I discussed at the beginning of this talk when relevant, I spend most of my time circulating around the class making sure that students have understood my directions and are doing the activity correctly, making sure that students are practicing the target language, correcting student errors, and answering questions. Often students don't understand an activity even after it has been modeled, so I have to explain it to them in pairs or groups. Sometimes I provide three or four such activities per class, but one or two per hour of class is more common.

Document Analysis

When I was writing this speech, I had an elementary school teacher send me the textbooks that are currently being used in the school system. They arrived after my speech was basically written, so I just had time to add a few comments. I was surprised by how much of the textbooks are in Korean. I realized that the government approach tacitly supports exactly the kind of teaching one sees on TV in that a vast majority of the language in the current English textbooks is in Korean, not English. To condition my comments, I realize that the textbooks were made by the previous government, so, despite the current government's shortcomings, one cannot blame it for the quality of the current textbooks. Page 103 of the 영어 *Elementary School English 5*, illustrates my point, as it is a page of activities with all instructions written in Korean. The textbooks should be mostly in English, possibly with a glossary at the back. Also, little target language is provided in the textbooks. I hope there is more provided in the teachers' books. Another page, page 166, from 영어 English 5 (교육 인적 자원부), illustrates my point well, as it contains a page with activites that need students to complete information that could easily be translated into English, some modelling could also then be provided. (e.g., Translations – Survey your friends, Friend's name, What s/he did on Monday. Modeling:

A: What did you do <u>on Friday</u>?
B: I <u>played Maple Story on Friday</u>).

Now, I realize that these shortcomings with the textbook are a government problem, and the government should rewrite the textbooks and make some other changes that I'll address later on. (Note: since this was written, I have seen an announcement in the newspaper that new textbooks are forthcoming. I'll wait until they come out to pass further comments on them.) Another problem I have with the textbook is that the content taught in the 영어 5 book seems to be about the level that many kids are studying when they are kindergarten age these days. In a day and age when just about every child is attending some English Hogwan, can we justify wasting our students' time like this in class? We are teaching to the lowest common denominator. A curriculum revision is certainly needed. In the meantime, the only solution I can come up with to this problem is teaching multi-level classes, which I realize many of you are already doing. These, of course, are the most difficult classes to teach. Since I'm trying to provide practical advice here, I'd suggest intentionally choosing activities with some vocabulary and grammar points that are more difficult than what is taught in the textbooks so that students at a variety of levels are served. One is reminded of Stephen Krashen's maxim of i+1, however you interpret his '1' (1981, 100). I'm thinking more of i+1.5, wherein I assume what would be normally taught if you were using the textbook would be considered i+1. That is, the implied readers of the textbook, or make that *implied learners* of the textbooks currently used are below the level of the *actual learners*, so supplementary materials are required (see Wolfgang Iser, 1980, for a treatment of implied and actual readers).

Systemic Problems

Despite my previous comments about the textbooks and the curriculum, from an educational perspective, the textbooks must be taught, so materials should be integrated with what is being taught in the textbook and with the national curriculum. Now, the activities provided in the elementary school books are not that bad, despite being at the wrong level, and being in Korean. When I taught the current high school text books, I honestly thought the textbooks were woefully lacking in providing conversational materials. The materials provided barely touch on the grammar being taught, it is often not clear how the grammar relates to the topic of the lesson, and the books do not give enough practice for students to master the patterns. Often it is difficult to spot the educational objectives of a lesson without reading the Korean guide, which suggests that the lessons are poorly designed if an experienced teacher cannot readily see what the point of the lesson is. The conversation activities in these books can also usually be taught in about 10 minutes of class time, at about which time the students become numb from boredom. In addition to rewriting the main textbooks, I think the government should make a rather minimal investment and get 3 or 4 of the more experienced native English teachers who are currently working as co-teachers in the schools to work full-time developing supplementary conversation textbooks to accompany the existing textbooks. As it is, every co-teacher in the country is spending hours every week coming up with similar lesson plans. These lesson plans should be consolidated and made available to everyone in the system. Alternatively, bonuses could be paid for particularly good lesson plans so that you may not even have to hire people to write a textbook. However, from a publishing perspective, it will be extremely difficult to have any continuity in the lesson plans if they aren't coordinated somehow at the textbook design level. Still, having even just a resource bank of activities would be extremely helpful. I hope someone with the authority to make this decision is here today-I couldn't recommend it more. This would provide integration with the existing curriculum as well as a proper foundation in the grammar points and vocabulary studied. As it is, native English speaker co-teachers, whom should also be given the power to assign grades if educational reform is truly to be achieved, are left to plan all of their lessons from scratch.

Having co-teachers assign grades might also solve one of the problems that I witnessed in the high school program: it is very difficult for English native speaking teachers to get students to pay attention in class. I often saw classes in which only six out of thirty students were paying attention to their teacher. This is because the English conversation component is not viewed as being important to the students. It is not on the CSAT (College Scholastic Aptitude Test), and the co-teachers do not assign grades. Thus, the government sends a (c)overt message to students that English conversational abilities are not important. If these teachers assigned grades, and those grades were a part of university entrance requirements, students would pay much more attention in class. Another benefit of this suggestion is that it would be prohibitively expensive to introduce a speaking component beyond the simplest measure of a multiple choice test to the CSAT: just paying assessors to review that many exams would cost a fortune. It would also be subject to criticism because of the subjective nature of assessing conversational abilities. (For a discussion of the problems with rater training and rater agreement, albeit concerning writing, see Elder, Barkhuizen, Knoch and von Randow, 2007; the title of Wigglesworth's 1993 article alone attests to similar problems in oral testing). Koreans also attested mistrust of the subjectivity of oral testing procedures (Li, 1998, 695). While trained testers often agree on similar band ratings for students, 100% agreement is needed for a test such as the CSAT or parents will be in an uproar about the results. Having co-teachers assign grades would avoid this quagmire.

Another issue that also relates to curriculum and materials development is the short term contract nature of English native speakers in the Korean school system. It often takes a year or two of teaching materials to be comfortable with adapting the materials. To gain a sufficient knowledge of the situation, level of students, and their interests that is essential if one wants to write new materials that are effective requires teachers to work for quite a long time in an environment. This would involve hiring foreign teachers on a permanent basis in the school system such as in America or Europe. This would also involve negotiation of what a native speaker teacher is. The current system encourages 'backpacker' teachers who come here for a year, have little commitment to the system, and take the knowledge they gain with them home never to come to fruition in materials development and teaching skills. Now, this is not a critique of the teachers in the school system now; the vast majority of them are professionals who take their job seriously and strive to produce exciting lessons that captivate students' attention. That said, the country could gain more from them if it utilized them more efficiently. In addition, this move would involve changing the title from 'co-teacher' to just 'teacher'. It may also involve English native speaking teachers learning significant amounts of Korean as they would need to in order to participate effectively in meetings. A liaison officer may be needed to communicate between administration and teachers, but those are already in place. A thorough knowledge of Korean would greatly improve their English teaching abilities as they would readily spot instances of positive and negative transfer.

What to Teach?

This brings me to my next point: What to teach? Another problem I saw in the system is that many students at the middle school and high school levels are simply memorizing vocabulary lists. While I don't believe that learning vocabulary is a waste of time, and Keith Folse has gone so far as to call the belief that learning lists of vocabulary is unproductive a myth (2004, 35), when students learn by just memorizing vocabulary in isolation, they often do not learn the collocations of the words from the list. They then have to learn these later on when they attend university. I regularly have to teach students prepositions such as "on the second floor", "on Friday", and "in June" in university classes. It would be nice if students learned these properly when they first learned English so that the same lessons didn't have to be repeated throughout the entire educational system. Thus, when you teach, try to focus on which prepositions are used with which word, and what words commonly are found together (collocations). Also, only a passive knowledge of a lot of the vocabulary is taught in the textbooks. The same is partially true of cloze activities in which only visual reinforcement of vocabulary is provided, but no speaking/listening practice is given. This is not to say I am opposed to cloze exercises-they have their place. (It is also granted that there is a minimal amount of pronunciation practice in the textbooks that involves the native speaker reading a long list of words to the class). My problem with the current system is that often lists of vocabulary are taught, and students are expected to recognize those words, but students aren't given any practice using those words themselves in sentences. One method I use to practice new vocabulary is to generate lists of questions from any of the vocabulary learned in class, and provide sample answers to those questions. To return to that page from *Elementary English 5* we looked at earlier (page 103), I wasn't sent the teacher's guide, so I'm not positive about this, but it seems from the pictures and vocabulary on this page that the target language consists of *wash (my) hands, eat lunch, watch TV, in the kitchen, in the living room, in the bathroom, desk, table, chair, book, eat an apple,* and *read a newspaper.* One could make up additional questions such as "Where do you usually read books?", "How many chairs do you have in your kitchen?", "What kind of sandwiches do you like?", etc. This would give a little extra practice with the language. It would make everyone's job easier if the government prepared a supplementary textbook that did just that for every chapter of the set curriculum, and provided a variety of other activities linked to each chapter/page. If you're worried about the accuracy of the questions you write, you could try generating the questions yourself and then having the native English speakers at your schools, if you have some, check them for errors. If you have a native speaker at your school, you may want to ask him/her to produce these kinds of questions. Make sure to save the files so that you can use them next term when that teacher may have left for another job. You could also search the internet, which doesn't always yield the results you want. For more specific searches, try the Corpus of Contemporary American English (COCA), or MICASE (The Michigan Corpus of Academic Spoken English) for sample sentences with the words you have chosen. You could also generate extra lists of questions using the patterns and/or grammar taught in the textbook instead of basing your questions on the vocabulary. I often tell my university students that the textbook questions are boring, even if they're not, and ask them to come up with some more interesting questions than the ones we have been practicing. Sometimes they respond and generate the questions on their own. Other times, I have to generate them. Still, it's a productive activity to try and get students to generate their own questions. Sometimes it's even a little shocking, but I won't go into the strange and personal questions some of my students have asked in class. I still think the activity is worthwhile because it gets students to ask questions that they are concerned about and to which they often would really like to know the answer. This engages students in real conversation. Students would be far more interested in that survey activity we saw earlier if they generated their own questions to survey the class about, which is another activity I frequently use with higher level classes. It's a great activity because it can be used as both a speaking and writing activity.

Other sources of materials for lessons are resource books. There are many, many photocopiable resources out there that can be used in the classroom-you don't have to reinvent the wheel. Just go to your local English bookstore and spend a few hours going through the resource books. To return to that page of the book we saw earlier from 영 어5 (103), the topics covered are housing and daily activities, and the grammar point is the present simple to express regular activities. If I wanted to supplement it, I could choose either a topic based or grammar based supplement. Picture dictionaries, and there are many out there (*The Oxford Picture Dictionary, Let's Go Picture Dictionary,* and *Word by Word Picture Dictionary* jump to mind), provide quite a lot of activities to do with every room of the house. A look at the index of the *Word by Word Picture Dictionary* reveals the topics Bathroom, Dining Room, Everyday Activities, Extracurricular Activities, Home Supplies, Kitchen, and Living Room, and that's only looking at the first page of the index. One could supplement the elementary school book using either rooms of a house or regular activities. You could also use the glossary to choose any word from your book to plan a lesson around. The great thing about these activities is that they also provide target language at the bottom of every page to practice the vocabulary. In addition, there is often more difficult vocabulary mixed in with the regular activity, so even your higher level students can learn from these activities; they can be used with multi-level classes. If you wanted to link it by grammar point, Jill Hadfield's books are very useful. If you look at the index to her intermediate book, which I used today because I don't have her elementary and beginning books at home now, you will see that the structural index provides a grammar linked activity. This makes it very easy to use these books to find activities related to many items covered in your textbook. The drawback of using these books is that it can take a while to prepare the items. If you find some activity you use quite often, I strongly recommend you laminate the items. I have made the mistake of not doing that, and I can't tell you how many times I have ended up photocopying and cutting out the same activity. Also, students tend to write on the cards if you don't laminate them.

To introduce a point about teaching grammar, when I'm learning a grammatical pattern in a foreign language, I find that if I practice it at least five times, I may remember it, but ten times is even better. If I do it fifteen times, I will probably remember it forever. The old style substitution drills taught this well. It is a pity those substitution drill textbooks were so ugly, and the vocabulary rather boring. Unfortunately, I find that many modern conversation textbooks don't provide much repetition practice. Sometimes students are left to practice a pattern only about three or four times. I guess the authors of these books have far better memories than I do and can master grammatical patterns at amazing speed. Regardless, the supplementary books I already mentioned provide the same kind of repetitive practice with a more modern presentation. Moreover, since students are usually involved in some kind of task in these activities/games, it doesn't feel like one is just working through a long list of items when one is flipping over game cards or looking at color pictures like it did in the old substitution drill books; it becomes meaningful learning rather than rote learning.[2] Students still get the practice they need without the psychological burden of feeling they have to work through fifteen items, though they are still doing just that. All of the supplementary books are similar, so there isn't just one that I can recommend. You may want to pay close attention to specifically how much target language is provided in the supplementary materials when choosing these textbooks since it will make your job much easier if the textbooks already model the language. I could list a few textbooks and websites that do a good job of modeling the language, but then I might be guilty of product placement even though I am not currently working for a publisher.

Obviously, this approach of relying on supplementary materials is much more manageable than having to come up with 50 minutes of speaking per English class. Also, considering what I said about some explanations in Korean being alright after having attempted to explain in English, the new government policy is not as intimidating as it once was. The key is to teach mostly in English and to limit the use of Korean to explaining concepts that are difficult to teach. It may take a while to get used to using the supplements, but once you do, they can make your job much easier and may make your classes livelier. I find that I can now look at a textbook and 4 or 5 activities instantly come to mind. I usually have more activities I could use than class time, so I have to choose which ones will work best. I realize that your teaching situation is extremely difficult in that you have to teach multi-level classes while trying to follow a curriculum. In the short term, I hope the use of supplements will help alleviate this problem and reduce the amount of time you have to spend preparing for class. On a practical level, schools might want to consider buying a bunch of supplementary books and having someone index them to chapters of the textbooks. In the long term, I hope the government hires some people to produce supplements to the textbooks that are already linked to each level, and which provide the target language you need to teach to make your job much easier. Now that I'm done speaking, some of you may be awakening from your naps and thinking, "If he had spoken **less**, I would have remembered **more** of his speech." Probably!

End Notes

[1] This paper is slightly modified from one presented to a group of 250 elementary and middle school English teachers at the plenary session of the first Daejeon English Education Seminar: Qualitative Improvement of Teaching English in English (TEE) Proceedings (대전영어교육세미나; 영어진행수업의 활성화 방안) held at Paichai University on June 12, 2008. TEE = Teaching English in English; TEmE = Teaching English mostly in English

² It is very difficult to draw the line between rote and meaningful learning as it hinges on variables such as vocabulary choice, student level, and student age as well as immeasurable factors such as general student interest in the subject and motivation to learn.

References

Elementary English 5. Educational Resources Division (Korea; 영어 English 5. 교육 인 적 자원부).

Auerbach, E. R. (1993). Reexamining English Only in the ESL Classroom. *TESOL Quarterly* 27(1), 9-32.

Browning, R. (1855). Andrea del Sarto. *Men and Women*. Lancashire: F.E.L. Priestley. Retrieved from Representative Poetry Online: http://rpo.library.utoronto.ca/poem/264.html

Elder, C., Barkhuizen, G., Knoch, U., & von Randow, J. (2007). Evaluating rater responses to an online training program for L2 writing assessment. *Language Testing* 24(1). 37-64.

Canagarajah, S. (2004). Subversive Identities, Pedagogical Safe Houses and Critical Learning. In B. Norton and K. Toohey (Eds.), *Critical Pedagogies and Language Learning* (116-137). Cambridge: Cambridge University Press.

Fox, G. (1998). Using Corpus Data in the Classroom. In Brian Tomlinson (Ed.), *Materials Development in Language Teaching* (25-43). Cambridge: Cambridge University Press.

Folse, K. (2004). *Vocabulary Myths: Applying Second Language Research to Classroom Teaching*. Ann Arbor: University of Michigan Press.

Hadfield, J. (1987). *Elementary Communication Games*. White Plains, NY: Longman

Hadfield, J. (1997). *Advanced Communication Games*. White Plains, NY: Longman

Hadfield, J. (1998). *Elementary Vocabulary Games*. White Plains, NY: Longman

Hadfield, J. (1999). *Beginner's Communication Games*. White Plains, NY: Longman

Hadfield, J. (2000). *Intermediate Communication Games*. White Plains, NY: Longman

Hadfield, Jill. (2000). *Intermediate Communication Games*. White Plains, NY: Longman

Iser, W. (1980). The Reading Process: A Phenomenological Approach. In J.P. Tompkins (Ed.), *Reader-Response Criticism: From Formalism to Post-Structuralism*. (51-69). Baltimore: The Johns Hopkins University Press.

Krashen, S. (1981). *Second Language Acquisition and Second Language Learning*. Oxford: Pergamon Press.

Li, D. (1998). It's Always More Difficult Than You Plan and Imagine: Teachers' Perceived Difficulties in Introducing the Communicative Approach in South Korea. *TESOL Quarterly* 32(4). 677-702

Merriam-Webster Online. (2008). *Dictionary and Thesaurus*. Merriam-Webster, Inc. Retrieved from http://www.merriam-webster.com

MICASE: Michigan Corpus of Academic Spoken English. (2007). *Micase Online Home Page*. Retrieved from http://quod.lib.umich.edu/m/micase/

Molinsky, S. J. & Bliss, B. (1994). *Word by Word Picture Dictionary*. Englewood Cliffs, New Jersey: Prentice Hall Regents.

Nakata, R., Frazier, K. & Hoskins, B. (1999). *Let's Go Picture Dictionary*. Oxford: Oxford University Press.

Nida, E. A. (1964). *Towards a Science of Translating*. Leiden: E. J. Brill.

Phillipson, R. (1992). *Linguistic Imperialism*. Oxford: Oxford University Press.

Pratt, M. L. (1991). Arts of the Contact Zone. *Profession 91*, (33-40). New York: MLA.

The Bank of English. (2008). *Collins Word Web*. Retrieved from http://www.collins.co.uk/books.aspx?group=140

The Corpus of Contemporary American English. (2008). *Corpus of Contemporary American English (CORCA)*. Retrieved from http://www.americancorpus.org/

Wigglesworth, G. (1993). Exploring bias analysis as a tool for improving rater consistency in assessing oral interaction. *Language Testing 10*. 305-23.

Wikipedia. (2004). *Wikipedia: The free encyclopedia*. FL: Wikimedia Foundation, Inc. Retrieved from http://www.wikipedia.org

9. The New 21st Century Literacy: Problems and Challenges for the Digital Age
Thomas D. Clark

Literacy now has a new meaning in this digital age. The new literacy needed today is more broadly defined than the previous definition. Before, it simply meant understanding text—now it has a new meaning of being savvy enough to "... navigate the multi-dimensional and fast-paced digital environment" (Jones-Kavalier, Flannigan, 2006, 1). Moreover, with this new definition comes new challenges and problems to digital literacy such as resistance to change, implementation, complexity—problems which have to be addressed in order for the literate to stay proficient and the illiterate to acquire their skills.

Introduction
There is a new literacy in the 21st Century, whose mastery is crucial in our technical age, which seems to be a formidable foe to those who have not been exposed to it at an early stage in their life. Whereas children nowadays are "digital natives" who are at ease with texting, web chatting, and the like, today's adults and seniors may be found struggling to catch up. "Digital immigrants" now find themselves bewildered with today's technology and have become illiterate and passed up by a younger generation who have the technical savvy to thrive. (Jones-Kavalier, Flannigan, 2006). These two terms were recently coined by Mark Prensky (2001) to describe this new phenomenon taking place in our information age, and they highlight the problems of the discrepancies between those with and without technical skill and know-how.

Problems and Challenges

This digital divide can be clearly seen in our classrooms with teachers and students in developed countries such as the United States and Korea. According to Jones-Kavalier and Flannigan (2006), "A common scenario today is a classroom filled with digitally literate students being led by linear-thinking, technologically stymied instructors" (1). Students have been exposed to these technologies or similar ones early on during their formative years while their teachers have just been exposed to it only recently. As a result, the students are sometimes more capable with the technology. This can be seen in basic situations where students have a far greater learning curve with newly installed software in their classrooms compared to their teachers. Plus, while much funding goes toward the technology itself, very little goes toward the education on how to use it--teachers are given the tools, but not the knowledge. Teachers increasingly are learning the technology on their own time, to grasp the technical know-how without help from their school's administration (Jones-Kavalier, Flannigan, 2006). Haynes, an ESL instructor, adds, "We speak "digital" as a second language (DSL). We grew up in a drastically different text-based environment and even if we have tried to keep up with current technology, we speak this language with an accent" (Haynes, 2006, 1).

Though there may be difficulties with the implementation of the technology and the training of the instructors, the students typically have the confidence to use it effectively and prefer its use to more traditional methods of instruction (Jones-Kavalier, Flannigan, 2006, 2). The days of *only* using chalkboards and books in developed countries are approaching obscurity. Nowadays, there is the intermittent lesson with streaming video or audio-video interaction in our children's classrooms. Here the problem is how teachers should use this technology wisely to increase their students' competency, and to not be blinded by an extravagant new technology (also called a 'wow' factor). "Using the same skills used for centuries—analysis, synthesis, and evaluation—we must look at digital literacy as another realm within which to apply elements of critical thinking" (Jones-Kavalier, Flannigan, 2006, 2). One example of this is found with Haynes' composition class:

> With 5th & 6th grade groups, I use the software Inspiration. With the latest version, my students can research information for a report or other writing assignment and organize it on a template in Inspiration directly on their laptops. They can spell check their work, use a thesaurus or dictionary, change the organizer into an outline and export that outline to their word processing program. These outlines become their frame for writing (Haynes, 2006, 2-3).

Endemic to technical marvels of technology such as audio-video interaction, there is the issue of complexity. There is the variety, and the constant altering into faster and more powerful forms. "Our world today is about connecting the digital dots. The challenge is in dealing with the complexity—the dots are multidimensional, of varying sizes and colors, continuously changing, and linked to other, as yet unimagined dots." (Jones-Kavalier, Flannigan, 2006, 2). Clearly, the trend is towards more complex technology with multi-functions and uses requiring heightened aptitude. Being digitally literate will require constant diligence on the part of the learner.

Conclusion

It is crucial that these issues related to the new 21st century literacy be resolved. The technological resources in place today offer great potential for society in the sectors of education and business and especially to our schools for the beneficial role they provide in information, learning, and research. Clearly, however, the members of our technological society must be digitally literate in order to use these resources. For this to happen, the older generation must continue to maintain their technical skills learned later in life while the younger generation has already began to obtain them. With continuing education, digital immigrants can improve and acquire the technological capabilities needed to function with, and help educate, the forthcoming generation of digital natives.

References

Jones-Kavalier, B., & Flannigan, S. (2006). Connecting the Digital Dots: Literacy of the 21st Century. *Educause Quarterly, 29*(2), 1-3.

Haynes, J. (2006). DSL – Digital as a Second Language Essential Teacher. *Essential Teacher: Teachers of English to Speakers of Other Languages, 3*(4), 1-3.

Prensky, M. (2001). Digital Natives, Digital Immigrants Part 1. *On the Horizon, 9*(5), 1-2.

Part Three
TESOL Interfaces 3(1)
& TESOL Interfaces 3(2)

2009

10. Language is Used

Mark C. Love

This issue of the journal has seen us grow as editors. We found some of our contributors were resisting our efforts to force their prose into the stodgy mold the discourse rules the academic community tends to follow, rules that many perceive to reflect language use in the twentieth and even the nineteenth centuries. This led us to examine our role in the editing process. With the belief that language is an ever- evolving entity, we decided to follow a language-is-use policy and edit with much lighter hands (Ludwig Wittgenstein is attributed with the concept that language is use; see Mikhail Bakhtin for in-depth explanations of how language changes through use). We hope you like the new style and that the journal now more accurately reflects language as it is used in the twenty-first century.

For the current issue we have collated two research articles, and two forum articles, all contributed by Woosong students and faculty.

In *Responding to Behaviors of Resistance in Japanese University EFL Classrooms*, John Burrell surveys teacher and student attitudes towards the four frequently encountered disruptive behaviors of being late, sleeping in class, chatting in class and sending and receiving text messages as well as appropriate responses to each of these behaviors. The results are truly enlightening with students demanding for stricter action on the parts of teachers in handling some behaviors. Burrell finishes by calling for research into the effectiveness of disciplinary behavior.

In *Realizing the benefits of computer assisted language learning (CALL)*, Chris J. Brennan looks at the learning methods and benefits of CALL and critiques them. His table (Table 1) to use when evaluating 'effective interface design,' an aspect of the CALL design process that he feels is frequently ignored, will be of use to those engaged in designing interfaces for their educational projects.

Culture in English Language Teaching by JiaJia Ren again takes up the call to bring more culture training into the EFL classroom. Ren argues we need to introduce culture, create cultural environments, and compare cultures in the classroom. We should do this by using a variety of media

The need for a comprehensive SLA theory: What place does that theory have in TEFL? by Eric D. Reynolds attempts to define what factors an SLA theory needs to account for. The author provides brief synopses of the major theories of SLA and offers a brief critique of each one. The author then goes on to look at some possible new directions in which SLA theory could go. Of interest, the author calls for less theory, not more, and more testing of current theory. He states that "We need to search for alternate ways to ask the same questions" and finally calls for "more practical classroom based research to support a theory of second language teaching (SLT)."

The next issue of *Interfaces* will be published mid-December of 2009, and we look forward to all future submissions. As Korea is becoming an ever more important player in the global market, the Korean EFL market is becoming of greater and greater importance. Unfortunately, there is still a *relative* dearth of research written in English on Korea. We hope that will change, and *Interfaces* will provide a forum for fruitful discussion in this area.

References

Altbach, P. G. (2004). Globalization and the university: Myths and realities in an unequal world. *Tertiary Education and Management, 10*(1), 3-25.

Bautista, D. D. (2007). Editorial: There is a Place for Learning Experiences. *Interfaces, 1(1)*. Retrieved from http://interfaces.tesolmall.net/jarticles/one-one/editorial1-1.pdf

Brew, A. (1999). Research and teaching: Changing relationships in a changing context. *Studies in Higher Education, 24*(3), 291-301.

Brew, A., and Baud, D. (1995). Teaching and research: Establishing the vital link with learning. Higher Education, 29(3), 261-273.

Coaldrake, P., and Stedman, L . (1999). *Academic Work in the Twenty-First Century: Changing roles and policies.* Occasional Papers Series. Canberra, Australia: Department of Education, Training and Youth Affairs.

11. Responding to Behaviors of Resistance in Japanese University EFL Classrooms
John Burrell

This study explores how Japanese university EFL students and teachers believe the teacher should respond to four behaviors: coming late to class, sleeping in class, chatting in class, and sending and receiving text messages in class. 737 students and 19 teachers answered a four-part questionnaire to determine what they believed the teacher should do in each of the four cases. The results indicated that while the majority of students believed three of the behaviors warranted little or no action by the teacher, the fourth, chatting in class, was even less acceptable to the students than to the teachers. The teachers believed none of the behaviors were acceptable and the most common response to the repeated occurrence of the behaviors was to lower the student's grade. In carrying out the study it was found that there was a third party to the issue, the administration of the institution. However, the investigation of the beliefs about the correct response to the behaviors of the administration was beyond the scope of the study.

Introduction
New teachers at universities in Japan may find themselves thinking, *This is university?* when confronted by classroom behaviors such as lateness, absenteeism, chatting, sleeping, or use of cell phones in class. Petrucione and Ryan (2002) addressed this issue by developing a classroom exercise for their students to do in the first or second class of the semester. They had the students write and discuss what they thought the teacher should do when students engaged in various non-productive behaviors. They were asked what the teacher should do the first time the student did something and when the students did it repeatedly. From their presentation the author developed an anonymous

questionnaire and that was given to 737 university students and 19 university teachers to determine if students and teachers thought coming to class late, sleeping in class, chatting with friends, and sending and receiving email were acceptable in a university classroom, and if there were any differences between the two groups.

Literature Review

The impetus behind this study was the belief that it is important to determine what the students think about how their classes are conducted (Nunan, 1995). When there is a mismatch between what teachers and learners expect to happen in the classroom there is a negative impact on learning (Nunan, 1987). The research about this aspect of teaching, while not specifically aimed at behaviors of resistance, is extensive (Cathcart & Olsen, 1976; McCarger, 1993; Oledejo, 1993; Schultz, 1996). It is critical to a teacher's success to make informed choices about how to conduct their classes (Ryan, 1995) and this can only happen when the student expectations are known.

In the literature concerning teaching university EFL and ESL there is relatively little discussion of classroom discipline or behaviors of resistance (Crookes, 2003). Class management is covered but usually focuses on other aspects such as teacher language and lesson pacing. Davies and Pearse (2000) describe issues with classroom discipline as mainly the preoccupation of some who teach large groups of children and adolescents. An example that supports this is *A course in Language Teaching* (Ur, 2006) which has fifteen pages devoted specifically to classroom discipline, but all the examples are from secondary or middle school. It is probably accurate to describe Japanese university students as Carbone (1999) does American university students as "just big high school students" (36).

There is more information concerning disruptive student behaviors in regular classes in universities in the United States and Canada. Student incivility in universities seems to be growing (Morrissette, 2001; Perlmutter, 2004; Clark & Springer, 2007) and a significant source of faculty stress (Perlmutter, 2004; Lewis, Romi, Xing &Katz, 2005). International teaching assistants in American universities confront some of the same discipline problems in their classrooms as instructors do in Japan (Luo, Bellows, & Grady, 2000). In spite of the growing concern about the issue, university faculty members in the United States are rarely trained to deal with discipline problems in their classes (Center for Survey Research, 2000; Clark & Springer, 2007; Perlmutter, 2004; Seidman, 2005).

Methodology
Participants
Questionnaires were administered in June and July 2003. The participants were 737 university students from three private universities and one public university in Japan. Three of the universities were from Shizuoka and one was from Fukuoka. There were 406 male participants and 302 female. The majority (406) of the participants were first year students, 183 were second year students, 97 third year students, 48 fourth year students, and one graduate student.

Nineteen teachers participated in the study. They were from Shizuoka and Fukuoka. The number of teachers may be too low for any definitive statistical analysis, but the responses are included below. There were sixteen men, two women, and one non response. All were native English speakers.

Instrument
The researcher changed Petrucione and Ryan's classroom activity into a questionnaire because that while the presenters'

students, who were from a prestigious women's university and were of relatively high level, most students are non-English majors who are false beginners. It was not deemed feasible (cost effective in terms of class time spent and information gathered) to do the exercise in English and be able to have much meaningful discussion, especially at the beginning of a course where it would be of the most use. However, the author thought the information could be important so the questions were translated into Japanese and given as a questionnaire (Nunan, 1995).

Originally a close-ended questionnaire based on Petrucione and Ryan's activity was considered. Questionnaires often use closed ended questions because of their ease of administration and analysis (Brown, 2001). Previous experience with two other studies (Burrell & Goshi, 2003; Burrell & Goshi, 2004) with over one thousand participants each, comprised of mostly open-ended questions concerning student preferences for elective English classes, led to the desire to do something a little less time consuming. However, there was no idea how the participants would answer in this case, so there was no confidence that a questionnaire could be constructed that would not limit the participants' possible answers. This study was truly exploratory and so open-ended questions were the most suitable (Brown, 2001).

The questionnaire was essentially the same as the activity given by Petrucione and Ryan (2002) to their classes; however, there were a few changes made. In the student questionnaire, two demographic questions concerning gender and year in school were added. For the teachers there were four demographic questions added. The first asked the participants' gender. The second was open-ended and asked the participants' native language. The third was also open-ended and asked how long the participant had worked at the university level in Japan. The last demographic question asked if the participant had any children. The last question was added at the urging of one of my Japanese colleagues who insisted that he had become significantly more patient with his students after his child was born. Both versions of the questionnaires were anonymous.

In Ryan and Petrucione's activity there were five content questions and for this study two were eliminated and one other was added. The first question in the original was, "How should the teacher react when a student comes to class after the chime has rung?" For this study, the question was changed to "What should the teacher do when a student comes to class late?". The question was changed because of the realization that not all teachers start their classes with the bell and so the definition of late could not be so precise. The second concerned sleeping in class and was not changed. The third question in the original asked how the teacher should react when a student was doing work for another class. This was eliminated to include a question about chatting in class, something the researcher has found much more common. The last question in the original asked how the teacher should react when a student was slow to answer a question. In their presentation, Petrucione and Ryan stated that this behavior should not be seen in the same light as the proceeding ones and the researcher agreed. In order to make the questionnaire easier to administer it was decided to hold the number of questions to the four behaviors: coming late, sleeping, chatting, and sending and receiving email on mobile phones.

It was necessary to translate the questionnaire into the students' native language because of the relatively low level of English of most students (Nunan, 1989, 62). In addition, less class time would be taken if the questionnaire was in Japanese and this was very important because the questionnaire was voluntarily administered by a number of teachers at different institutions. The less intrusive the questionnaire was in terms of class time, the more likely they were to be administrated. The English version was translated into Japanese and then back translated into English by another person. No serious differences were found between the original English version and the version produced after the back translation. The teachers' questionnaire was only given in English.

Results

One of the reasons in the literature for not using open-ended questions was the possibility of the participants to write too much and present difficulty for analysis (McDonough & McDonough, 1997). In the student questionnaires, this was not the case. The answers tended to be succinct with about 10 to 15 characters in the average response. However, with the teachers it was true. The volume was impressive, with writing often crammed into the margins. Some of the teachers included quotes illustrating their teaching philosophies and almost all included information beyond the scope asked by the questionnaire. Certainly, the issue of dealing with these particular behaviors is one that concerned these teachers. The topic also apparently concerned the students as well because there were relatively few questions left blank on the questionnaires.

The responses to the first question highlighted a distinct difference between teachers and students, as seen in table one, in that while more teachers (68.4%) would lower the repeatedly late students' grade in some way, more students (53.7%) thought a warning or ignoring it was better. This corresponds to a study by Ryan (1995) that showed that a majority of Japanese university students expected even repeated instances of being late to class not result in any penalty that would lower their grade.

Interestingly, more students (7.5%) said the teacher should ask the student why they were late as opposed to the teachers (5.3%). This is actually quite insightful as there could be logistical considerations for the student, such as a previous class in a building far from the English classroom (Swetnam, 1999). It probably should be the first option the teacher takes before implementing others.

Sleeping in class had one of the biggest differences between teachers and students (refer to Table 2). Almost half of the students (41.5%) thought the teacher should ignore a student who repeatedly slept in class. Almost the same percentage of teachers (42.1%) indicated they would lower the students' grade in some way. In Ryan (1995) an even greater percentage (58%) of students thought sleeping in class should be ignored. In a survey of American students (Carter and Punyant-Carter, 2006) by far the most preferred teacher response to students sleeping in class was for the teacher to talk with the student privately after class; not common enough to warrant its own category in the present study.

The students were much less tolerant of other students repeatedly chatting in class than the teachers. This was also the case in Ryan (1995). More students (40.8%) than teachers (26.3%) thought the teacher should kick out of class those students who repeatedly chatted with their friends and did not participate. In another study, Carter and Punyant-Carter (2009) again found that the preferred response by the teacher to students chatting in class was for the teacher to talk with the student privately outside of class. That Japanese students were so much less tolerant of other students chatting, compared to the other behaviors, was the most surprising finding for the researcher.

Table 1.
Responses to: What should the teacher do when a student comes to class late?

Responses	First		Repeatedly	
	Stu	Tea	Stu	Tea
No answer	1.9%	0%	1.9%	5.3%
Ignore	46.1%	21.1%	12.6%	5.3%
Gentle warning	10.6%	52.6%	1.2%	0%
Warn	30.5%	15.8%	28.6%	0%
Strong warning	0.4%	0%	10.9%	0%
Ask why	6.6%	0%	7.5%	5.3%
Don't allow in	0.1%	0%	8.1%	68.4%
Mark absent/down/takeaway points	1.9%	26.3%	21.4%	0%
Fail/don't give credit	0%	0%	3.8%	0%
Writing assignment/written apology	0.1%	0%	1.2%	0%
Corporal punishment	0.3%	0%	0.7%	0%
Other	1.4%	0%	2%	0%

Table 2.
Responses to: What should the teacher do when a student sleeps in class?

Responses	First		Repeatedly	
	Stu	Tea	Stu	Tea
No answer	1.8%	0%	2.2%	0%
Ignore	47.6%	10.5%	42.5%	10.5%
Gentle warning	3.3%	5.3%	0.1%	0%
Warn	18.5%	5.3%	14.8%	5.3%
Strong warning	0.7%	0%	4.5%	5.3%
Wake	25.6%	78.9%	10.9%	10.5%
Ask why	0%	0%	1.9%	10.5%
Mark absent/down/takeaway points	0.7%	0%	10.2%	42.1%
Kick out	0%	0%	7.7%	5.3%
Fail/don't give credit	0%	0%	0.7%	5.3%
Make an interesting class	0.3%	0%	1.8%	0%
Corporal punishment	0.3%	0%	1.5%	0%
Other	1.1%	0%	2.3%	5.3%

Table 3.
Responses to: What should the teacher do when a student is chatting with their friends and not participating in the class activity?

Responses	First		Repeatedly	
	Stu	Tea	Stu	Tea
No answer	1.1%	0%	1.6%	0%
Ignore	13.2%	0%	4.7%	0%
Gentle warning	5.4%	26.3%	0.3%	5.3%
Warn	68.5%	42.5%	20.5%	26.3%
Strong warning	6%	10.5%	14.2%	10.5%
Separate students	0.4%	5.3%	1.4%	5.3%
Wait for them to be silent	0.4%	5.3%	0.7%	0%
Mark absent/down/takeaway points	0.5%	0%	0%	10.5%
Kick out	1.9%	5.3%	40.8%	26.3%
Fail/don't give credit	0%	0%	2.8%	5.3%
Ask why or what	0.7%	5.3%	1.2%	0%
Make an interesting class	0.4%	0%	0.8%	5.3%
Corporal punishment	0.1%	0%	1.2%	0%
Other	1.4%	0%	2.8%	5.3%

Table 4.
Responses to: What should the teacher do when a student is sending or receiving mail during class?

Responses	First		Repeatedly	
	Stu	Tea	Stu	Tea
No answer	3.5%	0%	3.8%	0%
Ignore	41.7%	0%	28.8%	5.3%
Gentle warning	3.8%	5.3%	0.4%	0%
Warn	44.8%	63.2%	22.8%	10.5%
Strong warning	2%	15.8%	6.8%	5.3%
Mark absent/down/takeaway points	0.1%	5.3%	5.2%	15.8%
Confiscate	1.9%	5.3%	14.1%	42.1%
Kick out	0.5%	0%	9.9%	5.3%
Fail/don't give credit	0%	0%	1.8%	0%
Corporal punishment/break	0.1%	0%	2.4%	0%
Other	1.6%	5.3%	4.1%	15.8%

Discussion

The majority of Japanese university students did indicate that three behaviors: coming late to class, sleeping in class, and texting in class, while maybe not actually acceptable in a university classroom, do not justify serious sanctions by the teacher. However, the students saw chatting in class as not acceptable. Most of the teachers surveyed did not see any of the behaviors done repeatedly as acceptable and the result was action that would affect the student's grade. One question that came from the study was why one of the behaviors was seen as unacceptable and not the other three.

It may be because the Japanese educational model has the students being very passive in their learning and quiet in the classroom (Snell, 1999). Therefore, the students do not see behaviors such as sleeping, being late, and texting as negatively as the teachers do because they do not bother the other students.

They hurt the particular student only. In contrast, chatting could disturb other students in the Japanese model, and so is viewed much more negatively by the Japanese students. Matsuura, Chiba, and Hilderbrand (2001) found that Japanese university students preferred a more traditional approach to English language classes with more of an emphasis on teacher centeredness. Chatting by other students would interfere with hearing the teacher and so is unacceptable.

The problem for the foreign teachers, who often favor a more learner-centered approach (Matsuura, Chiba, and Hilderbrandt 2001), can be when they attempt to implement a more active style of learning that utilizes pair or group work. To be effective this style of teaching requires complete student participation. Any of the four behaviors can have adverse consequences on the effectiveness of a more learner- centered style of learning. Japanese students have little experience with interaction in their classrooms, both with other students and the teacher (Snell, 1999). The Japanese system is very test oriented and the students may have a hard time understanding that in their university English classes (run by native speaking teachers) not only their test scores, but also their classroom behavior can influence their final grade.

Conclusion

In the course of this study, it became clear that there is an important third actor concerning the issue of responding to behaviors of resistance: the university administration. A colleague at another institution declined to administer the questionnaire because at the time he was embroiled in a dispute with his head teacher over allowing a student into the classroom when they were over 45 minutes late. He was afraid that the head teacher would see the distribution of this questionnaire as some sort of political move. Another colleague who is in charge of the part time instructors at his university was very wary of distributing the questionnaire for fear the instructors might think he was in some way checking up on them. A number of revisions to the cover letter were necessary before he was satisfied that they wouldn't. Classroom discipline issues involve not only the teacher and the students, but also the administration of an institution. The attitude of the administrations at the universities involved was beyond the scope this study, but should be the subject of further investigation.

Based on the interest shown by the attendance and attention paid in Ryan and Petrucione's original presentation and the amount written by the teachers on the questionnaires in the present study it is clear that responding to behaviors of resistance is an important issue for university EFL teachers in Japan. The issue of class discipline is certainly not just for those who deal with children. It is an issue for those who teach in Japanese universities and one in which they may have had little training.

A question for further study is what types of responses by teachers are actually effective. A majority of the teachers who responded gave the same (unsolicited) advice. They stated that they made the class rules very clear from the first day of class. The author believes it is probably also a good idea to reiterate the rules as the term or semester progresses. If the students' level of English is high enough, Ryan and Petrucione's (2002) original activity would serve as a useful basis for a first or second class activity to see what the students expect to happen in the classroom. Ultimately, those teachers coming from other teaching situations outside of Japan, when teaching required courses to non-English majors, should be prepared to deal with issues of class discipline.

References

Brown, J. D. (2001). *Using Surveys in Language Programs.* Cambridge: Cambridge University Press.

Burrell, J., & Goshi, M. (2003). An analysis of student preferences for elective English courses. *The Report of the Foreign Language Center, 23.* Japan: Tokai University.

Burrell, J., & Goshi, M. (2004). An analysis of student preferences for elective English courses part 2. *The Report of the Foreign Language Center, 24.* Japan: Tokai University.

Carbone, L. (1999). Students behaving badly in large classes. *New Directions for Teaching and Learning 77,* 35 – 43.

Carter, S. L. & Punyant-Carter, N. M. (2006). Acceptability of treatment for a student sleeping in a college classroom. *Education* 126 (3) 541-546 Retrieved from http://www.articlearchives.com/education-training/students-student-life- colleges/999394.html

Carter, S. L., & Punyant-Carter, N. M. (2009). College students' perceptions of treatment acceptability of how college professors deal with disruptive talking in the classroom. *College Student Journal* Retrieved from http://www.findarticles.com/p/articles/mi_mOFCR/is__1_43/ai_n31415091/

Cathcart, R. L., & Olsen, J. W. B. (1976). Teachers' and students' preferences for correction of classroom conversation errors. In J. F. Fanselow & R. H. Crymes (Eds.), On TESOL '76, 41-53. Washington, D.C.: TESOL.

Center for Survey Research, University of Indiana, Bloomington. (2000, June 14). A survey on academic incivility, preliminary report. Retrieved from http//www.indiana.edu/-csr/CivilityPreReport.pdf

Clark, C. M., & Springer, P. J. (2007). Thoughts on incivility: student and faculty perceptions of uncivil behavior in nursing education. *Nursing Education Perspectives*. Retrieved from http://www.articlearchives.com/education-training/curricula-medical- education/1658369-1.html

Crookes, G. (2003). *A practicum in TESOL: professional development through teaching practice.* NY: Cambridge University Press.

Davies, P., & Pearse, E. (2000) *Success in English Teaching.* Oxford: Oxford University Press.

Lewis, R., Romi, S., Xing, Q., & Katz, Y. J. (2005). Teachers' classroom discipline and student misbehavior in Australia, China, and Israel. *Teaching and Teacher Education 21.* 729 -741.

Luo, J., Bellows, L., & Grady, M. (2000). Classroom Management Issues for Teaching Assistants. *Research in Higher Education 41* (3), 353-383.

Matsuura, H. Chiba, R., & Hilderbrandt, P. (2001). Beliefs about learning and teaching communicative English in Japan. *JALT Journal 23*(1), 69-89.

McCarger, D.F., (1993). Teacher and student role expectations: Cross-cultural differences and implications. *The Modern Language Journal, 77,* (2), 192-207.

McDonough, J., & McDonough, S. (1997). *Research Methods for English Language Teachers.* London: Arnold.

Morrissete, P. (2001). Reducing incivility in the university/college classroom. *International Electronic Journal for Leadership in Learning,* 5(4). Retrieved from http://www.ucalgary.ca/~volume5/morrissette.html

Nunan, D. (1987). Communicative language learning: the learners' view. In K.D. Bikram (Ed.), *Communication and learning in the classroom community.* (176 – 190). Singapore: SEAMO Regional Language Centre.

Nunan, D. (1989). *Understanding Language Classrooms.* Hemel Hampstead: Prentice Hall International (UK) Ltd.

Nunan, D. (1995). Closing the gap between learning and instruction. *TESOL Quarterly, 29* (1), 133-158.

Oladejo, J. A. (1993). Error correction in ESL: Learners' preferences. *TESL Canada Journal, 10,* 71-89.

Perlmutter, D. D. (2004) Thwarting misbehavior in the classroom. *The Chronicle Review 50 (30).* Retrieved from http://chronicle.com/weekly/v50/i30/30b01401.html

Ryan, S., & Petrucione, S. (2002). Classroom discipline: what do learners think? Paper presented at the JALT national conference, Shizuoka, Japan.

Seidman, A. (2005). Misbehavior in the college classroom? A cross cultural survey of students' perceptions and expectations. *The Language Teacher 19 (11),* 13-16.

Snell, J. (1999). Improving teacher student interaction in the EFL classroom: an action research report. *The Internet TESL Journal 4* (4) Retrieved from http://tteslj.org/articles/snell-interaction.html

Shultz, R. A. (1996). Focus on form in the foreign language classroom: Students' and teachers' views on error correction and the role of grammar. *Foreign Language Annals 29*(3), 343-364.

Swetnam, W. B. (1999). Decreasing the likelihood of stragglers in your class. *The TESOL Journal 8(4)* 38.

Ur, P. (2006). *A Course in Language Teaching.* Cambridge: UK University Press.

12. Realizing the Benefits of CALL (Computer Assisted Language Learning) in English Language Learning Classrooms

Chris J. Brennan

The versatility and functionality afforded by new technology furnishes novel opportunities and activities for learning via Multimedia (animation, graphics, moving video, music), the Internet (treasure hunts, webquests, and moodle), Electronic communication (e-mail, key pals, forums, and instant messaging), and Intelligent tutoring and quiz systems. Lyotard (1984) has coined the phrase "Death of the professor" (1) – the envisagement that educators will inevitably be supplanted by the implementation of such new educational technologies due to their inherent efficacies within the disciplines of teaching and learning. This paper initially examines the optimistic perceptions of new technologies in education and a synopsis acquaints the reader with new learning methods and associated benefits within the context of CALL afforded by the contemporary technologies of multimedia, the internet, electronic communication, and adaptive learning. A critical appraisal examines the veracity of the purported beneficial claims of new technology in education from the perspectives of educational theory, design, and practical considerations. Deficiencies which conspire to encroach on the efficacy of educational technology are identified and discussed. This paper concludes that the hitherto prevailing 'Cut and Paste' approach to the implementation of new educational technologies does not constitute a panacea for teaching and learning. Conversely, until educational, design, and practical dimensions are inclusive themes within new educational technology implementations, benefits will not be uniformly realized. Accordingly, Lyotard's

(1984) fatalistic 'Death of the Professor' epitaph is considered to be a fallacious and unrealistic prognosis.

Introduction

In our contemporary society, the unabated proliferation and continuous inception of new and innovative technologies is certainly a testament to our modern day World. We reside in a global village, and live in virtual communities in virtual on-line interconnected Worlds. Today we possess the ability to interact with computers in ever increasingly sophisticated ways, from a simple mouse click, to speech recognition, to virtual reality.

Computers can avail the functionality of a learning vehicle by affording the transfer of information to learners by virtue of diverse modalities including written and spoken texts (Hasselgård, 2001), graphics (Phinney, 1996), pictures/pictograms with animations and sounds (Wendon, 1987), motion video (Arthur, 1999), and virtual reality (Bricken, 1991) constituting an audio-visual interaction experience.

Computer Assisted Language Learning (CALL) systems capitalize on these knowledge transfer modalities and exploit multimedia (animation, graphics, moving video, and music), the internet (treasure hunts, webquests, and moodle), electronic communication (e-mail, key pals, forums, and instant messaging), and intelligent tutoring and quiz systems. The benefits of such contemporary educational technologies in schools have included "Multisensory delivery, increased self-expression and active learning, cooperative learning, communication skills, multicultural education, and student motivation" (Barron & Orwig, 1993, 3).

Educational technology promises to democratize learning, increase access to multiple information resources, decentralize instruction, and remove hierarchies in communication and interaction in English language learning classrooms. Inevitably, the manifestation of these changes has translated into new and inventive pedagogies including cooperative learning (Yahya; Huie, 2002), group-based learning (Supyan; Hussin; Nooreiny; Maarof; D'Cruz, 2000), web-based education (Brown, 1999), multimedia learning (Huang, 2000), distance learning (Jones, 2000), asynchronous multimedia conferencing (Hahn,1995), and adaptive testing (Berberich, 1995).

As Lyotard (1984) espouses, such modernistic changes have prompted some commentators to envisage the prospect of, and proclaim the epitaph of 'Death of the professor' – an envisagement that educators will be supplanted as a result of the inherent efficacies that educational technologies possess within the discipline of teaching and learning.

Indeed, this prospect may not be so improbable,as Zepp (2005) articulates "In many instances, technology can outperform the teacher in terms of sheer efficiency – more information can be transmitted to more students in a shorter time span by technology than by teachers" (102) and studies of CALL implementations by Blake (1987) of University students revealed that educational technology employed in the learning environment served to increase learner motivation for University students studying language.

Based upon these premises and expectations that educational technology can enhance and facilitate the teaching and learning process (Benbunam-Fich, 2002), and afford learner-centered opportunities in the classroom (Lambert; McCombs, 1998), consequently education the world over has experienced an unprecedented rate of change (Ford; Goodyear; Heseltine; Lewis; Darby; Graves; Sartorius; Harwood, 1996), and

Thompson (1999) considers that consumption of computer mediated knowledge is increasing rapidly within all levels of education – this attest to the contemporary technologies' perceived utility and merits.

Indeed, this rate of change can be correlated with the fact that in 1999, 99% of all public school teachers had computers in their schools. Moreover, 84% of these teachers had computers in their classrooms (U.S. Department of Education, 2000). Further, in 2002, 92% of the public schools had Internet access in the classroom, computer labs and media centers (U.S. Department of Education, 2003), and according to the U.S. Department of Education (2000), it revealed that one third of teachers were "well prepared" or "very well prepared" to take advantage of computers.

Accordingly, this emergence of new technology and new learning methods afforded by multimedia, the internet, electronic communication, and adaptive testing have been embraced by education professionals eager to capitalize on the benefits of augmented learning in CALL.

Learning Methods and Benefits Afforded by Multimedia in CALL

The expression of 'multimedia' has its' origins in the domain of Computer Science, but is now resident in societies' contemporary diction. Multimedia affords a range of knowledge transfer modalities for supporting the learning process (Anderson; Smallwood; MacDonald; Mullin; Annemarie, O'Malley, 2000).

Multimedia describes an enriched media presentation format which is concerned with the computer-controlled integration of text, graphics, drawings, still and moving images (video), animation, audio (music or sound), and any other audio-visual media. Today multimedia is considered as being typically employed in the form of MP4, AVI, or MPEG format, and probably constitutes the majority of peoples' understanding of the definition. Other formats can also be employed to convey meaningful information. Such modes can employ pictures (usually in the form of BMP, JPEG, JPG, or GIF format), and Moving images (typically Flash or Animated GIF format, or Video), usually accompanied with sound or music (usually WAV or MIDI format), and Text (typically HTML or RTF format), (Kaskalis; Tzidamis; Margaritis, 2007).

The educational value of such simultaneous and amalgamated visual and auditory presentation can be correlated with the fact that research has revealed that people remember 20% of what they see, 40% of what they see and hear, but about 75% of what they see and hear simultaneously (Lindstrom, 1994). Further, studies in multimedia have also revealed the highest rate of information retention, equating to reductions in learning times (Ng; Komiya, 2000). Such empirical findings predictably elude to the conclusion that multimedia presentation can conceivably expedite the L2 language acquisition process.

Indeed, observations from experiments conducted even half a century ago concur with this notion. That is, Vernon (1946) played a 50 minute film to seaman concerning the methods of taking depth soundings. Subsequent testing of this group in comparison to a group who received conventional oral instruction of 3 hours, scored only 6 percent less than the 3 hour exposure group. Vernon invariably concluded from these observations that a 1 hour film could accomplish an identical quantity of information transfer as 3 hours of conventional oral instruction. Accordingly, such observations warrant investigation into their potential applicability within a language learning context.

Chun, Plass (1996a) also reported propitious results from 3 studies exploring the efficacy of multimedia with regards to vocabulary acquisition in an experiment exploring multimedia annotations (picture, text, video). A similar study by Tozcu, Coady (2004) also revealed that subjects who used computer assisted courseware, outperformed a control group in the areas of vocabulary knowledge, reading comprehension, and reading speed. Naturally, these accounts of efficacy, constitute obvious and compelling rationales to justify the implementation of multimedia based CALL applications. Furthermore, a value-added intrinsic property of multimedia pertains to the fact that it can also be represented, stored, transmitted and processed digitally, which equates to a convenient synergy of interoperability with the internet. This property translates to a prospective global user base for instantaneous multimedia learning content dissemination and utilization.

Multimedia is also interactive, enabling users of learning applications to regulate the content and flow of information (Vaughan, 1998) which is in contrast to content delivery in a traditional lecturer theater or classroom context. Thus, such a multi-modal, interoperable, and interactive delivery paradigm has correspondingly bequeathed diverse and potentially revolutionary approaches to accomplish content delivery to learners. That is, the seminal emergence of Virtual Reality (VR) which combines all aspects of multimedia (animation, graphics, moving video, and music) for total immersion in a computer generated environment may serve to afford uniquely expeditious learning opportunities and endow an additional fascinating dimension to CALL applications, however presently VR remains in its infancy.

Alternatively, Second Life, has the potential to stimulate global awareness of language, albeit as a technically inferior substitute to VR. That is, Second Life allows users to create their own virtual environment on the internet. Within this virtual environment users are able to interact in real time with more than 12 million subscribers interconnected via the World Wide Web (WWW). It is the environment and the avatar which individual users create which initially encourages cross-cultural and cross-social interest and stimulates social interaction across these traditional barriers, and social interaction can take place via speaking or typing. The virtual environment also furnishes users with a novel ability to move around this virtual world and visit virtual shops and parks, extending the social interaction experience beyond verbal or written communication. Second life offers an intriguing and unintimidating conceptualization into a potentially global interaction experience with others of differing cultures and language abilities.

Learning Methods and Benefits Afforded by the Internet in CALL

The world wide interconnection of computer systems bestows obvious global opportunities for language learning, and web-based education and training is currently a prolific research and development area (Khan,1997). Indeed studies by Mike (1996) have shown that just using the internet in the first instance increases higher order thinking skills. Brown (1999) advocates and articulates the value of internet treasure hunts. This task is characterized by Brown (1999) as students working in groups cooperatively, typically two or three participants sharing a workstation connected to the WWW, using Netscape or other browser to search for answers to an assortment of questions by searching various Web sites and pages for the answers. The value of treasure hunts with relation to CALL can be coupled with the succinct description by Moore (1996) who asserts that "there is little doubt that the Internet can bring access to a much wider range of information and resources than are currently available in most classrooms" (317).

Further, Holderness (1984) exemplifies that with regards to children, if they are given interesting project topics they will be motivated to search for meaning and explore in greater depth, translating to elevated learning experiences. It is conceivable and that such elevated learning experiences could also be extrapolated to adults. This novel internet learning methodology obviously places emphasis on the pedagogy of cooperative or collaborative learning sometimes referred to as Computer Mediated Communication (CMC) and McKay & Robinson (1997) advocate the view that CMC offers the strongest benefits with regards to CALL for co-operative and collaborative learning. That is, since language learning is implicitly an interactive and social activity, the value and applicability of encouraging collaborative learning within the natural context of language learning is obvious. Nunan (1989) contends that task-based learning afforded by CMC can change teacher-centered classrooms to more learner-centered environments as students are compelled to assist each other and become actively involved in their personal learning.

Hawisher (1992) concurs with this sentiment and articulates that in student-centered classes as opposed to teacher-centered classes, opportunities for collaboration increase. Further, research has revealed that adopting group and project-based activities are effective techniques to provide students with a particularly active approach to learning, Guzkowska, Kent (1994), and Hairston (1992) explains that real diversity arises from the students themselves and is expedited in a collaborative classroom in which students work together to develop their undestating. This view is also endorsed by Colomb, Simutis

(1996) who articulate that students experience a sense of learning, reading and writing as emerging from their collective activities. Moreover, Beauvois (1997) notes that computer communication increased total class participation to 100%.

Learning Methods and Benefits Afforded by Electronic Communication in CALL

The Internet has invariably empowered its' users with the capability to communicate virtually instantaneously across cultural barriers, availing the opportunity to progress EFL learners' reading and writing aptitudes and proficiencies. Such an enhancement to traditional learning attends to students' needs in terms of authentic audience, feedback, peer evaluation, and authenticity in writing (Trokeloshvili, 1997). Indeed, Hunter (1993) states that amongst educators many believe that computer-and-communications networking can be sucessfully employed to support and enable reform in education that is needed, and equally, research conducted by Lee (1998), shows that e-mail is a useful learning vehicle for teaching English. Further, Muehleisen, (1997) considers that internet use provides a practical real life language, bolstering motivation for ESL students to use English in their daily lives.

Furthermore, as Bacha (2000), argues there is also a need to ameliorate the teaching of writing skills for University ESL students and the internet and e-mail is a fitting technology that furnishes the possibility to progress EFL learners' reading and writing proficiencies, and there is a consensus that the linguistic nature of online communication is an effective method for promoting language acquisition. That is, analysis of electronic discourse has revealed a propensity for such discourse to be more lexically and syntactically complex than oral discourse (Warschauer, 1995) and such properties are distinctively conducive for language learning. However, it should be cautioned at this juncture that the provision of such features as emoticons will serve only to diminish the value of electronic discourse if students utilize them in their communications. That is, emoticons serve only to substitute written language with graphical visualizations. Accordingly, this form of 'shorthand' should be discouraged in L2 learners.

Electronic communication across the internet also provides the necessary conditions for learning to write, since it affords an authentic forum for written communication (Janda, 1995), and Warschauer (2000) has gone so far as to describe e-mail as the mother of all internet applications. Trenchs (1996) similarly advocates the notion that e- mail is an effective supplement to the learning curriculum for L2 students. Liao (1999) also contends that such a communicative approach amongst other themes are salient principles for the emphasis of fluency first, and grammatical accuracy second for L2 learners. Indeed, in Liao's (1999) study, it was emphasized that grammatical proficiency of sophomore students' e-mail to counterpart Chinese students, was easier to understand than before e-mail was exploited as a learning instrument.

In addition, Choi (1998) notes a study where Korean students had individual foreign 'Key Pals' and this methodology successfully enhanced their language proficiency, and as Rankin (1997) concurs, the additional interaction with foreign languages provided by e-mail affords ESL/EFL learners with more input than they would be able to expect from class time. Academics such as Belchamber (2007), Warschauer (1995), Beauvois, (1995), González-Bueno, (1998) have also noted that students who are reticent to speak in face- to-face contexts are increasingly willing and disposed to participate in an electronic environment.

Recently however, the increasingly popular and ubiquitous MSN messenger type (Nowlan, 2008) of synchronous methods of communication have also emerged, where individuals (or groups of participants) can collectively communicate in real-time, affording multi-user, cross cultural learning opportunities.

In addition, the MSN messenger genre of applications typically support the transmission of files and real-time images from Web-cameras – bequeathing a video- conferencing dimension to the learning experience. Microsoft Net Meeting can also empower learners in this regard, and affords what Counihan (1998) describes interaction which supposes real emotion and creativity, agreement and disagreement, gestures, etc, which facilitates and enriches the learning experience.

Finally, moving images can be "streamed" live or downloaded for later review. Clearly, with the advent of ubiquitous high-speed Broadband (such as ADSL), traditional methods of storage and retrieval associated with multimedia dissemination (DVD and CD-ROM) may be supplanted by internet access alone. It is envisaged that this prospect will encourage the proliferation of further learning opportunities including Video On Demand (VOD) type applications, web casts, digital stories and pod casts.

Learning Benefits Afforded by Adaptive Teaching and Testing in CALL

Sometimes referred to in the literature as Computer Adaptive Teaching (CAT) systems, such intelligent tutoring systems exploit modeling algorithms in order to identify and correct incorrect assumptions made by students. That is, contemporary educational technologies are able to 'get to know' their students which optimizes and tailors the learning experience for different individuals by focusing on the students' underlying strengths and weaknesses, and as Calvi, De Bra (1997) note, with such systems, different learners may get different content for the same learning object. In this way, this new educational technology assumes the role of a "cognitive tool" (van Jooligen, 1999), and as Leidner, Jarvenpaa (1995) note, such systems can be considered as enhancing the cognitive information processing of learners by tailoring the learning process to individual needs. Indeed, the effectiveness of such CAT systems has already equaled that of individual human tutoring methods (Spencer, 1999). Furthermore, continuous refinement of CAT systems has opened up new fronts in the domain of Artificial Intelligence (AI), and such AI-based intelligent tutoring systems have also demonstrated the capacity to teach as effectively as humans, even in advanced areas of academic study (Lajoie, Derry, 1993).

Similarly, the concept of intelligent tutoring systems can also be extrapolated to computer based intelligent testing i.e. the administering of quizzes. A fitting example is a system utilized by the Microsoft Corporation to test the technical competence of candidates seeking certification as Microsoft Certified System Engineers (MCSE).

Microsoft operates an intelligent quiz system or adaptive test that can judge the necessity to pose further questions on a given subject based upon correct or incorrect answers supplied in response to previous questions on the same subject matter. That is, if a candidate provided a correct response to a complex question on a given topic, the system's algorithm would 'know' it would be illogical to pose easier questions on the same subject matter. Accordingly, each candidate who is administered the adaptive test has a unique test of their knowledge, and quizzes typically administer variable numbers of questions for each candidate.

Critical Evaluation and Discussion

It is conceivable that when employed within CALL environments - multimedia, internet treasure hunts, e-mail and instant messaging, video conferencing, and computer adaptive testing constitute novel opportunities to enrich and enhance the language learning experience.

Further, based on proclamations of the intrinsic suitability of these technologies within education, and the myriad of academic research papers attesting to the efficacy of such educational technologies in language learning (Barron et al., 1993; Yahya et al., 2002; Supyan et al., 2000; Brown, 1999; Huang, 2000; Jones, 2000; Hahn, 1995; Berberich, 1995; Olson, 1974; Zepp, 2005; Lambert et al, 1998; Blake, 1987; Chun et al., 1996a) there is a propensity to be persuaded by the proponents of this technology and advocate the stance that capitalizing on educational technology constitutes an opportunity to actualize a panacea to learning that has hitherto not been afforded by preceding approaches and pedagogies, and antecedent technologies.

However, when examining the efficacy of technology within the contexts of educational theory, design, and practicalities, it transpires that advocating an ultimately optimistic view of educational technologies is an overly simplistic, premature, and parochial stance. That is, although it is accepted that the studies referenced above have demonstrated cases of successful implementations, yielding benefits, this does not invariably translate to the position that benefits are 'uniformly' achieved in every implementation of educational technology.

Indeed, the converse is also true, that is, the literature also attests to the fact that the implementation of educational technology is not so seamlessly and impressively pervading as one would initially be led to presume, and such observations inevitably elude to the conclusion that the introduction and adoption of educational technology does not constitute a panacea. Anecdotal observations also corroborate this conclusion, and Barnard (1999) amongst others espouse this converse scenario.

That is, Barnard (1999) argues that there are concerns pertaining to the under- utilization of technology in education and these perceptions are common across all educational sectors and many industrialized nations, and clearly, this actuality is certainly not consonant with Lyotard's (1984) prognosis that the professor will be supplanted by educational technology.

Beynon (2007) also shares the view of Barnard (1999) and concurs that despite many having shared high expectations for the impact of computer-based technology on educational practice, from a practical perspective, these expectations have not been realized. Kaufman (1998) also articulates that educational technology has failed to deliver on such robust claims of efficacy. Mohan (1994) similarly concluded from experimental data gathered over a duration of 9 years that the computers role as a tool for speaking may not be an appropriate one.

O'Hagan (1999) goes further and adopts the view that although few would deny that technology can furnish a flexibility and diversity of learning opportunities, controversy exists as to whether it can actually enhance learning of itself. This conviction has prompted some scholars to formulate analogies of this position, and in an influential paper authored some 20 years ago, it was proposed that the media are "mere vehicles that deliver instruction but do not influence student achievement any more than the truck that delivers our groceries causes changes in our nutrition" (Clark, 1983, 445). Similarly, Hannafin, Rieber (1989) also cautioned that "the emergence of computer- driven hybrid technologies has spawned unprecedented interest, yet advances in technological capability alone no more improve instruction than sharpened pencils improve prose" (102).

Thus, this disparity of consensus regarding the efficacy of educational technology articulated by Beynon (2007), O'Hagan (1999), and Hannafin et al., (1989) are suggestive that educational technology implementation strategy is based on nothing more academically substantive than a 'Cut & Paste' approach. Baker (1981) is consonant with this view and suggests that computer-based systems are out of context, in that, although such systems may appear rational when considered in isolation, they do not fit within the framework of the existing instructional context. Albirini (2007) elaborates further on this critique and elucidates that information technology remains to be appropriately placed into the educational context, despite the unabated efforts to 'fit' it. Albrini (2007) continues and considers that people have created the tools of educational technology. However, the underlying paradigm for its' effective use remains to be developed, and that the impetus should focus instead on what he describes as the "theoretical inadequacy" (231).

Albrini (2007) argues that concrete problems such as "lack of planning, paucity of funds, shortage of hardware, absence of standards, inadequacy of teacher preparation, need of software updates, lack of computer expertise, lack of knowledge of how to apply technology in the classroom, and insufficiency of access to computers" (p227) do not constitute the real obstacles that induce inefficacy of educational technology. Instead the problems reside at a more fundamental level and in the context of a paradigmatic conflict with regards educational theory.

Tipson, Frittelli (2003) views are consonant with those of Alberini and argues that Information and Communication

Technologies (ICT) offer significant contributions in education, healthcare, gender equality, environmental sustainability, but to be successful, that contribution should be considered along with a range of other non- technological considerations. Indeed as Koidl (2002) asserts, at present academia still does not fully understand the underlying mechanisms of how humans really learns, and similarly Alavi, Leidner, (2001) suggests the need for greater depth and breadth of investigation into technology-mediated learning as it has been suggested that improper use of technologies can adversely impact both the teacher and learner (Office of Technical Assessment, 1995).

Thus, endorsing a bankrupt logic that educational technology constitutes a panacea, when in fact such technology neglects underlying theoretical mechanisms of learning, will inevitably manifest only mismatches, incompatibilities, and deficiencies in achieving the target learning objectives. Beynon (2007) elaborates that, technology can only truly bolster the learning process if the technology embodies a relationship between human cognition and action, and at this present time, such technology fails to attend to engage with such universal facets of human learning. That is, current technology is, at best, according to Beynon (2007) unfit for purpose, and exists in a theoretical vacuum since the digital media does not map well onto existing constructivism and behaviorism theories of learning. Baynon's (2008) comments appear suggestive that educational technologies which neglect and fail to embody the underlying principles of learning tantamount to an endemic theoretical nihilism within the very conception of such systems.

A plausible explanation for this predicament is that software programmers who are commissioned to develop such educational systems may be oblivious to the fundamental underpinning of educational theories. Indeed they may possess no associated credentials with regards to learning theories, or even have an aptitude to develop a useful learning tool for use in the context of learning.

That is, such an approach to CALL system development will be susceptible to the developer's own fallibilities and limitations, and these inadequacies will inexorably be propagated to the end user 'victims' of the system. The ramifications of this scenario are that the target users' motivation to utilize a CALL system may be impaired as a consequence of the disincentive qualities endemic to the CALL system. Accordingly, such circumstances may only precipitate negative views by the target users of such systems, and be construed to afford only modest educational value or be construed as defunct.

Such undesirable consequences, have emboldened critics of CALL systems to contend that current approaches to education technology have took the control of learning out of the hands of the teacher and placed it into the hands of the computer software programmer (Valdez; McNabb; Foertsch; Anderson; Hawkes; Raack, 2000), and have in effect dehumanized the learning process, and ignored the characteristics including learner satisfaction, self-worth, creativity, and social values (Alessi; Trollip, 2001). Furthermore, these problems will be additionally compounded if the computer software programmer neglects interface design considerations, and it is an imperative that such design principles never be banished to the periphery of CALL system design since the interface exists as the specific locus where actual knowledge transfer occurs.

Accordingly, in order for learners (and teachers) to find CALL applications acceptable and useful, it is improvident for software programmers to trivialize and pay only cursory attention to interface design criterion. The adoption of such an insouciant approach to interface design will neglect fundamental ergonomic design considerations, diminishing the viability and efficacy of classroom and on-line learning, and exacerbate what Beynon (2007) refers to as a theoretical vacuum. This situation will only promote a litany of mismatches, incompatibilities, and deficiencies in achieving the target learning objectives. Naturally, to ensure user acceptance, the appropriate use of aesthetics, graphics, color, spelling, sound, highlighting, feedback and branching are imperative design constructs. Interface design must incorporate such usability heuristics as those endorsed by Nielsen and Molich (1990) in order to essentially prevent detracting the learners' attention from the core learning activities the system is designed to deliver in the first instance. Figure 1 presents a useful template which describes the rudiments for effective interface design for promoting user acceptance. Rigorously adhering these discrete cardinal design principles and marrying them together with the CALL system design is instrumental in mitigating the probability of system design being overly constrained by the personal design decisions of the software programmer, and acquiescing to a more intuitive and purposive design which is compatible with the needs of the target users (learners).

Viability of system status and feedback	Feedback satisfies the requirements pertaining to behaviorist theories of learning, and a paucity of feedback can only translate to an encumbrance and obstruction to learning, but many packages of computer assisted language learning fall short when it comes to providing the learner with individualized teaching and feedback (Murphy; McTear, 1997).

Match between system and the real world	Thorn (1995) advocates the view that programs have a requirement to be very simple in it terms of the interface dimension, so that learners don't have to compete between learning English and learning how the program works. Further, such systems should utilize language appropriate to the language proficiency of the target users and system- orientated terms should be avoided in order the emancipate users from requiring technical knowledge which is not related to the original target learning objective.
User control and freedom	The user must retain the ability to navigate forward and backward, and terminate the learning task at anytime. Users actions must also always be responded to immediately to reinforce the notion that the user is driving the interaction, and 'the system is waiting on the user' and not vice versa.
Consistency and standards	Titles, backgrounds, colors, buttons, captions, should all be uniform in appearance within the application to ensure consistency and avoid ambiguity.
Aesthetic and minimalist design	The information presented on the screen should be minimalist and be relevant only to the task in hand. Superfluous information to the task should be omitted, and avoidance of inundating the learner is paramount. Thorn (1995) endorses the design principle of the interface possessing a sense of beauty. Such a design consideration bolsters an effective learning environment.
Help users recognize, diagnose, and recover from errors	Rigidity of user applications means that users will rarely have the chance to make an error when using the application. It is invaluable to design into the system error traps that can help the easily user recover from mistakes.

Figure 1.
Usability heuristics which promote user acceptance

Realizing the Benefits of CALL | 187

In addition, as a corollary to the seemingly exponential proliferation of CALL technologies, it would be an exercise of prudence to require that such technologies be evaluated by corresponding professional bodies who would be responsible for awarding recommendations based purely on the suitability and benefits the technology purports to deliver. That is, such professional bodies would refrain from preoccupying themselves with considerations which are native to the domain of software development, and instead would preside over the evaluation of the effectiveness of the learning experience.

The age of the target user of the system is also another potential crucial theoretical dimension that could potentially compromise the efficacy of knowledge transfer of computer based information systems if not attended to in the systems' design. That is, there is prolific debate within the domain of language learning that children's brains have a 'plasticity' quality which adults unavoidably relinquish at adolescence as the brain reaches maturation. Chomsky (1965) refers to such a language specific learning ability as a Language Acquisition Device or LAD which accounts for the apparent mastery of language by children of a young age within such a compressed time frame, despite the highly abstract nature of the rules of language. Chomsky (1965) contends this LAD will 'mould' itself to any language to which is exposed. Thus it is a prerequisite that software designers be cognizant and sensitive of such influential theories of human learning when developing systems specifically for adults or children.

Technical issues of reliability, and download speed are equally important characteristics for user acceptance of CALL websites, especially for applications which involve some form of video-conferencing. Additional salient issues which are not divorced from user acceptance encompass equipment, lack of available time and knowledge of operating systems and hardware and internet software, ethics and privacy. Hernández-Ramos (2006) refers to such practical considerations as the invisible demands of technology. Furthermore, Backer (2001) prescribes that, to realize the efficacy of novel applications, practical considerations must also be addressed which concern such notions as access to internet enabled computers during class periods, or whether or not such facilities may only be partially available. That is, limited or unplanned contact with the system would inhibit and disrupt the user's learning of the commands that are required to use the system. Furthermore, it could also be contented that less technically endowed users of a system may only reluctantly submit themselves to and accept the technical demands of a system that imposes additional technical learning unrelated to their original target learning objectives.

That is, although technology does possess and afford tangible benefits for some learners, this vehicle of learning may not necessarily be a preferred methodology of learning by all. Accordingly, caution should be exercised when dictating to students which technologies they will utilize. Inattentiveness to such practical considerations may lead both teachers and learners to receive new technologies with skepticism (Sloep & Westeraadd, 2001).

Conclusion
The discussion contends that the implementation of educational technology is not optimistically deterministic. That is, although the ubiquity of technology meant that computer systems would inevitably pervade into the education sector for the purpose of ameliorating education standards, it is a fallacy that such benefits have been robustly and uniformly realized with the field of language learning in English language classrooms.

Consequently, the endeavor to successfully realize the objectives of democratizing learning, increasing access to multiple information resources, decentralizing instructions, removing hierarchies in communication and interaction, and obliterating the stringent structure of the classroom, have not been comprehensively achieved.

However, the discussion errs on the side of a cautionary warning as opposed to stipulating a pessimistic prognosis, and advocates the doctrine and strategy that if salient theoretical, design, and practical obstacles are surmounted then perhaps such a rectification will precipitate a 'reinvented' educational system, characterized by a transformation in curricula and pedagogic practice, culminating in an optimized teaching and learning experience for teachers and students respectively. Indeed, there is plenty of scope for further research in the areas which focus on the theoretical underpinnings of human learning and CALL system design. In addition, perhaps more importantly, the subsequent systematic evaluation of computer assisted language learning systems by canvasing the opinions of the target users themselves to elicit a measure of their efficacy in practice is also a fundamental requirement to remedy unforeseen issues of CALL system efficacy.

Thus as a prelude to any implementation, this paper prescribes that there is an emphasis to focus on and transcend such perennial problems in order to accrue the benefits of new technology in Computer Assisted Language Learning (CALL), and there is a requirement for an impetus which functions to elicit, decompose and scrutinize all encumbering endogenous issues which constitute impediments to realizing the efficacy of educational technology.

As Oliver (2006) states, the introduction of educational technologies although well intentioned in seeking to change curricula, pedagogic practice, and the learning experience, appears to have stalled in its hasty, ill-conceived introduction. Oliver (2006) continues to say that this does not have to be the case, and that all the above improvements can be realized if we attend to an appropriate level of analysis. Furthermore, this paper prescribes that a more realistic scheme to the introduction of educational technology is to graduate away from a 'replace the teacher with technology' mentality, to one which exploits technology as an aid to instruction rather as a way to supersede existing educational practices (Olson, 1974). Zep (2005) also reaffirms the value of the teacher within the learning environment and articulates the following responses in this regard: Computers cannot give the information more clear than teachers. Teachers give the information more clearer.

In order to transmit information or skills effectively, we need people to do so. Computers cannot express a motivational feedback or reinforcement. Teachers know how to teach specific information to a learner. Only another human can be cognizant of a learners needs and provide meaningful encouragement, reward, and motivation, and promote what Alessi et al., (2001) refer to as self-worth, satisfaction of the learner and creativity.

These factors inevitably allude to the proposition that Lyotard (1984) 'Death of the Professor' epitaph is therefore an inappropriate and unrealistic one. That is, if teachers bring useful benefits to the learning process which technologies are unable to reproduce and deliver themselves (and vice versa), then where is the justification for the mentality to replace teachers with technology (and indeed, vice versa)? Clearly under these circumstances, it would be more prudent and realistic to capitalize on the effective combined attributes of both teachers and educational technologies and exploit this mutually complementary synergy in the learning environment. In short, as Maloy (1996) succinctly argues in his paper, that in the struggle for the computer revolution in classrooms, it is the classroom which wins for now.

References

Alavi, M., & Leidner, D. E. (2001). Research Commentary: Technology-Mediated Learning- A Call for Greater Depth and Breadth of Research. *Information Systems Research,* 12(1), 1-10.

Albirini, A. (2007). The Crisis of Educational Technology, and the Prospect of Reinventing Education, 1 - *Special Issue on Technology and Change in Educational Practice,* 10, 227-236.

Alessi, S. M., & Trollip, S. R. (2001). Multimedia for Learning: *Methods and Development,* Needham Heights: Allyn & Bacon.

Anderson, A. H., Smallwood, L., MacDonald, R., Mullin, J., Annemarie, F. & O'Malley, C., (2000). Video Data and Video Links in a Mediated Communication: What Do Users Value? *International Journal of Human-Computer Studies.* 52(1), 165-187.

Arthur, P. (1999) Why use video? A teacher's perspective, *VSELT* 2(4), 4.

Barnard, J. (1999) Computers in FE biology – a study of how teachers' classroom practice can be affected by different types of software. *Journal of Educational Technology & Society,* 2(4), Special Issue on "Embedding Ubiquitous Use of Technology", 100-106.

Bacha, N. N. (2000). Developing learners' academic writing skills in higher education: A study for educational reform. *International Journal of Arabic-English Studies.* 2(2).

Backer, J. (2001). Using A Modular Approach to schMOOze with EFL/ESL Students. *Internet TESOL Journal, VII,* 5. Retrieved from http://iteslj.org/Lessons/Backer-SchMOOze.html

Beauvois, M. H. (1995). E-Talk: Attitudes and Motivation in Computer-Assisted Classroom Discussion. *Computers and the Humanities, 28,* 177-190.

Baker, F. (1981). Computer-managed instruction: a context for computer-based instruction. In H. F O'Neil, Jr. (Ed.), *Computer-Based Instruction: A State-of-the-Art Assessment.* New York: Academic Press.

Barron, A. E., & Orwig, G. W. (1993). *New technologies for education.* Englewood, CO: Libraries Unlimited.

Beauvois, M. H. (1997). Computer-Mediated Communication (CMC): Technology for Improving Speaking and Writing. In Michael D. Bush and Robert M. Terry (Eds.), *Technology-Enhanced Language Learning.* (165-184). Lincolnwood, IL: National Textbook Company.

Benbunam-Fich, A. (2002). Improving Education and Training with IT. *Communications of the ACM. 45*(5), 94-99.

Belchamber, B. (2007). The Advantages of Communicative Language Teaching, *The Internet TESL Journal, 13*(2). Retrieved from http://iteslj.org

Berberich, F. (1995). Computer Adaptive Testing and its extension to a teaching model in CALL. *CAELL Journal. 6*(2), 11-18.

Beynon, M. (2007). Special Issue on *Technology and Change in Educational Practice, 10*(1), 94-106.

Blake, R. (1987). CALL and the language lab of the future. *ADFL Bulletin, 18*(2), 25-29.

Bricken, M. (1991). Virtual Reality Learning Environments: Potentials and Challenges. *Computer Graphics 25*(3), 178-184.

Brown I, I. (1999). Originally presented at the 1999 ACTA-ATESOL National Conference - *TESOL Matters for the Millennium,* Sydney, Australia, 17-21 January 1999. Retrieved from http://iteslj.org/Lessons/Brown-TreasureHunts.html

Calvi, L., & De Bra, P. (1997). Using dynamic hypertext to create multi-purpose textbooks. Proceedings of *World Conference on Educational Multimedia/Hypermedia and World Conference on Educational Telecommunications*, Calgary, Canada, June 14-19, 130-135.

Choi, J., & Nesi, H. (1998). *The Internet TESL Journal*, 5(3). Retrieved from http://iteslj.org

Chun, D., & Plass J. (1996a). Effects of Multimedia Annotations on Vocabulary Acquisition. *The Modern Language Journal, 80*(ii), 183-198.

Chun, D. (1994). Using computer networking to facilitate the acquisition of interactive competence. *System*, 22(1), 17-31.

Colomb, G., & Simutis, J. (1996). Visible conversation and academic inquiry: CMC in a culturally diverse classroom. In Herring, S.C. (Ed.), Computer-Mediated Communication: Linguistic, social, and cross-cultural perspectives. John Benjamins Publishing.

Eastment, D. (n.d.). *Technology-Enhanced Language Learning: Hype or Gold Mine?* Retrieved from http://dspace.dial.pipex.com/town/square/ei11/tell.htm

Ford, F., Goodyear, P., Heseltine, R., Lewis, R., Darby, J., Graves, J., Sartorius, P., Harwood, D., & King, T. (1996). *Managing Change in Higher Education: A Learning Environment Architecture.* Buckingham: Open University Press.

González-Bueno, M. (1998). The effects of electronic mail on Spanish L2 discourse. *Language Learning & Technology 1*(2), 55-70.

Guzkowska, M., & Kent, I. (1994). Facilitating Team-work in the curriculum. In Thorley, L. & Gregory, R. (Eds.), *Using Group-based Learning in Higher Education* (49-53). London: Kogan.

Hahn, H. A. (1995). Distributed training for the reserve component: *Course conversion and implementation guidelines for computer conferencing.* ERIC Doc. ED359916.

Hairston, M. (1992). Diversity, Ideology and Teaching Writing. *College Composition and Communication, 43*, 2, 179-193.

Hannafin, M. J., & Rieber, L. P. (1989). Psychological foundations of instructional design for emerging computer-based instructional technologies. Part II. *Educational Technology Research and Development, 7*, 102-14.

Hasselgård, H. (2001). Corpora and their use in research and teaching. Retrieved from http://folk.uio.no/hhasselg/UV-corpus.htm

Hawisher, G. (1992). Voices in College Classroom: the dynamics of electronic discussion. *The Quarterly of the National Writing Project and the Center for the Study of Writing and Literacy 14*(3), 24-32.

Hernández-Ramos, P. (2006). How Does Educational Technology Benefit Humanity? Five Years of Evidence. *Educational Technology & Society, 9*(4), 205-214.

Holderness, J. (1991). Activity-based teaching: approach to topic-centred work. in: Brumfit, C. (Ed.), Teaching English to Children. Harlow: Longman.

Hymes, D. 1974. *Foundations in sociolinguistics.* Philadelphia: University of Pennsylvania Press.

Huang, S. (2000). Communicative Language Teaching in a Multimedia Language Lab. *The Internet TESL Journal, 6*(2). Retrieved from http://iteslj.org

Hunter, B. (1993). NSF's networked testbeds inform innovation in science education. *T.H.E. Journal, 21*(3), 96-99.

Janda, T. (1995). Breaking the ice: *e-mail dialogue journal introductions and responses.* In M. Warschauer (Eds.), Virtual Connections: Online Activities and Projects For Networking Language Learners (57- 58). Honolulu, HI: University of Hawai'i Second Language Teaching and Curriculum Center.

Jones, B. L., & Maloy, R.W. (1996). Schools for an information age: *restructuring foundations for learning and teaching,* Westport: Praeger.

Jones, G. (2000). How do I learn to speak? A review of the possibilities and constraints of online language learning. Unpublished essay submitted as coursework for the *Certificate in On-line Education and Training*, London University Institute of Education.

Kaufman, R. (1998). The Internet as the ultimate technology and panacea. *Educational Technology, 38*(1), 63-64.

Kaskalis, T. H., Tzidamis, T. D., & Margaritis, K. (2007). Multimedia Authoring Tools: The Quest for an Educational Package. *Educational Technology & Society, 10*(3), 135- 162.

Khan B. H. (1997). Web-Based Instruction, Englewood Cliffs, New Jersey: Educational Technology Publication.

Koidl, K. (2002). Adaptive Hypermedia Systems for e-Learning, *Proc of Seminar Telekooperation*, Germany. Retrieved from http://www.tk.informatik.tudarmstadt.de/Lehre/ss02/semtele

Lajoie, S. P., & Derry, S. J. (1993). *Computers as Cognitive Tools*, Lawrence Erlbaum Associates: Hillsdale, New Jersey.

Lambert, N. M., & McCombs, B. J. (1998). Introduction: Learner-Centered Schools and Classrooms as a Direction for School Reform. In Lambert, N. M. & McCombs, B. L. (Eds.), How Students Learn: Reforming Schools Through Learner-Centered Education (1-22). Washington, DC: American Psychological Association.

Lee, E. K. (1998). The Effects of e-mail mode on Korean high school students' task-based writing in English. *Paper presented at the annual summer conference*, Seoul, Korea.

Leidner, D. E., & Jarvenpaa, S. L. (1995). The Use of Information Technology to Enhance Management School Education: A Theoretical View. *MIS Quarterly, 19*(3), 265-291.

Liao, C. (1999). e-mailing to Improve EFL Learners' Reading and Writing Abilities: Taiwan Experience. *The Internet TESL Journal, 5*(3). Retrieved from http://iteslj.org/Articles/Liao-Emailing.html

Lindstrom, R. (1994). *The Business Week Guide to Multimedia Presentations: Create Dynamic Presentations That Inspire*, New York: McGraw-Hill.

Lyotard, J. (1984). *The Postmodern Condition: A Report on Knowledge* (trans). Benningtion, G., & Massumi, B., Minneapolis: University of Minnesota Press.

McKay, P., & Robinson, M. (1997). Language teachers and technology: The literature and teacher perceptions. In N. McMeniman & Viviani, N. (Eds.), *The Role of Technology in the learning of Asian Languages* (11-21). Canberra: Languages Australia.

Muehleisen, V. (1997). Projects Using the Internet. In College English Class. *The Internet TESL Journal*. Retrieved from http://iteslj.org/Lessons/Muehleisen-Projects.html

Mike, D. (1996). Internet in the schools: A literacy perspective. *Journal of Adolescent and Adult Literacy, 40*(1), 1-13.

Molich, R., & Nielsen, J. (1990). Improving a human-computer dialogue. *Communications of the ACM, 33*(3), 338-348.

Mohan, B. (1994). Models of the Role of the Computer in second Language Development. In M. Pennington & V. Stevens (Eds.), *Computers in Applied Linguistics*. Multilingual Matters.

Moore, P. (1996). Reading and Writing on the Internet. *The Australian Journal of Language and Literacy, 19*(4).

Murphy, M., & McTear, M. (1997). Learner Modelling for Intelligent CALL. In A. Jameson, C. Paris, and C. Tasso (Eds.), *Proceedings of the Sixth International Conference on User Modeling*, 301-312. Vienna: Springer.

Ng, K. H., & Komiya, R. (2000). Introduction of Intelligent Interface to Virtual Learning Environment. *Paper presented at the Multimedia University International Symposium on Information and Communication Technologies 2000* (M2USIC'2000), October 5-6, 2000, Petaling Jaya, Malaysia.

Nowlan, A. (2008). Motivation and Learner Autonomy: Activities to Encourage Independent Study. *The Internet TESL Journal, 14*(10). Retrieved from http://iteslj.org

Nunan, D. (1989). *Designing tasks for the communicative classroom.* Cambridge: Cambridge University Press.

O'Hagan, C. (1999). Embedding Ubiquitous Use of Educational Technology: is it possible, do we want it and, if so, how do we achieve it? *Journal of Educational Technology & Society, 2(2),* Issue: 4 - Special Issue on "Embedding Ubiquitous Use of Technology", 19-22.

Olson, D. R. (1974). Introduction. In D. R. Olson (Ed.), *Media and symbols: the forms of expression, communication, and education* (1-26). Chicago: University of Chicago Press.

Oliver, M. (2006). Editorial: *New pedagogies for e-learning?* ALT-J, 14 (2), 133-134.

Office of Technology Assessment. (1995). *Information technology and its impact on American education.* Washington, DC: U.S. Government Printing Office.

Phinney, M. (1996). Exploring the Virtual World: Computers in the Second Language Writing Classroom. In M. Pennington (Ed.), *The Power of CALL.* Houston, TX: Athelstan.

Rankin, W. (1997). Increasing the communicative competence of foreign language students through the FL chatroom. *Foreign Language Annals, 30*(4), 542-546.

Sloep, P. B., & Westera, W. (2001). The Concept of Educational Technology, Maatwerk met digitaal onderwijs. *Controllers Magazine,* June, 27-30.

Spencer, K. (1999). Educational Technology - An Unstoppable Force: A Selective Review of Research into the Effectiveness of Educational Media, *Journal of Educational Technology & Society, 2*(4), Special Issue on "Embedding Ubiquitous Use of Technology", 23-34.

Supyan H., Nooreiny. M., & D'Cruz, J.V. (2000). Sustaining an Interest in Learning English and Increasing the Motivation to Learn English: *An Enrichment Program. Universiti Kebangsaan Malaysia (Malaysia)*. Paper presented at The Millennium MICELT 2000, 3rd Malaysia International Conference for English Language Teaching, 15-17 May 2000, Melaka: Universiti Putra Malaysia.

Tipson, X., & Frittelli, C. (2003). *Global Digital Opportunities. National Strategies for "ICT for Development"*. New York: Markle Foundation.

Thompson, H. (1999). The Impact of Technology and Distance Education: A Classical Learning Theory Viewpoint. *Journal of Educational Technology & Society, 2*(3), Special Issue on "Learning by Doing" State of Distance Education", 25-40.

Thorn, W. J. (1995). Points to consider when evaluating interactive multimedia. *The Internet TESOL Journal, 5*(3). Retrieved from http://iteslj.org/Articles/Thorn-EvaueConsider.html

Tozcu, A., & Coady J. (2004). Successful Learning of Frequent Vocabulary through CALL also Benefits Reading Comprehension and Speed. *Computer Assisted Language Learning, 17* (5), 473-495.

Trenchs, M. (1996). Writing strategies in a second language: Three case studies of learners using electronic mail. *The Canadian Modern Language Review, 52*(3), 464-497.

Trokeloshvili, D.A., & Neal H.J. (1997). The Internet and Foreign Language Instruction: Practice and Discussion. *The Internet TESL Journal, 3*(8). Retrieved from http://iteslj.org

Vaughan, T. (1998). *Multimedia: Making it Work* (4th Ed.), Berkeley, CA: Osborne/McGraw-Hill.

Valdez, G., McNabb, M., Foertsch, M., Anderson, M., Hawkes, M., & Raack, L. (2000). *Computer-based technology and learning: Evolving uses and expectations*. Retrieved from http://www.ncrel.org/tplan/cbtl/toc.htm

Vernon, P. E. (1946). An experiment on the value of film and filmstrips in the instruction of adults. *British Journal of Educational Psychology, 16,* 149-162.

Vygotsky, L. S. (1962). Thought and Language, London. van Jooligen, W. R. (1999). Cognitive tools for discovery learning. *International Journal for Artificial Intelligence in Education, 10,* 385-397.

Warschauer, M. (1995). Comparing face-to-face and electronic discussion in the second language classroom. *CALICO Journal, 13*(2 & 3), 7-26.

Warschauer, M., Shetzer, H., & Meloni, C. (2000). *Internet for English teaching.* Alexandria, VA: TESOL Publications.

Wendon, L. (1987). Letterland - Changing the Language of reading instruction. In P. Smith (Ed.), *Parents and teachers together.* London: Macmillan Education

Yahya, N., & Huie, K. (2002). Reaching English Language Learners Through Cooperative Learning, *The Internet TESL Journal, 8*(3). Retrieved from http://iteslj.org

Zepp, R. A. (2005), Teachers' Perceptions on the Roles on Educational Technology, *Journal of Educational Technology & Society, 8*(2), 102-106.

13. Culture in English Language Teaching

JiaJia Ren

In EFL (English as a Foreign Language) teaching, the students are required to have cultural competence besides the basic language skills. Therefore, this paper introduces the importance of culture teaching in ELT (English Language Teaching) in China by the relation between culture and ELT. It also states the contents of culture teaching. Then it further expounds the different approaches to achieve the language acquisition through culture teaching.

Introduction

Culture teaching in EFL (English as a Foreign Language) has got more attention than ever before (Brooks, 1968), and teachers are aware that language learning is also a part of culture learning and that cultural competence is an integral part of communicative competence.

Researchers such as Byram (1989) and Kramsch (2001) have realized that the ultimate purpose of language teaching is to help students develop communicative competence (grammatical, discourse, sociolinguistic, pragmatic and strategic competence). As Brown (1994) points out, all these five aspects must work together for successful communication to take place. Spolsky (1989) proposes a necessary condition of dual knowledge for language learning, i.e. the acquisition of both language knowledge and skills in using that knowledge. In order to use the language knowledge appropriately, it is important for students to develop culture awareness in communication.

The Relation between Culture and English Language Teaching

Language teaching is related to bringing a target culture to learners, or, language learning is related to learning about another culture and acquiring knowledge of a target culture and an ability to communicate with native speakers. In order to achieve these objectives, it is important for teachers to teach culture and foster learners' communicative competence in ELT (English Language Teaching). Brown (1987) states that second language learning is often second culture learning.

Traditionally, foreign language teaching has long focused on the acquisition and on teaching techniques rather than on the teaching of culture. However, study (Stern, 199 2) shows that in many cases communication failures are caused by a lack of cross- cultural understanding, rather than the absence of linguistic competence. Irving (1986) points out, when communicating with foreigners, native-speakers of English are quite forgiving about pronunciation and structure mistakes, but they are much less forgiving about violation of rules and routines of communication. Such violations are often considered to be impolite.

Stern (1999) expressed the relationships between culture and English language culture as follows:
Language is a part of culture, and must be approached with the same attitudes that govern our approach to culture as a whole;

Language conveys culture, so that the language teacher is also of necessity a teacher of a culture; and, language is itself subject to culturally conditioned attitudes and beliefs, which cannot be ignored in the classroom.

Language and culture are closely associated with each other. Acquiring a target language is related to acquisition of a good command of target language culture. In this sense, acquisition of information about the target language culture is as important as language learning itself.

Content of Culture Teaching

First, let us look at a dialogue between a person from Chinese culture (*Man B*) with a person from another culture (*Man A*, a native-English speaker) who visits his home:

> Man A: *Your wife is very beautiful.*
> Man B: *No, no, my wife is not that beautiful.*

The embarrassment caused to *Man B* above is the consequence of cultural differences that shape responses to particular situations. When being complimented, native-English speakers would generally prefer to accept it by saying *thank you* or *I'm pleased to hear so*, to show their pleasure and appreciation; while the Chinese would generally prefer to refuse the complement to show their modesty and politeness.

Therefore, the contents of culture teaching should include aspects of cultural communication information. The cultural knowledge information can be gained directly through approaches of formal communication, which are concerned with the product of communication, and gained gradually through approaches of informal communication, which are concerned a process of communicative engagement (Ellis, 1982).

Those who were born in certain social-culture circumstances and naturally inherited their own common culture can easily understand their ways of behavior and avoid misunderstanding. That is the reason why the English-learners cannot easily use their English knowledge to communicate even though they have learned some history, geography and literature of English-speaking countries. While communicating in a foreign language, such learners are easily influenced and restricted by their native language, which is deeply rooted and works subconsciously even when these learners become familiar with the target language culture. Therefore, in this regard, learners ought to focus more on cultural communication information for the improvement of communicative competence.

Approaches Adopted in Culture Teaching
Introducing Cultural Background
Information about people from other cultures, their ways of life, their countries and their civilization is needed in the EFL classroom. Teachers should consider how such information can be used to develop learner ability in gaining knowledge about other cultures. Teachers should help learners come to know about the differences between other cultures and the home culture and guide them to turn externally available knowledge into their own internal knowledge. For instance, in American usage, a restroom is a room in a theater, department store or other building equipped with toilets, and washbasins and is for the use of customers and employees; restroom is a polite term for bathroom or a toilet; the English equivalent for the Chinese might be lounge, or sometimes lobby.

Creating Cultural Environments
The teacher should guide students to participate in the community in its cultural environment. However, this does not mean that a learner cannot be a participant of 'classroom culture' as Breen (1985) calls it, a simulative environment where the learner may begin to understand the foreign culture. The classroom is an artificially created cultural environment in which the learner's internal social reality meets a different external reality. As Kramsch says:
> in class, culture is created and enacted through the dialogue between teacher and students, Through their dialogue, participants not only replicate a given context of culture, but because it takes place in a

foreign language, it also has the potential of shaping a new culture (1993, 49).

Teachers can also motivate learners to participate in all kinds of English activities, such as English poem recitations, oral English competitions, and English drama performances.

Comparing Different Cultures
Teachers should make comparisons between cultures, which may help learners to understand other cultures, as well as their home culture, on the basis of previous experience and new knowledge. It is noteworthy that comparison helps learners better understand the target culture of different cultural judgments (Deng, 1989). Comparison also helps learners explain different culture behavior, avoiding just explaining another's behavior according to the learner's own standards. Only by comparison can one distinguish the differences and improve the ability of distinguishing acceptable culture and unacceptable culture, thus preventing learners accepting the target culture uncritically. For example, in China a dog is not considered to be a lucky animal, while native-English speakers are likely to praise somebody as a *lucky dog*. When saying someone is timid, Chinese tend to refer to him or her as a *mouse* while native-English speakers more likely using the phrase as timid as a *rabbit*.

Adopting Advanced Techniques
Mass media such as film, novels and especially newspapers and magazines, are also considered an insightful means for teaching culture, for they reflect people's way of life in terms of variety, contemporary issues and authenticity. Besides, audio-visual media materials and approaches, so different from the traditional chalk and black board method, are widely welcomed by teachers and students due to their vivid presentation of both

language and cultural knowledge based on authentic circumstances. Educationists have reacted with much imagination and enthusiasm in exploiting the capabilities of modern technology, teachers believe that using media in the teaching of EFL in the classroom is certain to bring about superior results (Mayer, 2001). It helps to simplify the teaching/learning process and can help to perfect it. Moreover, it can bring in cultured input in a clear and realistic way as compared with traditional, media-free instruction.

Teaching knowledge about other cultures in EFL education can strengthen a learner's intellectual power since the learner changes from being ignorant to being knowledgeable. Thus, the approaches suggested above can help to foster and improve a learner's cultural awareness and competence of cultural understanding.

Conclusion
The relation between language and culture influences culture teaching. It is necessary and urgent to teach not only cultural knowledge information but also cultural communication information as well. English-learners should be fostering cultural awareness and communicative competence through culture teaching.

References
Breen, M. (1986). The social context of language learning—a neglected situation. *Studies in second Language Acquisition,* 135–58.

Brooks, N. (1968). Teaching culture in the foreign language classroom.' Foreign Language Annals, 1, 204-217.

Byram, M. (1989). *Cultural Studies in Foreign Language Education.* Clevedon: Multilingual Matters Ltd.

Deng, Y. Ch. (1989). *Language and Culture*. Foreign language teaching and research press.
Irving, K. (1986). *Communicating in context*. New Jersey: Prentice Hall Regents.
Kramsch, C. (1993). *Context and Culture in Language Teaching*. Oxford: Oxford University Press.
Kramsch, C. (2001). *Language and Culture*. Oxford: Oxford University Press.
Mayer, R. E. (2001). *Multimedia learning*. Cambridge, England: Cambridge University Press.
Spolsky, B. (1989). *Conditions for second Language Learning*. Oxford: Oxford University Press.
Stern, H. (1960). *Fundamental concepts of Language Teaching*. Oxford: Oxford University Press.
Stern, H. (1992). *Issues and Options in Language Teaching*. Oxford: Oxford University Press.

14. The Need for a Comprehensive SLA Theory: What Place Does That Theory Have in TEFL?

Eric D. Reynolds

This paper seeks to sort out what is critical in forming a theory of second language acquisition. In addition, the author explores the history of SLA theory and describes the major theories of SLA. Moreover, in the process of description the author seeks to describe/evaluate those SLA theories. Finally, the paper offers some directions for future research for SLA in relation to a major end-user: second and foreign language education.

Introduction

Within the broad realms of academic study, second language acquisition (SLA) is still a relatively new field of study and continues to progress through a series of transitions. In practical fact, few, if any, researchers and scientists involved in SLA theory and research would argue that the field has reached a point of broad and solid consensus on a foundational set of facts from which a single unifying theory of SLA has been formed. In his recently published text, Long (2007) counts "as many 60 theories, models, hypothesis, and theoretical frameworks" (4) in the field of SLA, which is up from forty in Larsen-Freemen and Long in 1991. Clearly, many in the field are concerned about this situation as some of the titles of SLA texts would suggest: *"Issues* in SLA", (Beebe, 1988) *"Universals* in SLA", (Eckman, Bell, & Nelson, 1984) "The *Logical Problem* . . ." (Baker & McCarthy eds., 1981), or Long's (2007) *"Problems* in SLA" [emphasis added]. The purpose of this paper is to sort out what is critical in forming a theory, what the major theories of SLA are, and to describe/evaluate them, and, finally, to offer some directions for future research for SLA in relation to a major end-user: second and foreign language education.

What to Include in SLA Theory?

The question of what to include in SLA theory is an interesting one. Initially, one needs to distinguish between what a theory is (or *does*) and what it needs to account for. On that first issue of what a theory is and does, McLaughlin (1987) outlines several of the important features of a theory of second language acquisition. Initially, he outlines three underlying assumptions which are critical to understanding theory in general and for the purpose of this examination, should be interpreted and reframed in the light of contemporary terminology and perspective in social science research. Those assumptions are: "research is inseparable from theory", "there is no one scientific method", and "there is no single scientific truth" (3-5).

First, McLaughlin takes pains to point out that he refers specifically to a scientific theory. While he does not in this text elaborate on what constitutes "scientific," I would concur that a theory of SLA *does* need to be scientific in the sense that it needs to meet standards of rigor, evidence, and validity, etc. as established by SLA's scientific community. McLaughlin's first assumption, that research is inseparable from theory, is essentially a question in the philosophy of science—research builds theory and tests it, while simultaneously theory must account for the observed results of research as well as create the theoretical foundation that future research will be used to measure. Research that neither creates nor tests theory is meaningless—just as theory that neither accounts for nor predicts phenomena loses meaning. McLaughlin's second assumption, that no one scientific method exists, points directly to what has become the distinction between quantitative and qualitative research. His point, however, is deeper than the simplistic polarity implied by the two ends of our educational research methodology choices. SLA theory in particular needs to consider a variety of data for theory, as we will discuss later, because so many different and independent fields of study are in part responsible for the data that has been collected and the questions to be answered through a theory of SLA: general linguistics, neurobiology, cognitive psychology, etc. McLaughlin's third assumption, that no single scientific truth exists, is somewhat more difficult to grapple with in a field that includes many practitioners who are markedly "rational" – in a Cartesian sense – both their view of the world and consequently their approach to research and theory. Beyond the perspective of rationalists, McLaughlin (1987) points out that all researchers and theorist (including relativists) "feel that one's own approach and one's own point of view is better than other people's" (5). Thus, we need to bear in mind the variety of approaches that can help us peer into the murky workings of SLA. My personal metaphor for this theoretical pluralism is that of the blind men and the elephant. As new researchers in TEFL, we enter the study of SLA a little bit on the blind side; we would all do well to examine why we look at the elephant (assumption one – the relationship between research and theory), the lenses we use to explore the elephant (assumption two), and, perhaps most importantly, the sort of conclusions the other blind men are drawing in regards to the elephant (assumption three).

While the three assumptions elaborate well on the sort of thing theory is, McLaughlin goes further to define what theory does—in other words, the function of theory. He lists three characteristics: furthering *understanding, transformation,* and *prediction.* As the whole point of theory is to help us conceptualize the world in which we live, furthering understanding may be the most obvious—still, an incomprehensible theory is all too common! Secondly, the theory needs to transform. A new theory should allow us to reexamine our perspective and conclusions regarding the topic, and "change both the content and form of our knowledge" (7) –

reminiscent of a Kuhnian paradigm shift. This change generally should add parsimony, clarity, and "comprehensivity" – the inclusion of new and more complete data, as opposed to comprehensibility—to our understanding. Finally, and often problematically, the theory needs to allow for testable predictions. While McLaughlin does not frame his case in this fashion, I would add that any theory must face the criticism of the established scientific community and to withstand that scrutiny. McLaughlin refers to this in terms of *evaluation* with four different elements—we will use these notions later in section two for analyzing the major SLA theories. While asking the question about what to include in theory does not necessitate an exploration of the nature of theory, the question absolutely requires an examination of what a theory of SLA needs to account for. In other words, what sorts of research data has been generated that holds sway in the SLA community: What are some key "things" that we see occurring in a person's second language acquisition that appear to be sufficiently generalizable that we need to account for them in constructing a theory of SLA? Again McLaughlin (1987) lays the foundation by listing ten such generalizations. Allow me to paraphrase them with bullet points and McLaughlin's listed source:

- Predictable sequences of structural acquisition exist (Lightbrown, 1985).
- Learners create an "interlanguage" in which some errors mirror L1 learner's errors and other errors seem related to L2 transfer (Lightbrown, 1985).
- Interlanguage development is related to Universal Grammar, which makes some 'rules' easier than others (Ellis, 1985).
- A person's second language acquisition reflects an active and interactive process (Wong Fillmore, 1985).
- Any interlanguage stage reflects variable rules (Ellis, 1985).

- Knowledge of language rules does not imply the ability to use them (Lightbrown, 1985).
- Situational factors are a primary cause of interlanguage variability and in indirect relation to learning rate and ultimate proficiency (Ellis, 1985).
- Input affects language learning: simple, repetitive, and regular is better (Wong Fillmore, 1985).
- Motivation affects language learning (Wong Fillmore, 1985).
- Individual difference in personality and cognition affects language learning (Wong Fillmore, 1985, 155).

Similarly, Lightbrown and Spada (1999) list a series of ten questions "in terms of both personal characteristics and conditions for learning" (31) that need to be addressed to arrive at a clear understanding of an SLA theory. I will not list them here for brevity's sake, but state that they include many elements drawn from McLaughlin's generalizations above. Most recently, Long (2007) refers to this particular issue as one of content, or "the relative importance of internal or environmental factors" (6) where internal factors would include such innate items as universal grammar, individual differences, and age and environmental factors might include items like input, situation, and external motivation. Certainly, Lightbrown and Spada (1999) and Long (2007) raise at least three generalizations that are not on McLaughlin's list:
- Language acquisition is affected by critical periods.
- Level of metacognitive skill affects second language learning.
- A learner's use of recasts affects second language learning.

How then can I narrow down this increasingly long list of factors to account for in a theory of SLA? I would look broadly at a theory to account for at least four items:

- Innate, systemic, "universal" factors associated with second language acquisition (i.e. UG, critical period, and so on),
- Recognized differences in second language use (i.e. Interlanguage variability),
- Individual differences in learners (i.e. motivation, situation, etc.), and Impact of environmental input and teaching on acquisition.

Of course, these categories can be seen with significant areas of overlap and cross influence. Indeed, data from one could well be described with justification from another. However, moving from generalizations drawn for verifiable data, to constructing a sound theory of SLA that increases and transforms our understanding while simultaneously providing predictive power, these four items offer a terrific start.

SLA's Historical Framework

While a strictly chronological approach to describing and evaluating "the" major theories of SLA has some advantages, my personal preference is toward a more thematic framework for grouping these theories. Yet with sixty theories to first group and then determine the major theories, even the noted experts have difficulty—and end in a state that falls short of full agreement. A brief overview of the taxonomies that have been suggested for grouping SLA theories might include McLaughlin (1987), Beebe (1988), Lightbrown and Spada (1999), and Larsen-Freeman & Long (1991) – which was further refined by Long (2007). From this list, McLaughlin (1987) was the first to press, and he draws on early work by Lightbrown to create a taxonomy around the fields of study which had a perspective on SLA including: general linguistics, sociolinguistics, social psychology, neurolinguistics, and cognitive psychology. Similarly, the Beebe (1988) edited text draws on these "perspectives" to create a sort of taxonomy listing some of the same items as McLaughlin – sociolinguistics and neurolinguistics – and certainly several concepts in the psycholinguistics section are contained in McLaughlin's general and cognitive psychology groupings. Beebe's edited text, however, goes further to include perspectives from education—both in the general second or foreign classroom instruction as well the bilingual classroom. That McLaughlin based his framework on Lightbrown's 1984 work is interesting, because in 1999 Lightbrown and Spada would offer a different taxonomy for grouping SLA theories: behaviourism, innatism, psychological, and interactionism. Finally, Larsen-Freeman and Long (1991), with revisions by Long (2007), offer a similar framework to Lightbrown and Spada (1999), which is most interesting to me because of its simplicity. Larsen-Freeman and Long suggest we group theories of SLA as either nativist, environmentalist, or interactionist. So, finally, I am left to construct my own list of categories, which includes: behaviorist, nativist, environmentalist, and interactionist. Before moving ahead to describing, situating, and evaluating the major theories and their pedagogical implications, I would stop to provide a framework for evaluating theory. McLaughlin (1987) suggests four criteria for evaluating theory – three borrowed from Kaplan (1964), norms of correspondence, coherence and pragmatism – and one additional criteria, confirmation (testability or 'falsifiability'). My hope is to use this framework of evaluation to compare the character of each theories strengths and weaknesses.

Behaviorist Theories
In adding behaviorist theory to Larsen-Freeman & Long's category list of SLA theories, I wanted to emphasize some of the origins of SLA theory and note that behaviorism is not dead. It still influences SLA and particularly SL pedagogy. The most

famous name in behaviorist theory is B. F. Skinner, although important elements of the theory hearken back to Piaget, and as an educational psychologist, my experience includes working with general concepts of behaviorism. Clearly, the application of behaviorist theory to SLA is a case of applying general learning principles from a theory of cognitive psychology to the specific problem of language learning. Moreover, behavioral theories make no particular distinction between first and second acquisition, or child and adult acquisition. Rather the theories attempt was to relate the general principles of learning in the broader behaviorist theory, "imitation, practice, reinforcement (or feedback on success), and habit formation" (Lightbrown and Spada 1999, 35) and how they would apply to language learning. Certainly, significant evidence from each individual's life experience would indicate that imitation, practice, and reinforcement have tremendous impact on language learning— Lightbrown and Spada (1999) refers to this anecdotal support as the "intuitive appeal" (9) of behaviorism particularly in terms of child language acquisition. Additionally, current neurological research has demonstrated that neurons become "stronger" *through use*—or more efficient at transmitting signals through the process of myelination. A colleague at Indiana University, Jonathan Plucker and I have referred to this physiological fact in conversation as a sort of "new behaviorism."[1]

In terms of habit formation and SLA, however, behaviorist theory faced both a great opportunity and a great uproar. Logically, if one is "learning" a second language and the way that one "learns" is through habit formation, the habit of language use from the first language should have some influence on the second language learning process. In terms of specific theory, this constitutes an influence on, or perhaps reflection of, the Contrastive Analysis Hypothesis (CAH). Within the field of linguistics, contrastive analysis of different languages clearly predates the flowering of SLA as a field. So I would do well to point out that CAH has at least two fathers—one in descriptive linguistics and another in cognitive psychology. Lado, Weinreich, Fries and others are associated with this theory. Critical notions in the theory are transfer and interference.

When a phoneme, structure, etc. is common to L1 and L2, then the phoneme, structure, etc. will readily transfer to the new language. In other words, learning that phoneme, structure, etc. will be easy, or at least easier. When a phoneme, structure, etc. is not shared by the two languages, or is significantly different between them, then the L1 structure will interfere with the acquisition of the correct phoneme, structure, etc. in the new language. Certainly, (CAH) has the same intuitive appeal as the general behaviorist theory: "Anyone who has attempted to learn a foreign language will be able to corroborate Lado's claim. Foreign-language learners are all too familiar with the interfering effects of their NL [native language] causing everything from accented speech to inappropriate non-verbal behavior" (Larsen-Freeman & Long 1991, 53).

In evaluating the strengths and weaknesses of behaviorist theories, I want to look first at the strengths using McLaughlin's four criteria. The "intuitive appeal" Lightbrown and Spada discuss regarding behaviorist theory in general and the "familiarity" described by Larsen-Freeman & Long are surely pointing to the norm of correspondence. What is described in the theory matches up well to significant portions of our intuitive, implicit, and non-analytical understanding of the second language learning experience. Moreover, behaviorism in general offers a tremendous appeal in terms of coherence. Behaviorists describe all learning simply with a few tools and techniques that can be used in a variety of ways. That parsimony in the theory has strong power in terms of pragmatic norms, due to the straightforward implications for teaching, and, in turn, verification of the theory. In one sense, behaviorism is the most 'teacher friendly' of the four groupings of SLA theory—although interactionist theory comes close. Behaviorist SLA theory puts the SL/FL teacher in charge. Perhaps the most prominent examples of this are the audio-lingual method (ALM) and Richards' advocacy of task based learning (TBL) and it's precursor the PPP method (present, practice, produce) (Richards 1991). The 'present, practice, produce' of PPP exactly mirrors the "imitation, practice, and habit formation" referred to by Lightbrown and Spada (1999). Similarly, the CAH offers direct connections to second language teaching. All we would need to do is 'plug in' the two languages for contrastive analysis and understand the direction of L1 to L2, and the differences in a phonology, morphology, syntax, semantics, etc. between the two languages would create a ready-made program of study for the language learners. Teachers could spend less time on the readily transferable items and focus additional effort on the items that suffer from various levels of interference. Again with great certainty, the simplicity of the notions of how the behaviorist theory of SLA would function created a perfect opportunity for another criteria for evaluation—falsifiability. McLaughlin's notion of confirmation is where behaviorist theories fall short. The layman's understanding of language learning brings to mind a multitude of examples of effective learning through behaviorist approaches and plenty of examples of interference and transfer as indicated by the CAH. The question of whether the theory *always* works or at least *generally* works needs to be answered positively in order to confirm the theory. Therein lies what is probably the first great debate of SLA theory, although the debate was actually about language acquisition in general. Chomsky (1959) reviewed and, well . . . *dismantled* the general behaviorist language learning theory in an article in 'Language'.

Chomsky's concluding sentence is a sound summary of the problems of behaviorist theory: "If the study of language is limited in these ways, it seems inevitable that major aspects of verbal behavior will remain a mystery" (57). In other words, Skinner has oversimplified the problem. One particular conclusion often drawn from Chomsky's critique is the idea of creativity in language. If everything a child learns in terms of language comes from imitation and practice, then how does language grow? How do humans create beautiful but completely new language patterns? The oft-cited sentence "colorless green ideas sleep furiously" is referenced to indicate that humans can generate completely new language—and moreover, others can make some sense out of it. Chomsky concludes and I concur that behaviorist language learning theory is insufficient. The CAH was in part caught up in the harsh reaction to behaviorist learning theory: "Ironically, while the association of CAH with behaviourism gave it academic legitimacy, it ultimately led to its downfall" (Larsen-Freeman & Long 1991, 55). Aside from the problems in general with behaviorist theory and language learning, the CAH predicted certain types of errors associated with interference. As studies inspired by Corder's (1967) notions of error analysis were undertaken and completed, evidence began to mount indicating that the predictions of CAH were not accurate. Dulay and Burt's (1974) research indicated that the CAH over predicted errors, and other research showed that it failed to predict errors in other cases (Hyltenstam, 1977).

Ultimately, the strict version of the CAH has been largely abandoned—by strict, I mean the version where CAH predicts *all* errors. However, Brown (2000) points out that weaker versions of CAH were not only possible, but continue to hold some influence— referring specifically to the notion of cross-linguistic influence (CFI) and Eckman's Markedness Differential Hypothesis (MDH). Given our naïve positive response to the central notion of behaviorism and CAH and the fact that *some* evidence supports the theory, a revised, if diminished, theory remains—not an unnatural result.

Nativist Theories

A brief explanation of the category of "nativism" is in order. Brown (2000) suggests, "The term nativist derives from the fundamental assertion that language acquisition is innately determined, that we are born with a genetic capacity that predisposes us to a systematic perception of the language around us, resulting in an internalized system of language" (24), or more directly Larsen-Freeman and Long (1991) suggest, nativist theories "explain acquisition by positing and innate biological endowment" (227). Looking ahead, the next grouping, "environmentalist," echoes of the nature versus nurture argument are plainly heard in the development of SLA theories. While most educated people take a middle of the road view on the nature v. nurture debate, the argument continues and certainly language acquisition is an area of special interest. As Chomsky contends, language itself is one of if not *the* key distinction between humans and animals—"a special faculty has a specific biological basis and that has evolved only in humans" (Harley, 1995, 19). A spate of recent texts has been published in support of the nativist perspective in recent years, even as relativism seems to be growing in our culture overall. Pinker's (1994) *The Language Instinct*, Jackendoff's (1994) *Patterns in the Mind*, and Pinker's (2002) subsequent *The Blank Slate* are examples of these recent publications. The oft cited example of an orphaned infant raised in a different country by parents from the new country that is able *innately* to learn the different language of the new country *perfectly* is the natural experiment that gives rise to many of the questions that nativist theories seek to resolve. What is it that makes humans natural language learners? I will look at Chomsky's Universal Grammar and Krashen's Monitor theory in this section.

Chomsky's Universal Grammar

To begin with, I should say that Chomsky's theories are properly theories of language acquisition in general—perhaps with more emphasis on first language acquisition—but they have been interpreted in terms of second language acquisition in many influential ways. Moreover, Chomsky himself was/is a linguist and the Universal Grammar (UG) theory arises out of that field of study. A final background point is that UG is at some basic level a reaction and a response to the weaknesses that Chomsky has elaborated in Skinner's behaviorist theory of language learning.

The first concept that needs to be considered in discussing UG is the language acquisition device (LAD). Chomsky initially posited that there is something in the human brain—a sort of unknown "black box"—that enables every normal child to learn the language that they are exposed to as infants. He called that the LAD. Different proponents of nativist theory have different perspectives regarding the applicability o the LAD in second language acquisition. Some argue that once an individual has mastered a first language that he/she no longer needs the LAD for L2. Others argue that—in a manner reminiscent of the critical period hypothesis—the LAD does not apply to adult language acquisition (Brown 2000). In either event, the proponents have downplayed LAD's role in second language acquisition and instead have emphasized the role of UG: "In recent writings, Chomsky and his followers no longer use the term LAD, but refer to the child's innate endowment as *Universal Grammar* (UG)" (Lightbrown and Spada 1999, 16).

The core principle of UG is that because every normal child can learn every language, that all languages themselves are based on a single deep grammar that can be traced back through analysis. A metaphor shared with me is that, from the UG perspective, if aliens somehow landed on Earth and were trying to figure out how to communicate with humans, they would perceive great similarities between the world's languages and infer that indeed we all spoke the *same* language—that the differences amounted more to *accent* than to wholly different languages! The point for language acquisition is that all children acquire language in a *systematic* fashion—somewhat reminiscent of interlangauge. Moreover from the UG perspective they are able to do so from language input that is insufficient for the purpose that they use it for in two significant ways. First, the quality of the language input that they receive is not particularly high— communicative English is full of fits and starts, incomplete sentences, slips of the tongue—yet children arrive naturally with a strong comprehension of the structure of the language. Second, and more telling is that fact that children arrive at this good structural understanding without much corrective feedback from adults regarding whether their sentences are ungrammatical or not (Larsen-Freeman and Long 1991). Proponents of UG differ regarding what sorts of effects they imagine UG will predict in language learners; however, many of the predictions revolve around "comparing judgments of grammaticality" (Lightbrown and Spada 1999, 36). The point is that the learner's judgments of grammaticality will avoid the pitfalls associated with measuring the learners unreliable and variable language performance and instead focus on their more reliably measurable knowledge of grammar. Of course the grammar questions involved are much more complicated and I do not have sufficient space or time to review them here. Larsen-Freeman and Long (1991) and Ellis (1994) provide good reviews.

Krashen's Monitor Theory

Finally, a homegrown SLA theory! Krashen's Monitor Model is arguably the most influential of the SLA theories that I will discuss here. Certainly, in my twenty years of professional experience in language learning, Krashen has been the subject of more discussions on the acquisition of language than any of the other theorists reviewed here—even Chomsky. Krashen built upon some of the notions of UG and was initially developing a theory that was a model of second language performance rather than a model of second language acquisition (Larsen-Freeman and Long 1991). Specifically, Krashen was trying to account for two issues that were uncovered through SLA research studies. One issue regarded the fact that a sort of "natural order" of morpheme acquisition was becoming apparent through research. The second issue was that some differences were found in the way that the natural order was being acquired in terms of reading and writing skills versus listening and speaking skills. In the end, Krashen's (1982) Monitor Model of SLA was generated to help explain those issues and others.

The Monitor Model itself is a constellation of five different hypothesis—making it arguably the most complex and comprehensive of the major SLA theories. The five are:
1. The acquisition – learning hypothesis,
2. The natural order hypothesis,
3. The monitor hypothesis,
4. The input hypothesis, and
5. The affective filter hypothesis

The first two match the particular research issues described in the previous paragraph. The differences shown in Larsen-Freeman's (1975) study in the "natural order" of acquisition of specific skills by adult learners led Krashen to posit that there were two separate—and innate—systems involved in SLA: one for *acquisition*—naturally "picking up" the language, and another for *learning* in a structured educational setting. So what is the difference? For Krashen, the acquisition system was primary, because it actually produces the language. The learned system on the other hand serves to monitor and correct the output from the acquired system. The second hypothesis, the natural order hypothesis, refers to the data suggesting that certain morphemes are acquired at specific stages in an individual's language acquisition. The natural order hypothesis appears at least on the surface to be a sort of innate developmental process related in kind to LAD and UG. Moreover, other researchers have worked to extend natural order notions determined around morpheme acquisition order to other linguistic categories like phonemes and syntax. The Monitor Model would view the natural order as an innate product of the acquisition system rather than the learned system (Gass & Selinker 2001). The final three hypotheses are original to the Monitor Model. The monitor hypothesis is the core of the model. As described above, the learned system serves to monitor the acquired system in regulated language output. However, the monitor itself is not entirely automatic, at least three conditions need to be met (and even then the monitor may not "kick in"). One, the learner needs the *time* to think about the language. Two, the learner needs to *focus on the form* of the language as it is being produced - reminiscent of Albert Bandura's *attention*. Finally, the learner has to *know the rule*! In this way the monitor serves to link the acquired and learned systems. The input hypothesis elaborates on how learners are able to improve their language skills, and is to a large extent a response and reaction to the claims of UG. Where UG postulates that language input is generally insufficient (re: not comprehensible) for learners to acquire the target language, Krashen argues that comprehensible input is a *critical* factor that allows for language acquisition. Moreover, he links that comprehensible input to the question of

The Need for a Comprehensive SLA Theory | 223

natural order hypothesis suggesting that if the learner at a particular state of knowledge (i) receives input at the next stage in the natural order ($i + 1$), then progress, learning, can occur—a model not at all removed from Vygotsky's zone of proximal development. Krashen's final hypothesis is the affective filter hypothesis. The affective filter that Krashen postulates is a barrier to the language acquisition system. When a learner is suffering from negative affect, which might include things like a bad day, low motivation, a poor attitude in general, then an affective filter will be raised between the comprehensible input and the acquisition system and learning will not occur. Putting together all of the hypotheses of the monitor model creates a scenario of language learning that might be generalized as follows:

- First, if the learner is in a state of low negative (and high positive?) affect [affective filter hypothesis], and
- If the learner receives *comprehensible input* [input hypothesis], then
- Both the acquisition and learning systems will be able to function [acquisition-learning hypothesis], and
- Learning will proceed in *the* natural order [natural order hypothesis], and finally
- The learner's learned system can serve to monitor the output of the acquisition system [monitor hypothesis]

When looked at in this way one could easily be reminded of a Rube Goldberg contraption, but clearly Krashen went a long way to providing the sort of complex and rich description of second language acquisition that had been missing.

Evaluation of Nativist Theories

Both UG and the Monitor Model have tremendous appeal in terms of their ability to describe aspects of the language learning process that we are familiar with from the anecdotal evidence of our normal lives—the norm of correspondence. The broadest elements of these theories seem certain to the layman's analysis. That children have an innate and remarkable ability to learn the language of their environment is undeniable—lending credence to UG. That acquisition is different from learning, that negative affect gets in the way of learning, that people learn a second language in a similar order, that comprehensible input is critical, that metacognitive monitoring of language use is also essential all add correspondence appeal to the Monitor Model. Moreover, each has a strong measure of parsimony and internal coherence. In terms of pragmatic appeal to language teachers, UG has a significant weakness: if UG is true, what does a teacher do? Implications for what to teach or how to teach from UG are limited—and arguably not within Chomsky's intentions. McLaughlin (1987) refers to this issue as "the learnability problem" (105). A stronger pragmatic case can be made for the Monitor Model, as described above, a teacher can see the steps that need to be undertaken to apply this model in their language classrooms. The teacher needs to determine the learner's current level to provide comprehensible input at somewhat above that level, and to ensure that the learner's affective filter is 'down,' and then the learner's innate processes can take charge. Indeed, the natural approach teaching method of Krashen and Terrell (1983) proved widely influential.

In terms of confirmation, however, neither UG nor the Monitor Model fares well in terms of falsifiability. At some level this problem is due to the fact that a nativist theory, by definition, postulates an unknown genetic/biological mechanism for language learning—just the sort of thing that Skinner was hoping to avoid by restricting his theory to observable data. These LAD/UG sorts of mechanisms serve as a *deus ex machina* to rescue the theories from failure, but the mechanisms themselves are unknown and, therefore, inherently not falsifiable.

The Need for a Comprehensive SLA Theory | 225

So clearly UG suffers from weakness in terms of learnability and falsifiability. Similarly, Aspects of the Monitor Model are equally unfalsifiable, and difficult to quantify. What is a UG? Where is the Monitor? How much is $i + 1$? McLaughlin (1987) takes a much harsher view toward the monitor model[2] denying it on all four criteria and denying each individual hypothesis. However, McLaughlin and others (Brown 2000, Ellis 1994, Gass & Selinker 2001, Larsen-Freeman & Long 1991, and Lightbrown & Spada 1999) concur that UG and the Monitor Model have been highly influential in both SLA and SL teaching. Moreover, Krashen and his Monitor Model, in particular, have exerted great influence on SL teaching with significant beneficial effects.

Environmentalist Theories

As we have already discussed, environmental theories stand in a sort of opposition to nativist theories as they mirror the nature v. nurture debate: "Indeed, they typically deny that innate contributions play any role at all other than that of providing the animal with the internal structure which environmental forces can proceed to shape" (Larsen-Freeman & Long 1991, 249). Environmental theories in general seek to explain language learning in terms of how various environmental factors influence language learning. Included in this category would be much of Schumann's work including the Acculturation Model and the Pidginization Hypothesis, as well as Gardner's work through social psychology on motivation, attitude and language learning which he called the Socio-Educational Model. For the sake of brevity, I will focus on Schumann's notions.

Within the environmentalist framework the questions "if" and "how" one will learn a second language are to a great extent questions of individual difference and process. Schumann's paired theories, the Acculturation Model and the Pidginization Hypothesis, explore these questions. Schumann's fundamental assumption in the acculturation model is that the "closer" one is to the target culture and language, the easier it will be to learn the language and therefore, one is more likely to achieve a high level of L2 proficiency, which echoes the CAH. The genesis of the model lies in a case study which Schumann conducted of a Costa Rican immigrant who never reached a very high level of language proficiency. The acculturation model formulates this notion of "close" in a concept called *distance* and further divides that distance into two types: *social distance* and *psychological distance*. Schumann offers eight group factors that characterize social distance: social dominance, integration pattern, enclosure, cohesiveness, size, cultural congruence, attitude, and intended length of residence. In addition, four individual factors are offered to characterize psychological distance: language shock, culture shock, motivation, and ego permeability. Table 1 summarizes what each factor might "sound like" for the language/culture learner's perspective. Schumann then argues that with each factor the relative difference creates positive or negative effects for the language learner, and clearly he is looking primarily at immigrant populations which would imply ESL over EFL. If in each category the learner perceives that they are quite similar or that the cultural attitude or other characteristics are on the positive side, then they will reach a higher level of proficiency. A good situation would be one where the learner and the members of the target culture perceive that neither is dominant, that they want the learner to integrate, that the learner's culture group is not closed and cohesive, that the origin culture population is small, that the cultures share many things, that they have mutually positive attitudes about the other culture, that the learner will have an extended stay, that the target language and culture do not cause anxiety for the learner, that the learner perceives the ability to be integrated into the other's culture and vice versa!

Table 1.
Factors in the acculturation model (adapted from Ellis 1994, 232)

Factor	Expression
Social Distance	
Social dominance	Politically, culturally, technically or economically, my culture is the same, or superior, or inferior than the "other's" culture
Integration pattern	I am going to *assimilate* (be like the other) or *acculturate* (act like the other when interacting, but retain an in-group lifestyle as well) [or attempt to completely retain culture 1?]
Enclosure	My culture group has its own space (high enclosure), or we do not (low)
Cohesiveness	In general, I keep more in group contacts (high cohesion) or more other group contacts (low cohesion)
Size	My group is numerically larger or smaller than the other group
Cultural congruence	My culture group is generally similar or generally different than the other group
Attitude	My group and the other group have generally positive or negative attitudes about each other
Intended length of residence	How long do I intend to stay in this "other" culture?
Psychological Distance	
Language shock	How high is my anxiety around using the other's language?
Culture shock	How anxious and disoriented does the other's culture make me?
Motivation	My motivation is to integrate into the other's culture. (*integrative motivation*—more beneficial) My intention is to gain knowledge of the other's culture and then use it for my benefit (*instrumental motivation*—less beneficial)
Ego permeability	To what extent will my sense of self and culture allow me to be like the other?

Thus as an individual or an entire immigrant group moves toward greater assimilation or acculturation, they would move to greater language proficiency, Schumann offers the pidginization hypothesis to explain how a process of pidginization—the incomplete and inaccurate acquisition of the target language— might function. Essentially, learners move to a pidgin, which is in some ways similar to interlanguage, and then with a change in status to depidginized proficiency. Several other terms became involved in the general acculturation literature: "nativization" to better describe the social process of acculturation and language proficiency and the confusing use of "creolization" - a creole is a mature language learned by the children of speakers of pidgin, but it is not nativization (McLaughlin, 1987). Ultimately, the movement of both creoles and pidgins toward the target language through the process of increased social contact and an improvement in the positive status of the various social and psychological distances can be seen as the same process.

Evaluation of the Acculturation Model and the Pidginization Hypothesis

Arising from social psychology, the questions raised and the character of the acculturation/pidginization theory is markedly different than the previous theories discussed here. While grammatical data has been used to support the theory, the theory itself is not essentially language based, rather it is a social explanation of relative language achievement. Returning to McLaughlin's criteria – correspondence, coherence, pragmatism, and confirmation - how does Schumann's environmentalist theory fare? The method of origin for this theory—the case study of the Costa Rica immigrant – points to a different sort of data that needs to be interpreted. Clearly, Schumann has isolated factors of distance that work in the one case, but do they correspond to other cases? As Ellis (1994) indicates, the data from subsequent research does, at best, weakly support the acculturation model. However, Ellis also concedes that at the root of the problem is the relative character of the *distance* factors. Finding an absolute quantitative characterization of such qualitative factors is problematic. Acton (1979, cited in Brown 2000) offered a solution to this problem. Instead of attempting to measure the *absolute* social and psychological distance—which is a plainly relative factor—why not measure the *perceived* distance? Thus, he devised a questionnaire, the "professed difference in attitude questionnaire" (PDAQ), to measure these relative factors. "That Acton's PDAQ did not predict success in language is no surprise since we know of no adequate instrument to predict language success or to assess language aptitude. But the PDAQ did describe empirically, in quantifiable terms, a relationship between social distance and language acquisition" (Brown 2000, 187). Of course, part of the issue with correspondence and the acculturation/pidginization model is that Schumann's model only looks at a small portion of the second language acquisition issue—specifically the social and psychological factors that affect one's progress toward language proficiency. Although the acculturation/pidginization model is hardly a comprehensive theory within the set parameters, we have some reason to support correspondence. Moreover, the model has internal coherence for exactly the same reasons. In terms of pragmatic criteria, however, while the acculturation/pidginization theory has a great deal to offer in regards to the broader sociological questions surrounding migrant populations and immigrating individuals, one finds little in the theory to aid classroom teachers. Long (2007) argues strongly that not every SLA theory needs to satisfy classroom teachers, and some portion of classroom teachers must find Schumann's acculturation theory unsatisfying. In conclusion, McLaughlin points out a final issue of confirmation. Since the social and psychological factors of distance are clearly intertwined, how are we to determine causality? Is the learner positively disposed to the target language/culture and therefore successful at learning the language, or has their success in acculturation made them positively disposed to the target culture? Without an answer to this question, the premise cannot be confirmed.

Interactionist Theories
The final category of theory I explore in this examination is that of *interactionist* theories. Such theories seek to combine elements of both nativist and environmentalist theories—extracting the best of both the nature and the nurture camps. For this exam I will explore the *Zweitspracherwerb italienischer und spanisher Arbieter* (ZISA) group's Multidimensional model and Long's Interaction hypothesis.

The ZISA Multidimensional Model
The ZISA Multidimensional model is based on a project built around a wonderful set of participants through the University of Hamburg in the late 1970s. Methodologically, the study was part cross-sectional, with 45 participants, and part longitudinal, with 12 participants. While the original data collection focus as grammatical, the researchers ultimately created a model that argued that "the learner's position relative to the target language is defined by two dimensions the learner's *developmental stage* and the learner's *social-psychological orientation*" (McLaughlin 1987, 115). Where the notion of *social-psychological orientation* harkens back to Schumann, the notion of *developmental stage* reminds one of Piaget, and Krashen's natural order hypothesis.

Without going deeply into the specific grammatical details (see Larsen-Freeman & Long 1991 for more detail) of the developmental stages, the ZISA group was able to determine that the study participants followed a clear developmental path in word-order rules in five stages. Moreover, when one stage had been mastered it was not lost and the progressive stages were mastered in order. Subsequent work revealed similar developmental stages in eight other grammatical categories. For this set of data at least the results were remarkable. In terms of the participants social-psychological orientation, ZISA explored only a few environmental factors, but the major factor was one that is on Schumann's list: the relative integrative disposition versus segregative disposition. In fact, one could easily see that several factors listed separately in Schumann's model could be grouped together under the relative integrative vs. segregative disposition. Additionally, these dispositional differences were mirrored in some grammatical practices of standard versus simplified usage and restrictive versus simplified output. The ultimate conclusion of the ZISA group's model is that individuals can theoretically move freely through the different variability dimensions and developmental stages, but they always progressed forward—albeit at different rates dependent on their social- psychological orientation (Larsen-Freeman & Long 1991).

The Interaction Hypothesis
A final theory remains to be discussed in this exam: Long's (1996) Interaction hypothesis. The "interaction" in the title of this hypothesis is about the interaction between the language learner and their teacher, other native speakers and non- native speakers—*not* the interaction between theory types on a range between nature emphasis and nurture emphasis. The manner in which Long's interaction hypothesis is an interactionist theory arises from how the hypothesis expands upon Krashen's notion of *input*, by contending that input in general is made comprehensible through *modified interaction*. Essentially, the negotiation of meaning that occurs between the language learner and their teacher or other native speaker or more advanced adds

the interlocutors to arrive at the appropriate level of language input. Clearly, this mechanism is reminiscent of Vygotsky's (1978) zone of proximal development. Moreover, the emphasis on learner language and interaction reflects social constructivist learning theory in general. More specifically, the interaction hypothesis posits a three-step process:
1. Interactional modification makes input comprehensible;
2. Comprehensible input promotes acquisition. Therefore,
3. Interactional modification promotes acquisition. (Lightbrown and Spada 1999, 43)

This simple syllogism is the heart of the interaction hypothesis. Lightbrown and Spada (1999) continue to elaborate three types of modified interaction that facilitate the creation of comprehensible input: 1) comprehension checks—where the native speaker (NS) makes sure that the non-native speaker (NNS) understood, 2) clarification requests—where the NNS ask the NS to clarify, and 3) self- repetition or paraphrase—by the NNS.

Evaluation of Interactionist Theories
How do the interactionist theories fare under the microscope of McLaughlin's four criteria? Both do well in terms of corresponding to the data they hope to explain. The Multidimensional Model has the benefit of being more comprehensive and specific in the characteristics that it describes. The Interaction hypothesis is rather sparse in where it tends to be applied—one could argue that it is limited solely to the area of language input and is mute on cultural or innatist concerns. Similarly in the area of coherence, both theories have some strength, as they are strongly internally coherent. A case can be made against the Multidimensional Model because it tries to do too much—the clear intention of the ZISA group in including the additional variable is to account for variability—

which puts it in the range of the Monitor Model in its attempt to be more comprehensive.

Both theories have pragmatic appeal to teachers, but in strikingly different ways. On the side of the Multidimensional Model, like CAH and the natural order hypothesis, the ZISA group seems to offer a clear and concise curriculum based on empirical research. On the side of the Interaction hypothesis, the teacher is, as in the behaviorist model, much more responsible— and unlike the behaviorist and Multidimensional Model, the teacher is an active player in the learner's efforts to learn the language, to socially co- construct their language, rather than an automaton that regurgitates the predetermined curriculum. Ultimately, that role is the most respected and appealing role that any of the SLA theories reviewed here have offered the language teacher.

New Directions for Research

In 1987 noted second language scholar McLaughlin contended that "Over the past two decades or so, the number of studies concerned with second language learning has increased exponentially," (1); therefore, we infer, the members of this scientific community need to explore the character and quality of theory in SLA—and metaphorically clean up their academic act. In 2007 noted second language scholar Long contended that SLA "has become increasingly fragmented in the past 15 years, and is characterized by a multiplicity of theories ... [therefore] identifying faulty understanding, and amending or culling the theories concerned constitutes progress, whereas persistence of a plethora of theories, especially oppositional ones, obstructs progress" (3-4). Given that those two "noted scholars" are making such comments, I would not argue for a slate of new and different theories. Long (2007) does make a strong case that SLA needs to do a bit of pruning in the garden. Simultaneously, I am fearful that since McLaughlin's gauntlet calling for focus first fell some twenty years ago, and the field has yet to rise to his challenge of focus, that SLA as a field may have difficulty in attaining that goal, which Long would urge us to. The reality of the academic world for young scholars is that 'niche' research and writing can help resolve the publishing imperative on non-tenured faculty. Simultaneously, 'niche' writing provides tremendous backpressure to the minimalist urge. In creating a plan for conducting that pruning of theory, I will suggest a few ideas — these are not, however, new ideas.

SLA should test some of these oppositional theories. One possible way forward is to replicate some of the earlier studies and focus specifically on studies that gave mixed results in the attempts to verify one or another of the theories. Tools and techniques have changed in the forty years or so chronicled by McLaughlin and Long, so that the results this time provides a good chance to reveal more valid and offer more reliable conclusions.

The methods and techniques of our research need to be submitted to a second review for rigor. We need to search for alternate ways to ask the same questions. One technical area of research that has been explored only in the most minimal of ways is neurological research. SLA has good reason to want to use those fMRI machines to look at the brains of NNSs: our current methods do not allow us to look at the brain (remember the three blind men and the elephant?)! "But what emerges is the notion that processes that may be seen as separate and independent at the psychological level may be united or at least highly integrated at the neural level" (Schumann, 1997, 237). Theoretically our language learning processes could be the other way as well – similar psychological processes may be dissimilar at the neurological level. Certainly, fMRI based brain research has in the past few years provided biological evidence supporting the critical period hypothesis in previously unimagined ways (Strauch 2004). Along those same lines, I believe that research into emotion has demonstrated that emotion is not only a help or hindrance to language learning – as in Krashen's affective filter, but an element of communication as rich and unexplored as nonverbal communication has proven to be.

Finally, in this process of conducting research, to "prune the garden," I believe that continuing to explore ways in which interactionist theory development can provide an opportunity to consolidate some of the competing theories. To borrow an analogy from physics where theories to unify the forces were not possible until sufficient research had shown specifically what forces needed to be unified. SLA is hardly as mature as physics, so the field may not be sufficiently mature for that step—but in the same breath the unification of forces seems to happen every hundred years or so in physics (1860s, 1960s), so while I feel the urgency suggested by Long, I believe that we have time. Perhaps theory unification for SLA is waiting around the right around corner in a Kuhnian paradigm shift.

A final comment regards the relationship between SLA theory and SL/FL teaching. Long (2007) again makes a strong argument that SLA theory need not include or be overly concerned with SL/FL teaching: And whereas the goals of most SLA theorists is the least powerful theory that can handle the facts (i.e. identify what is *necessary* and *sufficient* for language acquisition), the language teacher and the language teaching theorist alike are interested in the most *efficient* set of procedures, the combination of conditions and practices that will bring about language learning fastest and with the least effort, whether or not strictly necessary or sufficient (16).

Point well taken, but I have to disagree. That the world of pure science and the world of applied science are clearly different is no revelation. Moreover, I know that Long is a great friend to the language teacher—as we noted earlier in the fact that the Interaction hypothesis is clearly the most teacher respectful and friendly. However, the pragmatic norm requires that the theory have practical value—aside for the lack of confirmation, lack of pragmatic application was the major grounds on which to reject several of the theories reviewed here. Let me conclude by offering a direct question to Dr. Long:

> If I cannot get you to agree to a reasonably pragmatic theory of SLA, would you sign on for more practical classroom based research to support a theory of second language teaching (SLT)?

End Notes

[1] Perhaps it should be 'neu-behaviorism'?

[2] And throws in a few, perhaps deserved, ad hominem comments.

References

Acton, W. (1979). *Second language learning and perception of difference in attitude.* Unpublished doctoral dissertation: University of Michigan.

Beebe, L. M. (Ed.). (1988). *Issues in second language acquisition: Multiple perspectives.* New York: Newbury House.

Brown, H. D. (2000). *Principles of language learning and teaching.* White Plains, New York: Pearson.

Chomsky, N. (1959). A review of B. F. Skinner's "Verbal Behavior." *Language, 35* (1), 26-58.

Corder, S. P. (1967). The significance of learner's errors. *International Review of Applied Linguistics, 5,* 161-91.

Dulay, H. & Burt, M. (1974). Natural Sequences in child second language acquisition. *Language Learning, 24,* 37-53.

Ellis, R. (1985). *Understanding second language acquisition*. Oxford: Oxford University Press.
Ellis, R. (1994). *The study of second language acquisition*. Oxford: Oxford University Press.
Ellis, R. (1997). *SLA research and language teaching*. Oxford: Oxford University Press.
Gass, S. M., & Selinker, L. (2001). *Second language acquisition: An introductory course*. Mahwah, New Jersey: Lawrence Earlbaum.
Harley, T. A. (1995). *The psychology of language: from data to theory*. Hove, East Sussex: Psychology Press
Hyltenstam, K. (1987). Markedness, language universals, language typology and second language acquisition. In C. Pfaff (Ed.), *First and second language acquisition process*, (55-78). Cambridge Mass.: Newbury House.
Jackendoff, R. (1994) *Patterns in the mind*, New York: BasicBooks.
Krashen, S. (1982). *Principles and practice in second language acquisition*, London: Pergamon.
Krashen, S., & Terrell, T. (1983) *The natural approach*, London: Pergamon.
Larsen-Freeman, D. (1975). The acquisition grammatical morphemes by adult ESL students. *TESOL Quarterly, 9*. 409-30.
Larsen-Freeman, D., & Long, M. H. (1991). *An introduction to second language acquisition research*. New York: Longman.
Lightbrown, P. M. (1984). The relationship between theory and method in second language acquisition research. In A. Davies, C. C., & A. P. R. Howatt (Eds.), *Issues in Interlanguage*, (241-252). Edinburgh: Edinburgh University Press.
Lightbrown, P. M. (1985). Great expectations: Second language acquisition research and classroom teaching. *Applied Linguistics, 6*, 173-89.

Lightbrown, P. M., & Spada, N. (1999). *How languages are learned.* Oxford: Oxford University Press.

Long, M. H. (1996). The role of linguistic environment in second language acquisition. In W. C. Ritchie, & T. J. Bhatia (Eds.), *Handbook of second language acquisition,* (413-68). Cambridge: Cambridge University Press.

Long, M. H. (2007). *Problems in SLA.* Mahwah, New Jersey: Lawrence Earlbaum.

McLaughlin, B. (1987). *Theories of second language learning.* London: Edward Arnold. Pinker, S (1994). *The language instinct: How the mind creates language,* New York: Harper Collins.

Pinker, S. (2002). *The blank slate: The modern denial of human nature,* New York: Viking. Richards, J. C. (1991). *Reflective teaching in TESOL teacher education.* ERIC Document ED370357.

Schumann, J. H. (1997). *The neurobiology of affect in language.* Malden, MA: Blackwell.

Strauch, B. (2004). *The Primal Teen: What the New Discoveries about the Teenage Brain Tell Us about Our Kids.* New York: Doubleday.

Vygotsky, L. S. (1978). *Mind in society: The development of higher psychological processes,* Cambridge Mass.: Harvard University Press.

Wong Fillmore, L. (1985). Second language learning in children: A proposed model. In R. Eshch & J. Procinzano (Eds.), *Issues in English language development,* (33- 44). Rosslyn, VA: National Clearinghouse in Bilingual Education.

15. Special Issue: Workshops from the 1st Woosong Mini-Conference
(Held in Association with the KOTESOL Daejeon-ChungCheong Chapter)

**DAEJON-CHUNGCHEONG CHAPTER
MINI-CONFERENCE
SEPTEMBER 19, 2009**
Woosong Tower, Dong-gu. Daejeon
www.kotesol.org

It's coming.
Get ready.

16. Research Skills

Mark C. Love

The Research Workshop of the conference was attended by about 15 people and was very much a form of discovery learning. Eric Reynolds briefly introduced the concepts of qualitative, quantitative and mixed methods research and had attendees individually fill out a form on the writing process. The goal of this instrument was to identify possible areas of research attendees may have overlooked in their environments. It also asked each attendee to reflect on her/his individual writing process to try to identify ways to improve the writing process. Each person who attended then briefly introduced him/herself and described her/his teaching and/or research interests. After this the group broke up into three groups roughly on the grounds of interest in quantitative (David Kim), qualitative (Mark Love) or mixed methods (Eric Reynolds) research.

While the other groups were being chaired concurrently, a lively discussion of a *very* qualitative nature ensued in my group. One attendee, Kristina Krauss, is interested in dance and another, John Gartland, is very interested in the theater and drama. Both had successfully used the arts in teaching English. The principal issue that emerged from this discussion was how difficult it is to conduct research into this kind of activity. One can design surveys that query students about their experiences or their perceptions of the efficacy of various pedagogical activities, but there is always that nagging feeling that the depth of the experience is being completely overlooked in the research. These comments later led me to reflect, again, on how the role of pleasure is sadly lacking in (most) academic analysis and is a factor underlying almost everything we, and our students, do but is hidden in the academic literature behind phrases such as *motivation, resistance* and *the affective barrier*. This is completely in accord with Dorothy Coe and Jane Strachen (2002)'s experience in attempting to research dance. As with all reflections, I wonder if this isn't just limited to experiences such as dance, and if we might be missing out on the experiential dimensions in a lot of the work we do.

References
Strachen, J. (2002). Writing dance: tensions in researching movement or aesthetic experience. *Qualitative Studies in Education, 15*(5), 497-511.

17. Digital Storytelling: Making Meaning from Experience

David Kent

This workshop explores the use and applicability of digital storytelling in various educational contexts, but particularly as it relates to EFL/ESL. Several examples specific to EFL/ESL, and Korea, will be introduced. Topics discussed will revolve around the types of digital storytelling that exist, effectiveness of digital storytelling in the classroom, means for evaluating student produced content, and utilization of the required tools, creative procedures, and the necessary resources that must come together to culminate in the development of multimedia literacy in terms of digital story production.

18. Online-English Activities for the Classroom and at Home

Michael Peacock

This presentation aims to provide you with online activities for you and your students. These activities can be done during class time or given for extra help at home. I will show you where to find these activities and how to embed them into your personal/school website

MES English
(www.marks-english-school.com/games.html)
MES English is an English school in Japan. They offer a wide variety of English videos, games, and printable resources. The games require the user to have flash installed on their computer.

Youtube
(www.youtube.com)
You can use Youtube in many different ways to teach English. By searching "English for Children" you can find thousands of different videos dealing with songs, chants, and stories. By searching a particular song plus "lyrics" you can create a personalized *norae bang* for your classroom.

Elllo
(www.elllo.org)
Ello is a great website for English listening practice. It contains hundreds of English conversations and games that require the student to focus on listening skills. Most of the videos give the student the option of reading subtitles while they watch/listen. Elllo is more suited for older students and requires flash.

East of the Web
(www.eastoftheweb.com)
East of the Web has various short stories, games, and interactive activities for students. The games range in difficulty level and include hangman, word searches, and others. The actives require flash.

Bradley's English School
(activities.bradleys-english-school.com)
This site contains many flash and java games including hangman, word searches, and word jumbles. It also has some great matching activities. The activities require flash.

Breaking News English
(www.breakingnewsenglish.com)
This site is geared for students in higher grades. It provides users with updated news articles as well as a complete lesson plan to use with it. It also includes an audio recording of the article.

Voice-it
(www.voice-it.biz/homepage)
Voice it is an amazing tool that allows your students to record their voice online. Once recorded, the user has the option of listening to their voice and sending the audio file to an email address.

If you would like to embed Voice-it into your website, here is the code:

```
<object width="550" height="400">
<param name="movie" value="http://sugaraudio.kumbe.it/flex/recorder.swf?PARAM_host=www.voice-it.biz&PARAM_cliversion=web2mail2" />
<embed width="250" height="150" src="http://sugaraudio.kumbe.it/flex/recorder.swf?PARAM_host=www.voice-it.biz&PARAM_cliversion=web2mail2" />
</object>
```

Vocaroo

(www.vocaroo.com)

A lot like Voice-it, however the user also receives an online link to the recording. You cannot embed Vocaroo into your website.

Embedding

To embed a flash file into your website you first need to find the file on the website. You can do this by using the Firefox internet browser. When you are on a website, click Tools→ Page info→ Media. This step will display all media files on a website. Flash files end in ".swf". Once you have found the file name, add it to this code:

```
<object width="550" height="400">
<param name="movie" value="somefilename.swf">
<embed src="somefilename.swf" width="550" height="400">
</embed>
</object>
```

Once you have embedded the code onto your website the flash file should be displayed.

19. Task-Based Blogging: An Invaluable Asset to the EFL/ESL Teacher

Adam Parsons

In the age of technology students are starting to use the internet for day to day tasks. Students shop online to save money, have formed many online communities for social interactions, and rely on the internet to find employment. Many students have set up weblogs or more commonly blog to make their voices in the global internet community heard. As EFL/ESL teachers we need to take advantage of this developing language tool. Blogs are a very beneficial tool to the language teacher in today's world. We can utilize our student's familiarity with blogs to promote language acquisition by having students communicate in the languages they are learning. By creating and developing language learning based blogs, we can have students practice language in a useful and meaningful way through Task-Based-Blogging.

Task-Based-Blogging combines the theory of Task-Based Language Learning with blogging. Teachers can create blogs focused on students performing meaningful tasks in the target language. Many language books have sections on doing tasks in the language classroom; however teachers are required to gather media and other materials which are not always available. The teacher can adapt these task based activities into a blog, which can be used in and out of the classroom. The internet has a wide variety of material, such as videos, newspapers, and images which are easily attainable and require time to photocopy and distribute. Rather than spending two hours searching for menus for a restaurant lesson, teachers can find and implement menus from the internet on their blogs.

There are a variety of useful tasks a teacher can use a Task-Based-Blog for. A task can be something as simple as posting a comment on an image or as complicated as finding a job. A teacher can incorporate video to provide models for meaningful discourse and embed videos that they would not have time to show students in the classroom. Teachers can create apartment hunting tasks to teach housing vocabulary and gauge students' comprehension by having student seek out apartments for assignments. A great way for creating blog assignments is to design assignments around the theme the students are studying. A teacher can easily create an assignment using directions around a city by having students do a search on MapQuest, which is straight-forward to use and provides most of the vocabulary for navigating around a city. I have only mentioned a few ideas, but the possibilities for creating blog assignments are limitless.

It is very simple to check homework because completed assignments are all on one page. Instead of spending countless hours running to the copy room wasting paper, teachers can post homework on blogs and format their blog assignments in any way they wish. It is very fast and efficient to reuse blog assignments. All teachers have to do is copy and paste into a new post. Once a teacher has been using blogs in the classroom, the will have numerous assignments to alter or copy for future use. A teacher that uses Task-Based-Blogging for a semester will wonder how they did without it.

> *A blog is a website usually maintained by an individual with regular entries of commentary, descriptions of events, or other material such as graphics or video* (Wikipedia definition).

Why use a Blog in an ESL/EFL Class?
- It's free and no copies are required.
- Minimal technical expertise is necessary to create/reply to a blog assignment.
- It's very easy to link to various websites to help with assignments.
- Blog assignments make great supplementary homework.
- It is very simple to check homework, as the comments in the blog are all on one page.
- You can easily incorporate multimedia into your assignments.
- Assignments can be as easy or as difficult as you make them.
- Easy to make surveys and get student input.

Simple Blog Assignments
1. Self-Introduction.
2. Watch the video and answer questions.
3. Describe the painting.
4. Continue the story.

Self-Introduction Assignment
This is a great first assignment. In this assignment, students just type a short bio. This short assignment will help students figure out how to comment on the blog. I usually make a handout with the blog address and simple instructions. I also post the simple instructions on the blog.

Task-Based Blog Assignments
Task Based Blog assignments can be as simple as finding the demographics of a city or as complicated as finding a Korean restaurant in Boise, Idaho. Task Based Blog assignments can involve both language skills and life skills.

Here are a few examples:
- Find a gym in New York City
- Find a restaurant in New York City
- On-line Shopping
- You just moved to a new city; use MapQuest to find things close to your new home
- Find a job
- Apartment hunting in San Diego
- Grocery Shopping
- Find a tour package

Apartment Hunting
Assignment
Guess what, you just accepted a nice job in San Diego, California. You now have to find a place to live. Look through the house listing on this page: San Diego Housing
(Click on the location link, then explore the apartment. Pay attention to the Listing Information and information under the photo.)

Answer these questions in your comment.
1. How much is rent?
2. How many rooms does it have?
3. How many bathrooms does it have?
4. What type of housing is it?
5. What is the address?
6. Who do you contact/phone number about the apartment?
7. Why did you choose this particular place?
8. Post the URL in your comment.

Completed Assignment
1. Rent is $1,340
2. It has 2 bedrooms.
3. It has 1 bathroom.
4. It is an apartment.
5. The address is: 4247 Nobel Drive La Jolla, CA 92122
6. I need to contact (858)638-0105
7. I chose this place because it is close to shopping, beach, and restaurants. It has a pool and fitness center. The place looks wonderful in the photo.

Grocery Shopping
Assignment
You have $100 to spend at a grocery store.
Go to: *The Grocery Store* (link to an online store)
1. Search for products that you want to buy by clicking the menu on the left.
2. Go through various items, if you want to buy them, hit the add to cart button.
3. Hint: The add to cart button will add up the $$$$ for you.
4. When finished after you have found $100 worth of groceries, hit Secure check out under your cart menu, this will bring up your cart shopping list, which you can change at anytime.
5. Retype your shopping list in the comment section. And put X(Number) for quantity. Then put the total.

Completed Assignment
- Minute Maid Apple Juice 6 - [10oz bottles] $5.21 USD x2
- Apple Streusel Pie [9 inches] $8.99 USD x2
- Kraft American Singles [3 lbs.] $13.40 USD x1
- Hamburger Helper - Salisbury [6.2 oz.] $1.61 USD x1
- Tyson Breaded Chicken Breast Tenderloins 25oz $11.96 USD x1
- Tyson Buffalo Style Chicken Wings 64oz $19.79 USD x1
- Cream of Wheat: Farina 2-1/2 Minute, 28 oz $4.79 USD x6

Total:$103.90 USD

To see Task-Based Blogging in use, go to:
   http://woosongparsons.blogspot.com

20. Evaluating and Selecting Internet-Based Instructional tools for the EFL Classroom: Where to Go, and How to Get There

Ezekiel Mentillo

This presentation and discussion will be focused on the evaluation and selection of internet based instructional tools for use in Korean EFL classrooms. In the field of EFL education there are numerous evaluation models for software, websites, and documents, but is there a need for an evaluation system tailored to fit the needs of EFL instructors? Is there a need for more streamlined evaluation models? Is there a need for a database that would provide easy to interpret evaluation feedback from colleagues and students in the field of EFL? Several evaluation models will be asserted and discussed as well trials and tribulations that were involved in the creation and selection of these evaluation models. This discussion is based on ongoing Master's research and will include a personal narrative of my experiences in the pursuit of a Master's degree.

There is little doubt, that CALL and, more important, networked language-learning environments offering a variety of modes for communication and interaction have changed the face of the language classroom. These changes have had a profound and irreversible impact on language tutors and their perceived role(s)—in the classroom and beyond (Hauck & Stickler, 2006).

Welcome to the Computer age
- CALL: Computer Assisted Language Learning
- MALL: Multimedia Assisted Language Learning
- TELL: Technology Enhanced Language Learning
- CMC: Computer Mediated Communication
- CAI: Computer Assisted Instruction

Computers in the Language Classroom:
To Use or Not to Use?
- Do we, as EFL instructors, need to use computers in our classrooms?
- What are the advantages and/or disadvantages of using computers in the EFL classroom?
- Where does an EFL instructor begin in their quest to utilize computers in the language classroom?

Technology especially computer technology has brought challenges to our educational system. Universities are traditionally at the center of initiating change. However, this leadership role, traditionally played by the universities, is being challenged continuously. Nowadays students are generally more knowledgeable about the use of technology than teachers. Consequently, there is a mad scramble to incorporate technology into the teaching process, so as to appear up-to-date and ethical. Coping with such a large number of changes within our institutions does not mean simply making teachers incorporate technology so that they can be as good as the learners. Rather it means reconsidering our paradigms of learning and teaching (Zhang, 2003).

Bridging the Gap:
Digital Immigrants and Digital Natives
- Digital Natives: individuals raised with technology present in their lives from a young age.
- Digital Immigrants: individuals who have been introduced to and forced, to a certain extent, to integrate technology into their lives (Prensky, 2007).

Teachers generally teach the way they were taught (Mehlinger & Powers, 2002) and infusing technological tools into instruction poses unique challenges to teachers who are not willing and ready to change from their traditional instructional practices (Mehlinger & Powers, 2002, 17 in Keengwe, J., Onchwari, G. & Onchwari, J. (2009).

Challenges in Selection and Integration
- The sheer volume of resources available on the internet and their constantly changing state can make the selection of CALL materials a daunting process (Hauck & Stickler, 2006).
- Do Google searches alone suffice as a means of finding quality materials to use within our classrooms?
- How do EFL instructors select CALL materials to use in their classrooms?
- What should EFL instructors be looking for in the selection process?
- What tools are there to aid EFL instructors in the selection process?

Some Means of Selection
Word of Mouth
Suggestions from friends or colleagues.

Personal Research
Utilizing search engines and browsers to sift through materials.

Utilizing Reviews and Evaluations
Visit sites such as CALICO (Computer Assisted Language Instruction Consortium), TESOL Quarterly, AEFL Journal, and/or other independently run websites like Dave's ESL Café and eslHQ.

Benefits and Challenges with Some Means of Selection
Word of Mouth
While this may be reliable within a select and trusted group, it is ultimately limited to that group.

Personal Research
This may yield some hand-selected resources, but it can be extremely time consuming.

Utilizing Reviews and Evaluations
Evaluations and reviews found in some journals and consortiums, while insightful and detailed, can be both long winded and jargon laden. Evaluation standards and criteria can vary from journal to journal. Locating independently run websites that offer reliable evaluations can be as time consuming as personal research for websites.

Some Existing Evaluation Criteria Software

CALICO emphasizes 4 different areas when evaluating educational software:
1. Technical features
2. Activities (procedure)
3. Teacher fit (approach)
4. Leaner fit (design)

(CALICO, 2005 in Mentillo, 2008)

Websites

There are numerous different sets of criteria with regards to the evaluation of websites, including:

- Authority
- Accuracy
- Objectivity
- Currency
- Coverage

(Davis, 2000 in Son, 2005)

- Reliability
- Accuracy
- Authority
- Currency
- Fairness
- Adequacy
- Efficiency
- Organization

(McKenzie, 1997 in Son, 2005)

Website Evaluation Sheet

Dr. Jeong-Bae Son examined the above mentioned sets of criteria and many others to create a Language Learning Website Review Form (Son, 2005). It was Dr. Son's research and set of criteria that truly sparked my interest in the area of evaluating internet based instructional tools.

The form is available online at:
http://www.usq.edu.au/users/sonjb/papers/Son_ch13_2005.pdf

Son (2005) 15 Website Evaluation Criteria

1. Purpose (i.e., Is the purpose clear? Is the content in line with the purpose? Is the Website appropriate for its targeted learner?)
2. Accuracy (i.e., Is the content accurate? Are spelling and grammar accurate?)
3. Currency (i.e., Is the Website current? Is the Website updated regularly?)
4. Authority (i.e., Is there information on the author? Is the author well-recognized for his or her work?)
5. Loading speed (i.e., Does the Website download fast? Do the content pages download efficiently?)
6. Usefulness (i.e., Does the Website provide useful information? Are the language activities or tasks useful?)
7. Organization (i.e., Is the Website well organised and presented? Is the Website interesting to look at and explore? Are screen displays effective?)
8. Navigation (i.e., Is the Website easy to navigate? Are on-screen instructions easy to follow? Is it easy to retrieve information? Are hyperlinks given properly?)
9. Reliability (i.e., Is the Website free of bugs and breaks? Is the Website free of dead links?)
10. Authenticity (i.e., Are the learning materials authentic? Are authentic materials provided in appropriate contexts?)
11. Interactivity (i.e., Is the Website interactive? Are methods for user input effectively employed?)
12. Feedback (i.e., Is feedback on learner responses encouraging? Is error handling meaningful and helpful?)
13. Multimedia (i.e., Does the Website make effective use of graphics, sound and colour? Is the level of audio quality, the scale of graphics or video display appropriate for language learning?)

14. Communication (i.e., Can the user communicate with real people on-line through the Website? Is on-line help available?)
15. Integration (i.e., Can the learning materials be integrated into a curriculum? Does the content fit with curricular goals?).

My research Origins

I truly began my research in evaluation with the 15 evaluation criteria put forth by Son (2005). Based on his work and others, a set of evaluation standards for websites was generated and asserted in 2008.

PWELT Criteria Technological Orientation
Appeal/First Impression:
- Does the website hook your interest? Are you interested in looking further?

Accessibility/Navigation:
- Are activities easy to access?
- Is the site easy to navigate?
- Are instructions clearly labeled and easy to read?

Organization:
- Is the site organized?
- Are links easy to access and conveniently placed?
- Are activities logically organized?

System Requirements:
- Are system requirements clearly defined?
- Does the site specify exactly what software/hardware is needed?

Reliability:
- Is the site free of bugs or breaks? Is loading speed reasonable?

Currency:
- Is the website current?
- How often is the site updated? Is the site free of dead links?

Commercialism:
- Is the site obscured by advertisements?

Interactivity:
- Does the site utilize Web 2.0 technology?
- Are there interactive aspects to the site? (Chats, forums, etc.)

Multimedia:
- Does the sight effectively use a variety of different graphics, sounds, colors, videos, and so on?
- Is the level of audio, video, or graphic quality appropriate for language learning?

Usability:
- Is the sight easy to use for both native and non-native English speakers, both teachers and students?

Educational Orientation

Purpose:
Is the purpose clear? Is the content in line with the purpose?

Scaffolding:
Are activities properly scaffolded?
Are learners provided with warm up activities, vocabulary, and/or other materials to prepare them for the activity?

Authenticity:
Is material authentic?
Are voices, dialogues, topics, graphics, videos, etc. authentically represented contextually?

Integration/Application:
Are materials and lessons easily integrated into an existing curriculum or educational system?
Does content reflect curricular goals and objectives?

Feedback:
Is feedback provided to the learner?
Is feedback meaningful and supportive?

Validity:
Do tasks and activities reflect a pedagogical or theoretical underpinning?
Is content in line with a specific approach or approaches?

Accuracy:
Is content correct?
Are grammar, vocabulary, reading, and writing accurate?

Entertainment:
Is the site interesting or entertaining?
Is the site going to encourage further and extended use?

New Research Questions
1. How do EFL instructors in Korea select internet based tools for use in their classrooms?
2. Is there a need for a streamlined set of evaluation standards with regard to internet based instructional tools?
3. Is there a need for an easy to use presentation of feedback, based on the above mentioned evaluation standards, in the field of EFL instruction in Korea?

Is there a need?
- CALICO Software Reviews
- www.eslHQ.com
- www.englishclub.com

1. Do you think there is a need for change in the evaluation of internet based materials?
2. What do you think would aid EFL instructors in the evaluation and selection of internet based materials?

References
Hauck, M., & Stickler, U. (2006). What does it take to teach online? *CALICO Journal, 23*(3), 463-475.

Keengwe, J., Onchwari, G., & Onchwari, J. (2009). Technology *and* student learning: towards *a* learner-centered teaching model. *AACE Journal. 17*(1), 11-22.

Mentillo, E. (2008). Multimedia and language learning websites and their place in English education: evaluation strategies for EFL teachers. *Interfaces, 2*(1).

Son, J. (2005). *Exploring and evaluating language learning Web sites*. In: Son, Jeong-Bae and O'Neill, Shirley, (Eds.), *Enhancing learning and teaching: pedagogy, technology and language* (215-228). Flaxton, Australia: Post Pressed.

Zhang, F. (2003). The contribution of a multimedia language learning environment to the language learning process and outcome. In D. Lassner & C. McNaught (Eds.), *Proceedings of World Conference on Educational Multimedia, Hypermedia and Telecommunications 2003* (1891-1895). Chesapeake, VA: AACE.

Part Four
TESOL Interfaces 4(1)
& TESOL Interfaces 4(2)

2010

21. A Petition for Practical Pedagogical Projects
Mark C. Love

It was while reading Jennifer Ewald (1999) lamenting the dearth of practical applications of critical pedagogy to language study that I was struck by the notion that this applies to so much more in EFL than just critical pedagogy. As such, the title of this edition of from the editors echoes her article. While there is a preponderance of theory in journals such as *TESOL Quarterly*, actual applications of the theory are limited. It is to counter this imbalance in the literature that the editors hereby issue a call for practical pedagogical projects. With this issue the journal will introduce a new section to the journal: Lesson Plans. It is envisioned that these will be short 'articles' that present a pedagogy project along with a very brief rationale for the project and a description of the teaching situation for which it is designed. Since most of our students teach in Korea, most of the projects we receive will be directly applicable here or will report on creative teaching undertaken in Korea. However, we are not limited to just Korean projects and welcome submissions that report on any creative teaching project A template to guide submissions is downloadable from the journal's website, and special thanks go to David Kent for providing the template.

The Current Issue
For the current issue we have collated a research article, a review and two pedagogical projects to kick off this new section of the journal, all contributed by Woosong students and faculty.

Research Article
P. Badenhorst's *Sacred, scared, scarred: An autoethnographic portrait of teaching as unbecoming amidst the ambiguities of life* is a deep autoethnography in which the author grapples with the meaning(s) of critical incidents that have significantly shaped his identity as a teacher. Badenhorst also examines how teaching identities are enmeshed in the social and vice-versa and how they relate to the flow of power and ethics, in teaching and in life. Along the way, he raises many taboo topics in an effort to better himself by 'unbecoming' himself, a lesson from which all teachers can learn if they are brave enough to submit themselves to this process, however unbecoming it may seem.

Review
In *The JungChul Cyber English Learning Program*, M.S. Gu and D. Kent look at an internet based language teaching program. They examine how well the program teaches listening, speaking, reading, and writing and list the programs shortcomings. Vocabulary and pronunciation are also dealt with.

Lesson Plans
Two articles begin this section, and we hope many more will follow. J. Hopkinson's *English quest – a large-scale, task-based activity* provides practical advice in setting up an English quest. He also reports on problems and solutions his teaching team encountered in three separate trials in Korea. Filled with practical advice, this will prove especially helpful to beginning teachers who may have never set up a scavenger hunt before.

Y. Sohn proposes a lesson plan that examines An Na's *A Step from Heaven* that incorporates reader-response criticism, feminism, and cultural criticism. While this may seem ambitious, Sohn succeeds in crafting a lesson plan that teaches fairly advanced critical thinking skills to middle school students in a manner that touches very lightly on the theory as to not overwhelm the students. Sohn succeeds in teaching advanced concepts in a subtle manner by using a text that is very appropriate for her students.

References

Ewald, J. D. (1999). A plea for published reports on the application of a critical pedagogy to 'language study proper'. *TESOL Quarterly*, 33(2), 275-279.

22. Sacred, Scared, Scarred: An Autoethnographic Portrait of Teaching as Unbecoming Amidst the Ambiguities of Life

Paul Badenhorst

A virtual self reflects upon its past and considers its struggle to grasp the dynamics which inform the use and abuse of power within society. Simultaneously, thoughts, feelings, experiences and expectations are introduced to the retrospective autoethnographical narrative; especially as these relate to the politics of teaching. Always mindful that it is a product of social construction involving a relative degree of agency, the virtual self attempts a wilful deconstruction of itself. Later, the virtual self embarks on a brief quest to define its teaching as a process of critical *unbecoming* amidst the ambiguities of life. This work espouses a critical approach to the discursive matter at hand and regards subjectivity as integral to this approach, allowing the virtual self to be cast as an actor in a dramatic landscape of peculiar occurrences, none of which can be described vividly through the sole use of traditionally valued methods of qualitative enquiry. As the virtual self consumes the memory of time passed, a new kaleidoscope of pedagogy begins to emerge. The content of *true* teaching is both that which flows *into* and *out of* the teacher who has accepted the inner call to strategically create influence from meaning. This requires the teacher to consistently remain critical of her socially constructed *Weltanschauung* so as to take an ethical stance going beyond that merely informed by lived experience – an ethical stance sensitive *to*, and protective *of*, difference.

Introduction

The teacher is *human*.
Humans are *social*.
The social is *political*.
Therefore, *teaching is a political act.*

Since human experience is intrinsically "chaotic and messy" (Spry, 2001, 727), autoethnographic work cannot be accomplished through a cold, theory-saturated pedagogical underpinning detached from lived experience – that kind associated with traditional methods of qualitative research in which the author attempts to hide in the shadows of supposed 'objectivity' by detaching subject from text, before shoveling the former under layers of hypotheses. Instead, postmodern-oriented autoethnographic writing strives for reflexivity by which the researcher moves beyond the second person pronoun, yet remains constantly aware of her role as researcher. Devault frames autoethnographic reflexivity as follows:

> When talking about their lives, people lie sometimes, forget a lot, exaggerate, become confused, and get things wrong. Yet they are revealing truths. These truths don't reveal the past 'as it actually was,' aspiring to a standard of objectivity. They give us instead the truths of our experiences (1997, 261).

Furthermore, this writing enterprise is informed by personal narrative that situates the "socio-politically inscribed body as a central site of meaning making" (Spry, 2001, 710). Consequently, in this current work, I recognize that I am but a microcosmic part in an ever-changing discursive medley of interrelated macrocosmic wholes which have exerted, and in some instances continue to exercise, a relative degree of influence over me.

Ultimately, this article does not intend to be an idealistic smorgasbord serving the reader with unrealistically optimistic maxims, highly sentimental anecdotes and a barrage of terse aphorisms. On the contrary, this exploration is as much a study in humanity as it is of what it means to be a teacher since, as will become apparent, these two concepts are highly interdependent and mutually inseparable. Therefore, it is imperative that this work adopts an introspective and critical narrative approach that provides a perspective-based understanding of the role of teacher's humanity in the development of her discovering and pursuing the calling of *teacher*. Due to the highly personal, historical nature of the narrative endeavor, frequent voyages will be undertaken into the realm of the poetic; the metaphoric. Aesthetic and evocative imagery has the ability to graphically communicate meaning beyond the level of dispassionate intellectual formalism, paving the way for a transubstantiation of the read word into read experience. This read experience allows the reader to share glimpses into the lived experience of the writer; ultimately allowing both writer and reader to share in a highly intersubjective journey of discovery leading towards a deeper appreciation of the teacher as a human among humans. This insight however carries along with it profound implication – that, in light of her position among other human beings, the teacher carries a social, ultimately political, responsibility to lead society to wholeness beyond that brokenness so visible in, for instance, the marginalization of minority discourses and the exploitation of society's vulnerable. The following poem, and the video[1] that accompanies it, metaphorically allude to the reality of this highly fragmented nature of life – one in the midst of which the teacher is called to serve.

THE OWL[2]

The night I arrived

Was cruel and cold and dark

Wolves hunting

Your wooded labyrinth for blood

And flesh and warmth

Beneath the blanket

Of your snow-cove**red** trees

Wailing like banshees in the wind

A doe had given birth to her fawn

Sac**red**. Sca**red**. Sca**rred**.

But you could not protect them

From fang and tooth and claw

The hungry bear that ate mother and child

Colo**red** your whiteness

A rosy, bloody **red**

Note: **bold** words colored red in the original

Standing in the Wind

Outside, a foreboding bitter wind has descended like the angel of death. People are hiding behind closed doors. Other than the ghostly song of the wind, the streets have turned silent. The impressions left by our footsteps have formed coded patterns in the light snow like the black letters running across this sheet of paper. These symbols of intent lead deep into the cold and eventually turn indecipherable. Yet, these footsteps will not be here for long, for whether by snow or by sun, the memories of this journey will soon be covered, or simply melt away. Disappear. I see your footprints next to mine and I know that – given sufficient time – no one will even know we were here. These footprints are prophetic. They remind us of the impending fate of both the largest, brightest star as well as that face which is still able to smile with innocence and purity. And they are beautiful – these footsteps – especially yours. Yet, there are things – unlike footprints in the snow – that cannot be erased from the mind. Impressions that have fashioned the geography of memory and remain obstinately present like granite rock towering high above the clouds beneath which everything else has been forgotten. Images that will surely endure until our expiry date . . . that number, the latter of two, engraved into tombstones and the walls of mausoleums.

Shit! It's so cold today and I know you're tired. I can see the size of your breath every time you exhale. Here. Have my coat while I have this cigarette. Will you sit here with me for just a moment while our footprints are still here? I'm asking you to look back at our path in the snow . . . to try and think back . . . to try and remember the 25th of December.
Do you?
Do you remember?
Do you remember the 25th of December?

Innocence and Guilt

December 25, 1989. On a cold winter's day they executed the tyrant. I was 4607 days – or twelve years, seven months, and ten days – old. That was twenty years ago to the day. As media reports and graphic images filtered through the airwaves in the months that followed, a deeply disturbing portrait of reality began to unfold. It was this event – the death of the tyrant – that served as catalyst for the very disclosures that awoke the dawn of my deep disillusionment . . . that moment when I looked back on myself for the first time and had to ask: 'What's the meaning of this *fucking* madness?' After 24 years in power, and following in the path of the despot who preceded him, Nicolae Ceausescu had left behind a legacy of the most abhorrent abuse and neglect, all directly precipitated by domination of the avaricious *few* over the bleeding multitude. Around 150,000 children were institutionalized in Romanian state-run orphanages – or *leagans* – throughout Ceausescu's regime. The orphanages, like factories, were designed to manufacture adult workers void of loyalty to family or religion; who would owe allegiance only to the state. The healthy among the children "were groomed for the secret police's special units; the sick and disabled wasted away in their own filth – the flotsam of an uncaring, insane society" (Glovinski, 2004, 3). By 1989, over a thousand children had contracted AIDS through blood transfusions and the use of unsterilized needles, even though the regime had denied any significant infection among members of the population (see Greenwell, 2003).

In early 1990 I remember watching a televised feature on the frightening plight of these children, many who shared my age, but not my build or size. I was a child of privilege. They were the projected dirt beneath my feet. I remember retiring to my room shortly afterwards. I left the light off and crawled under the covers. I had been infected by the horror I had witnessed. My body started to shiver. Then, through the barely visible silhouette of branches outside I became aware that in the dark there were trees where birds sat perched staring silently; waiting. I lay in the embrace of black, staring through the waxing crescent of the barely open closet door. *That alluring waxing crescent.* It was dark inside there – like molasses. Mesmerized by the intangible black canvas before me, I was pulled into it. And there I had a virgin glimpse of my – of our – awe-inspiring, occasionally terrifying, place in this cosmos.

I have seen the dark universe yawning.
Where the black planets roll without aim –
Where they roll in their horror unheeded,
Without knowledge or lustre or name (Lovecraft, 2002, 336).

A ghostly battalion of images arrived shortly thereafter and lay siege to my mind.

> (D)espite the heat of the day, several of the children are wrapped in dirty blankets. From one still bundle, only a bluish patch of scalp is visible. Asked if the child inside is alive, an orderly says, 'Of course,' and pulls back the cover. The tiny skeleton stirs, turns onto its side and groans (Glovinski, 2004, 117).

I cried. I pleaded with Jesus and his band of angels to deliver them . . . to stop their suffering. The knowledge of one's own good fortune and privilege set against the misfortune of others has the uncanny ability to be a source of sorrow. I sobbed bitterly. I fed my pillow the soggy weight of my naivety in tears. And then, somewhere in the silence of the quietest hour of night, my well ran dry. The grave robbers had come for my sleep, leaving me to lie staring searchingly into the black void. By dawn I felt dreadfully tired, yet I purposed to walk into the new day bearing the fresh wound of my initiation into reality, feeling that I now shared a bond with those whose suffering I had witnessed only a few hours before, yet whose humiliation I could never comprehend. That morning the sky was Pacific; the air fragrant and placid. And yet – in spite of the sun – my sadness continued to grow into the year.

One dark day – sometime later in 1990 – a group of mixed-race children who were begging, knocked on the front door of our house as they occasionally did. Usually, while my mother would prepare food for them to take home, my brother and I would follow the example set by my father and talk with them; be friendly and caring. Before long we were regularly inviting them to join us on the front lawn for a game of cricket or football, and some snacks. Yet, this day I was alone. It was winter again. The six of them asked for something to eat – gently, kindly, trusting – as they always did. Their faces, dirty. Their eyes desperately hungry like a hunger I have never known. I promised to give them all the food they could carry if they would fall down on their faces and beg of me [3]. They left empty handed. I stood by the open door and watched my friends as they walked down the road . . . away from me. My gaze fixed on the rapidly fading silhouette of their tiny bodies; my ears searching through the wind for the sound of their voices. Then the air grew quiet and they disappeared. I closed the door and decided to leave it unlocked. Stunned at the impulsive overtone of this most dehumanizing of actions I sat staring at myself in the mirror for a long time. I too had the darkness of a Ceausescu inside of me. I too held the potential for evil. I had demonstrated to myself that I was capable of great harm, and that my heart could alternate between colors twice in the space of a few minutes; twice within a year. This knowledge terrified me. I wondered if somewhere deep inside me there was a beast lurking in the shadows – a Minotaur that had breeched the restraining confines of its labyrinth. Yet, I cannot inflict hurt, without hurting myself. And I cannot draw blood, without bleeding myself. There was no other knock on the door that afternoon, and I spent the rest of the day alone, haunted by my conscience, seated at the foot of a bed, in silence.

Many winters passed; my eyes turned dark. Forward into the unknown I continued to walk, increasingly becoming preoccupied with an inner struggle to grasp the dynamics which inform the use and abuse of power within society.

As strange as it now may appear, the insight I gained from both these deeply personal, yet ultimately polar moral experiences, would later – in reflection – serve to convince me to follow the true yearning of my heart. In my confusion, I desired to move beyond the shadows cast by black wings and dark clouds. I wanted to venture into a world unprotected and devote my life *for* people, and more specifically, for the *other*. This noble intention however requires an ability to judge distance, especially in times when the charted skies hide their signs. Often, I have lost my way. Occasionally, I have found it again.

I think of the *six* – often – and wonder if they still think of me. Though I was too young to be a teacher by profession, I had undoubtedly taught those six children that day. Whether it was a lesson about the capricious quality of the human heart, the fact that friends cannot always be trusted, or that white people should be avoided – this I cannot know. However, through my callous actions – and the way they interpreted these – I undoubtedly taught those *six*, who were around the same age as I, a lesson. One I deeply regret. Of course, my culpability and subsequent remorse is a cautionary lesson in itself.

Ultimately, teaching goes deeper than a role we decide to take upon ourselves. It starts fundamentally from those actions that flow from us based on who we are at a particular juncture in space-time, and realizing that these actions will leave an impression – for better or worse – upon those we relate to.

Disconnection and Reconnection
Recently, while earnestly contemplating my life in order to write these words with my heart, I have become deeply aware of the profound frustration of many of those around me. Their words, set against the memory of my experience, have generated a comparison I can touch.

Several years spent in service of the Church had brought me to my knees at the edge of a very dark abyss, gasping for oxygen while trying to hold onto the frayed ends of my sanity. Many willingly fall to their knees as an act of faith. Some, however, collapse to their knees at that moment when the last remaining flame of faith – or belief in an absolute explanation *of* and *for* life – has finally been extinguished.

In 1996 I enrolled to study theology and in 2000 I entered full-time Christian ministry as a minister of religion. Far from being motivated to *save souls*, the burden of my heart lay in feeding stomachs and wiping tears, and to this end – with an overgrown beard, an optimistic mindset, and the basic necessities I needed to get by – I toiled with both heart and hand. I was determined to fight inequality and remedy suffering, naively believing that I could change the world; oblivious to the fact that the world would continue to change me.

For seven years I labored in the poor community to which I had accepted a call. I cherished the people I worked with and actively sought out opportunities to aid and assist wherever I could.

Yet, I could not escape from beneath the dark, sanctimonious shadow of religious dogma, and the subsequent demands placed upon me by a church hierarchy that covertly regarded 'caring' as a means of manipulating people into becoming converts. If I had found any value in the narrative pertaining to Christ it was of a man who supposedly lived his life for the *other*; a man who shunned the institutionalized, religious power-hierarchy of his day – not the symbolic man-whore of *sanctified* religious consumer culture. That flashy icon of personal salvation and comfort fired from the canons of grand narrative into the minds of those persuaded not to question. That popular image flaunted by denominational Christian churches over the centuries, often for little reason other than to fill their pews and coffers in the misguided hope of simultaneously filling *heaven* as well. Contrary to the hubris so characteristic of the hierarchy, the religion I encountered among many of the poor was a humble albeit opiate, pragmatic affair, yet nonetheless one vulnerable to social control and abuse.

The suffering I daily encountered in my work was emotionally exhausting, and humbling, yet it fueled my desire to persevere. The frustration, on the other hand, brought about by a church that expected me to preach the *blood* and the *spirit* – that heavenly *deus ex machina* that would magically heal the wounds of society through reciting the Sinner's Prayer – was intense, and both psychologically and emotionally stifling. Increasingly, as time passed, I found it impossible to reconcile the simple black-white dichotomous paradigm so characteristic of Christian soteriology with the complex social dynamics I witnessed in people operating from – and interacting – within a host of radically different discourses.

In hindsight, my disillusionment with the church had started during my first year of studying theology. However, back then I felt that I could remedy my discontent by devoting myself fulltime to the practical human needs so evident in the world I desired to serve. Often, my anger at the social *status quo* willfully left unchallenged by the church would boil over into passionate, recalcitrant sermons that verbally challenged *comfortable white people*; encouraged the need to *make conversation with our Muslim colleagues at work and invite them to dinner so we could come face-to-face with their humanity* (the Sunday after the September 11 attacks), and protested *our filthy hypocrisy*. On several occasions my teaching drew a measure of scorn from my colleagues, and more than once individual congregants seated within the pews rose to their feet and loudly interrupted my passionate diatribe. That I had chosen to work within the context of a very conservative denomination did not simplify my cause in any way, though I had managed to both guide the listening *few* to a greater social awareness, as well as elicit strong reactions from the *many* who otherwise would have left the service as quietly and piously as they had entered. Yet, by late 2006 my patience with the frivolities of religious power structures had expired. Late one evening I vented an instalment of my deep frustration by *pissing* gratuitously all over the pulpit. I went home and had a few more beers. Then, I awoke and resigned.

These past months, on several occasions, I've touched the callous imprints of disillusionment like stigmata yet again. Here, I am specifically referring to some among the high, middle and elementary school EFL teachers I have worked with over the course of the past year at a teaching training facility who have confided the depth of their despair to me. They speak the same message and use the same words, as though they were all reciting lines from the same tragic script. Yet, beyond their words, eyes convey unspoken emotional signals colored in tones of grey – sadness, disappointment, meaninglessness; futility. Most of them entered the teaching field filled with fiery passion and promise, only to encounter the betrayal of a hierarchical education system bent on mass-production – one that crushes the desire to be creative, expressive, personable, critical and relevant; creating instead a continuum ranging from mild despair to outright apathy. In short, a system that denies language teachers the very freedoms they need to perform their calling in an efficient, motivated, and passionately-engaged manner; a system which catalyzes the mutation of those who once were prepared to devote their lives for *others* into a generally learner-detached group of *teaching machines*[4] provided with little opportunity other than to teach from the cold pages of a book for tests designed to accomplish no more than create a measurable database of social stratification. I remember the weight of the feeling of despair. I remember it all too well. And I wonder what my role should be – as a teacher trainer – in the lives of those who claim to find no meaning in their inner calling anymore; those who look to the future and can rightfully find no evidence to suggest that this Rube Goldberg beast-of-a-machine will be replaced anytime soon.

For these teachers, I give myself, often suspecting that what I have to give may be no more than a bandage for a wound that will not heal by itself. Occasionally, that which I have passionately given of myself has not been accepted by some. However, it is *my hope* that through my humanity, persistence, the sensitivity with which I listen, as well as the diligent quality of the critical opportunities I provide them with, some teachers will come to take a degree of authority over their circumstances so as to cultivate the root of change in their individual classroom contexts. In this regard, Palmer speaks of linking the *role* with the *soul* (2003, 380) – a responsibility I recognize I have seen before. Just as the religious worker ideally uses her position as a funnel through which to channel her heart into situations thirsty for hope, the role of teacher is the means by which educators convert themselves from messengers of change into *messages* of change.

Becoming and Unbecoming

The dominant motivation behind this autobiographical enterprise is to establish a deeper understanding of the dynamics behind my social construction for the purpose of gaining humble new insights that may both facilitate and broaden my ability to address oppression and alleviate human suffering; especially so through my teaching. This requires that I *think about my own thinking* by becoming an *action researcher* of myself (Kincheloe, 2005, 5-6). Ultimately, humans are "the constructs of relationships, not fragmented monads or abstract individuals" (Kincheloe, 2005, 17). It follows then that, since human identities do not enter the world in the form of some neatly packaged unitary self, we need to undertake that work which deconstructs the *virtual self* (see Kincheloe, 2005) by viewing it in context to the ever-shifting series of relationships and patterns that have constituted – and continue to constitute – the construction of identity. Here, the concept of *virtual self* is an extension of Deleuze's definition which posits the virtual as a kind of surface effect produced by actual causal interactions which occur at the material level, so that the self is a potentiality constantly being fulfilled in the actual (see Deleuze, 2002). The virtual self is never self-coherent, fixed, or bounded since it does not rely on any objective point of reference. Instead, it is a phenomenon of loose accumulation, coagulation, and sedimentation that can be both produced (what Deleuze calls a *'Body without Organs'*) and dismantled. This process of stratification is constant so that the subject is continually being recreated in the process manifesting a complex configuration of multiplicities being defined from the outside – what Deleuze terms the 'line of flight' (see Deleuze,

2002; Deleuze & Guattari, 1992). It follows that the virtual self is intrinsically a product of social construction involving a relative degree of agency, requiring regular critical self-analysis that allows the virtual self to be cast as an actor in a dramatic landscape of peculiar occurrences.

It is undeniable that who I am as a teacher – my philosophy, approach and action – has been molded by over three decades of participation in a wide configuration of discourses that have served as "a punch line, running gag, and an exercise in the construction of meaning" (Ceisel, 2009, 667). Hence, it is expedient that I embark on a journey of *unbecoming* – undertaking a critical self-evaluation that allows me to see myself in context to the world in which I live from the vantage point of the world from which I come. For instance, born melanin-free in a country – much like most other countries either once colonized or inhabited by European colonizers – which historically provided legislated privilege on this context, I have been allowed far greater social mobility than most who do not share my skin color or genetic heritage. I therefore have a responsibility to redress this injustice beginning with the quality of my word and action in the way I relate to people who have traditionally been marginalized because of the color of their skin. Only once I take this step towards authentic self critique can I become conscious of the reasons for my thoughts and actions; only then can I deconstruct myself so as to construct a world more just than the world from which I come; only then can I cut through the fetters of ignorance and maladjustment that prevent me from walking like a teacher should. That is, to walk beside . . . to walk beside others . . . to walk beside all others with integrity.

However, the question *'Why do I choose to teach?'* still remains? While I hold the concept of traditional education with a large degree of contempt since the institutionalized nature of education directly contributes to the crystallization of a disparate, class-orientated, production-driven global society (see Illich, 2000), I strongly agree with the protest expressed by Mali (2005) when he engages with the slanderous view which chooses to degrade teaching as the preferred profession for those who supposedly lack the ability to do anything else. Much as the action of *cutting* is largely determined by the quality of the blade, effective teaching is determined by the qualities of the teacher. *Teacher* is more than a professional category – it's a calling!

Eisner suggests that the work of the teacher "is related to achieving the deep satisfactions of teaching" (Eisner, 2006, 46). Yet, he describes these satisfactions in generically abstract and overly optimistic terms – for instance, "to realize a form of immortality"; to "make a difference in students' lives" (Eisner, 2006, 44-45) – none of which engage with that inner turmoil which so often accompanies deep, heartfelt teaching. In short, these vague descriptions fail to engage the task of teaching with the *heart* of the teacher.

For a more appropriate grasp of teaching we need to focus our enquiry inward, and this is a journey every teacher should undertake. It is as though, on our way back in time, we introspectively reverse the order of *becoming*; we sort through a lifetime comprised of layers of social influence in a process towards *unbecoming*. When we critique the way the self has been – and often continues to be – situated in context to others (see Spry, 2001), we are enabled to come face-to-face with our own fears, biases and prejudices, and confront these with a view towards purging ourselves from every attitude that can potentially restrict the personal freedom and social development of others. This process of *unbecoming* allows us to begin the work of disentangling ourselves from those constraints of knowledge in which we have been caught – constraints that marginalize specific discourses through rules of exclusion, and maintain a disproportionate and uncritical reproduction of power. Of course, power is ubiquitous and integral to the way humans relate to one another; society will never be power-*less*. However, since power ultimately operates within social networks – enmeshed in a plurality of relationships between contexts where participants are both able to be subjects as well as be subjected, power always holds potential for emancipation since it is not a constant; power is productive in more than one way (see Foucault, 1979). In this sense, the process of *unbecoming* is both a deconstructive and moral exercise. Foucault remarks: "I am a moralist, insofar as I believe that one of the tasks, one of the meanings of human existence – the source of human freedom – is never to accept anything as definitive, untouchable, obvious, or immobile" (Bess, 1980, ¶ 2). This implies that we critically engage with ourselves by examining those discourses of which we form part – discourses that are ultimately rooted in alternating configurations of power.

One of the earliest vivid memories I have of myself is a set of images in motion mentally recorded sometime between my first and second birthdays at a time when I had just started walking with a limited, albeit respectable, degree of proficiency. *I can see grass. I'm in a park. I see brightly painted swings. Red. Then blue. Then yellow. I see some other children. I make my way to the swings. It feels like I am laughing. I hug the other children. I see my mother calling me. I am happy. I hug all the children. The children hug me back.* The memory fades. I come to understand that I've always craved a deep sense of *oneness* with the world around me – a desire both never fulfilled and never to be fulfilled, or as Zizek describes in Freudian / Lacanian terms: "(D)esire's *raison d'etre* ... is not to realize its goal, to find full satisfaction, but to reproduce itself as desire" (1997, 39). This inner thirst is inevitable and is what draws us deeper into life like Hamlet following the elusive ghost down silent cobbled passageways, deeper into the womb of Elsinore; deeper into time; deeper into the unknown.

Another memory sourced from an event that occurred approximately ten years later has me standing before a class of my peers in an all-boys school. *The male teacher has called me to the front to comment on the perfectly-combed side path in my hair (a product of my ultra-perfectionist home environment). I have recently entered puberty and am feeling very self-conscious. The teacher places both his hands on my shoulders and directs a question at the class: 'Do you see this thing standing before you?' The class is silent. He continues in a stern, though mocking tone not dissimilar from that used by the whip-wielding dominatrix: 'This thing is a homosexual! Gay from top to bottom! Look at him carefully. Disgusting!' Abrupt giggles are sporadically heard around the class. The sadist laughs. The pervert dismisses me. In a silent state of humiliation I walk back to my desk. I can feel my face is not hiding my inner Armageddon . . . the pain I am feeling. I do not hate him though I sense I soon will. Men hate gays. I must not be gay.* At that moment I experienced shame at something that should never have provoked shame in the first place. That a teacher should project his undisclosed sexual insecurities onto an innocent boy by alluding to a totally natural sexual orientation in such a prejudiced manner – that is shameful. Unfortunately, homosexuality often finds itself used as a cheap slur among *dudes* in a male-dominated society that refuses to make peace with its own diversity; impinging upon the freedom of individuals to live authentic lives free from stigma and shame. I now gain a little more insight into why I hate the abuse of influence, power, and trust. This situation may also hint at the mockery I make of machismo and masculine bravado.

The former of the two experiences I have alluded to was my first spiritual experience; the latter of the two experiences was deeply meaningful as well, though it only gained an existential dimension several hours later, once the shock had settled. It may appear contradictory that an agnostic should choose his words this way. However, use of the word *spiritual* should not be confused with Platonic or religious and theological designations of this word. Palmer defines spirituality as the "human yearning to be connected with something larger than our own egos" (2003, 377). The subject as social construct does not exclude the reality of a desire to experience a connection that draws us *out of* ourselves. This desire – whether biologically or psychologically informed, or a combination of both – often stirs us to seek participation in meaningful relationships with both that which is and those who are *other* to us. This urge for self-transcendence – or conscious desire to go *beyond* the secure landscape of one's personal world – requires those brave enough to *open up* to it, to live passionately, sensitively and *searchingly* in spite of the uncertainties which linger incessantly in the darkness of the unknown. To this end, Albert Camus wrote of the accumulation of quality life experiences, all projected as ultimately meaningless and absurd in view of the inevitability of death, yet validated none the less by the very moment-in-space-time reality that they were lived in the first place. He writes: 'Being aware of one's life, one's revolt, one's freedom, and to the maximum, is living, and to the maximum' (Camus, 2000, 61). Social expeditions to establish relationships – connections – through dialogue and understanding with those who are *other* to us most certainly qualify as meaningful, quality life experiences, especially if these lead us to a deeper appreciation of the kaleidoscope inherent in life.

True *teaching* reflects this desire for connection through the relationships it seeks to establish and affect. In the process we are drawn *out of* ourselves and into the new *community of practice* (Cox, 2005, 527-528) we share with our learners which itself represents "a microcosm of the larger social and cultural world" (Pennycook, 2003, 479). It is at this very intersection where our humanity is both laid bare, shared and exchanged, allowing the opportunity for us to view and interact with human beings as they really are, whether they be hurting, fragile, insecure, prejudiced, naive, ignorant, angry, confused, or oppressed within their lived racial, gender, class, sexual-orientation or economic experiences and social realities.

Only once we have opened up to the *other* and allowed the *other* the space to open up to us have we earned the right to demonstrate what Block refers to as "standing ethically" before our learners (Block, 2008, 425). For an effective teaching environment to take shape – one that connects knowledge of the *world* beyond the classroom to the *word* represented by the curriculum; one that overrides a *banking* approach to teaching in which students are regarded as little more than empty bank accounts that should remain open to authoritative deposits made by the teacher (see Freire, 2000) – this necessary stand needs to be taken. This stand is rooted in political practice and implies the strategic creation of influence from meaning. It extends beyond the content of what is taught, to also include the content of what one is and how one treats others both in the classroom and out of the classroom. Giroux observes:

> Pedagogy is a moral and political practice that is always implicated in power relations and must be understood as a cultural politics that offers both a particular version and vision of civic life, the future, and how we might construct representations of ourselves, others, and our physical and social environment (2004, 33).

Sacred, Scared, Scarred: An Autoethnographic Portrait | 287

The teacher is called to help accomplish this; it is a *calling* from deep within her own humanity that needs to be discovered, unwrapped, developed, and ultimately accepted.

I firmly believe that if teaching does not *hurt* you, you are not teaching. Teaching implies the sharing of one's full self in the effort and practical resources one exhausts – a requirement symbolized by a certain wise man who, according to legend, offered his own flesh to a starving litter of tiger cubs – even when all one devotedly gives is not always accepted or appreciated. Furthermore, teaching entails sharing in not only the joys, but especially the suffering of others, and strategically creating greater public awareness of these living varieties. This is what I believe distinguishes teaching from a mere job. Teaching implies responding to a deep urge, a deep passion, and deep compassion within the core of one's being. It is the apparent equivocation of a selfish act performed for the sake of others, both because of and in spite of oneself. To be a teacher is to orientate oneself both *through* and *in spite of* the world *to* the word, and especially *through* and *in spite of* the word *to* the world (Freire, 2000, 32-33). Block notes:

> To teach is to assume an ethical position in an immoral world. To teach is to be a prophet in a degraded world. To teach is not to suffer silently, but to suffer nonetheless. To teach is to change the world student by student and paper by paper (2009, 425).

Paolo Freire speaks of the realities of both *humanization* and *dehumanization* in our world, pointing out that only the former is a vocation – one affirmed by the very existence of those struggling to regain their lost humanity (2000, 43-44).

As I ponder my final words in this "narrative of the self" (Richardson, 1993, 521), the presence of winter is showing a stubborn resilience. Admittedly, I have only barely broken the ice of the profound meaning teaching has come to represent for me. It is the stories I hold deep within which incite me to respond to the inner call to serve the world around me. A bittersweet path – thirty-two years traversed and riddled with many experiences and events – has left me empty of absolutes and the "swindle of fulfilment" (Giroux, 2009, 275). I have, as it were, chosen to dump all traditional notions of certainty into the dark abyss of a bitter existential confusion, and this I willingly embrace. Yet, in the absence of naïve grand narratives I have discovered a deeper and entirely fluid meaning to life. This meaning finds itself as much in the questions I ask, as in the questions I endeavor to awaken within others – questions that point us beyond ourselves towards a greater sensitivity and awareness of the world we form part of. Though questions like *'Who am I?'* and *'Why am I here?'* have traditionally formed the backbone of personal existential exploration, the questions I am alluding to extend beyond the preoccupation of self to include a recognition of society as an organic entity comprised of an interrelated association of co-existing organisms – both human and non-human; each affecting the outcome of the other. These questions are framed outwardly first in both the belief that the process of seeking to answer them may indeed result in the wellbeing of others, as well as the hope that the insights we are bound to discover will help us understand ourselves better by seeing ourselves in perspective to the intricate tapestry we form part of. Paradigmatic questions like *'Who are **you**?'* and *'Why are **you** here?'* enable us to break out of the metanarrative of self – that practice whereby our experiences and perspectives become the exclusive, rigid and uncritical normative lens through which we view the world – towards a deeper awareness of those peculiarities surrounding the existence of the *other*. This paradigm shift in turn allows us to ask even deeper questions that expose disparity and complacency. In fact, if we are serious about developing a greater understanding of the world around us, as well as becoming proactive participants in the process, our questions need to be relevant to our contemporary milieu, especially in context to specific social configurations and the way in which these relate to power: ways of relating affected by factors of race, gender, language, culture, class, sexual orientation, age, physical challenge, and even species. 'In what ways are others being deprived of equal benefit relative to me?' and 'What can I do to bring about greater equality?'; alternately, 'In what ways do others draw unequal benefit in context to me?' and 'What can I do to help address this imbalance?'. Especially the last two questions provide an opportunity for the cultivation of "resistance" (Dreyfuss & Rabinow, 1983, 342). At its most basic level, teaching is a political act. At a pragmatic, socially-sensitive level though, teaching is about exposing difference among learners, and cultivating a respect for diversity, while seeking to dismantle socially conditioned negations of difference and frozen configurations of power. To this end it is imperative that teachers and learners share in authentic and meaningful communication that allows learners to "connect their own lives and everyday experiences to what they learn" (Giroux, 2004, 44). I am aware that critical pedagogy is vulnerable to cultural imperialism if it is imported by those external to the discourse community in which it is being disseminated. Consider how critical theories have, for instance, demonstrated intolerance when individuals outside of Western culture are not given freedom of choice (as exemplified by the contemporary controversy raging throughout Europe surrounding Arab women wearing the *burqa*), yet remain blind to those gender-based pressures that are firmly embedded in Western culture (such as the relentless onslaught of corporate advertising which compels women to undergo plastic surgery, cosmetic implants, and Botox injections) (see Zizek, 1997; Etcoff, Orbach, Scott, & D'Agostino, 2004). Consequently, while I need to remain cautious of questioning specific aspects of Korean culture, I work to create a pedagogical climate in which the learning participants in my classes are able to view the cultural specifics within their own discourse communities and critically engage with these before, hopefully, extending this critical approach to their learners as well. Therefore, I view my responsibility in context to the Korean EFL teachers and students I daily relate to as being one of encouragement – the encouragement of greater social awareness through working to increasingly establish a kaleidoscopic pedagogical environment conducive to questioning, research and, ultimately, dialogue.

Critical Introspection (Towards Unbecoming)
I have attempted to position this performative writing as a form of "scholarly representation" demonstrating a critical approach (Pelias, 1998, 4). However, to this end, this work will be an ongoing investigation, even after I have typed the last letter of the last word of the final paragraph.

I am reminded of the recent words of the holocaust survivor, Elie Wiesel, who said: "You know how many reasons we have to be desperate and despairing. The world is not learning anything" (2004, online). I know this to be true, and I have long abandoned both the belief in salvation as well as the hope that the world can be 'fixed'. Yet, I want to learn to improve myself, especially in context to the way I relate to others in the face of injustice and exploitation, and hopefully, challenge those within reach of my teaching to aspire to the same. In this sense, teaching is both a reaching *inside* and a reaching *outside* – an event simultaneously seeking to affect personal and interpersonal growth and change. Foucault speaks of "a care of self, which thinking of itself, thinks of others" leading relationships to be "as they should be" (1988, 8-9).

I wonder about the *blind spots* in my life – those parts of my attitude and behaviour obscured by that ignorance within I have yet to discover. And I contemplate those parts of me that are in the process of changing, yet remain obstinate in their occasional manifestation. Unless I resist manifestations of power imbalance, my wilful complicity will be undeniable hypocrisy; a trait that cannot in any way be reconciled with what it means to be *teacher*.

Living a critical life means being just as critical of ones world – ones *Weltanschauung* – as of the world around oneself, and it requires that we be willing to "combat fascism within the self" (Widder, 2004, 427). Only then do we proceed from *unbecoming* to a new *becoming*. To this end, teaching *is* a process of critical *unbecoming* amidst the ambiguities of life since it is in orientating ourselves to teach with integrity that we are orientated to change.

Concluding Thoughts: Walking into the Snow

So here we are. The heavy shower of snow has covered us in cloaks of white. We've been standing alone in this blizzard for a while now. Perhaps we should go. Perhaps we should walk south. And *never forget*.

I remember December. And I still think of the *six*, only able to suspect the role I play in the stories they have told.

End Notes

[1] The video claims *fair use* as a document created for educational purposes and can be viewed at the following online location: http://www.youtube.com/watch?v=TEmTNt7fmzQ

[2] By Paul Badenhorst

[3] Though the reader may be shocked at the graphic nature of such candor, this paper as an authentic performance piece necessitates it. Says Park-Fuller: "In autobiographical narrative

performances, the performer often speaks about acts of social transgression. In doing so, the telling of the story itself becomes a transgressive act – a revealing of what has been kept hidden, a speaking of what has been silenced – an act of reverse discourse that struggles with the preconceptions borne in the air of dominant politics" (2000).

[4] Some Korean secondary school teachers often jokingly reflect upon their situation by referring to themselves as *teaching machines*.

References

Bernauer, J., & Rasmussen, D. (Eds.). (1988). *The final Foucault*. Cambridge: MIT.

Bess, M., & Foucault, M. (1980). *Power, moral values, and the intellectual: An interview with Michel Foucault* (Interview transcript). Retrieved from http://www.vanderbilt.edu/historydept/michaelbess/Foucault%20Interview

Block, A. (2008). Why Should I Be a Teacher? In *Journal of Teacher Education, 59,* 416-427.

Camus, A. (2000). *The myth of Sisyphus*. London: Penguin.

Ceisel, C. (2009). Checking the box: A Journey through my hybrid identity. *Cultural Studies – Critical Methodologies, 9*(5), 661-668.

Cox, A. (2005). What are communities of practice? A comparative review of four seminal works. *Journal of Information Science, 31*(6), 527-540.

Deleuze, G. (2002). The actual and the virtual. In G. Deleuze., & C. Parnet. *Dialogues*. New York: Columbia University.

Deleuze, G., & Guattari, F. (1992). *A thousand plateaus*. London: Continuum.

Devault, M. (1997). Personal writing in social research. In H. Rosanna (Ed.), *Refexivity and Voice*. Los Angeles: Sage.

Dreyfuss, H., & Rabinow, P. (Eds). (1983). *Michel Foucault: Beyond structuralism and hermeneutics.* Chicago: University of Chicago.

Eisner, E. (2006). The satisfactions of teaching. *Educational Leadership, 63*(6), 44-46.

Etcoff, N., Orbach, S., Scott, J., & D'Agostino, H. (2004). *The real truth about beauty: A global report – Findings of the global study on women, beauty and well-being.* Retrieved from http://www.campaignforrealbeauty.com/uploadedfiles/dove_white_paper_final.pdf

Foucault, M. (1979). *Discipline and punish: The birth of the prison.* New York: Vintage.

Foucault, M. (1988). The ethic of care for the self as a practice of freedom. In J. Bernauer., & D. Rasmussen (Eds.), *The Final Foucault.* Cambridge: MIT.

Freire, P. (2000). *Pedagogy of the oppressed: 30th anniversary edition.* New York: Continuum.

Giroux, H. (2004). Critical pedagogy and the postmodern/modern divide: Towards a pedagogy of democratization. *Teacher Education Quarterly, Winter 2004,* 31-47.

Giroux, H. (2009). Afterword: End times in America – Religious fundamentalism and the crisis of democracy. In S. Steinberg., & J. Kincheloe (Eds.), *Christotainment: Selling Jesus through Popular Culture.* Boulder: Westview.

Glovinski, P. (2004). Ceausescu's children: The process of democratization and the plight of Romania's orphans. *A Worldwide Journal of Politics, Fall 2004.* Retrieved from http://lilt.ilstu.edu/critique/Fall%202004/Peter_Gloviczki.pdf

Greenwell, K. (2004). *The Effects of Child Welfare Reform on Levels of Child Abandonment and Deinstitutionalization in Romania (1987-2000).* Unpublished doctoral dissertation, University of Texas, Austin, TX. Retrieved from http://www.crin.org/docs/Greenwell%20-%20Romania.pdf

Gutting, G. (Ed.). (1994). *The Cambridge companion to Foucault.* Cambridge: Cambridge University.

Illich, I. (2000). *Deschooling society.* London: Marion Boyars.

Kincheloe, J. (2005). Autobiography and critical ontology: Being a teacher, developing a reflective persona. In W. M Roth (Ed.), *Auto/Biography and Auto/Ethnography: Praxis of Research Method.* Rotterdam: Sense.

Kritzman, L. (Ed.). (1988). *Politics, philosophy, culture: Interviews and other writings 1977-1984.* New York: Routledge.

Lukes, S. (2002). Power and agency. *British Journal of Sociology,* 53(3), 491-496.

Lovecraft, H. (2002). *The call of Cthulhu and other weird stories.* London: Penguin.

Mali, T. (2005). What teachers make. Retrieved from http://www.ted.com/talks/taylor_mali_what_teachers_make.html

Palmer, P. (2003). Teaching with heart and soul: Reflections on spirituality in teacher education. *Journal of Teacher Education,* (54)5, 376-385.

Park-Fuller, L. (2000). Performing absence: The staged personal narrative as testimony. *Text and Performance Quarterly, 20,* 20-42.

Paton, A. (2003). *Cry, the beloved country.* New York: Scribner.

Pelias, R. (1998). *Performative writing as scholarship: An apology, an argument, an anecdote.* Paper presented at the National Communication Association Convention. New York.

Pennycook, A. The social politics and the cultural politics of language classrooms. In P. Richard-Amato (Ed.), *Making it happen: From interactive to participatory language teaching.* White Plains: Pearson Education.

Rabinow, P. (Ed.). (1984). *The Foucault reader.* New York: Pantheon.

Richardson, L. (1993). Writing: A method of inquiry. Y. Lincoln & N. Denzin (Eds.), *Handbook of Qualitative Research*. Thousand Oaks: Sage.

Rosanna, H. (Ed.). (1997). *Refexivity and voice*. Los Angeles: Sage.

Richard-Amato, P. (Ed.). (2003). *Making it happen: From interactive to participatory language teaching*. White Plains: Pearson Education.

Smith, D. (2009). Categories are not enough. *Gender & Society, (23)*1, 76-80.

Spry, T. (2001). Performing autoethnography: An embodied methodological praxis. *Qualitative inquiry*, 7(6), 706-732.

Warren, J. (2001). Absence for whom? An autoethnography of white subjectivity. *Cultural Studies – Critical Methodologies, (1)*1, 36-49.

Widder, N. (2004). Foucault and power revisited. *European Journal of Political Theory*, 3(4), 411-432.

Wiesel, E. (2004). Interview. Retrieved from http://nobelprize.org/nobel_prizes/peace/laureates/1986/wiesel-interview.html

Zizek, S. (1997). *The plague of fantasies*. London: Verso.

23. The JungChul Cyber English Learning Program

MiSug Gu
David Kent

These days there is an increasing desire for foreign language learning in South Korea, particularly for English. With widespread availability of technology in Korea, the computer has come to be regarded by many as an indispensable study aid that, when coupled with access to hi-speed broadband, provides a wealth of internet-based learning systems. As cyberspace increasingly becomes a popular way of easily finding and interacting with language learning content, it is important to consider the basic factors of available foreign language learning systems, particularly in light of the advantages and limitations of providing access to these systems via the internet. The potential of one such system, the JungChul cyber English learning program, to provide internet-based English education was reviewed. It was found that the program was partially useful for studying but that it did have some limitations. Overall, the program provides useful content for listening and pronunciation skill development. However, it was not as efficient in delivering writing or conversation training, and especially for conversation, lacked support for interaction between presenters and learners. So too, for reading and grammar the content is too similar to what can be found provided by off-line methods of education.

Introduction

The English education sector in Korea today needs to search for a new and efficient way of providing learning due to recent developments of multimedia. Learners need this new variety of methods as education courses are being provided using the internet and computers and as the learning requirements and interests of a new generation are changing. The rapid growth and development of the web has become an important issue in recent computer-assisted language learning (CALL) research and practice, along with discussions of the potential role of the web in the learning and teaching of English as a Foreign Language (EFL). In this regard, a number of researchers and practitioners (Allodi, 1998; Bell, 1998; Felix, 1999, 2001; Li & Hart, 1996; Murray & McPherson, 2004; Son, 2005, 2007) argue that the web offers a global database of authentic materials that can enhance language learning and teaching. There is thus a need for developing ways of using the web effectively and efficiently (Son, 2007).

As cyber lectures and cyber colleges have been appearing, web based education has been used in many areas (Son, 2007). Also in the foreign language education sector, web based education has allowed for personal learning possibilities through digital means, from which it is possible to educate students according to their level. Even though it is possible to learn from such computer-based classes, if the content is not pedagogically sound and students are computer illiterate, studies show the effect of this education to be low (see Yeh, 2004). So, in this regard, many cyber-based educational learning systems may need to be supplemented with traditional learning materials, and their benefits and detriments for learning identified. Therefore, in this article, we will briefly touch on the advantages of using the Internet for English language learning before providing a concise review of the JungChul cyber English learning program.

Using Internet-Based Systems for English Language Learning
A number of researchers highlight the advantages of using the internet for foreign language learning (see Felix, 1999, 2001; Son, 2005, 2007). These advantages include no restrictions on the place and the time of learning, interoperability, flexibility for

updating learning data, diversity of data, and the relatively low ongoing costs of delivery (Davey, 2005; Graves, 2001; Kim, 2006; Pai, 2005).

Further, Davey (2005) claims that many of the precepts of current pedagogy are satisfied by using the internet to learn English, for example material is up-to-date, readily available, and the language used is authentic. Having outdated materials is a problem which course planners often have to face when using the traditional sources of classroom materials. If material becomes too outdated, it can also prove demotivational for students, particularly younger learners. On the other hand, authentic material can prove motivational, interesting, and useful to learners. A large amount of authentic content useful to English language learners can be found on the internet from newspapers, to travel timetables, as well as online shopping sites, and even weather forecasts information. Teachers can also use student-centered internet-based publishing tools such as blogs and wikis to allow learners to become creators rather than passive recipients of learning. In this regard, one of the most important facets of the English education using the internet is Computer Mediated Communication (CMC). CMC allows for anywhere anytime interaction using everyday contexts that can foster communicative competence by increasing target language output and student motivation (Ware, 2005; see also Davey, 2005).

Contrary to the advantages of learning English that are made available through the internet, there are also a number of limitations stemming from use of the internet to access programs for learning English. These limitations include the dynamic nature of the internet itself, along with a lack of regulation, technical problems, and ongoing financial costs (Belz, 2003). While the dynamic nature of the Internet ensures that the latest information is available it also means that web pages and links often change or disappear, with a lack of regulation ensuring that it is not easy to be certain that the information being accessed is accurate or correct (Davey, 2005). One way to help minimize such a problem is to ensure that teachers and students can effectively evaluate the content they access for learning on the internet. As for technical problems, slow access speeds or inadequate support or training in hardware use can lead to frustration for both teachers and learners trying to use systems for learning (O'Dowd, 2003). Costs, although quite low in Korea, can still prove prohibitively high for some parents and individuals. The financial burden associated with internet access through conventional means include the cost of the computer hardware itself along with content provider charges, and ongoing learning program subscription fees (Ware, 2005).

A Brief Overview of the JungChul Cyber English Learning Program

This section details a brief evaluation of an internet-based English language learning system. This system is the JungChul Cyber English Learning Program (JungChul Language R & D, 2010).

General Characteristics of Listening and Conversation Provision through Internet-Based Software

A characteristic of some internet-based learning systems regarding listening and conversation provision is that learners can listen to and repeat out loud the contents to which they are listening, although this method works equally well with mp3 or cassette provided material. Learners can also hear explanations provided by content experts or native speakers just as readily with local market produced offline systems. However, learners may find internet-based systems can be used more readily due to the nature of access and content provision, as off-line systems provide static content that is generally not updated. So too, internet-based systems can be used at times of convenience for learners and allow them to select content for themselves that matches their levels (Son, 2005, 2007; Yeh, 2004). As such, for English conversation, on-line systems largely offer self-training. This sees learners just listening and repeating the sentences presented to them, so many on-line programs (unless providing real-life tutors via chat or webcam) are still not readily usable foreign language conversation practice (Pallos, 2005; Yeh, 2004).

The JungChul Listening and Conversation Component
The JungChul cyber English learning program material presents listening and conversation material through several steps. These steps are: (a) Get Ready; (b) Listen In 1; (c) Listen In 2; (d) Conversation 1; (e) Conversation 2; (f) Conversation 3; (g) Expressions; (h) Mission; and, (i) Wrap Up.

In 'Get Ready', learners can hear the overview of the lesson, see and animation preview, and hear a simple conversation in this step. In 'Listen In 1', learners can listen to three kinds of conversations presented by an animation in each lesson. If learners want to listen again, they can click the picture that is on the right side of the screen. So, learners can practice English conversation skills repeatedly through this step. In 'Listen In 2', learners can listen to the conversation in 'Listen In 1' again. Learners can also check and test for memorization regarding the repeated conversation they have been reviewing for learning purposes. In 'Conversation 1', 'Conversation 2', and 'Conversation 3', learners can review and check three different kinds of conversations. The 'Conversation 3' step is composed of the three stages of Strategies, Practice, and Role Play. The Strategies stage shows a skit in which the presenter explains the content to be learned before translating each sentence from the previous step. The Practice stage allows for practice of conversation skills along with Role-Play where the user can select one dialogue and play the role of a person in the conversation. In 'Expressions', learned expressions can be practiced by clicking on the words or expressions from a list. In 'Mission', learners can say a sentence to their partner in a conversation using the appropriate expressions from those previously provided through the system. Finally, in 'Wrap Up', learners can review the sentences that they acquired from the program, and complete the conversation, completing cloze exercises using appropriate expressions.

General Characteristics of Reading and Writing Provision through Internet-Based Software

In reading and writing, internet-based systems are often similar to off-line systems, especially when users repeat and memorize new words for themselves and repeat reading sentences as needed. Yet one advantage of online systems over offline systems is that learners can ask questions on forums or message boards in written form (Johnson & Heffernan, 2006; Son, 2005, 2007; Yeh, 2004), and this advantage is applied in the JungChul Cyber English language learning program.

The JungChul Reading and Writing Component

The JungChul cyber English learning program reading engine is composed of: (a) Start up; (b) Read the Text; (c) Dividing chunk; (d) Lecture; (e) DIY; (f) Speaking in Word Order; (g) Absorbing Listening; and, (h) Write It Up.

The software uses Flash for reading elements of the program. The 'Start up' section is composed of 'before we start', 'question', and 'listening to explanation' components. In 'before we start', the presenter introduces the program, and in 'question' provides vocabulary test that will be given again in the reading comprehension element of the program. After this, in 'listening to explanation', the presenter explains the vocabulary that was previously tested. In 'Read the Text', a text file is provided for reading and the user should read the sentences in a set time. After that, a test of vocabulary based on the sentences is presented. In 'Dividing Chunk', the user is tasked to divide sentences into appropriate learning chunks, while in 'Lecture', the presenter explains how to read and interpret the whole text sentence by sentence, dividing the sentences appropriately chunk by chunk. In 'DIY' learners can hear the sentences if they click the speaker button in front of each sentence, and in 'Speaking in Word Order', they can repeat the previously studied sentences out loud in English after hearing the sentence spoken in Korean by the presenter. In 'Absorbing Listening', users can just relax and listen to the sentences previously studied. Finally, in 'Write It Up', learners can type translations of important sentences in English after they are first provided to them in Korean. Through these steps, practice is provided for not only reading but also listening and writing.

General Characteristics of Vocabulary and Pronunciation Provision through Internet-Based Software

Learning vocabulary and pronunciation using an off-line system is possible utilizing word practice and pronunciation drills. When using word practice exercises it is possible to practice a variety of words and the sentences related to the subject, and link these to pronunciation drills. However, generally with internet-based systems, word practice exercises revolve around showing word lists combined with exercises that practice the pronunciation of the main words (Johnson & Heffernan, 2006; Chun & Plass, 1996a, 1996b; Cropp, Cumming, & Sussex, 1994; Gupta, Olohan, & Zahner, 1994; Son, 2001, 2005, 2007; Yeh, 2004).

The JungChul Vocabulary and Pronunciation Component

The JungChul cyber English learning program vocabulary and pronunciation engine is composed of: (a) Mind Mapping; (b) Self Training; (c) Mini Test; (d) Actual Test; and, (e) Sum-Up.

The vocabulary software engine introduces everyday vocabulary, special vocabulary, and business vocabulary. In 'Mind Mapping', the program uses mind maps as a means for learners to absorb new vocabulary items. In the program, they take an example, such as traveling, and then the presenter presents one word. After that, the presenter extracts the vocabulary items which are related to the word. So, the user can begin to think about the words related to one special subject here. It is a useful method for students to learn many kinds of words. In 'Self Training', users can listen to and repeat words which the presenter provided in the previous step. Also, in this portion of the program learners can listen to the sentences and repeat them using these words. In 'Mini Test', users are tested on vocabulary and review items learned. This is achieved by presenting learners with a cloze exercise that must be completed within a set five-second period. In 'Actual Test', ten questions based on the previously learned sentences are asked and by each there is a blank that must be filled in with an appropriate vocabulary item. Finally, in 'Sum-Up', a summary of the words and sentences previously presented is provided with the method for learning based on repetition.

General Characteristics of Grammar and Speaking Provision through Internet-Based Software

On-line grammar programs offer learners an abundance of material but some provide an overwhelming amount of information that learners may find difficult to understand and work through effectively. So too, the importance of practicing pronunciation when studying vocabulary is recognized (Son,

2005, 2007; Yeh, 2004), and for this it is useful to use internet-based programs because in the conventional method it is very difficult to practice pronunciation by oneself without access to partners or feedback.

The JungChul Grammar and Speaking Component
The JungChul cyber English learning program grammar and speaking engine is composed of: (a) Lecture; (b) Exercise; (c) Activity Time I; and, (d) Activity Time II.

In 'Lecture', there are three kinds of lecture listed at the top of the screen that include 'First Try', 'Today's Point', and 'Speaking Practice'. In 'First Try', there is a picture which shows some materials in a room. The presenter provides a word list that matches the materials in the picture with the presenter providing prepositions and words according to the position and content of the material. In 'Today's Point', there are some pictures that represent the position of the materials. In this step, the presenter asks the user to practice the sentences by saying the aloud with the prepositions and the words previously shown. In 'Speaking Practice', the presenter reviews and repeats the prepositions and the words that have been studied. In 'Exercise', expressions learned in the previous step are reviewed and tested. In 'Activity Time I ', questions and answers are practiced using expressions studied in the previous steps. Finally, in 'Activity Time II', expressions previously studied can be practiced with online partners.

Conclusion
The internet has developed into something that plays a very important role in our everyday lives. On the internet there are very many foreign language learning programs to practice speaking, listening, writing, reading, vocabulary and other language skills. Although these programs may contribute to

learners' acquisition of English as a foreign language, a number of programs have limitations. We sought to outline the basic advantages of using internet-based systems for English language learning, and briefly provide an overview of one program that provides English language learning.

The JungChul cyber English language program is representative of on-line English programs available in Korea, and was thus reviewed. The program provides a variety of methods for practicing reading, writing, speaking, vocabulary learning, and pronunciation practice, and uses a number of materials to do so efficiently. However, for grammar and reading practice the program provided learning in a similar fashion to off-line education methods. So, for these skills it may prove better to actually work with existing off-line contents rather than using the program. This was also found for the writing and conversation sections. For writing, the method of education is similar to that applied for offline grammar education in many contexts. For conversation, the education method of the program lacked interaction between the presenter and the learners with learners just watching a video and being expected to repeat the conversation.

In conclusion, for some parts of English education, an internet based education method is useful, but for others it is not. Ultimately, it may prove better for many educators to use both internet available materials along with offline contents in a complementary fashion.

References

Allodi, A., Dokter, D., & Kuipers, H. W. A. E. (1998). WELLS: Web-enhanced language learning. In S. Jager, J. Nerbonne, & A. V. Essen (Eds.), *Language teaching and language technology* (123-135). Lisse: Swets & Zeitlinger.

Bell, C. (1998). Everone's using the web, so why aren't we? Web design and the ESOL teacher. *CAELL Journal, 8*(4), 8-12.

Belz, J. A. (2003). Linguistic perspectives on the development of intercultural competence in telecollaboration. *Language Learning & Technology, 7*(2), 68-117.

Chun, D. M., & Plass, J. L. (1996a). Effects of multimedia annotations on vocabulary acquisition. *Modern Language Journal, 80,* 183-198.

Chun, D. M., & Plass, J. L. (1996b). Facilitating reading comprehension with multimedia. *System, 24,* 503-519.

Cropp, S., Cumming, G., & Sussex, R. (1994). On-line lexical resources for language learners: Assessment of some approaches to word definition. *System, 22,* 369-377.

Davey, I. (2005). The Use of the Internet in CALL: Opportunities and Limitations. *Ritsumeikan Studies in Language and Culture, 17*(1).

Graves, W. H. (2001). *Framework for an E-Learning Strategy.* ELI Meetings: Educause Publications.

Gupta, G., Olohan, M., & Zahner, C. (1994). Lexical resources in CALL. *Computers & Education, 23,* 75-80.

Johnson, A., & Heffernan, N. (2006). The Short Readings Project: A CALL reading activity utilizing vocabulary recycling. *Computer Assisted Language Learning, 19*(1), 63–77.

JungChul Language R & D. (2010). JungChul Cyber. Retrieved April 07, 2010, from http://cyber.jungchul.com

Kim, J.Y. (2006). A survey on mobile-assisted language learning. *Modern English Education, Modern English Education, 7*(2), 57-69.

Li, R. C., & Hart, R. S. (1996). What can the World Wide Web offer ESL teachers? *TESOL Journal, 6*(2), 5–10.

Murray, D. E., & McPherson P. (2004). Using the web to support language learning. Sydney: NCELTR.

O'Dowd, R. (2003). Understanding the "other side": Intercultural learning in a Spanish-English E-Mail exchange. Language Learning & Technology, 7(2), 118-144. Retrieved from http://llt.msu.edu/vol7num2/odowd

Pai, H.K. (2005). *E learning, U-Learning, Community and School Education*. Seoul: Sejin Publishing.

Pallos, L. (2005). Speak to the Computer: Speaking Practice for the Language Learner. In P. Kommers & G. Richards (Eds.), *Proceedings of ED-MEDIA 2005: World Conference on Educational Multimedia, Hypermedia and Telecommunications*, Norfolk: Association for the Advancement of Computing in Education (AACE), 3292-3297.

Son, J. B. (2001). CALL and vocabulary learning: A review. *English Linguistic Science, 7*, 27-35.

Son, J. B. (2005). Making web-based language learning meaningful. *Paper presented at the Second International Conference on Pedagogies and Learning*, The University of Southern Queensland, Toowoomba, Australia.

Son, J. B. (2007). Learner Experiences in Web-based Language Learning. *Computer Assisted Language Learning, 20*(1), 21–36.

Ware, P. (2005). 'Missed' Communication in online communication: Tensions in a German-American telecollaboration. *Language Learning & Technology, 9*(2), 64-89. Retrieved from http://llt.msu.edu/vol9num2/ware/default.html

Yeh, J. (2004). Suggestions for effective methods of teaching webbased college practical English. Modern English Education, 5(2), 154-172.

Young, R. (1980). Modular course design. In ELT documents: Projects in Material Design. Hemel Hempstead: Macmillan.

24. English Quest – A Large Scale, Task-Based Activity

Joel Hopkinson

As teachers we often think about creating fun, educational activities for our students, especially as a reward for completing a large body of work or an important test. Starting with the basic idea of a scavenger hunt, various pedagogical theories inspired a framework that led to the development of a special, educational event called "English Quest". English Quest could be described as an activity that is teacher-guided, Task-Based, large-scale, and potentially can be used with multiple classes at the same time. It works well with any Communicative Language Teaching (CLT) curriculum, involves pair-work or group-work in Cooperative Language Learning type activities, can include Topic-Based or Content-Based themes, and can also involve activities that are inspired by the Total Physical Response method (see Nunan, 2003 for a description of CLT, Richards, 2005, and Richards & Rodgers, 2001, for descriptions of Cooperative Language Learning, Content-Based Learning, Task-Based Language Teaching, and Total Physical Response).

There are elements of learner-centeredness in this activity as well. The students learn through practical application and multiple learner strategies are needed to complete different tasks. The students can choose who in their group is going to do certain tasks and at various times mix between doing them as a group or as an individual. However, these activities are also teacher-guided in that the teacher sets up the entire activity and spends a lot of time planning it. There is the potential for many paths to be run by the students but in the end, it is the teacher who has planed the parameters of the activity and makes sure that the students do not get lost or wander too far off-task.

Learning Context

The English Quest activity was conducted three times in three slightly different contexts. However there were some common factors in all of them, namely:

1. The activity involved was held in a South Korean university using students who were Korean learners of English as a foreign language.
2. More than one teacher was involved in the activity.
3. There were multiple classes that participated in this activity sometimes on the same day.
4. English Quest was run after the midterm test.
5. For the first two English Quests, on one of the days of the week a class would do the English Quest and on at least one of the other days of the week, their class would be interrupted by another class who was doing the activity.

English Quest 1 (EQ1) was conducted using students from the same faculty and year (Tourism and Convention Major second year students). Each class did the activity separately. There were two teachers involved: an Active or Teaching Teacher whose class was running the activity and the Support Teacher.

English Quest 2 (EQ2) used three teachers, the Teaching teacher and two Support teachers, one who looked after the tongue twister/ food challenge; and the second in charge of the physical challenge. This was the first time that we had three teachers and that we used costumes as a challenge in which the students had to dress up to complete an activity. The students involved were all from the same faculty and year. Each class did the English quest separately. We had learned a lot from the last time and this one ran a lot more smoothly. We also looked at parts of the building that we did not use in the first one. This time, there was also a lot more returning to a teacher to check that certain tasks had been completed satisfactorily so that the students' progress could be monitored to prevent them from becoming lost.

English Quest 3 (EQ3) had four teachers involved in the planning process, although on the actual day of the event only three ran the activity. The event was held in a single, large room and involved each teacher working a station with the students moving between stations to complete tasks. Three classes participated in the event at the same time. They were from different majors and probably did not know each other.

Materials and Resources
When planning each of these English Quests, we tried to keep the costs down to below 10,000 Korean won per teacher (roughly $10). The resources for English Quest can be organized under several categories: Place, Surroundings, Human, Office Supplies, and Other.

Choosing the place to hold your English Quest is going to be one of the most important decisions that you will have to make. Early incarnations used an eight story university building and had clues, tasks, challenges and/ or directions on nearly every floor including the basements. The third English Quest, as mentioned before, did not leave the room.

We considered having an English Quest on a soccer field but were worried about weather and the difficulties of ensuring that the space would be available on the day. A few of the activities also involved the students going into nearby buildings, to complete tasks that asked the students to record the price of one of the menu items in the school cafeteria, or asked what art exhibit was on the second floor of a certain building.

English Quest – A Large Scale, Task-Based Activity

The furniture, fixtures and other miscellaneous items that make up the environment of the space where you will do your English Quest are also a resource. An old bookcase, an empty locker, and a large mirror may be a great place to hide a clue or directions. Vending machines and posters may provide useful answers to questions that the students have to fill out on a worksheet to show that they have completed a task. If there are any distinguishing features, gardens, or equipment that you can use as a reference in a clue or direction, you should seriously consider doing so. Dark corners in basements may provide a great setting for a spooky Halloween jack-o-lantern with a clue sitting beside it, or a small pine tree in the garden can be decorated like a Christmas tree and have clues hidden underneath it.

The human resources include the teachers who are participating in the English Quest, other teachers who may have their office in the building, the students themselves, or other staff that may be able help. Every English Quest has had at least two teachers actively involved in its creation and implementation; however, we found using three teachers added an extra dimension to the event that was dynamic and interesting.

Although you may not want to bother other people who are not involved in your English Quest too much, some may be interested in helping out. EQ3 had a Halloween challenge that involved the students dressing up in costume and 'trick or treating' the office staff. The staff then gave the students a chocolate bar that had the next clue wrapped around it. We also gave directions to different professor's offices and asked the students to record information on a worksheet. This information can be in the form of a simple question like: "Whose office is it?" to more detailed questions about their contact hours, schedules or any pictures they might have on their door.

Another group of people that you are going to have to communicate with are the security and cleaning staff. You do not want to go through all of the effort of setting up your clues and props just to find out that the cleaners have thrown some of them in the garbage. A letter translated into a language they can read is a good start and maybe some signs saying that this pile of what looks like scrap paper is actually part of an activity.

The students themselves are a resource although it is best to not rely too heavily on them bringing their own supplies and to always have a back-up plan. Many students have mobile phones with English/Korean dictionaries on then that they can use during the English Quest. Also they may call you if they get lost or even as one of the tasks they have to do. When making groups for the English Quest it might be best to make sure that there are members of mixed English ability.

The facilities and equipment needed for the English quest will depend on what sort of tasks and challenges you have in mind. You will need enough paper for clues, directions, puzzles, worksheets and anything else that the students need. You might also need envelopes to put the clues in but you can also get creative and put clues in balloons and boxes. You might need colored card to make displays and props with. Costumes and face paint are useful if you want to include this in some sort of challenge. Halloween jack-o-lanterns, Christmas ornaments or decorations from other festive occasions can be used too.

Aims and Goals

The goals of this lesson are to provide an interesting method of active learning that requires the students as a group to use English to solve various puzzles and problems, complete tasks, follow directions, gather information and answer specific questions. These tasks require additional skills other than

English ability thereby allowing students with low levels of English skill to meaningfully participate in the group. Some cultural information and vocational skills may also be used in the themes and tasks of individual activities.

Creating a fun and energetic activity was an important goal of English Quest because we wanted to reward the students for the hard work they had done towards their mid term examinations, and to create a relatively stress-free environment for learning to take place. Of course, any activity that involves winning and losing cannot be said to be stress-free however, in this case the stress involved was relatively low level and part of the fun. The students were not stressed about using English, rather they were driven by a willingness to complete tasks and reach check points before the other groups they were competing against.

The aims of this lesson are therefore as follows: to give the students a fun and positive experience learning English so that they feel more confident, have a more positive attitude, and be more inclined to study autonomously; to use language items from the course text book such as language for giving directions, money, food, and other new vocabulary in various tasks, puzzles and clues so that the student gains experience using them in a context other than the traditional classroom; to encourage class cohesiveness; and to encourage the students to develop the creative-thinking, problem-solving, clue-finding, and team-building skills that are useful in many other contexts of everyday and working life.

Implementation

For a pair or small group of teachers to successfully run something as large as English Quest takes a lot of preparation and organization. From start to finish, you should plan two to three weeks ahead of time. The first thing you have to do is find other teachers who are willing to work with you. There will be a fair bit of work done so everyone has to be sure that they are going to contribute some time to the preparation, pre-teaching their students, supplying or creating materials, and setting everything up on the day.

Once you know where you will hold your English Quest, you are going to have to walk the area and find things that you can use in the English Quest. When we were using an entire building, we walked every floor looking for things that we could use.

You should also plan where all of the teachers who are participating will be at that time, so that the students can visit their classrooms or offices. It may be a minor interruption to their class but it can be incorporated into the lesson. For example, we had a task that involved the students saying a tongue twister, and then having to eat a food challenge before gaining the next clue. The teacher who was running the activity would teach their class tongue twisters that day, getting the students in the class to come up and say the tongue twisters in front of the class. Then in the middle of all this performance anxiety, there is a knock at the door. Three to five students walk in the door asking about a clue, but to get it they have to go in front of the class and recite one of the tongue twisters that was taught.

All of the teachers involved will have to meet together after walking around the building and create a flow chart of all the clues, puzzles, tasks, road blocks, challenges, and directions that the students will encounter during the English Quest. Once you have a rough flow chart, a script should be created. This document is for the teacher so that they can monitor the students' progress through the English Quest and help them if they get lost or confused. Furthermore, all of the clues, task explanations, tongue twisters, directions, worksheets, puzzles, and codes that might be used in an English Quest will need to be made, photocopied, and distributed or positioned so that each team has one copy on the day of the event.

Once you have a clear idea of what sorts of things that your English Quest will contain, you will have to develop ways that you can scaffold this activity with your class so that they have a good idea about what to do on the day. I have used a vocabulary sheet as homework with lots of useful language for following directions and common items that the students may encounter in the building during the English Quest.

If you are going to use codes or hidden message word searches, then you should give the students some experience doing these things in a non-competitive environment before the English Quest. I use the discovery education puzzle maker (Discovery Education, 2010) to create a hidden message word search that has the sentence: 'The first student to stand behind their chair and put their book on their head wins a prize' as a scaffolding exercise. I tell the students that they should complete the word search made with vocabulary from their textbook and do what the hidden message says. Note that, you may have to adapt this activity depending on the context, putting things on a person's head might not be appropriate in some cultures.

Two things you want to avoid are helping the students too much during the English Quest, and having them lose hope and interest because they cannot figure out how to do an activity or puzzle. Another thing that is also useful to do is to remind the students to wear comfortable clothes and sensible shoes so they can run around on the day that they do the English Quest.

On the day of the activity, it is good to give the students a worksheet with questions regarding the activities they did to fill out as they complete the English Quest. During the English Quest the clues might have questions that the students have to write down the answer too and show the teacher later. For example, a list of directions might take the students to another professor's office, and the students have to record whose office it is, or the directions might take the students to a sign or poster, and the students have to write down what it says.

You might also want to think about having a 'passport' or a sheet that the teachers sign to help you monitor their progress. As the students go to different teachers (and/ or the same teacher multiple times), the teacher signs that they have completed the task. Finally, tell the students to keep every clue, worksheet, puzzle etc. that they find. This helps you see where they made mistakes and also makes cleaning up afterwards less work.

Remind the students the day before that the next class is the English Quest. Ask the students to make sure they arrive on time for the event because if they arrive late they will miss out on some of the fun. Have the students make their teams before the event so that the team members can remind each other about the event and make sure that everyone arrives on time.

Lesson Plan
A minutely detailed lesson plan is impossible for an English Quest because it will greatly depend on your individual circumstances and the activities that you have designed for the class. Of all the incarnations of English Quest, the event has never gone the same way, even when you are using the same clues. However, as a general guide, the following can be used and an example of a script can also be found in the appendix to this article.

Time
Planning for around one and a half hours is good, with 10 minutes allotted to each puzzle or task. Some students will be quicker than this but for the majority, this is a good time.

Preparation
In addition to what has been previously mentioned in the implementation section, you are going to have to arrive approximately thirty minutes early to set up all the clues. Additionally, you might want to be a bit secretive about it so that the students do not see you setting up the clues.

Introduction
When everyone is ready, give the students the worksheet that they will have to fill out and explain to the students what they have to do. Make sure that they know to come and talk to you if they get confused. Also make sure that they know to keep all the clues that they find to show you afterwards. The first clue we give is usually a code or hidden message word search because it takes some time and spaces out when the students leave to find the next clue so they cannot follow each other. Alternatively, it may be a good idea for the first few clues to send each group of students to different places and tell the students that this will happen so that they are less tempted to cheat.

Troubleshooting
Make sure that your clues are clearly worded. Also make sure that the directions are right and each step links up with the next one properly. Walk through the English Quest in your imagination before the event so that you are sure that everything is in order.

As with any sort of competition you have be on the watch for cheating. Sometimes this is just laziness on the students' behalf or a desire to avoid embarrassment. If you explain to the students that they can come back to the classroom at any time to get help and that they are not to cheat, then most of this sort of thing can be kept to a minimum.

Clean Up
After each event is over you are going to have to walk through the building and pick up any leftover clues or garbage that may be left behind.

Acknowledgements
The author would like to thank Ezekiel Mentillo, Curtis Desjardins and Isaac Bretz for their help with the English Quests.

References
Boggleseworld. (2010). *Boggles World ESL.* Retrieved from http://bogglesworldesl.com
Brown, H. D. (2007). *Principles of Language Learning and Teaching.* New York: Pearson Education.
Discovery Education. (2010). *Puzzle Maker.* Retrieved from http://puzzlemaker.discoveryeducation.com
Nunan, D. (Ed.). (2003). *Practical English Language Teaching: International Edition.* New York, McGraw-Hill Companies, Inc.
Richards, J. C. (2005). *Curriculum Development in Language Teaching.* Cambridge: Cambridge University Press.
Richards, J. C., & Rogers, T. S. (2001). *Approaches and Methods in Language Teaching.* Cambridge: Cambridge University Press.

25. Making Students Critical Readers in a Korean Middle School Reading Class
YooJin Sohn

I think teaching students critical thinking skills is very important because through this teaching students become more active during class and expand their breadth of knowledge. While teaching critical thinking skills, I believe students will increase their ability to think from various perspectives and to think more deeply and widely. To accomplish this, I believe teachers' guidance is also a very important factor that we should not forget. The things that teachers should consider to design a successful critical reading class, I think, are the choice of the book and the design of some questions to accompany the book. Casting tips, questions to help students engage with the material, will provide them with fresh views of the issues they are going to discuss, help them break out of stereotypical ways of thinking, and help them open up their minds to new or different views of the issues. I chose the novel "A Step from Heaven" by Anna as material to use for a critical reading class because I thought it deals with issues that students are interest in and that many students might have encountered or soon will. I also tried to apply several criticisms of this book into their reading to help students have more critical views of the contents of the book.

Literature in the Korean Middle School Classroom

There are many benefits of using literature in an EFL class, and notable among them is that teachers, expose students to target language, encourage students to empathize with different characters and the viewpoints these characters embody, and provide them with plentiful issues to stimulate thinking. Along these lines, Collie & Slater found that "extensive reading increases a learner's receptive vocabulary and facilitates transfer to more active form of knowledge" (1987, 4). As for personal involvement, Collie & Slater found the following:

> Engaging imaginatively with literature enables learners to shift the focus of their attention beyond the more mechanical aspects of the foreign language system...the reader begins to 'inhabit' the text...he or she feels close to certain characters and shares their emotional responses. The language becomes, 'transparent' – the fiction summons the whole person into its own world (5-6).

It is this personal involvement in reading literature that I am interested in fostering in my students.

What Kind of materials do teachers provide students with? and *How important is teachers' well planned guidance to have a successful class?* These are the questions and thoughts that came up my mind while reading the article, "Exploring the possibilities for EFL Critical Pedagogy in Korea: A Two-Part Case Study" (Shin & Crookes, 2005). I was one of those people who thought Korean students are passive, and this is because we Koreans have learned according to Confucian learning styles; being critical of teachers or their lessons is regarded as rude behavior. To tell you the truth, I thought this pattern of thinking came from students, and even when I was a student in middle and high school, I never blamed teachers but myself. Also, the atmosphere which encourages students to freely talk about issues or how they think of something is usually not made in class, or at least was not when I studied. Students are afraid of sharing their opinions in front of teachers and peers because they do not want to be criticized or judged. In addition, they have not had enough opportunities to share ideas but usually get them from teachers in a direct way as in most banking models of education. In most lessons, students have not been given enough time to think about the issues on their own; this is especially true in English language class because students are busy working solely on the language itself, which is merely the transmission of knowledge from teachers to students. For these reasons, I locked myself in as a student, and others seems to have done the same thing as well. Also, as a teacher, though in my first year as a full-time teacher I am a relatively new teacher, I still haven't even made a good trial lesson to attempt to elicit students' capabilities and abilities to think and read critically. Based on Freire's thinking, Shin and Crookes suggest a problem-posing model of critical pedagogy as opposed to the so-called banking model (2005). They say it helps students "identify the issues they themselves see as problematic, and rather than 'solve' problems, reflects back these problems (problem-posing) as the driving force for a process of collaboratively constructed knowledge" (Shin & Crookes, 2005, 114). According to Freire,

> A problem-posing view of education sees the identification and analysis of problematic aspects of reality as central to the curriculum. The teacher's role is not to transmit knowledge, but to engage students in their own education by inviting them to enter into the process of thinking critically about their reality (as cited in Auerbach & Burgess, 1985, 165).

In many Korean classes, however, many teachers still conduct their classes using the Grammar Translation Method (GTM) and focus on an intensive reading of the text. After reading, in turn, they check the students' comprehension. Therefore, many classes are limited to teaching grammar and translation of English texts into Korean. Nonetheless, students do not acquire the level of grammar that the system expects them to obtain, and they still have difficulties translating texts. I was wondering why,1 despite all this effort, students' language proficiency levels are still unsatisfactory. GTM doesn't seem to fully motivate students to learn and use the language. Many teachers and students agree. This is especially telling in light of Laufer and Hulstijn's comment that "Motivation promotes success and achievement in L2 learning and that students who experience high amounts of an external or intrinsic drive or need to learn, will achieve higher levels of proficiency than students with low levels of drive" (2001, 1). In most schools, little class time is devoted to look at interpretation in depth and provide an opportunity for students to meaningful engage with texts by thinking of the issues themselves and how the issues relate to their own lives. I was one of those teachers who eliminated opportunities for students to expand their own knowledge, share their own opinions, and connect issues raised in class to the larger issues in life by not providing a venture for them to think deeply about various aspects of the literature listening to their peers' thoughts.

However, after taking some courses and becoming a teacher, I found myself thinking about the issues differently from what other teachers, professors, and some of my peers think, and thinking differently is not wrong at all. I know my students can think and have their own opinions to share, but I have realized that perhaps they think they are not allowed to do so as I thought before in my middle or high school years. I believe one of the roles of a teacher is to lead students to think critically and create an atmosphere that encourages students to do so. One of the best ways to do this is to design a class which has discussion activities. Once you apply critical theories to reading and let students share their thoughts with certain critical views during the discussion, the participation of students will increase, and students will have the chance to read literature more meaningfully and be motivated to use language more authentically. According to Collie and Slater,

> Helping students explore their own responses to literature helps students not only to acquire the confidence to develop, express and value their own response but also to become less dependent on received opinion and therefore more interested in and more able to assess other perspectives (1987, 9).

This led me to think what ways of approach I can adopt in middle and high school classes that to make my students into critical readers. First of all, I believe the materials should not be too burdensome, yet they should be appropriate to students' cognitive levels. This is because students here in Korea face difficulty even with English itself. The language they use as a tool to communicate with each other about critical issues requires high cognitive levels, so takes careful planning if one is to expect them to think critically about issues that they are going to discuss about the reading. At first, to be dreadfully honest, I thought critical reading is impossible to adapt to the language learning class where members are elementary or junior high school students since critical thinking itself is the hard thing to do for them, but I don't think this way anymore. Students have their own points of view no matter how old they are. Moreover, the materials should be interesting to evoke responses from students. The more they are related to students' interests, the better students' participation and likelihood of sharing their opinions will be. In other words, the lesson becomes more meaningful for students, and there are more things for students to talk about because those issues relate to their lives, or the themes that may emerge reflect issues that they have been through before. In addition, teachers need to provide students with appropriate guide lines for the materials provided that students can easily follow, which will help them to keep on track. Teachers can do this by casting appropriate questions which will lead students to think critically or elicit them to do so.

Some exemplary questions are these: open-ended questions, which enables students to think more deeply since it don't end with a single word, or evaluative questions, which don't have a certain correct answers but stimulate students' freer responses.

Using Reader-Response Criticism, Feminism, and Cultural Criticism to read *A Step from Heaven*

With the criteria for selecting teaching material I mentioned above in mind, I chose An Na's *A Step from Heaven* to use for teaching critical reading. The protagonist of this book is a girl who emigrated from Korea to America. I believe this book is interesting for students in Korea not only because it is a young adult novel, which matches the age of my students and their cognitive levels, but also because emigration and studying abroad are issues that students are interested in these days as many Korean students study abroad and emigrate. Alsup states similarly on the benefits of using this kind of literature, "Young adult literature seems to have special potential to help students understand their tumultuous time of life…YA literature often mirrors adolescent problems" (2003, 160). My Korean students can relate to the protagonist of *A Step from Heaven* because she is a Korean studying abroad. So, they can experience life in America vicariously through this character and more readily understand how she feels about cultural differences. Moreover, as the story depicts the life of a young adult, it consists of happenings that are similar to those students encounter in their homes in their relationships with their parents, brothers and sisters. Therefore, I believe not only does this content match students' cognitive levels, and the English level does not impose too much of a burden on them even if they are asked to read it with critical views, but this book also draws out students' active participation in discussions since the topics the book deals with are related to students' lives.

With this book in mind, I made a lesson plan which I can adopt to my class that would familiarize students with several critical theories: reader-response, feminism, and cultural criticism. Reader-response criticism, of course, centers on readers' responses to literary texts. The book that I am using functions as a stimulus that evokes students' responses gets them to think about the events that occur in the book. Teachers should encourage students to share their interpretations of the text so that the students can perceive how other student interpret the same text. Lois Tyson says "reader-response theorists believe that even the same reader reading the same text on two different occasions will probably produce different meanings because so many variables contribute to our experience of the text" (2006, 170). Letting students have open group discussion will develop interpretation of the book, and it will open various gates that enable students to think about the issue differently. Meanwhile, their original interpretations will become more dynamic and multi-dimensional.

By using feminist criticism when reading, we can talk about the gender roles depicted in the story and lead students to think about them and perceive oppression toward females portrayed in the novel. Also, teachers need to lead student to see the "gender role as a complex system of social relations and discursive practices, differentially constructed in local contexts" (Norton & Pavlenko, 2004, 504). I think it's important to get students to perceive the patriarchal factors illustrated in this novel because this will provide them with a viewpoint they can use to see the oppression of women in their own lives as well. It is much like lifting a veil: once the veil is lifted, the world is never seen with the same outlines again. Students can also notice the social aspects which change as the novel progresses, and by doing so, they will have some notion of how society is not static and how feminism can be a force for change. However, having students do this is not as easy as just saying it. Lois Tyson raised a pertinent question concerning feminist theory: "If patriarchal ideology influences our identity and experience so strongly, how can we ever get beyond it?" (2006, 93). While I cannot answer this on a theoretical level, on a practical level, the teacher's role is very important to prepare the students to engage in feminist readings. Teachers need to design questions or tips which stimulate students thinking and allow them to reconsider how stereotypes and gender roles.

Cultural criticism is also especially applicable to *A step from Heaven*. Not only does it readily suggest comparing the cultures of America and Korea, but as cultures change so rapidly, teachers can have students find aspects or events described in the story that do not match each culture any more. In other words, as time goes by, because culture changes, students can find some aspects of the cultures described which are not taken for granted any longer in the current period when they live.

I believe students mature in how they think while doing critical reading, and it becomes one of the ways that they can use to notice their own identity. While engaged in critical thinking, students have a chance to find themselves by thinking about issues and expanding their interpretative abilities while listening to others' interpretations. This is possible as Margaret said, "individuals bring lived histories to activities and events in situated environments, and it is through communications and interactions with others in these environments that learners negotiate and co-construct their view of themselves and the world" (2005, 61). Students will definitely have some moment in which they break their stereotypical thinking during class discussion because each student has a different identity and different reading style that is a result of her/his lived experiences. According to Hawkins,

> Situated environments have their own institutionally and culturally defined categories, ranked hierarchically through the community's values, beliefs, and practices...their forms of participation contribute to shaping and defining the environment (2005, 62).

Students will have a chance to shape their own identity through critical reading, which will in turn shape their larger environment: society at large. Not to mention, critical reading and the discussion that ensues from it will also "help students gain a multifaced view of the world and themselves" (Kincheloe, 1998, 13).

Conclusion

Hammond stated, "Critical pedagogy investigates the connections between knowledge, power, and culture" (2006, 545). Therefore, it is a teacher's roles to have students think about those connections while reading and help them take and state their own positions on the issues and be open to others' opinions. Critical reading will enable students to look at the same issue from alternative perspectives as well. To accomplish this goal, teachers need to create an open discussion atmosphere as well as choose appropriate materials that is are not too beyond students' cognitive levels nor language levels.

References

Alsup, J. (2003). Politicizing young adult literature: Reading Anderson's *Speak* as a critical text. *Journal of Adolescent and Adult Literacy*, 47(2), 158-166.

Auerbach, R. E., & Burgess, D. (2004). The Hidden Curriculum of Survival ESL. In Shor, I. *Freire for the Classroom: A sourcebook for a liberatory teaching* (150-167). Portsmouth, NH: Boynton/Cook Publishers.

Collie, J., & Slater, S. (1987). *Literature in the Language Classroom: A resource book of ideas and activities.* Cambridge: Cambridge University Press.

Hammond, K. (2006). More than a game: A critical discourse analysis of a racial inequality exercise in Japan. *TESOL Quarterly, 40*(3), 545-571.

Hawkins, R. M. (2005). Becoming a student: Identity work and academic literacy in early schooling. *TESOL Quarterly, 39*(1), 59-82.

Kincheloe, J. L., & Steinberg, S. R. (1998). Lesson plans from the outer limits: Unauthorized methods. In J. L. Kincheloe and S. R. Steinberg (Eds.), Unauthorized Methods: Strategies for Critical Teaching (1-21). New York: Routledge.

Laufer, B., & Hulstijn, J. (2001). Incidental vocabulary acquisition in a second language: The construct of task-induced involvement. *Applied linguistics, 22*(1), 1-26.

Na, An. (2002). *A Step from Heaven.* New York: Speak.

Norton, B., & Pavlenko, A. (2004). Addressing gender in the ESL/EFL classroom. *TESOL Quarterly, 38*(3), 504-514.

Shin, H., & Crookes, G. (2005). Exploring the possibilities for EFL critical pedagogy in Korea: A Two-Part Case Study. *Critical inquiry in language studies: An international journal, 2*(2), 113-136.

Tyson, L. (2006). *Critical theory today: A User-Friendly Guide* (2nd ed.). New York, NY: Routledge.

Appendix
Lesson Plan

Book Title: *A Step from Heaven* (Young Adult Novel, Winner of the 2002 Michael L. Printz Award)

Level: Middle school advanced class, probably best for a supplementary class after school with 8 to 10 learners

Synopsis
Young Ju travels to American, a land they regarded as 'heaven on earth,' only to discover that life is also full of adversity there and is not as different from life in Korea as they imagined. Young Ju has to deal with three kinds of conflict: conflict with her parents, cultural conflict, and her own internal conflict about her identity as a Korean/American.

Before Reading
Students freely share their thoughts about going to study abroad at a young age and problems they would expect to face. Students can do this as a pair work or as a small group activity. Teachers encourage students to talk about conflicts which they have had in relationships with their parents at home and the way they solve those problems. By doing this before reading, students will come personalize the content of the novel, and can draw on this material when they adopt certain criticisms while reading the novel. Here are exemplary questions:
- *What would be probable problems that you would face when you go abroad?*
- *How will you solve these problems?*
- *What would be cultural differences you will get through?*
- *Which country do you want to go abroad? And why that country?*

- *Have you ever thought your whole family emigrates to America? If yes, then what would your family's living look like in America?*
- *What do you think of going abroad at a young age?*
- *Why do you think people want to emigrate into other countries?*
- *When your parents are in a big fight and you witness the scene, what would be your reaction?*
- *What does your relationship with your parents look like?*

Criticisms that I want to Apply
Reader-response criticism, feminism, and cultural criticism are the main criticisms that I want my students to apply while reading this novel.

Imagine Being the Characters in the Book
First of all, have students find any scene that they think doesn't make sense from their point of view. Encourage students to find the characters' reactions to each conflict and to think and talk about the reasons why they act the way they do. Then have students put themselves into each character's place so that they can impose their own thoughts on that situation. After small group talk, they can reconstitute the story from their own, and they can do some role-plays.

Analyze the Cover
After reading, have students analyze the cover of the book as well. Their interpretation of the cover of the book will vary because their impressions will be different (Collie and Slater suggest this activity on pages 8-9)

Making Students Critical Readers | 331

Looking for the Parts which Show Oppression of Female Characters
In this novel, there are two female characters, Young Ju and her mother, and two male characters, Young Ju's brother, Joon Ho, and her father. Young Ju's father is quite patriarchal and female characters' reactions to his conduct changes throughout the novel. Have students find the scenes which show it and talk about their thoughts about that situation. Also, have them guess what their reaction would be if they were in that situation.

Analyzing Cultural Differences and Cultural Similarities
Ask students to find the parts of the novel where two cultures or at least two people who have different nationality coexist in the novel. It is easier to find cultural differences and similarities. For example, in Mr. Doyle's car coming back from the ceremony, Amanda never hesitates to express her feelings; Amanda groans, "Daaad!" (119). Amanda's relationship with her father, who is an adult, is very different from Young Ju's, for whom disagreeing is a sign of disrespect. By comparing two cultures, students will analyze current society as well, for example, how Korean society has changed compared to that in the novel.

Further Applications
Further group discussions, role play activities, and dialogue journals would also work well with this novel. Make my students discuss a chapter of the novel in small groups. Discussion needs to precede going on to a role play activity or dialogue journal because group discussion gives a chance for students to think deeply, develop their thought, and broaden their ideas by listening to the other members' opinions. Their speaking proficiency and comprehension of a presented chapter can be checked through viewing their recomposed role play. Having students write dialogue journals in a way they rewrite the chapters given allows them to recast the story in ways that

are meaningful for them and match their personal identity matrix. *A Step from Heaven* depicts only Young Ju's point of view. Moreover, as a female protagonist, she stands in the position of defending her mom, so it is a bit hard to clearly understand her father's worries or inner thoughts. In fact, we can see positive aspects of her father only once in the chapter entitled "Blob." Considering this, we can rewrite some chapters from her father's point of view. Through this tool, a teacher can check not only students' writing proficiency but also their creativity. Moreover, as it gets students to re-read the novel from various points of view, and it leads them to be critical readers as well.

26. Special Issue: Workshops from the 2nd Woosong Mini-Conference
(Held in Association with the KOTESOL Daejeon-ChungCheong Chapter, and Introducing The Multimedia & CALL SIG)

**DAEJON-CHUNGCHEONG CHAPTER
MINI-CONFERENCE
SEPTEMBER 11, 2010**
Woosong University, Daejeon
www.kotesol.org

It's back!
Get ready.

Three strands of content:
- Multimedia & CALL
- Research
- Practical Activities

27. Getting Started with Your Research Project

Eric D. Reynolds
Josephine Mirador

This workshop is the first installment of a series of workshops entitled: TEFL research: Design to publication in one year. In this workshop participants will work on the early stages of their research projects. Participants will do a lot of brainstorming today, because the goal is of this workshop is to generate the basic ideas of their topic. Those basic ideas will include: a narrowed thesis and set of research questions, an understanding of the broad research methodologies they might wish to use to develop their project, review the basic skills of conducting a literature review in their individual Korean situations, establish a timetable and task list for their project including a Gannt chart, and finally develop the rudiments of a community to support their project.

In future conferences in the next twelve months—at Thanksgiving in Cheonan, during March in Seoul, and in May at the national conference— participants will work on additional topics in this twelve month process through conference sessions which will include topics such as: data--informed consent, pre-post test design, demographic data collection, survey design, interviews skills, observation schemes, ethnographic observation; analysis – SPSS, NUDIST/TAMSanalizer/others, traditional Qualitative/ethnographic analysis techniques, CA/DA techniques, the interpretation of results; write-up-- interpretation of research results, setting up peer revision support groups, survey of available EFL publications and conferences, avoiding publication pitfalls, the review process.

28. Getting Online with Moodle in the EFL Context

Michael Peacock

The presence of computers in the classroom has become commonplace over the past decade. Combined with the Internet, computers have opened a wide range of teaching resources, one of which is the modular object-oriented dynamic learning environment, or Moodle. Moodle allows teachers to create an online course for their students. Educators who use Moodle can create online lessons, assignments, quizzes, forums, blogs, as well as many more activities. It also allows educators to upload files such as Microsoft Word, PowerPoint, and Excel. This presentation will show the ways in which the culinary arts department at Woosong University uses Moodle alongside its general English conversation courses. It will also show educators how they can set up their own Moodle in less than 15 minutes.

29. Digital Storytelling for Your Classroom!

Justin McKibben

Digital storytelling is a method of using common modern technology to tell a story. There are a wide range of uses for this technique in any type of classroom and for any type of student. The focus for the presentation will be ESL classrooms. This presentation will explain the many uses of digital storytelling, the types of digital storytelling that can be done, and show real examples made by students. There will be practical tips for using digital storytelling in the classroom as well as a sample timeline with steps for using digital storytelling as a class project. References for examples of digital storytelling will also be given.

30. Webquests as a Task-Based, Inquiry-Oriented, Computer Assisted, Language Learning Exercise

Joel Hopkinson

WebQuests are one way in which a teacher can let students follow the threads of their own investigation into a topic. As part of an individual exercise, a pair, or a small group, the students work towards completing the task of the WebQuest and reporting on it to the rest of the class. WebQuests can be made on just about any topic and this presentation will walk the audience through the process of creating a WebQuest as well as the practical lessons that were learned by running it as a lesson for both Koreans and Foreign Faculty that are Native-Speakers of English. Feedback from a particular WebQuest entitled, "the History of the English Language", that has been taught several times, and formed a part of an action research project on the subject, will also be part of the presentation. WebQuests fit in well with current trends towards a more Communicative, Task-based or Topic-based approach to language learning as well as being one of the many ways that computers can be used to assist in language learning.

31. Replacing the Workbook with Blog Homework

Adam Parsons

Many textbooks come with standardized workbooks. The workbooks may vary in difficulty and content, which can make it a burden to use in the classroom. This study focuses on replacing workbooks with blog assignments. There are numerous benefits for both teachers and students using a blog rather than a workbook that will be addressed. One of the central issues when introducing a new type of homework into the classroom is the students' attitudes towards it. This presentation will present difficulties students may face and their attitudes towards using the blog system, students' assessment of CALL in relation to their learning, and suggestions for blog use in the language classroom. The presenter will introduce practical assignments that language educators can use and adapt to fulfill the needs of their students.

32. Science and English integrated Learning Based on Topics

ChanMi Park

Korean national English curriculum for elementary sixth graders in public school does not include enough content yet. It still focuses on improving conversation skill, which might be helpful and useful for daily life based on functional syllabus. However, in EFL situation students do not even have chance to have an English conversation in their daily lives, which means the current content are mostly reckless. Also as they grow, the gap between cognitive and linguistic development is getting bigger, so students need something more to deal with rather than learning language itself. In addition, the Ministry of Education, Science and Technology released concern about lack of literacy area, and tried to include more reading and writing in the curriculum. Against this backdrop, as one of the possible alternatives, integrating content and language is able to meet the situations. If the contents are taught in the target language, learners are exposed to both contents and language, so that learners are afford to make connection to their knowledge using target language simultaneously. This will motivate students to learn both content and language more effectively. In this project, the researcher will try to figure out if science and English integrated learning improve students' learning for both and thinking skill in public school.

Part Five
TESOL Interfaces 5(1)

2011

33. Particularity, Practicality, and Possibility in TESOL

Josephine Mirador

In his article entitled 'Toward a Postmethod Pedagogy' Kumaravadivelu (2001) proposed adopting the principles of particularity, practicality and possibility to transcend what he noted as the limitations of the concept of method in second language teaching and teacher education. Essentially, the three Ps highlighted what he saw as the need for a context-sensitive pedagogy, sensitization of teaching to the current socio-political realities in which teachers function, and emphasis on the interconnectedness of theory and practice as dialectically informing each other, with the possibility of enabling teachers to construct their own theory of practice.

The articles in this issue may provide examples of teachers engaging with the principles that Kumaravadivelu has proposed in that the practices examined and documented here inevitably find importance in the notions of particularity, practicality and possibility in variable L2 teaching contexts.

Mat Terrett's article (which he describes as a one-sided critique of existing local practices in the teaching of English for academic purposes in an English-medium institute of higher education in China) is a clear example of how one's practice (both as teacher and coordinator of an academic writing program) has had him sensitized to the particular needs of students in his teaching context. Inevitably, his critique becomes targeted at the adoption of a curriculum that follows an exam-practice orientation and utilizes a segregation approach on the teaching of academic skills. He presents accounts of his colleagues' reflections on the micro-political context of EAP and their perceptions of how decisions from the top have had such an impact on responding to the language needs of students. His provisional conclusion is that low-level learners in the university need English for specific academic purposes (and not English for general academic purposes or EAP) to get students to acquire effective vocabulary for an academic context. It seems that this article's significance further lies in the possibility of parallels in the trajectories of teaching EAP as experienced in China and in other contexts in the northeast Asian region.

Michael Armstrong and *Gerald Von Bordeau* both address practicality and provide relevant ideas on building interest and motivation in the EFL classroom. Armstrong's work targets the all-important issue of motivation and the possibility that it can be created through the adoption of role-play in the classroom. He stresses that "students of English often lack motivation and find it difficult to learn through role-playing situations and hypothetical imaginations". He believes that if students are provided with a learning model that lets them actively participate in creating fictional characters in a game setting, students are not only intrinsically motivated to acquire new language. More importantly, their desire for learning increases in that they are given the opportunity to 'own' their chosen character and the chance to go for a win.

Von Bordeau draws from a popular television program and shows how this can be linked to the specific context of Korean classrooms, hence addressing the notion of practicality in pedagogy. He claims that "too often EFL students view writing class as mundane and are unable to envision writing as the effective and creative form of communication that it is". He points to the issue of 'banal materials' and instructional methods adopted by most teachers in EFL composition courses. Instead, he argues for applying a socio- cultural approach which he thinks is more compatible with the goals of a university sophomore EFL composition course.

Neil Briggs takes aim at the source of potential and real conflicts in our midst by reviewing Simpson's article on east-west classroom culture conflicts. He examines some of the misconceptions and generalizations about the cultural conflicts which can arise when a native English-speaking teacher works with students in an 'eastern' classroom. Further, he explores the possibility that there may be hope in eventually constructing 'cultural harmony' in the classroom despite seeming polarities through the adoption of a critical pedagogy and CLT.

We hope that the articles in this volume resonate with your own teaching experiences, provide a springboard for other practical ideas in the classroom, and generate further interest in examining our roles as participants in the social process involved in teaching.

References
Kumaravadivelu, B. (2001). Toward a Postmethod Pedagogy. *TESOL Quarterly, 35*(4), 537-560.

34. Adoption of Famous Characters in an RPG Setting

Michael Armstrong

Students of English often lack motivation and find it difficult to learn through role playing situations and hypothetical imaginations. This lesson plan addresses those issues by providing students with a learning model that lets them actively take part in the creation of a fictional character, while intrinsically motivating them to acquire new language. Giving student's ownership over their newly made characters dramatically increases students desire to learn. This ownership is transferred by giving the students creative control over their characters looks, actions and desires. Once the students have an emotional connection, their characters are put into a game setting with an element of chance involved, students become even more motivated to compete and acquire language in order to increase their chances of winning. A carrot and stick effect is created by rewarding second language acquisition with points that further increase the characters' chances of success. During the final stages of the lesson, students can begin learning about their characters' inner motivations by employing the use of basic literary theories. And by the end of the lesson students will be hooked on the game system, emotionally attached to their characters and able to role play and examine hypotheticals in any number of ways.

Rationale

I currently teach students from age 18 to 60, yet despite the age gap, I keep running into the same problem. That problem is that students seem to lack the ability to experience any sort of deep pathos. While my students can understand surface motivation of protagonists, they are unable to process their inner motivations and put themselves totally in the "shoes" of the characters they study. I think it is important for students to be able to understand critical thinking skills and be able to view what we study in class from a variety of perspectives. As a result, I have created a unique way of leading them step by step to a state where they are capable of not only visualizing a character choice, but also understanding it on an empathetic level. The process I have developed helps them open their collective minds and break out of their neo-Confucian ways of thinking. The process begins by using a stripped down version of Dungeons & Dragons: Players Handbook 3.5 edition (D&D) (PHB) for use in designing and imagining hard copies of famous fictional characters. This role-playing game (RPG) system allows for immediate understanding of task-based learning (TBL) and gives students motivation to study because of the inherent "game" aspect. Once a character has been created we can subject that character to a multitude of perspectives and critical theories through the use of the D&D RPG system and changing the various settings in a fusion of styles and postmodernist themes (Barry, 2009).

Aims and Goals

The main goal of this lesson is to get the students thinking outside the box when it comes to examining characters in literature or film. The aim is to increase the sense of emotional attachment from the point of view of the participants and enable students to understand multiple perspectives and various critical theories. By creating a number of avenues in which characters can be understood, I hope to maintain student interest by using a variety of methods. Role-playing, risk taking, creative writing, discussions, visuals and world building will all come into play (Collie & Slater, 2005). The anticipated outcome is that students will be able to empathize with characters, settings and situations from outside of their own first person perspective, while participating in a TBL environment. This is a multi-platform lesson creating a strong foundation in basic-intermediate English. The lessons below total at least ten hours of instruction and possibly over forty if all supplementary exercises are taken into account. Ideally the students could ascertain their newly created characters' moods, motivations and desires through a postmodernist lens.

Learning Context

For this lesson the teaching environment is irrelevant. This lesson can be taught using information and communication technology (ICT), over online computer-mediated communication (CMC), or in individual or group face-to-face (FtF) classroom settings. However, the ideal learning environment would be eight students, four males and four females, sitting at four tables in a medium-sized room. In any class of English language learners (ELLs) I prefer either using groups consisting of dyads because of the inherent comfortable nature and equality of discussion that takes place among them (Collie & Slater, 2003). This can be enhanced by matching one female with one male in each partnership. This gender division has the benefit of improving inter-group participation, communication, self-efficacy and classroom manageability (Hunter, Darryl, Gambell, Trevor & Randhawa, Bikkar 2005). The only real necessary thing for a functional teaching and learning environment for this class is more than one student. Though it could be done with only one, having a plural number of students creates an environment that is conducive to discussion, comparison and multiple perspectives. There is also the game aspect and its goal orientated and achievement-based structure which provides intrinsic motivation through reward and competition, especially among larger groups of students (Brown, 2007).

Materials and Resources

The materials needed for this lesson are quite minimal and variable depending on the classroom environment. For a CMC class, computers, internet cameras and microphones with internet hook ups would be needed as well as several programs like Skype, maptool-1.3 and scanned pdf files of the PHB. However, for the ideal version of this class listed above, the only thing necessary would be paper, pencils, some 4, 6, 8, 10, 12, & 20 sided dice, a stripped down version of the D&D PHB for each student pairing and copy of the Dungeon Masters Guide (DMG) for the teacher. That is for the basic class; however, more advanced technology like overhead projectors, PowerPoint screens and miniature maps can only enhance the lesson for the students.

Implementation

Once all the dyads have been created and everyone is in their seats and at their tables the method of implementation begins. The steps are as follows:

Step One

Explain to the students that they will be taking control of a fictional character from any movie, comic, cartoon, video game, book or T.V. show. In the last stage of this lesson, once the groups understand their chosen characters' motivations, moods and desires, they will take them out in a four character "party" seeing if they can complete a series of tests and challenges.

Step Two

Give the students ten minutes to come up with a fictional character from any genre of film or literature. Some examples include: Sponge Bob, Batman, Superman, Protagonist from "Iris", The Joker, Wolverine, Thor, Sailor Moon, Homer

Simpson, Joey from "Friends", Charlie Brown, Master Chief from "Halo", and so on.

Step Three
Once the various pairs of students have their character they must understand his/her/its motivations and they can do that by discussing the following list of questions:
- *How old are you?*
- *What ethnicity are you*
- *Where were you born?*
- *Are you religious? What religion?*
- *Who is in your family and where are they?*
- *Are you introverted or extroverted?*
- *Have you ever committed serious crimes? What? Been caught*
- *Have you ever done violence to/killed another? Many times? Why?*
- *What are your vices?*
- *What are your virtues?*
- *What general goals motivate you? (career, love, ideals, money, fame etc..)*
- *What specific goals motivate you? (a new item, put a person in jail, etc..)*
- *What do you fear*
- *Do you have any secrets?*
- *Do you use your head or gut more?*
- *Are you more selfish or selfless?*
- *What was your education*
- *What are your favorite foods and drinks?*
- *What are your most hated food and drinks?*
- *What are your favorite activities?*
- *What are your most hated activities?*
- *How is your sense of humor? What makes you laugh?*
- *Who is your character's role model?*
- *How do you feel about marriage?*

- *How do you feel about friends?*
- *How do you feel about sex?*
- *How do you feel about your family?*
- *How do you feel about your country?*
- *How do you feel about yourself?*
- *Are you superstitious?*
- *What's a good catch phrase for your worldview? (e.g., life's a bitch, what goes around comes around, live fast die young and leave a beautiful corpse, carpe diem, and so on ...)*
- *What kind of music do you like?*
- *Do you have hobbies?*
- *Do you believe in capital punishment?*
- *What are your attitudes towards monsters?*
- *What are your attitudes towards the various races?*
- *What are your attitudes towards the afterlife?*
- *What would you die for?*
- *What is your general political view?*
- *What are best three adjectives to describe you?*
- *How do you feel about the Monarchies?*
- *What is your attitude towards the law?*
- *Would you eat people if stranded on an island?*
- *Do you believe in an absolute good and evil, or is it all relative?* (Armstrong, 2009, 6).

Answering these questions should take up the majority of a two-hour class and also provide some homework/group work. The questions may seem mundane, but the students will immensely enjoy answering them, because they will be not only discussing a character that they like, but also gain satisfaction in finding or creating answers that are not immediately obvious. The process of answering all these questions will enrich the students with more personality-themed vocabulary, while imprinting each dyad's chosen character in their minds, creating the beginnings of pathos.

Step Four

Once the inner workings of the character have been created, the outer looks must be created. Using a list of physical attributes and or fashion items or if you have it, the descriptive vocabulary chart from Jazz English 2, (2006) on pages 102-104 by Gunther Breaux, get the students to describe their character. Starting from the hair and going down, describing physical attributes first and then later fashion items or accessories. They should follow normal grammar rules, but an easy format to remember is quantity, quality, texture/pattern, color and noun, e.g., long silky beautiful wavy black hair. In addition, the students should do their best to produce a visual image of their character, either through drawing or image download. Get the students to use as many adjectives as possible when describing their character and remind them to include any equipment they may have on them. As a last step, mix the groups up and let them describe their character while the listeners draw it using only the audio cues to create the image.

Step Five

Now that the characters have been created both physically and mentally, it is time to assign their attributes into the game system and assess their skills. Using the character creation guide in the PHB the students should assign each character 6 ability attributes (Strength, Dexterity, Constitution, Intelligence, Wisdom and Charisma) with a score of 1-20, with a 1 being the lowest possible and a 20 being just above the normal human maximum of 18. There are several methods of point allocation listed in the PHB, but the easiest one is to get the students to assign a 20, 18, 16, 14, 12 and 10 to a corresponding ability. The students must also decide what skills the character possesses. Here the teacher must be wary, as this can be a tedious lesson, assigning meaningless numbers into empty boxes can steal quite a bit of motivation from the class. A good way to increase the

Adoption of Famous Characters in an RPG Setting | 351

motivation is to give other groups "veto power" over any suspiciously high ability scores. This not only keeps game balance, but it creates open discussion for English language learners. The best way to keep the motivation and momentum going is to end the two-hour lesson with a series of challenges that each dyad must put their character through. Here, each dyad is given 1d20 which they are to roll and add their characters' final skill score to, creating the element of chance, which all students love. For example if Soo Yun and Jin Ha's character of Spiderman is attempting to jump over an elephant they must roll the 1d20 + 10 (Spiderman's Jump Skill), they must beat a static number of 15 for difficulty. So they need to roll 5 or higher on the die 20. Ending the lesson like this serves two purposes. First, it keeps the intrinsic motivation flowing, and second, it reinforces the game system and action/verb vocabulary in a fun way, using repetition to aid in memorization.

Step Six
During the next lesson the RPG can begin. Create a setting in which all the pairs of students' characters meet. Rifts in the time-space-continuum always work for me and select a beginning genre: murder mystery, crime, science fiction, fantasy, historical fiction; spy; romance, etc. Put the characters into that world and using the die-20 system the group of characters, through challenges that require the player-dyads to think how their character, not themselves, would act. Some example challenges might be crossing a ravine using only the materials at hand or freeing a princess from a tower guarded by giant frogs. Other examples to include if the characters are inherently good are to give them moral choices. If they are cowards, give them choices of courage. It is important to remind them again and again that they should play their character and not follow their own choices. The best way to encourage this is to assign points called

'experience points' to them at the end of each lesson. Dyads that take actions similar to how their character would have taken those actions, based on their 44 answered questions receive more experience points, while those that misplay their character receive none. I suggest repeating this lesson 2-5 times, each time going for 2 hours.

Step Seven
Once the students feel comfortable in the skin of their characters you can begin examining them back in their original surroundings. Use script or video from the internet and have your class examine each character's motivation using the various literary theories: postmodernism, feminist, with psychoanalytical criticism being the obvious choice for this lesson. You will find that the students will have vastly improved senses of pathos and creativity in regards to the characters. Even pairs of students who played different characters will innately understand characters played by other dyads.

Further Applications
As a last note, this lesson can spring a whole crop of other assignments. Short stories about the character adventures together, copied dialogues from previous sessions, world-building, genre fusion through a postmodernist lens, visual artwork, conversation hypotheticals and sequencing. By including a writing component to these further applications, it inherently applies a reading component as well. Students can review each other's work and create open discussions of opinion in agreement/disagreement of said characters' actions. Once the students have fully grasped the characters and the system you can take the next step. Have them create their own characters, fully fictional representations of inner desires and fantastic dreams (Sherman, 2003). By assigning your students this task you are freeing them completely from 'thinking within their own

shoes' and enabling them to think from a truly multi-perspective by adopting a famous character.

One of my favorite secondary applications is to teach the students a set of themed idioms, vocabulary or phrases and give them experience point rewards for using their newly learned English in the correct context within the storyline of the "game." This form of task-based learning resonates with students and increases their SLA. For example, knowing that the characters they have created must masquerade as waiters and cooks to get into a hotel to accomplish some plot goal an educator can teach vocabulary and phrases from this theme ahead of time. Providing the students with a list of these words and awarding them additional experience if they are able to incorporate any of these items into the challenge scene creates an ideal environment for learning.

References

Appleman, D. (2009). *Critical encounters in high school English: Teaching literary theory to Adolescents* (2nd ed.). Teachers College Press, New York & London.

Armstrong, J. (2009). *Plutocracy: 2060* (4th ed.). (unpublished). Retrieved from https://sites.google.com/site/plutocracyrpg

Barry, P. (2009). *Beginning theory: An introduction to literary and cultural theory* (3rd ed.). Manchester & New York: Manchester University Press.

Breaux, G. (2006). *Jazz English 2: Freestyle conversations using real world English* (2nd ed.). Seoul, South Korea: Compass Publishing.

Brown, D.H. (2007). *Principles of language learning and teaching* (5th ed.). White Plains, New York: Pearson & Longman.

Collie, J. & Slater, S. (2005). *Literature in the language classroom: A resource book of ideas and activities.* Cambridge: Cambridge University Press.

Dorpond, T. (2010). *Maptool and Tokentool*. Retrieved from http://www.rptools.net/index.php?page=downloads #MapTool

Hunter, D., Gambell, T. & Randhawa, B. (2005). Gender gaps in group listening and speaking: issues in social constructivist approaches to teaching and learning. *Educational Review 57*(3), 329.

Sherman, J. (2003). *Using authentic video in the language classroom.* Cambridge: Cambridge University Press.

Tweet, J. Cook, M., & Williams, S. (2004) *Dungeons & dragons: Players handbook. Core rulebook 1 v.3.5*. Washington: Wizards of the Coast Printing.

35. Composition of the Modern Family
Gerald Von Bourdeau

Too often EFL students view writing class as mundane and are unable to envision writing as the effective and creative form of communication that it is. This lesson defense argues that this is partly the fault of the banal materials and instructional methods common in EFL composition courses. This lesson plan applies a sociocultural approach to meet the goals of a university sophomore EFL composition course. During the course of the lesson students should further their understanding and application of the five-step writing process, explore compare and contrast strategies, and acquire vocabulary which students can meaningfully employ during composition and daily communication. The lesson is divided into two parts. The first lesson applies a materials-light approach referred to as 'unplugged' teaching while the second lesson includes authentic video in the form of a popular U.S. sit-com. Finally, students will showcase what they have learned by composing a compare and contrast essay as homework after each lesson.

Rationale

Too often EFL writing courses and textbooks do not ask students to think critically about the subject they are writing on. Students learn the writing form or style from a sample essay, which is generally written at the students' writing level but beneath their cognitive maturity. They focus on writing techniques, vocabulary, grammar, lexical items, or elements of the essay, yet very rarely is writing taught to them as a communicative outlet for critical thinking and analysis. This stifles their creativity and hinders acquisition of the goals taught because students dread or become frightened by composition. Simply put, students have no connection to the theme or material they are asked to write on; therefore, writing becomes a chore instead of a useful form or tool of communication. The goal of this lesson is to impart common teaching aims of a first semester sophomore composition course through culturally and personally relevant themes, culturally relevant vocabulary, and various media. If the material is not relevant to the students' lives, it has no place in the composition classroom. The technical aims of the lesson are to further students' production and understanding of the writing process, production of a descriptive 'compare and contrast' essay, impart compare and contrast strategies, and acquisition of relevant vocabulary.

The overarching theme of the lesson will be 'family.' The lesson will span two class periods with each lesson lasting three hours. The target students are first semester sophomore English majors at Gimcheon University. The writing level of the class ranges from beginner to high-intermediate. The first lesson will apply a 'grassroots' pedagogy (Rubdy, 2009, 157) through 'unplugged' teaching (Thornbury, 2000). In grassroots pedagogy the local concerns, realities, and cultures of the students take precedence, creating a more inclusive environment in the classroom (Rubdy, 2009, 167). Unplugged teaching is a form of language instruction that discourages teaching from textbooks or from materials created outside of the classroom and instead promotes material-light lessons which focus on emergent language that is of immediate relevance to the students (Thornbury, 2000). The second lesson will move away from Unplugged teaching and employ the use of video and online resources. First, I will show students clips from the American sit-com Modern Family (IMDB, 2010), then the students will watch season 1 episode 24 of the series. Students will write two compare and contrast essays and participate in activities which will hopefully improve sociocultural communicative strategies and inter-cultural comprehension and tolerance.

Aims and Goals

The technical aim of the class is to strengthen student composition skills and production of the writing process. The students are required to complete two descriptive, compare and contrast essays. Compare and contrast signal words as well as the effective use of adjectives and adverbs will be taught. In the first of the essays students will write from an interpersonal standpoint in which they will compare and contrast their families with mine, while in the second of the two essays, students will write from an intercultural stance comparing and contrasting the 'modern' Korean family with the 'modern' American family. I also want to break the stigma that writing is a chore. I want students to view writing as a creative and valid form of communication and as an outlet for personal opinion, emotion, and ideas. Another aim of the lesson is sociocultural in nature. I want the students to learn how to express their culture in English and promote inter-cultural understanding and tolerance. Brown (2007) outlines eight questions ESL/EFL teachers should ask themselves while teaching culture in the language classroom.

1. Does the activity value the customs and belief systems that are presumed to be a part of the culture of the students?
2. Does the activity refrain from any demeaning stereotypes of any culture, including the culture of your students?
3. Does the activity refrain from any possible devaluing of the students' native language?
4. Does the activity recognize varying degrees of willingness of students to participate openly due to factors of collectivism/individualism and power distance?

5. If the activity requires students to go beyond the comfort zone of uncertainty avoidance in their culture, does it do so empathetically and tactfully?
6. Is the activity sensitive to the perceived roles of males and females in the culture of your students?
7. Does the activity sufficiently connect specific language features (e.g., grammatical categories, lexicon, discourse) to cultural ways of thinking, feeling, and acting?
8. Does the activity in some way draw on the potentially rich background experiences of the students, including their own experiences in other cultures? (213).

In pursuit of the educational goals, I must ask myself these questions before, during, and after the lesson to make certain that the cultural aims of the lesson are being met.

Learning Context

The lesson will be carried out at a Korean university and will be directed at sophomore English majors. The class is three hours long with two 10-minute breaks. This lesson plan will span two classes. The class is held once a week. Twenty-five students make up the class and their writing level ranges from beginner to high-intermediate. The learning format will include individual, pair, group, and class discussion. Because of the wide range of student levels, the groups will consist of various levels, so the higher level students can assist the lower level students. The higher level students will benefit from this as well because they will be teaching to the lower level students, thus furthering their comprehension of the material. I have been teaching the same students for four semesters, so the teacher-student rapport is generally strong. The students all began at the same time in the department, so they are generally open and comfortable with one another in the classroom except for a few introverted young men. Students are also familiar with my teaching style and most know what to expect from my unconventional (in the Korean university 'professor' context) teaching style.

Materials and Resources

The first half of the lesson will solely apply 'unplugged' teaching. On the materials used in 'unplugged' teaching, Thornbury (2000) states, "teaching should be done using only the resources that teachers and students bring to the classroom - i.e. themselves - and whatever happens to be in the classroom. If a particular piece of material is necessary for the lesson, a location must be chosen where that material is to be found (e.g., library, resource centre, bar, students' club ...)." The only materials to be applied in this lesson are: pencil, paper, whiteboard, and board markers. The purpose for such a 'bare bones' approach is to elicit ideas, emotions, and vocabulary that is relevant to the students' lives and connected to the lesson's theme (family). Thornbury (2000) further argues the merits of materials-free instruction. He states, "learning, too, takes place in the here-and-now. What is learned is what matters. Teaching, like talk, should centre on the local and relevant concerns of the people in the room, not on the remote world of coursebook characters, nor the contrived world of grammatical structures."

The second half of the lesson will employ authentic video. The class will watch clips of the American sit- com Modern Family as well as season one episode twenty-four of Modern Family in its entirety (Levitan, Lloyd, & Wernick, 2010). I have chosen Modern Family because of its up-to-date cultural themes, vocabulary, and lexical items. Viewing Modern Family will aid in the students' comprehension of contemporary English and

English language culture. According to Sherman (2003),
> video is a window on English language culture. Apart from giving access to global cultural products like feature films, it also shows how people live and think and behave—local culture with a small 'c.' A small amount of showing is worth hours of telling from a teacher or a course book (2).

Though Modern Family does play on some cultural stereotypes, I believe it is as close to an accurate representation of the modern, middle-class, suburban American family a sit-com can portray. The students could not acquire as current or accurate representation of American, familial culture from the standard EFL textbook. Students will have the opportunity to digest the information and decide for themselves what is relevant to their lives and learning. Handouts intended to aid with comprehension and eliciting opinion will be given to the students.

Implementation
First Lesson: Unplugged Teaching
Write 'family' on the board. Leave several board markers in the class for the students. Tell the class that I am going to leave the classroom and come back in ten minutes and that I would like them to pre-write together as a class on the topic of family. Students should brainstorm whatever comes to mind on the topic. Tell them that the whiteboard should be filled up with their collective thoughts (Thornbury, Scott's beginners class).

When I return, a class discussion will take place on the emergent language written on the board. I will add any new vocabulary necessary and help with any grammar, syntax, and lexical items (Thornbury, Scott's beginners class).

Next, we will move on to step two of the writing process—organization. I will write "Bourdeau's Family" on the whiteboard. Next, I will inform students that they will be working in groups and writing about my family, yet I am unwilling to give out information freely. In order to find the information about my family which they will need to complete their outlines, they will need to write questions and bring them to me. All questions must come in the written form. I will answer the questions in written form. The only information they can use is what I give them in the written answers. They should create an outline of my family. After the outline is complete, they should write a paragraph describing my family which includes topic, detail, and closing sentences. After writing the paragraph, students will share with the class. We will discuss the differences and similarities between the writings and correct any grammatical or vocabulary errors. I will teach vocabulary or lexical items as needed (Thornbury, Olwyn's interview writing).

For further development, students will use the paragraph they wrote about my family to write a descriptive, compare and contrast essay. Students should compare and contrast their family with mine. The essay should be three to five paragraphs long and include an introduction, body, and closing. Unlike the paragraph written about my family, this essay should be done individually.

Class 2: Modern Families
At the beginning of class, I will collect homework and inquire as to how it went. Then a few students will summarize their essay. The class will learn not only how my family compares but also how each student's family compares with his or her classmates' families. Finally, I will help the students with any difficulties before moving on.

I will explain that we will continue our lesson on descriptive, compare & contrast writing; however, instead of writing on our personal families, we will look at family from a cultural standpoint. I will let the students know that I am going to introduce them to a fictional American family by watching the sit-com Modern Family (IMDB, 2010.). Before watching the sit-com I will introduce several of the sit-com characters to the class via clips from season 1 episode 24 which do not explicitly state how the characters are related or their relationships with one another. After viewing paired clips, I will have students answer how the characters are related on a handout provided to them. After students have viewed all of the clips and written their thoughts on how the characters are related, I will reveal their true relationships. After students learn the correct nature of each character's relationship, I will have them share their thoughts and feelings within groups before presenting to the class. Next, I will explain the sit-com to the class to prepare them for comprehension (Sherman, 2003, 39). Important vocabulary, collocations, and expressions will also be given to students in a handout (Sherman, 2003, 121). Finally, before viewing the episode, we will brainstorm some cultural stereotypes of Korean and American families then, I will tell students to watch closely for similarities and differences between the family on the screen, their own families, and the modern Korean family.

After viewing the video, I will have class work as partners or in groups to write any comprehension questions they have about the video. Then, group or partners will work with others to answer any questions they can. Finally, I will answer any remaining questions.

After the comprehension check, I will inform students they are to write a compare and contrast essay on what they learned about the modern American family and the modern Korean family. If fewer students were in the class and if they were primarily the same level (intermediate to advanced), I would allow more freedom in choosing the cultural theme; however, I feel more structure is needed in such a large class and because of the wide range in writing level.) Students will then begin the writing process. Students will individually use a Venn diagram to brainstorm on the topic for a few minutes. Then, they should outline their essay. I will walk around the class and help students with their outlines and answer any questions about the assignment. The first draft will be assigned as homework, but students may begin writing in class if they finished their outline.

References

Appleman, D. (2009). *Critical encounters in high school English: Teaching literary theory to Adolescents* (2nd ed). Teachers College Press, New York & London.

Barry, P. (2009). *Beginning theory.* Manchester, UK: Manchester University Press.

Brown, H. D. (2007). *Principles of language learning and teaching.* White Plains, NY: Pearson Education, Inc.

Collie, J., and Slater, S. (2005). *Literature in the language classroom: A resource book of ideas and activities.* Cambridge, UK: Cambridge University Press.

Levitan, S., Lloyd, C., Wernick, I. (Writers), & Winer, J. (Director). (2010). In S. Levitan & C. Lloyd (Producers), *Modern Family.* Los Angeles, CA: 20th Century Fox.

Rubdy, R. (2009). Reclaiming the local teaching in EIL. *Language and Intercultural Communication,* 9(3), 156-174.

Sherman, J. (2003). *Using authentic video in the language classroom.* Cambridge, UK: Cambridge University Press.

Thornbury, S. (2000). *A dogma for EFL.* Retrieved from http://www.thornburyscott.com/tu/ Dogma%20article.htm

Thornbury, S. (n.d.). *Olwyn's interview writing.* Retrieved from http://www.thornburyscott. com/tu/resources.htm

Thornbury, S. (n.d.). *Scott's beginners class*. Retrieved from http://www.thornburyscott.com/tu/Scott'sbeginners.htm

Appendix
Lesson Plan 1

Class: Sophomore Composition – Semester 1

Time & Day: 9 AM – 12 PM, Wednesday

Materials and Equipment: Pencil, paper, whiteboard, and board markers.

Objectives: Students will produce relevant vocabulary on the topic of 'family.' Students will practice interrogatives and gathering information. Students will write a cohesive paragraph containing a topic sentence, supporting sentences, and closing sentence with the gathered information. Students will practice the writing process. Students will gain a basic understanding of and produce a compare and contrast essay.

Implementation
Introduction

09:00 Welcome students and direct attention to the whiteboard where 'family' is written. Tell the class *I am going to leave the classroom and come back in ten minutes and that I would like them to pre-write together as a class on the topic of family*. Students should brainstorm whatever comes to mind on the topic. Tell them that *the whiteboard should be filled up with their collective thoughts*.

09:05 Leave Class

09:15 Return to class. Lecture and class discussion on the emergent vocabulary. 30 to 35 minutes

09:50 10 minute break

Primary Lesson

10:00	'Bourdeau's Family': Students will work in groups to create written questions to learn information about my family. I will answer their questions in written form. I will encourage students not to write yes/no questions.
10:20	
10:40	In groups or as partners, outline and write a paragraph describing my family.
10:50	Students will share their paragraphs with the class. We will discuss the similarities and differences between the paragraphs.
11:00	
11:20	
	10 Minute Break
	Lecture: Compare and Contrast essays
	Students will use the writing process to write essays comparing and contrasting their families with mine. Help students as needed.

Review

11:50   Review the assignment and what was learned. Help students with anything they need before the end of class.

Lesson Plan 2

Class: Sophomore Composition – Semester 1

Time & Day: 9 AM – 12 PM, Wednesday

Materials and Equipment: Pencil, paper, whiteboard, and board markers, projector, laptop, audio, Modern Family season 1 episode 24 (IMDB, 2010.), and student handouts.

Objectives: Compose a compare and contrast essay applying the writing process. Students should view writing as a creative and valid form of communication and as an outlet for personal opinion, emotion, and ideas. Students will learn how to express their culture in English and promote inter-cultural understanding and tolerance.

Implementation
Introduction
09:00   Collect homework, essay summarization, question and answer
09:15   Introduction of lesson

Primary Lesson
09:20   Introduction of characters via clips from season 1 episode
09:35   24 and handouts
09:50   Reveal the characters true relationships. Group
10:00   discussion and class discussion
          10-minute break
10:10   Give students background information on the series and pertinent information needed to understand the
10:40   episode. Give students useful vocabulary handouts.
10:55   Watch the sitcom, pausing two or three times for
11:05   comprehension checks and clarification.
11:15   Group work: Clarification questions
11:25   Ten-minute break
          Venn diagram pre-write
          Essay outline
          Work on draft.
          Help students with anything they may need.

Homework
Finish 1st draft of the compare and contrast essay.

36. Is Conformity really the Answer? On Simpson's East-West Classroom Culture Conflicts

Neil Briggs

This article examines some of the misconceptions and generalizations about the cultural conflicts which can arise when a native English speaking teacher works with students in an 'eastern' classroom. In contrast to Simpson's pessimistic report about the cultural struggles that Western teachers should expect to encounter in Eastern countries, this article explores the possibility that there is indeed hope of harmonizing the seemingly polar cultures in the classroom. Teaching pedagogies and their inherent cultural connections are discussed, with a specific focus on the role of communicative language teaching (CLT) in the east. This article suggests that through critical pedagogical practices, including the negotiation of testing procedures and the use of CLT, the students can make the adjustments needed to engage with more Western style teaching methods. On the other hand, the teacher must also adjust their teaching in order to be considerate of not only the needs and desires of the students, but of their specific ability levels as well. The teacher must also remain conscious of the possibility that their teaching content can often contain socio- political ideologies which students commonly meet with resistance. This paper shows that western teachers and eastern students are not as incompatible as Simpson portrays them to be.

In his article, "Western EFL Teachers and East-West Classroom Culture Conflict" Steven Simpson attempts to provide an overview of the east-west cultural conflicts which commonly occur when teachers from western cultures move to 'the east'. While Simpson has many valid points and raises important issues that all western teachers should be aware of before teaching in the East, he also shoots himself in the foot by basing most of his evidence on over-generalized assumptions about both teaching cultures. Ultimately, he provides us with little more than a history of the issues and little hope for progress in this area, or a teacher's guide to maintaining the status quo. If teachers, regardless of cultural background, are not pushing for positive change and progressive educational methods, then are they really doing their jobs?

The first overgeneralization can be found in the title of Simpson's article. The term 'Westerner' places many people with very diverse cultures and backgrounds into one group and fails to recognize the many cultural changes which have occurred in recent years as a result of globalization. Although the term serves the practical function of identifying a culture that is foreign to Asian countries, the ambiguous nature of the term can be quite marginalizing to minorities within the culture. Liu carefully crafts his sentence to avoid such a pitfall in his article 'Teaching English in China: Conflicts and Expectations'. He explains that "if teachers hold biased judgment based on their own cultural backgrounds and stereotypes, NES (native English-speaking) teachers who teach in China will inevitably encounter conflicts in their teaching and in their relationship with their Chinese students (2010, 92). Liu's use of the conditional 'if' is very important because it allows for the possibility that at least some of the so-called westerners can be exempt from holding such highly biased and stereotypical attitudes. The term NES seems a much more appropriate description of the teacher than the term 'western EFL teacher' because it identifies the common attribute for which the teachers were hired. Simpson's consistent use of the term 'Westerner' strips the teachers of their individuality by overgeneralizing their characteristics and identifying them as mere members of a supposedly homogeneous group.

The East-West Conflict

Simpson begins his explanation of the east-west conflict in Chinese EFL education by explaining a key misunderstanding. He explains that "western EFL teachers interpret Deng Xiaoping's invitation as a call to bring their pedagogical expertise, while the Chinese typically intend it only as an invitation to bring their linguistic and cultural expertise" (Simpson 2008, 382). Again, this strikes me as a rather sweeping generalization which implies that all Western teachers are uniform in their beliefs and intentions. It also paints a rather closed-minded picture of the east by leading us to believe that they are completely opposed to the influence of western teaching methodologies. Liu (2010) presents an explanation as to why Western methodologies are often met with resistance in Chinese classrooms. He explains that student motivation will be negatively affected if the teacher sets goals that are too high or too different from students' expectations: "If students are not comfortable with a new teaching approach, low motivation and high anxiety can prevent learners from learning effectively"(Liu 2010, p 93). Indeed, these findings are significant and are worthy of careful consideration by the NES teacher when working in foreign contexts. Although some teachers may be guilty of unsuccessfully attempting to force more western teaching approaches upon their students, this does not mean that small changes and the introduction of new techniques will necessarily be met unfavorably by the students. "Effective NES teachers should teach across cultures by recognizing their historical and cultural distinction and should teach in communicative approach by considering students' needs and cognition that can really create communication"(Liu 2010, 93).

Simpson's statement about Deng Xiaoping's invitation also suggests that the Western teacher's 'desirable attribute' of cultural expertise is somehow independent of their much less desired pedagogical expertise. Simpson explains that the separation of culture and pedagogy is not possible in reality by explaining that Chinese pedagogies are deeply rooted in history and culture and insisting that they are inseparable.

Such a tight connection between culture and pedagogical preference has strong implications for the east- west classroom-culture conflict. Asking western teachers to abandon their pedagogical expertise, in reality, is asking them to abandon their own culture, which apparently was the attribute that was attractive to the east in the first place. Neither the teacher nor the students should, or need to be asked to completely abandon their cultural or educational values and beliefs. Holliday (1999, 237) offers a viable solution to the issue by introducing the concept of large culture paradigms and small culture paradigms:

> This large culture paradigm is by its nature vulnerable to a culturist reduction of 'foreign' students, teachers and their educational contexts. In contrast, a small culture paradigm attaches 'culture' to small social groupings or activities wherever there is cohesive behavior, and thus avoids culturist ethnic, national or international stereotyping.

By making this adjustment to our conception of the term 'culture', NES teachers and students can begin to work together to negotiate a middle ground within this 'small culture' context. In such a way, neither party is asked to abandon their 'large culture' beliefs, but both parties are asked to negotiate meanings, and make compromises based on the specific goals and needs of the specific learning context. Although the east-west pedagogies may be 'polar' they are not necessarily incompatible.

CLT and Cultural Conflicts

Simpson first attempts to explain the cultural conflict of western teachers in China by contrasting the differences in teaching methods. He outlines the CLT issue as three-fold in China: (1) CLT is designed for ESL, but China is an EFL environment (2) CLT is bound up in and founded upon Western ideals (3) The need to teach to the test (2008, 384). Simpson overdramatizes the differences between the Traditional Chinese Method (TCM) and the more 'western' CLT method. Although the deep history of English teaching in China cannot be completely ignored, Simpson admits that the 'Development period' has been introducing western-influenced teaching methods to China since the 70's, and has incorporated Grammar-Translation (GT) and Audio-lingualism (ALM) without great difficulties. This is evidence that the East, or more specifically China, is not completely closed to more Western methodologies. Simpson argues that such methods were accepted because they are the only methods that "fit naturally into the already well-established TCM" (2008, 383). He then goes on to describe CLT and TCM as being completely incompatible and mutually exclusive. There is, however, evidence to the contrary.

Canagarajah (1999) explains how socio-politics can play a role in the resistance of CLT: "Learning cannot possibly be considered an entirely innocent activity, since it raises the possibility of ideological domination and social conflict" (14). I argue that in this quote lies the true reason that GT and ALM were easily integrated into TCM. These methods can be taught quite independently of such social conflict simply by using materials relevant to the dominant local culture. In contrast, CLT presents more opportunities for the teacher to, whether consciously or not, teach a "hidden curriculum of values, ideologies, and hinking"(Canagarajah, 1999, 14). In order to avoid the social conflict that these practices may lead to, the teacher should critically evaluate their own teaching practices as well as to make an effort to "relate learning to the larger socio-political realities, and encourage students to make pedagogical choices that offer sounder alternatives to their living conditions (Canagarajah, 1999, 14). Canagarajah's point here is one that I feel is overlooked by Simpson, as well as many NESTs in EFL. When communicative tasks are based on text-book activities, which are predominantly based on American or other Western cultures, social conflict is likely to arise, thus hampering student ability to learn. Therefore, a critical approach to CLT is essential to its successful use in EFL.

To dispel another one of Simpson's broad generalizations, it is noteworthy to point out that CLT is not necessarily a rigidly defined teaching approach. Rao (2002) explains that there are both strong and weak versions of CLT. The strong version, which is most commonly scrutinized, is not only used to activate existing knowledge, but also to stimulate "the development of language itself" (Rao, 2002, 87). The weak version, which Simpson neglects to adequately acknowledge, allows for traditional teaching approaches to be utilized, while highlighting the need to provide opportunities to develop communicative competence. Simpson's disregard for the adaptable and dynamic nature of CLT strongly undermines the arguments which he pits against it. Simpson first argues that CLT is designed for ESL learning, and that it is not well suited for EFL learners. This is true for the strong version of CLT, which is most often and appropriately reserved for ESL teaching environments. In contrast, the weak version can be appropriately adapted to EFL environments as mentioned previously. Secondly, the weak version of CLT corrodes the strength of Simpson's second argument that CLT is necessarily based on Western ideals. He lists autonomy, egalitarianism, self-reliance and individualism as the ideals on which CLT was founded. While it may not fit well with TCM, in the name of progress would it be asking too much to give it a try, least in small doses? At this point, I feel it is important to admit my bias as a 'western EFL teacher' before making the assertion that it seems evident that if teachers in the East want to improve their effectiveness in teaching foreign languages, they must also have an open mind to accepting newer and progressive teaching methods.

Another issue which Simpson claims prevents the successful implementation of CLT is the East's testing culture. Simpson leads the reader to believe that CLT is not at all compatible with the Eastern testing culture. By employing a combination of methods, including the CLT approach, most of the traditional testing system does not have to be abandoned. Vasilopoulos (2008) outlines such an approach to implementing the CLT activities in Korean universities. He stresses that it is important to combine CLT with more traditional approaches in a country with a long history of AS and GT teaching methods.

Teachers can use communicative activities to re-enforce and further develop students' understandings of the vocabulary and grammar concepts that will appear on the more traditional written exams. In this way, students are more likely to view communicative tasks as a help rather than a hindrance. Despite CLT's potential to improve both test scores and communicative competence, it is unlikely to gain acceptance in a culture where test-based pedagogies dominate. According to Jin (2005), this is because both teachers and students, although interested communicative activities, do not attach great importance to them. Here it is important to note the difference between the terms 'attached importance' and 'attached interest'. Jin surveyed a Chinese university class of thirty students which were subjected to grammar-based exams. All of students indicated that they did not attach importance to communicative activities, but they all had interest in them. This outcome is quite predictable, because placing a high value on test scores naturally increases the levels of instrumental motivation among students. It is surprising that Simpson can list dozens of suggestions for harmonizing East and West teaching, yet omit this critical point. Harmonizing communicative approaches with traditional Eastern pedagogies can be made possible by negotiating with the students. The teacher and students can decide together upon including a suitable amount of communicative competence testing in addition to traditional testing. Of course, the implications of changing the test structure can raise many other issues, such as the subjective nature of evaluating communicative abilities, which goes against the traditionally objective nature of Eastern testing. However, if Western teachers can be afforded the responsibility of teaching a class of students in the East, would it not also be fair to afford them the freedom to negotiate a modified testing format with their students? A little bit of subjectivity seems to be a reasonable price to pay in order to promote higher levels of 'attached importance' among students. When the students already existing 'attached interest' is combined with increased levels of 'attached importance', student motivation to develop communicative competence is sure to improve.

Keeping with the theme of generalizations, Simpson seems to passively accept the notion that Eastern learners are by nature passive learners. Cheng (2000) offers significant evidence which suggests that this is not necessarily the case. A study showed that eight out of ten teachers surveyed enthusiastically challenged the stereotype that Asian learners are reticent and passive. Park and Oxford (1998) also reported the strong success of a communicative based program in Korea. This study suggested that when students are put in the right environment, they are willing to participate actively. Perhaps then, the problem is not the pedagogical approach, but the school environment which students have become accustomed to. Can the cause of student passivity truly be attributed to culture? Evidence suggests that it is more likely that it is years of conditioning from the school system which leads to such passive attitudes among the students.

Acculturation and Adaptation

Next, Simpson refers to the three phases of acculturation (as cited in Wong, 2000, 90) that are commonly experienced by foreigners when they move to a foreign country. In the first stage, Baggage Brought, Westerners are again generalized as expecting students to be highly motivated to learn. While it is likely true that many western EFL teachers complain that students lack motivation, do not participate, cheat, and use go-betweens, I do not feel that it is fair to conclude that the western teachers are negatively judging the students based on their cultural background. Western teachers typically expect participation and motivation on the behalf of the students because that is their culture, and that is what they know to be teaching. They usually do not know how to use the same teaching methods as the eastern instructors. Classes led by the 'westerner' are inherently different in a few ways. First, traditional methods get thrown out the window when the teacher cannot effectively utilize the L1 of the students. Especially in lower level EFL classrooms, the students cannot be expected to listen to the teacher speak for long periods of time in the students' L2. Native English-speaking teachers (NESTs) are essentially left with two options. They can attempt to use the traditional methods in a less effective manner than non-native English speaking teachers (NNEST), or they can teach according to the way they were trained to teach, in a less TCM way. This begs the question : For what reason are Western teachers in China in the first place? Are they doing anything that the local teacher cannot do if they are completely conforming to cultural expectations, or are they doing the same thing worse?

While Simpson provides sound advice for the 'westerner' moving to the 'East', he also paints a bleak picture of the work environment by suggesting that change is unattainable. The western teacher simply cannot take on the same role as the eastern teacher. Language and cultural differences make total assimilation impossible. The best we can do as teachers is to develop a sound understanding of cultural differences, adapt appropriately, but continue to do what a teacher should do, and that is push for progress. The students' voice is powerful and often overlooked, as in the case of Simpson's article. The solution could be as simple as the teacher asking the students what they want and what they need, followed by an appropriate pedagogical response. The results, as others have found, may turn out to be quite the opposite of what the generalized stereotypes of 'eastern' students may suggest.

References

Canagarajah, S. 1999. *Resisting linguistic imperialism in English teaching*. Oxford: OUP.

Cheng, X. (2000) Asian students' reticence revisited. *System* 28(3), 435-446.

Holliday, A. (1999). Small cultures. *Applied Linguistics*, 20(2), 237-264.

Liu, S. (2010). Teaching English in China: Conflicts and expectations. *The International Language, Society, and Culture*, 31, 90-97.

Jin, L., Li, L., & Singh, M. (2005). Communicative language teaching in China: Misconceptions, applications and perceptions. A paper presented at *AARE' 05 Education Research*. The Australian Association for Research in Education. Retrieved from http://www.aare.edu.au/05pap/jin05646.pdf

Park, Y.& Oxford, R., (1998). Changing roles for teachers in the English Village Course in Korea. *System, 26*(1).

Rao, Z., (2002). Chinese students' perceptions of communicative and non-communicative activities in EFL classroom. *System, 30*, 85-105.

Simpson, S. T. (2008). Western EFL teachers and East-West classroom-cultural conflicts. *RELC Journal, 39*.

Vasilopoulos, G. (2008) Adapting communicative language instruction in Korean universities. *The Internet TESL Journal, 14*(8), 8. Retrieved from http://iteslj.org

Wong, M.S., (2000). The influence of gender and culture on the pedagogy of five western teachers in China. (Unpublished doctoral dissertation) University of South California.

37. Issues with Academic Vocabulary Acquisition Suggest Low Level Learners Need English for specific Academic Purposes (ESAP) not English for General Academic Purposes (EGAP)

Mat Terret

This paper summarizes the findings drawn from a series of interviews with English for Academic Purposes (EAP) teachers on a foundation year program in China. The four EAP skills consisted of random topic content that operated independently of the others, and was similarly unrelated to the students' subject study. This randomness and irrelevance de-evolved into 'the exam-practice approach', which is heavily criticized by EAP teachers, particularly with respect to academic vocabulary acquisition. This 'approach' is further criticized by comparative studies of IELTS test writing and the kind of writing expected at universities. An ESAP approach with an explicit focus on academic vocabulary and target situation genre awareness work is proposed as the leading solution.

Introduction

This paper summarizes the findings drawn from a series of interviews with English for Academic Purposes (EAP) teachers and managers as part of an ongoing case study into the development of academic literacies practices. The context is a foundation year EAP program at an English language medium higher education institute, which awards university degrees and is located in China. From the first year (the foundation year) students are streamed into two subject pathways – Business and Engineering – so the target situation of all students is known. Complex ethical issues were raised in the collection and presentation of data, which stemmed from institutional politics and the challenge it presented to managers who had presided over the development of the EAP program (the details are not included in this paper). Despite conscious and explicit attempts to gather positive data, very little was collected. This paper therefore reads like a one-sided critique of the existing local EAP practices. Nevertheless, the findings reported are consistent with the literature on academic reading and vocabulary learning in EAP, and strongly suggest that with low-level learners, in contexts where the target situation is already known, English for General Academic Purposes (EGAP) is inappropriate. Rather, EAP *is* subject – specific English – English for *Specific* Academic Purposes (ESAP), or at least EAP teachers think it should be.

Context and Background to the Study

In 2008, when I first started researching the academic reading and writing programs, the EAP program was divided into four distinct skills (Reading, Writing, Listening and Speaking), with each 'skill' operating independently of the others on its own calendar schedule. It rapidly became apparent that it was not only the *randomness* of the reading texts that made coordination of the reading and writing programs difficult, but also their *relevance*. *Randomness* and *relevance* (or *irrelevance*) have become key words in this case study and are used to describe topics (as opposed to the specific skills targeted in the separate academic reading and writing 'skills' classes).

The rationale behind this approach, which has become known locally as the 'Exam-Practice Approach', appears to be that learners' need to be able to deal with random texts because the texts they will deal with in their EAP gate-keeping examinations will be similarly random and very similar to the IELTS test. However, in a comparative study of IELTS score gain across different "course types (IELTS preparation, pre-sessional EAP and combination)", Green (2005) concluded that "there were no significant differences in score gains by course type" (11). Due to the different requirements of university writing and IELTS style tests, Moore and Morton (2005) unambiguously state that "it would be most unwise to view test preparation on its own as an adequate form of EAP writing instruction" (64). Prioritizing IELTS test practice over locally situated EAP "could work against the best interests of learners and receiving institutions by undervaluing the more local competencies that these courses may foster" (Green, 2005, 13). Without clearly distinguishing between Academic Purposes and exam-practice "such programs run the risk of presenting students with a confusing model of university writing" (Moore & Morton, 2005, 64).

In the local context, the focus on exam-practice does appear to have caused confusion and led to a situation where *there was no systematic vocabulary or language exploration* (Teacher 1).

> *We don't, in my opinion, we don't actually do any teaching ... at all! ... We just go in every single class and we give them a test ... and then the next day we go in and give them **another** test that's not related to the previous test...it's not skills development* (Teacher 2).

This seems to have led to a rejection of an off-the-shelf course-book, a decision supported by the fact that *there isn't [a specific] one that fits* (Teacher 3). Teacher 4 points out that:
> *there are [very few] ... integrated EAP course-books on the market, whereas there are masses and masses of separate ones, like reading, speaking, listening and writing separated. ... I don't know if it is a good thing but it seems to be a fairly entrenched convention.*

Alexander and Argent (2010) agree that "published EAP course books for low level learners do not currently meet this challenge" (10) and Mayor (2006) argues that the majority of textbooks fail to address the specific linguistic issues faced by Chinese learners, indicating "a gap in provision" (119). Moreover, Hyland's (2009) call for specificity makes it extremely unlikely that any off-the-shelf textbook could be fully relevant to any specific EAP program.

The lack of a fully relevant textbook gave rise to *people with no formal positions scrabbling around for materials* (Teacher 4), and seems to have led to the further disintegration of the EAP program with an *isolated person with **different** material and a different topic* (Teacher 2) *coordinating* a skill.

The result is that EAP is *not especially well integrated with the subject courses* (Teacher 5). The *discrete readings selected from this book and that book and any other book we could get our hands on* (Teacher 1) has de-evolved into a random ***deluge*** *of papers with words on them that are actually not related to anything in particular* (Teacher 2).

There appear to be two main problems with this approach. First, the "common core hypothesis" (Flowerdew & Peacock, 2001, 16-18), which claims the required academic vocabulary and reading skills can be learnt using any appropriate text, does not have to be interpreted as meaning "random texts are okay". Second, "[o]ne of the most consistent implications of two decades of reading and writing relations is that they should be taught together and that the combination of both literacy skills enhances learning in all areas" (Grabe, 2001). Coxhead and Byrd (2007) even claim that "[a]cademic writing does not exist as a task on its own but is inextricably linked to the reading of academic texts" (133). Thus, randomness, irrelevance and separation of the EAP skills are likely to cause a site of confusion for students (discussed further below in relation to *transferability*). This has implications for both the EAP gate-keeping examinations and academic vocabulary acquisition, which Baumann and Graves (2010, 5) explicitly associate with "academic literacies", "academic language" and "academic domain knowledge". This is the focus of this paper.

The time constraints on a typical foundation year program make it very difficult for learners to effectively acquire a large vocabulary on a wide range of *general* topics and the issues of randomness, irrelevance and segregation EAP skills as exemplified by the 'Exam-Practice Approach' are likely to reduce the possibility of EGAP still further. Grabe and Stoller (2002) point out that "L2 students will not develop a very large recognition vocabulary until they have had thousands of hours of practice reading L2 texts" (78). One of the interviewees (Teacher 5) raises concerns about *how much any students read **anything** in English outside of what we give them*, a point that Teacher 4 reinforces with a greater degree of certainty:

> *With a different type of student, from perhaps a different socio-economic background, of a different age, with a different type of motivation, they could practice ... by themselves- they're not going to do that ... even though ... the amount of material – self-access material – is so much improved, they still don't practice very much by themselves.*

Teacher 4 also mentions *Krashen and roughly tuned input* and the problem faced by lower-level students:

> *to really develop reading and listening, you really need to read and listen to a lot of stuff ... extensively not intensively. And by having a lot of different topics I think we are actually providing that but, as I said, at the same time we are, especially with students at this level, taking away the opportunity for recycling vocabulary.*

Thus, Teacher 4 postulates a possible *trade-off between challenging higher level students* **skills** and ensuring that lower level students receive the maximum amount of **vocabulary** re-encounters.

> *maybe at a higher level it is possible to split those four skills and it may even be desirable and useful and I think it is at the lower level where it starts to create more problems* (Teacher 4).

At this point it might be useful to document the only piece of relevant positive data collected about the 'Exam-Practice Approach': the *little bit of a positive effect* that reading even random texts will slowly develop a familiarity with words (Teacher 1). However, given the dearth of reading going on outside class and the overwhelming amount of off-topic vocabulary due to the randomness of the topics, any incidental vocabulary acquisition is likely to be limited and inefficient. It seems, therefore, that focus on the texts the students need to learn for their subjects should be prioritized. Grabe and Stoller (2002) suggest that instruction "can focus on the 2,000 to 3,000 most common words as an essential foundation for word-recognition automaticity, and then focus on vocabulary that is appropriate to specific topics and fields of study" (79).

Academic Vocabulary, Genre and Transferability

> Interviewer: *How important is vocabulary work in Year 1 EAP?*
> Teacher 2: *Number one...*

One could perhaps argue, given that the course is a foundation year, that it would be sufficient to expose students to organized (i.e. not random) general topics that would be assumed knowledge in a university context (e.g., basic introductions to geography, humanities, the scientific method and even my original proposal – health). However, to achieve this without adding extra **content** to the students' workload would be impossible without changing the entire structure of the year one program (far beyond the scope of this study) because the students already study their chosen specialist subject alongside their EAP classes. Besides, Alexander and Argent (2010) question the assumption that "general English" needs to be mastered before students can move to genuine academic texts, arguing that EAP "materials should demonstrate that the language students are learning is high frequency and transferable to their academic disciplines" (2). This idea of **transferability** is also strongly echoed by the subject teachers and is, surely, the main point of the 'AP' component of EAP.

Looking at vocabulary alone is probably insufficient because words do not operate in isolation; it is also important to analyze how vocabulary is used in the textual context. Biber (1999) shows that there are many "lexical bundles" or sequences of words that are frequently used in academic writing and Hyland (2007) shows how words and lexical bundles are used in different ways, and occur at different frequencies in different subjects, thus strengthening his argument for specificity. Nor does subject-specificity stop at the level of lexical bundles, but also the rhetorical structures of whole texts. Indeed, the local academic writing practices seem to have become divorced from the target academic subjects.

There has been a tendency to categorize essay "types" and to teach "rules" for each type which, incidentally, is also a major criticism of one of the textbooks recommended in the syllabus in that it exacerbates the existing "confusion between 'genres', 'text types' and 'rhetorical structures'" (Gimenez & Haywood, 2010, 336). Indeed, the disassociation of EAP from tangible academic subject language goals has led to the teaching of conventions that are not only lacking relevance, but which are arguably "non-academic genre types: expository essays ... argumentative essays ... newspaper writing" (Loi, 2010, 267). Selected reading texts can be particularly contentious:

> newspaper and magazine articles ... are usually chosen as texts but these are not the main genres that students have to read at university. The audience and purpose of journalistic texts are very different from academic texts so the layout ... and organization are inappropriate and the language is often difficult and culturally loaded (Alexander & Argent, 2010, 2).

Such commentary supports Teacher 3's observation that the *'exam-practice approach' is not unique to [this institution]*, at least in terms of its random reading content. However, it appears that this problem may have been particularly acute in this context with students reportedly feeling *that English is a really difficult subject* (Teacher 1) rather than language support for their subjects.

Different subjects have different requirements for the macro-structure of the written texts they expect students to produce and these features are not made explicit in the EAP program, which leads to a loss of transferability of knowledge and skills. It is as if a new 'EGAP genre' has been artificially created, which fails to address the genuine academic purposes of the students' courses. The broad differences in taught writing structures are clear in the figure 1.

By "identifying the kinds of writing that learners will need to do in their target situations" (Hyland, 2007, 152), and by explicitly focusing on those language features, the randomness and irrelevance of the EAP program could be reduced and the sites of learner confusion minimized. This suggests that EAP instruction should be specific, moving towards an ESAP approach with an explicit focus on academic vocabulary and target situation genre awareness work, and thus raising the transferability of skills from the EAP classroom to the subject classroom. Failure to do could be interpreted as failure to satisfy the 'AP' component of EAP.

Written Structure Taught in EAP	Written Structure Taught in Business	Written Structure Taught in Engineering
Essay:	Essay:	Laboratory *Report*
Introduction	Definition D	
Body	Explanation E	
Conclusion	Example E	
	Diagram D	
	(from 2011)	
	Evaluation	

Figure 1.
Differences in taught writing structures

The discussion so far is probably sufficient to set out the basis of my own argument that the use of subject-specific texts would be more appropriate to EAP than random exam practice:
- the 'common core hypothesis' states that the most common words will be encountered in a subject text just as well as an irrelevant text
- the weaker students will not do the amount of reading required to raise their vocabulary to a level where they can cope with the random EGAP vocabulary load
- the target fields of study are known and subject-specific texts can therefore be prioritized over random input
- recycling subject-specific vocabulary and macro-textual structures in EAP classes should help learners to more

quickly become familiar with the words they need and to understand the transferability of EAP skills

Teacher Perceptions 1: Randomness, Irrelevance and Separateness

Interviewer: *So you're saying make it more meaningful and*

Teacher 2: *Well, just **meaningful**, I don't know about **more**! I don't think it's got any meaning whatsoever at the moment ... and I'm not trying to be negative! What we ask them to do is a waste of time.*

At a meeting between the principal and the EAP teachers, it was noted that students' academic needs and purposes are not currently supported by EAP and nor are EAP skills reinforced in subject classes so the relevance of EAP is lost and the students do not get the exam practice required for Year One EAP gate-keeping exams (Meeting Notes, 2010). Eventually, this line of evolutionary EAP development was reflected in the principal's question, *Is the system that we've got a handicap?* (Meeting Notes, 2010), to which Teacher 2 offers a very unambiguous answer, *It's a system **designed** not to be successful.*

There seems to be a general agreement that better integration of the four EAP skills and subject study is necessary, with mention of ESP tending to elicit the response, *you're preaching to the converted* (Inter-departmental Integration Committee Chairman). The principal remarked, *I want to see integration on Year One* and the dean said, *I want ESP* (Meeting Notes, 2010). Another manager stated that *integration is essential [and] it wouldn't be that hard to change* (Meeting Notes, 2010). Nevertheless, it is worth documenting some EAP teachers' comments because this appears to be a particular cause of frustration.

Teacher 2 was scathing:
> I don't understand it, I really don't **understand** ... I've never worked anywhere, **anywhere** where they try to devise some .. totally separate, separate, separate ... input and I just don't get **why** you'd want to do that! Also, when I did ask about that last year they said that that was a requirement, so I got the syllabus out and it doesn't say that! It actually says ... it gives a breakdown on how time and investment might be **weighted** but it **doesn't** say teach them in isolation.

Teacher 5 clearly relates the problems with the distinct skills to students' vocabulary acquisition:
> well, one thing that I've noticed is because there are these divided skills – very little connection between any of the different classes from what I can see, and that will impact the vocabulary ...

On many EAP courses it is often assumed that teachers can teach reading and writing skills and that students "will build their vocabularies on their own as they engage in other activities; and that this will happen particularly in the context of academic reading" (Parry, 1991). Alexander & Argent (2010) make the problems of such a segregated, random approach very clear:
> The attempt to include a range of subjects results in a random collection of texts that does not mirror a university context, where texts and activities are related and sequenced in terms of their content. This random selection leads to incoherence in the development of understanding and linguistic repertoires (2).

Issues with Academic Vocabulary Acquisition | 389

All of the interviewees explicitly commented on the relationship between reading random texts and the possible retardation of vocabulary acquisition. Even the architect of the 'exam-practice approach' asked if *the students are learning despite what we do?*

> *A series of randomly chosen texts and discrete lessons doesn't provide a ... step by step development cycle for kids to move from one ... range of vocabulary knowledge – by say 2000 words – we don't help them move to 3000 words* (Teacher 1).

> *It's clear ... **intuitively**, that ... if you encounter a lexical set related to one topic and you then, you know, five minutes later, go into another class and encounter another lexical set, you're not going to learn vocabulary because you need to re-encounter it several times and have the opportunity to recycle it. So I think in that sense it can only have had a detrimental effect in terms of vocabulary acquisition.* (Teacher 4)
> *I have looked at [student] portfolios again ... and there are still random lists of unidentifiable, decontextualized lexical items* (Teacher 2).

> ***random** topics with no targets, in what vocabulary [inaudible]? – and no recycling. And my impression is the teachers are disjointed so how can [the students] cope in the subjects when they're supposed to use it? (Teacher 5)*

Randomness is also problematized in relation to purpose – the 'P' of EAP:

> *generally speaking, people have a purpose in reading and we don't encourage that. And again, having these isolated skills and **random** texts that nothing ever happens to ... you know, they're not even required to **comment** on the*

> text that they read ... whether they thought the actual contents was interesting or useful ... which is what you'd **normally** do with, with input in some way (Teacher 2).

Finally, two teachers are clearly leaning towards ESAP as a solution to this unwanted randomness:

> I think reading is extremely important but, as far as here, the reading – if they couldn't be more related to the topics the students will study, like business texts, economics texts that we could recycle from their subject courses [laughter] that seems better to me than sort of **randomly** ... finding ... topics (Teacher 5).

> Why wouldn't engineers find reading about an engineering topic interesting? Why would a business student find reading about the derivation of Roman names more interesting than ... something about the financial crisis or something like that? ... we can choose the materials that meet the students' interests and that's not a ground-breaking approach in education. I don't know anyone in the world who says [chuckling] 'it's better to do something random than [inaudible] the students' interests.' We seem to ... have gone down that route ... (Teacher 1).

This leads to the relevance of an ESP approach which would ensure that all students at least encounter the bare minimum of subject texts, *getting back to that ESAP side of engaging the students, showing them the relevance of [EAP]* (Teacher 1).

Teacher Perceptions 2: ESAP

When the EAP program was first established *there were* **two** *hours of ESAP* (Teacher 4), enjoying more time allocation than any other EAP skill, and the ESAP coordinators were the only managerial positions below the Head of Department. Specific academic vocabulary appears to have been of some concern from the earliest days, with the ESAP classes *testing [students'] comprehension, ensuring their understanding and working with their vocabulary* (Teacher 1).

However, *the fact that the students weren't performing very well in the exams* meant *that we dropped our ESAP module ... to give the students more chance to focus on the exam-based stuff* (Teacher 1). Teacher 4 suggests that the ESAP program may have been a victim of its own success from an operational or political perspective:

> *its advantage is kind of part of the reason why it was abandoned, which may sound odd, but ... there was an* **impression***, and I don't think that there is any data to support this, but it was certainly my impression in the classes and ... I'd say pretty much the* **only** *aspect of their subjects that the students fully understood was the part that was covered in EAP class, so I believe that there was a feeling of EAP being made responsible for learning outcomes which were not their responsibility.*

In other words, *it was good for the students ... but it wasn't really that good for EAP* (Teacher 4). Thus, disputes over departmental responsibilities appear to have been prioritized over the students' learning in the decision to drop ESAP. This is further complicated by the fact that EAP teachers are paid less than subject teachers and the implicit challenge to the relevance of the EAP gate-keeping examinations (if teaching specific 'academic purposes' is not part of EAP responsibility, then how is EAP any different to teaching general English?).

As Teacher 2 pointed out that *the subject teachers as **well** have things to learn about what the learners can do* and Teacher 4, responding to the issues of departmental responsibilities highlighted by ESAP provision, challenged the distinct division between EAP teacher and subject teacher:

> *is it really necessary that all those so called EAP hours are really delivered by EAP teachers? Like, really rather than having 15 hours of EAP, maybe the subject teachers should be better trained to be teaching in a way in which students will be developing the same skills.*

Teacher 2 takes this line of reasoning further and challenges the very notion of a distinct EAP department at all, *I would disband EAP ... I would shoot it like a sick dog!* Instead, at foundation year level, subject teachers should also be EAP teachers (or vice versa), effectively making **all** classes ESAP. In other words, subject reading passages "should not focus exclusively on the content of the reading but also include study of the academic language, along with work on strategies for vocabulary learning" (Coxhead & Byrd, 2010, 133). Whilst further exploration of this point is beyond the scope of this paper, it clearly lends weight to the claim that **integration** is valued by EAP teachers.

Finally, comments on an ESAP task piloted in 2010 as a precursor to this present study suggest subject – specificity may have raised student motivation levels and that this was particularly marked for the Engineering students. Whilst subject-related readings meant that Business students *were kind of inspired ... to find out more things*, it was *not so noticeable as with engineers, engineers it was **really**, **really** noticeable* (Teacher 2). One student is described as experiencing a *breakthrough or an **aha!** moment* and making a transition from being *bored, comatose* or *a waste of space* to *bright ... active and engaged as a learner* (Teacher 2).

Perhaps this finding is unsurprising given that the EAP assessments targeted by the 'exam-practice approach' include the comprehension of non-scientific texts and essay-writing skills, which form **no part** of the Engineering subject program or assessment.

An ESAP approach would help weak students obtain sufficient highly scaffolded reading to pass the assessment requirements whilst also ensuring that higher level students are not restricted. Whilst any wider reading need not be subject-specific, there is no harm in higher level students reading beyond the subject course requirements, which is, surely, the very aim of higher level academia.

Is ESAP the Answer?

Every informant commented on the remarkably low level of English proficiency amongst the students and several senior managers commented on the numbers of students who are consistently accepted onto the program despite being too weak to realistically achieve any of the goals. *They start Year One at a lower level than they could do or, perhaps,* **should** *do ... The language skills are weak, ehh ...* ***tremendously weak*** *and their study skills are probably even weaker* (Teacher 1). There is also evidence that this issue may be relevant beyond the immediate context and Teacher 4 explicitly relates this to observed trends in student entry levels and global EAP provision:

> *it is quite logical that you would probably not consider going to university to study in a foreign language unless you had a fairly good command of it –* ***That's changed!*** *And it's changed, particularly in China, it's changed **fast**!*

Alexander and Argent (2010) claim the "minimum level of competence ... tends to be set around IELTS 4/4.5" (1). However, Mayor (2006) points out that "Chinese candidates performed relatively poorly on the IELTS Academic test when compared to other language and nationality groups" (105) and Green (2005, 11) claims that Chinese learners statistically tend to make less progress during EAP and/or IELTS preparation courses. Recent reports from two institutions related to the context of study suggest that Alexander and Argent's (2010) estimate may be unrealistically high (personal communication). The Chinese continue to represent the largest group of overseas students in the UK (HESA, 2011) and Dooey (2010) reports findings from Australia showing that the primary concern of students enrolled on pre-tertiary EAP programs was "having too many speakers of Chinese languages". A trend that seems set to continue with economic factors that encourage international institutions to tap into the lucrative market of low-level Chinese students. It is, therefore, clearly important that solutions to low-level Chinese learners are found.

> If Chinese students are to be more successful – not only in the IELTS test but also in their future academic study in English – they need to be provided with models of what will be expected from them in Western academic writing, reflecting contemporary practices across the disciplines (Mayor, 2006, 118).

Whilst the simple non-admission of weak students would no doubt prove popular with teachers and solve many of the documented problems, perhaps of greater value (and economic benefit?) would be a system capable of accommodating these low-level unmotivated learners while also maintaining the capacity to challenge higher-level learners. The argument above suggests that ESAP is probably the strongest contender to achieve this balance, but how can it be implemented?

Extensive reading is seen as essential to vocabulary acquisition (Grabe & Stoller, 2002, 78) but, since the majority of students are not motivated to engage in such activity, the EAP programme seems to be ethically obliged to focus on the **intensive** study of subject-related texts, prioritising the **Academic Purposes** over the general **English** of IELTS-style test preparation. The data suggest **relevance** and **purpose** would be particularly highly valued by EAP teachers, and that language development is valued as much as skills practice, possibly even more so for the inevitable numbers of low-level students. ESAP provides a straightforward solution to the question of relevance and purpose, and can provide the opportunity to practice EAP skills whilst recycling and reinforcing academic vocabulary.

Baumann and Graves (2010), who present several ways of categorizing and "identifying academic vocabulary for instruction" (8), imply that this should be done at the level of the curriculum (8). "Intuitions about academic language can be checked using an online concordance with an academic corpus ..." (Alexander & Argent, 2010, 2). Corpus linguistics and the use of computer concordances have revolutionized such approaches to vocabulary instruction by enabling researchers and practitioners to statistically measure frequencies and patterns of usage rather than relying on intuition. This is important because intuition is often "not in accordance with the newly observed facts of usage" (Sinclair, 1991, 4). It also strongly supports the use of "authentic" texts (here understood to be "target situation texts") because "[i]nvented examples would ... appeal for their authenticity to a non-existent context, which would eventually be evaluated by someone's intuition, with all the misleading consequences of that" (Sinclair, 1991, 5). At the time of writing, the measurement and comparison of word frequency and 'lexical bundles' in subject, EAP and ESAP texts represents an ongoing 'course development' project.

While we wait for the context-specific results of the 'course development' work, Coxhead's (2000) AWL and Haywood's (2007) online AWL Highlighter and AWL Gapmaker provide ready-made user-friendly resources. Attempts have already been made to introduce the AWL to the Academic Writing and Listening programs as a means of systematically prioritizing vocabulary instruction.

Teacher 2 argues that Coxhead's (2000) AWL provides a ready resource for introducing a systematic approach to vocabulary teaching:

> Whether or not it's the best system, it's a widely used system ... because of the fact that you can copy and paste any text, **any** text into the highlighter, and in a **second** you have a frequency – based lexical resource **identified** ... learners ... **aren't** capable of deciding for themselves what lexical items they meet frequently so therefore if there's a **tool** that identifies that the most frequently words ... and it is non-strand-based, so ... if you want a common **core** that both business and engineering students would have to use.

This is obviously highly consistent with Coxhead and Nation's (2001) claim that "an academic vocabulary list ... deserves a lot of attention in a variety of ways from both the learners and teacher no matter what their specialist area of academic study" (256). Teacher 2 points out that if EAP teachers concentrated on Coxhead's (2000) AWL, *because the academic word list* **excludes** *specialist language ... therefore if we had the specialist language input from subject teachers*, ESAP vocabulary input could be coordinated across an **integrated** curriculum. This differentiation of AWL and 'specialist' vocabularies may prove important because "[a]cademic vocabulary is generally not as well known as technical vocabulary" (Coxhead & Nation, 2001, 255), and is strategically useful because it allows EAP to evade the challenge of trying to learn another discipline (often attributed to Spack, 1988).

> Academic vocabulary is the kind of specialized vocabulary that an English teacher can usefully help learners with. This is in contrast to technical vocabulary where the teacher can often do little because of the teacher's lack of background knowledge of the subject (Coxhead & Nation, 2001, 256).

Thus, my provisional conclusion is that the 'exam-practice approach', exemplifying an EGAP orientation, can be usefully replaced by a fully integrated ESAP approach where EAP teachers focus on the academic vocabulary, 'lexical bundles' and macro-rhetorical structures of **subject** texts. Subject teachers can then focus on specialist technical vocabulary and content. With such a system in place, a future can be envisaged where foundation year integration is made complete by having both EAP and subject lessons taught by **the same** ESAP teacher and where a clear distinction is made between 'EAP' and 'English for IELTS-style tests'.

References

Alexander, O., & Argent, S. (2010). *Making EAP accessible for lower level learners*, paper presented at the University of St Andrews 2nd ELT Workshop: The Challenge of Teaching EAP to Lower Level Students.

Baumann, J. F., & Graves, M. F. (2010) 'What is Academic Vocabulary?. *Journal of Adolescent & Adult Literacy, 54*(1), 4-12.

Biber, D. (1999). *University language: A corpus-based study of spoken and written registers*. Retrieved from http://www.books.google com

Coxhead, A. (2000). A New Academic Word List. *TESOL Quarterly*, 34(2), 213-238.
Coxhead, A., & Byrd, P. (2007). Preparing writing teachers to teach the vocabulary and grammar of academic prose. *Journal of Second Language Writing, 16*, 129–147.
Coxhead, A., & Nation, P. (2001). The specialized vocabulary of English for academic purposes'. In Flowerdew, J. & Peacock, M. (2001) *Research Perspectives on English for Academic Purposes*. Macmillan.
Dooey, P. (2010). Students' perspectives of an EAP pathway program. *Journal of English for Academic Purposes, 9*, 184-197.
Flowerdew, J., & Peacock, M. (2001). *Research Perspectives on English for Academic Purposes*. Macmillan.
Gimenez, J., & Haywood, S. (2010). Review of: Uncovering EAP. How to teach academic writing and reading, Sam McCarter, Phil Jakes. Oxford: Macmillan Education (2009). *Journal of English for Academic Purposes, 9*, 335-338.
Grabe, W., & Stoller, F. L. (2002). *Teaching and Researching Reading*. Pearson Education Limited.
Grabe, W. (2001). Cited in Hyland, K. (2007). Genre pedagogy: Language, literacy and L2 writing instruction. *Journal of Second Language writing, 16*, 148-164.
Green, A. (2005). EAP study recommendations and score gains on the IELTS Academic Writing test. *Assessing Writing, 10*(1), 44-60.
Haywood, S. (2011). *AWL Highlighter*. Retrieved from http://www.nottingham.ac.uk/%7Ealzsh3/acvocab/awhighlighter.htm
HESA (2011). *Press release 155 - Students in Higher Education Institutions 2009/10*, retrieved from http://www.hesa.ac.uk/index.php?option=com_content&task=view&id=1943&Itemid=161

Hyland, K. (2007). Genre pedagogy: Language, literacy and L2 writing instruction. *Journal of Second Language Writing, 16,* 148-164.

Hyland, K. (2009). Writing in the Disciplines: Research evidence for specificity. *Taiwan International ESP Journal, 1*(1), 5-22.

Loi, C. K. (2010). Research article introductions in Chinese and English: A comparative genre-based study. *Journal of English for Academic Purposes, 9,* 267-279.

Mayor, B. (2006). Dialogic and Hortatory Features in the Writing of Chinese Candidates for the IELTS Test. *Language, Culture and Curriculum, 19*(1), 104-121.

Moore, T., & Morton, J. (2005). Dimensions of difference: a comparison of university writing and IELTS writing. *Journal of English for Academic Purposes, 4,* 43-66.

Parry. (1991). Cited in Grabe, W. & Stoller, F. L. (2002) *Teaching and Researching Reading.* Pearson Education Limited.

Sinclair, J. (1991). *Corpus Concordance Collocation.* Oxford University Press.

Spack, R. (1988). Initiating ESL students into the Academic Discourse Community: How far should we go? *TESOL Quarterly, 22*(1), 29-51.

Part Six
TESOL Interfaces 6(1)

2012

38. Eclecticism in TESOL

Eric D. Reynolds

Thank you all for reading the first issue of *TESOL Interfaces*. The journal used to be called simply *Interfaces*, and our hope is the new title will help disambiguate us from other journals in the field. In another beginning, this is my first issue as editor in chief, and as such I want to extend my earnest thanks to all of the people that submitted papers for this issue, particularly those that you find here, but also those that did not make this issue. I sincerely want to encourage those researchers and writers to continue their efforts: You can do it! This issue has a bit of an eclectic flair, bear with me as I briefly introduce the contents.

Tory S. Thorkelson considers how motivation works in EFL classrooms. Additionally, he examines the Korean EFL environment, in particular, relative to the issues of intrinsic and extrinsic motivations. Finally, the author offers us insights from the one he is most familiar with, his own.

Sarah Elizabeth Seitzinger opens up a world of opportunities by showing us how to use film-making to teach English at an English camp. The project utilized a project based approach primarily through student centered activities. Moreover, she tells us how to take advantage of readily available technology without sacrificing quality. Ultimately, she lays out a cost-effective and highly motivating way to engage young students in learning English.

Eric Reynolds, that's me, offers advice on conducting researching, particularly that first step of searching the literature. Many researchers find a big difference in the access they have to academic research in TESOL after they arrive in Korea. The article provides some advice for using free Internet based tools – e.g., Google Scholar—and integrating those tools with the more traditional access sources that may be available. But most important he points out how to leverage your community to the best literature search possible. This serves as the first installment of a new section of the journal, *On Research*, which will prove snapshots of how we do qualitative and mixed methods research in the field of TESOL.

Oh, one last thing: do you like the wordle recently introduced to the top of the *TESOL Interfaces* home page? For those of you who do not know, Wordle creates a word cloud where the most common words in the text appear larger. Thus, as a way to summarize the issue, I plugged the complete text of volume six of the journal into the application, and this is what came out ... What are we focusing on? Clearly, our *'students'* matter more than anything else. *'English'* was in second place and then the topics of the individual papers – *blogs, motivation, film camp*, and *research and writing* – rise out of the wordle. It looks like we did our job. We have put our students first.

39. Intrinsic and Extrinsic Motivation (and Discipline) in the EFL Environment
Tory S. Thorkelson

What are the theories behind motivation? How can motivating your students, or helping them find their own motivations for learning, make your job in the classroom easier? By reviewing some of the more dominant theories on motivation, and showing how they can be actualized for classroom use as well as dealing with some of the more common classroom problems the author has heard about or encountered in 16 years of teaching Adults in Korea, this paper aims to offer some of the strategies and approaches that have worked well for both the writer and his colleagues over the years.

Introduction

> *And if education is always to be conceived along the same antiquated lines of a mere transmission of knowledge, there is little to be hoped from it in the bettering of man's future* ~ Maria Montessori (1870-1952), Italian Doctor and Educator.

> *Time is a great teacher, but unfortunately it kills all of its students* ~ Hector Berlioz (1803-69), French Composer.

We all know that every student is different, every class is different and every term is different, but how many of us actually treat them as such? For new teachers who are forced to test and reinvent themselves, this is probably a daily truth but for older, more experienced teachers this is something we need to remind ourselves of on a regular basis. Therefore, the purpose of this paper (and the accompanying workshop) is to address how motivating our students, and ourselves, is an essential element of keeping our teaching fresh, relevant and worthwhile for ourselves and our students. To address this best, I will first need to define motivation and review some of the more popular theories related to educational psychology (as well as some new ideas on the science of motivation) and then show how a few simple things have made all the difference in my own classroom over the years.

Part One: Definitions and Theories of Motivation

According to Woolfolk (2004), motivation can be defined as, "an internal state that arouses, directs and maintains behavior" (351). Further, there are two types of motivation, "**Intrinsic:** Belonging to the nature of a thing, like a game which is fun and inspires interest and curiosity. Activities are their own reward. *Extrinsic:* external or coming from outside the activity, like punishments and rewards" (351).

From an educational perspective, intrinsic motivation is far more powerful than extrinsic which is the theoretical equivalent of the carrot and stick, and we all have had students who excel because they love English for its own sake rather than being motivated by the teacher, the test, the desire to get an A+, or whatever other external factors may be pushing them to do well in our classes. This (preference for intrinsic motivations over extrinsic ones?) is also reflected in the four dominant theories of motivation as summarized in Figure 1.

Four Theories of Motivation

Behavioral Approaches
Assumes that our basic physiological needs motivate us, and that when hunger, thirst and so on are satisfied, we will behave in certain ways because they are associated with these needs. (Skinner and Pavlov, for example)

Humanistic Approaches
Emphasize personal choice, freedom, self-determination and striving for personal growth. Stresses the importance of intrinsic motivation. (Maslow and Carl Rogers, for example)

Cognitive Approaches
People respond not to external events or physical conditions like hunger, but rather to their interpretations of those events. Cognitive theorists believe that behavior is determined by our thinking, not simply by whether we have been rewarded or punished for the behaviors in the past. People work hard because they enjoy the work and want to understand. Once again, motivation is intrinsic.(Ulric Neisser, for example)

Social Learning Approaches (or Sociocultural)
Combine behavioral and cognitive approaches so that both the effects of outcomes and the impact of individual beliefs are taken into account. Motivation is seen as a product of the individual's expectation of reaching a goal and the value of that goal to him or her. (Bandura, for example)

Figure 1.
A brief summary of the four major approaches to motivation (adapted from Woolfolk, 2004, 352-8)

As Behaviorism was replaced by less punishment and reward oriented approaches which valued the students as self motivated 'partners' with their teachers and classmates in the learning process, students gained more autonomy over their learning and the teacher stepped back out of the center of attention and took on more of a facilitative or 'coach' role rather than the more traditional one as the authority or 'reservoir of knowledge' on and for their subject area. Both Maslow and Bloom offered their own individual interpretations of this process and trend which became staples of Educational psychology from when they were originally proposed up until the present day. Maslow's (1954) original Hierarchy of Needs is shown below along with the newly revised version:

Maslow's Original Hierarchy of Needs	Maslow's Revised Hierarchy of Needs
	Parenting
	Mate Retention
Self actualization	Mate Acquisition
Esteem (respect)	Status/Esteem
Love (affection, belongingness)	Affiliation
Safety	Self-Protection
Immediate Physiological Needs	Immediate Physiological Needs

Figure 2.
Maslow's Original and Revised Hierarchies of Needs

Anyone who has dealt with tired or hungry students in their classrooms can appreciate what Maslow was trying to get at in his original work. The revised version leaves a lot to be desired in terms of what education is all about. Bloom's *The Taxonomy of Educational Objectives* (1956) and Gardner's *Multiple Intelligences* (1983) along with Gardener's *Five Minds for the Future* (2007) are all seen as attempts to show how to teach students to think critically and function at higher levels of 'intelligence' (Bloom's taxonomy) while acknowledging that students are unique individuals with unique needs (Gardener's multiple intelligences) that go beyond simply being well educated members of a given society (Gardner's five minds). Unlike Maslow, Bloom has been re-interpreted and reworked to be more directly applicable and useable by the classroom teacher. For proof of this see both the revised Bloom's taxonomy and Dalton and Smith's (1986) interpretation of the original taxonomy in Appendix 1.

First, the new taxonomy takes the original nouns and transforms them into verbs (or more active words), which are much easier to teach to and integrate into the curriculum, objectives, classroom and activities per se. Also, creativity certainly ranks higher than the ability to simply sythesise or analyse what has already been learned, so it becomes the top skill and final destination of the educational process itself.

Old Version	**New Version**
Evaluation	Creating
Synthesis	Evaluating
Analysis	Analyzing
Application	Applying
Comprehension	Understanding
Knowledge	Remembering

Figure 3.
Bloom's Original Taxonomy (1956), and the Krathwol and Anderson (2001) revised version

Second, Dalton and Smith take a slightly different approach by creating questions to stimulate the critical and higher order thinking at each stage of the original taxonomy, while also providing tasks and activities for classroom use at each stage as well. While this works well in many ways, at least two vital questions remain. Do students evolve and move up the taxonomy naturally, or do they need to be 'pushed'? If teachers can help, then how can they assist students to advance from one stage to the next? For me, the answer to the first question rests again with motivation.

Motivated students are curious students and will explore and discover things for themselves – but as Vygotsky (1978) argues letting the teacher "point them in the right direction" or guide them only when students truly need it will facilitate the process. One answer to the second question would be for teachers to vary tasks from lesson to lesson and move up the taxonomy as students develop more advanced skills which ties in well with Vygotsky's Zone of Proximal Development (ZPD) which is defined as "... the distance between the actual development level as determined by actual problem solving and the level of potential development as determined through problem solving under adult guidance or in collaboration with more capable peers" (86). In this way, both teachers and students can have input into when an adjustment in tasks done in class moving up the taxonomy is both desirable and advisable.

While Gardner's multiple intelligences typology has been criticized by some for its lack of academic rigor (see Morgan (1996) as just one example), it allows for addressing students' needs through effective use of their "talents" (alone or in combination) while making explicit the idea that students have both strengths and weaknesses that need to be developed and addressed for the educational process to be truly effective. The "5 minds" only take this even further by showing what students should come out of the educational process being able to do as effective members of a given society.

Intrinsic and Extrinsic Motivation (and Discipline) | 409

                Bodily-Kinesthetic
Verbal-Linguistic   Musical-Rhythmic
Visual-Spatial   Logical-Mathematic
Interpersonal   Intrapersonal
                        Naturalistic

Figure 4.
Gardner's original Multiple Intelligences

The five minds take this a bit further by showing marked similarities to Bloom (synthesis and creating) and also addressing many of the social skills we expect from the best members of a given society. I particularly like the visual inspired by the figure below because the brain needs to be 'plugged in' and it is the teacher's job to do this by harnessing students' curiosity, desire to learn and finding what motivates them. Only then can our classrooms, lessons and schools be filled with the best that education can offer to present and future generations.

Five Minds for the Future

Disciplined		Synthesizing
Mastery of key subjects		Arraying information to make sense to self and others
Respectful	Creating	Ethical
Seeking to understand differences	Beyond existing knowledge and syntheses to pose new questions	Striving toward good work and good citizenship

Figure 5.
Gardner's Five Minds

Finally, I would like to discuss Daniel Pink's (2009) *Drive: The Surprising Truth about What Motivates Us* about the science of motivation. For me, his work epitomizes the best of what we need to accomplish in our classrooms and beyond. While Pink focuses mostly on business environments, his three tenets of motivation are highly relevant to fostering motivated learners, in my opinion. His ideas can be summarized as follows:

> When it comes to motivation, there's a gap between what science knows and what business does. Our current business operating system–which is built around external, carrot-and-stick motivators–doesn't work and often does harm. We need an upgrade. And the science shows the way. *This new approach has three essential elements: 1. Autonomy – the desire to direct our own lives. 2. Mastery — the urge to get better and better at something that matters. 3. Purpose — the yearning to do what we do in the service of something larger than ourselves.* (Italics mine) (218-219).

Personally, I would add 'recognition' to this list, as we need also to acknowledge publicly those who do well in big ways and small in our classrooms, boardrooms and lives. Praise in public and chastise in private where possible is my view on this. If our students have some independence in how they do the tasks we set them, see their skills evolve in some ways during their time with us, and understand the purpose of what we and they are doing in the classroom, I firmly believe that they will become co-enthusiasts and true partners in their own and other students' learning rather than obstacles to our teaching and other students' learning.

Part Two: Putting the Theories into Practice

Now, in part two, I would like to show how setting clear rules for your classroom, treating your students as people, and expecting more from your students than they expect from themselves will help you deal with many of the 'problems' that most often get in the way of education – especially in an environment where teachers and students have very different goals, cultural backgrounds, and expectations for their classroom experiences.

First, let me describe my day one. As with many teachers, I spend maybe half the class period going over the details of the class content, and grading scheme, but of particular importance to understanding my students' motivation, I will discuss my standard class rules in some detail. Let me explain each of the seven rules briefly in turn.

1. Be on time. (Western time, not Korean!)
This teaches students to respect their classmates' time as well as yours. Late students lose points after 15 minutes in my classes and absences also count against them (although I do give them one free absence per class per term as an acknowledgement that we are all human and some things can't be controlled).

2. Ask questions. (In this case, silence is NOT golden).
Korean students are notorious for being silent even when they have a question because they don't want to stand out or look foolish. I make sure they know I expect questions in class but also offer office hours and have my email and office number on my syllabus in case they are more comfortable asking questions outside of class.

3. Speak English ONLY. (This is NOT a Japanese, German, French, or Korean class).
Even though I expect some L1 to slip out sometimes, I do not encourage it unless absolutely necessary.

4. Attendance and participation are important, and will be reflected in your mark
Some students still expect that they will get an A+ just by being in class every day. My students need to be in class and doing what I ask them to do to get full credit for both of these.

5. Cell phones MUST be turned off. (Need I explain?!)
While I do allow some use of their dictionaries (especially in a writing class), I monitor carefully and will take points off if I catch them sending messages or visiting Facebook during class – except during exams when no cell phones are allowed to be on or in use at all.

6. This is OUR class, so let's make it interesting and fun
A happy class is a productive class. I am also known to joke with my students on occasion (which tends to make the point better than yelling or getting angry might when something goes wrong).

7. Bring ALL class materials every day
Many of my classes do not have textbooks, and making handouts is both time consuming and can be costly, so students who don't bring materials can copy or share a friend's materials but – if the problem occurs more than once – they will lose points for this as well.

Let me offer one more tip: I used to get a lot of students who would say, *Teacher, I did not understand the rules*, when I had to enforce something. Then a friend said he made a Korean version and had his students sign two copies – one for him and one for them. I did the same thing, and rarely had a problem after that, and when I did, the signed rules on file solved it!

Problems and Solutions discussed in the Workshop
Now, let us look at some of the more common problems that teachers have told me that they have in their classrooms—based on my 16 years of teaching adults here in Korea.

Reticence
What do you do when despite your best effort, a student in your class refuses to speak any English? Take them aside, and remind them that their mark is based on English usage and participation--not simply attendance. More importantly, try to find out why they are refusing to use English in class. Use a 'Red, Yellow, and Green' card system and allow students to monitor each other. Assign one group member as a 'Language monitor' during group activities.

Lateness
A student, or students, continuously comes late to class and/or always takes 15 minutes instead of the 10-minute break everyone else takes. Lock the door when you start your class, and then take points off if a verbal warning after the incident does not work.

Cell Phones
What should you do when a student's cell phone is constantly going off while you are trying to teach, and sometimes s/he actually answers the phone or makes calls during class? Give the students one verbal warning, then take the phone away for the duration of the class. If it occurs again, require a letter of apology before returning the phone. One friend used a 'Cell Phone Jail' at the front of the class to great effect. Another made the student in question buy them a coffee by way of apology. Answering their phone yourself might also work.

Sleeping

What do you do when a student comes on time everyday but then sits in the back and sleeps through the entire lesson? Remind the student of the class requirements for participation. If that does not work, kick them out until they decide they want to learn. Be sure to check if they have a part time job as well, since many students work nights to pay for tuition, living expenses, and other issues.

Long Bathroom Breaks

What can you do when students go to the 'washroom', and do not bother to come back for 30 minutes or more? Mark them as absent, and make a point of noticing their absence so that their friends will tell them what happened when they were not there. Be sure to welcome them back to class if and when they return.

Forgotten Materials

What do you do when a student never brings their textbook, a pen, or other necessary materials for class? Remind them that they need to bring their materials to class, and perhaps lend them a book once. After that, I ignore them and let them be bored or ask their friends for help.

Evaporating Students

What do you do when a couple of students come for the roll call (attendance) and then slip out while your back is turned? Mark them as absent, and make a point of noticing their absence so that their friends will tell them what happened.

Coffee Break Spies

What do you do when you catch some students going through your bag and looking at your attendance sheets when you return to class after break? Remind them it is impolite to do this, and then kick them out of class if it happens again. A letter of apology may be used to give them a chance to come back.

Sweet Pleaders
What should you do when your students are constantly pressuring you to let them go early or have outdoor classes when the weather is nice? Reward them for doing a good job or finishing early, but be sure that the outdoor classes are well structured and induce learning. My solution for this pleading was an 'infohunt' activity where the students did a scavenger hunt all over Hanyang's hilly campus, while I read my newspaper. See appendix 2 for the list of questions and items they had to collect in a 50-minute period.

Complaints About Grades
What do you do when students complain that grading is unfair? I hand back all homework, as well as going over at least the midterms in class. I also keep notes of what rules they broke: cell phones, late arrivals, and the rest. Finally, I break assessment into categories spread throughout the term including Quizzes, Presentations, Journals, Interviews, and others depending on class type. I often give some kind of bonus work related to the class, but the bonus is never worth more than 5% of the overall grade.

Boredom
What can you do when students say that the topics are boring? My best solution has been to give students two lists of topics for discussion in groups. I use *Instant Lessons* (MacAndrew & Martinez, 2003) and *Taboos and Issues* (MacAndrew & Martinez, 2001) and have the students choose up to eight from each list of forty as a group and then I mix the groups up and have them negotiate to choose five to six topics they like in their new groups. I use all three lists to decide what to teach –

supplementing with material from *Breaking News English* and other sources. Then when they say, *Teacher, this is boring*, I can say, *You chose it!* For other classes, I give lots of choices, but they must confirm all topics with me first before they present, write a paper or the other classroom tasks. An example of how confirmation is critical arose when a student wanted to demonstrate how to commit suicide in a variety of ways. Because this was clearly inappropriate, we changed the topic to how to help someone who is thinking of committing suicide stop thinking this way.

Mixed Level Classes
What do you do when you have a large, class with wide differences in skill level? I provide a variety of activities about the same topic for beginner, intermediate, and advanced students or create open-ended materials and questions that let students engage at their own level. Try to get to know your students' names and use the space/classroom to your advantage. Use nametags to keep attendance and recognize students. Be organized and prepared and use the board/AV effectively as well as provide effective outlines/handouts. Have a routine so students know what to expect.

Conclusion
In conclusion, I would offer the following general tips and advice for any teachers dealing with students in Korea. I sincerely hope they work as well for you and your students as they have for me and mine.

Know something about the theories and research available on motivation: autonomy, mastery, purpose (Pink, 2009) and recognition where appropriate, for example. Keeping every student motivated at all times is an impossible task, but addressing their needs specifically, helping them to find their own reasons for learning and allowing them to apply their talents (and develop new ones) are all important to having a good classroom experience for you and them.

Inspiration starts with you, not your students. Passionate teachers are usually successful teachers. Combined with knowledge of your subject and a genuine regard for and concern about your students as people, it is a very successful combination of factors.

Move from more strict to less strict as the class progresses. The class rules are meant to keep students focused and on task. They should not be arbitrary in either their contents or their application. One of my former bosses told me I had a reputation among students for being 'Firm but Fair'. I strive to maintain that to this day with all my classes and students.

Students do not care what you know: they care whether you care. Some flexibility is a good thing (e.g., my Hanyang Infohunt story). Get to know your students as people and treat them with kindness and respect. Be aware of what is going on in their lives--exams, projects, assignments, and sometimes even who just broke up with their boy/girlfriend and has a part time job at nights and are always tired in class. Tone your lessons up or down accordingly, and do not be afraid to go off topic on occasion as long as learning is still going on.

Remember students' names and get to know your students as people. Many articles over the years have stressed that knowing students' names is important. When you have 200 or more students a term, it can be hard to do, but nametags and photos that are used to keep track of attendance or a seating chart are good ways to 'cheat' and speed up the process.

Teach by example, by finding ways to relate to your students in ways they will understand, and then the lessons you conduct will be much easier and more fulfilling. Always relate classroom topics to their experience where possible. Give them autonomy over topics they speak or write about where possible, and they will often surprise you with how much they accomplish as a result.

Learning is a cooperative process. Learn from your students as they learn from you, and both of you will get far more out of the process than you put in. Let your students teach you something about their language and culture, and they will be far more open to learning what you have to teach about English and your culture in turn. Do not worry too much about making mistakes. You are going to make them, so learn from them and carry on.

Discipline and extrinsic motivation go hand in hand – Carrot & Stick – but only use them sparingly and when absolutely necessary. It may only take one or two public instances of taking points off for being late or not bringing their textbook to class to make the point for the rest of the class at the beginning of term, so take the time to set a high standard of expectations at the start. You can always ease off later in the term when the class knows each other and you much better.

My philosophy is this: Teachers do not fail students: students fail themselves. I start every class/term with every student at an 'A+'. I remind them that their actions will influence their grades, so it is up to them to keep their participation, attendance and quality of work high to earn that high grade they all want at the end of the term. Finally, a recent article rated "Friendliness" as the most highly valued quality by students when rating excellent teachers. Are you friendly and caring without necessarily being a 'friend'?

References

Anderson, L.W., & Krathwohl, D. R. (Eds.). (2001). *A taxonomy for learning, teaching and assessing*. Boston, MA: Allyn & Bacon.

Banville, S. (2004). *Breaking News English*. Retrieved from http://www.breakingnewsenglish.com

Bloom, B. S. (1956). *Taxonomy of Educational Objectives, Handbook I: The Cognitive Domain*. New York: David McKay.

Dalton, J., & Smith, D. (1986). *Extending children's special abilities: Strategies for primary classrooms*.

Gardner, Howard. (1983) *Frames of Mind: The Theory of Multiple Intelligences*. New York: Basic Books.

Gardner, H. (2007). *Five minds for the future*. Harvard Business School Press: Cambridge, MA.

Gronlund, N. (1990), *Measurement and evaluation in teaching* (6th ed.). New York, Macmillan.

MacAndrew, R. & Martinez, R. (2003). *Instant discussions: Photocopiable lessons on controversial topics*. Hove, UK: LTP

MacAndrew, R., & Martinez, R. (2001). *Taboos and issues: Photocopiable lessons on controversial topics*. Hove, UK: LTP

Maslow, A. H. (1954). *Motivation and personality*. New York: Harper and Row.

McLeod, S. A. (2007). *Simply psychology Maslow hierarchy of needs*. Retrieved from http://www.simplypsychology.org/maslow.html

Morgan, H. (1996). An analysis of Gardner's theory of multiple intelligence. *Roeper Review 18*, 263-270.

Pink, D. H. (2009). *Drive: The surprising truth about what motivates us*. New York, NY: Riverhead Books.

Pohl, M. (2000). *Learning to Think Thinking to Learn*. Victoria, Australia: Hawker Brownlow Education.

Vygotsky, L. S. (1978). *Mind in Society*. Cambridge, Mass.: Harvard University Press.

Woolfolk, A. E. (2004). *Educational psychology* (9th ed.). Boston: Allyn & Bacon.

40. Giving Creative Control to EFL Students through Short Film-Making

Sarah Elizabeth Seitzinger

Inter-session camps and after school classes are ideal settings for conducting English short film- making projects. Putting creative control of the filmmaking process into students' hands can inspire students to take charge of their own learning and to exceed their task requirements. By teaching students the basics of genres, storyboarding, character design, script-writing, camera techniques or angles, light and sound, setting, and editing, and then employing that information in a hands-on project, instructors can empower students to use English in an engaging task-based learning activity. Taking advantage of readily available technology (digital cameras or smart phones), this project puts tools in students' hands to create a meaningful final product using English in every step of the production. Students will gain confidence with English speaking by interacting with the teacher and by seeing their efforts come to fruition in a tangible and lasting way through film. Additionally, teachers often work with limited budgets and facilities, but a film-making unit can be cost-effective and conducted with relatively limited financial resources. This project was carried out by public school high school students during a 7-day English camp, though it can apply to other levels and settings.

Introduction

> *I hear, and I forget I see, and I remember I do, and I understand* ~ Confucius.

What inspires a person to create? Perhaps we find scope for the imagination in creative works of others that we desire to imitate. Maybe there is an inner desire to take pieces or materials and compose a piece of art greater than the sum of its components.

Giving Creative Control to EFL Students

Possibly we see an opportunity to play in a proverbial sandbox and are surprised by what we can produce when given the opportunity, encouragement, and tools we need. Movies have captured the imagination, and the desire to express oneself in a moving, visual narrative has inspired the creative efforts of many aspiring filmmakers. With the Digital Revolution, the technology able to make movies grew in accessibility as it fell in price, and today's students have access to tools our forerunners could not have envisioned outside of science fiction. South Korea has embraced this technology even as English language study has vaulted into a booming area of commerce. Amidst all the changes, it is easy for the needs of students to get lost, yet students can reap many rewards from a student-centered EFL pedagogy that embraces the technology of digital film making and puts students at the wheel of creativity in driving their English studies.

In 2011, I encountered several native English teachers (NETs) who incorporated short filmmaking into their public high school English camps. Only having casually studied film as an art form, watched many behind-the-scenes featurettes, and co-created home videos with friends and siblings in high school, I knew little about filmmaking from experience. However, watching some EFL student- made films inspired me to take the plunge, unprepared as I was, and run a short filmmaking summer English camp at Sorae High School. I took the idea and ventured out with it, drawing from the ideas of others and my own amateur video-making experiments. I was overwhelmed by the positive verbal and written response from students who attended the camp, and by the quality of films they produced with limited time and resources. It is my goal to share some ideas from that process to encourage EFL teachers to try similar projects, and to show that it does not demand prior expertise or expensive equipment to accomplish a meaningful, creative, student – driven English learning activity using short film making.

Few educators have published research thus far on using student-driven filmmaking in the EFL classroom. McKenney and Voogt (2011), EFL teachers in the Netherlands, wrote, "When it comes to integrating video-making into the language arts curriculum, no other support materials, in English or Dutch, have been located after extensive searching in both research and practice publications" (711). McKenney continues to conduct training seminars for teachers to encourage them to explore such projects with their EFL students, but few other educators seem to be publishing their results. Part of my motivation in writing is to build onto a young field of research and to encourage fellow educators to join in the ongoing dialogue to explore the possibilities of project-based short film activities.

This dearth of research does not seem caused by incompatibility between EFL classrooms and short film projects. Consider the following research findings gathered by Hofer and Swan (2005), "Digital video projects can promote student creativity, accommodate students with different learning styles and ability levels, and connect students with their out-of-school interests" (105). The benefits of a short film camp for fostering student creativity outweigh the costs of time investment and front-end planning work. Many students who attend English camps or after school classes do so because they are interested in learning English, but some students have other favorite subjects, and they have enrolled in the English class for other reasons. Students generally have a broad array of learning styles, and it is almost guaranteed that NETs will find several English proficiency levels within a single class. A film project can bridge some of those gaps.

A helpful place to begin facilitating a film project is by determining the learning goals you have and setting the film requirements to coincide with those goals. For example, if a teacher wants students to develop skill with second-language storytelling, then he or she should emphasize character development, plot structure, and dialogue. One of the strengths of this project is that it makes students think about the message design process. McKenney and Voogt (2011) describe the process as follows: "(1) formulating a message goal; (2) considering the audience; (3) mapping necessary elements; (4) collecting and organizing content; (5) reducing the elements to the essentials (editing and revising); and (6) publication" (710). This process can be used in any message medium, whether audio, video, text, or others. Students in my project experiment did not deal with the final step, but they addressed the other steps that McKenney and Voogt outline.

Camps about filmmaking are also beneficial to students because they tap into all four language skills: listening, reading, writing, and speaking. The first is listening. Students must listen attentively to get directions from the instructor, though this may be aided by some L1 explanations from fellow classmates with higher listening proficiency. Some of the supplemental games and warm-up activities also help students develop listening skills. During the production stage, the ELL students in charge of directing their film need to use listening skills to decide if a line of dialogue was clearly pronounced enough, or if another take is necessary for listeners to understand. Students will also listen to example films along the way, and perhaps listen to video tutorials about using editing software or other skills.

Not only does the receptive skill of listening play a role, but reading is also an integral part of filmmaking since students read directions, re-read the English script after they complete it, read it with the intention of memorization or performance in mind, and read the film pack or workbooks to discover project requirements. While focusing on specific reading strategies was not a major element of this particular film camp, reading practice is clearly present in filmmaking camps or after school classes. Students even have the opportunity to combine reading and listening comprehension through following the subtitles on the student films as they watch the end results.

Perhaps an even more strongly emphasized language skill in a film camp is writing. Students must begin by writing a well-plotted storyboard narrative, using visuals and text together to communicate meaning. Other stages of pre-production require script writing, including using grammar, dialogue, idioms, informal speech, and storytelling elements. Students in my camp wrote brief reflections about their film making and collaborative working experience. All of this writing had relevance to the project, and was more meaningful than simply making the students write for the practice. If given another few days to complete the project, I would have allotted more time for students to write character descriptions as well; writing for character development took a back seat.

Fourth, while a film camp may not use conversation in the same way a debate camp or other speaking-emphasis classes do, it still requires numerous conversations. Spoken interaction takes place from teacher to student, from student to teacher, and from student to student. Even though a finished EFL movie may not have thousands of words of spoken dialogue, a look behind the scenes reveals plenty of conversation used for clarification, problem solving, topic vetting, giving instructions, and other planning purposes. I made a conscious effort to stop lecturing at key points, and to let students discuss their projects. Much of the discussion was in English, with a switch to Korean taking place mainly for comprehension checks. Pronunciation and enunciation in the second language become more important when students have to be understood by multiple audiences, and English camps include speaking activities that can improve the actual film dialogue.

Second language students benefit from short film projects in other ways besides practicing the four language skills and message creation. Student creativity and autonomy come into play with character design, film genre selection, amount of dialogue used, locations for shooting, costume design, filming technique, directorial decision-making, post-production editing and use of special effects. The filmmaking process is outstanding for teaching to ELLs because it provides opportunities for behind-the-scenes creativity and design in addition to the end result that the public sees. From the beginning of camp, I emphasized that I was not the director; I was the producer—the money person, the negotiator with the "studio" (in this case, our high school), and the one keeping everything on a budgeted schedule. Students were the directors, camera operators, assistants, actors, concept designers, scriptwriters, costumers, and all the other roles they filled in various ways, sometimes with 2-3 different jobs per student. Learners needed to choose their roles and type of involvement in the project according to their talents and interests for it to provide a meaningful experience of creative freedom.

This selection of roles early in the project helps students feel more secure about their responsibilities and more aware of your expectations for them. EFL students will nearly always have different levels of comfort with speaking and writing, and even among native speakers, some teenagers will be less willing to place themselves in front of a recording camera than others. For each short film group, students were allowed a maximum of two members who were not participating as actors. Even with this behind-the-scenes crew option, most of the students chose to participate in the acting roles, but the more bashful students were relieved not to have to perform in front of a camera or classmates they barely knew. They were still active contributors to the group as cinematographers, scriptwriters, directors, and other roles. It may seem that these students missed out on the English learning opportunity, but the students still had to communicate with me about the project, listen to presentations in English about filmmaking methods, contribute to English games, and watch the final product in English along with students who did jump at the chance to be actors.

Depending on the ages and skill levels of the students, the responsibilities attached to each role may vary between camps. Directors in my camp served as important liaisons between their group and me, either asking me their questions directly or delegating the responsibility to other students. Elementary students might have less directorial power, while university students can be given more responsibility. Actors had the task of checking their own dialogue and scenes for errors and the weight of carrying the story. Camera operators or assistant directors sometimes switched between creative control and acting jobs.

Regardless of their film cast and crew roles, students all needed to learn the filmmaking process together so they could work more effectively towards the finished product; therefore, it's wise to take enough time on all the pre-production elements. A teacher who collaborated on a filmmaking project for ELLs writes, "Kim required the proper steps of planning, storyboarding, script writing, and, finally, viewing the iMovie tutorial. Sounds logical, but too often those essential ingredients are ignored by both teachers and students" (Anderson, 2002, 19).

Students and instructors naturally want to move to more interesting production stages, but the project moves more smoothly with attention to pre-production.

Providing general film topics for students to consider might keep them from thinking outside the box in this early stage, but it gives them a jumping off point if the topic suggestions stay non-specific (Appendix E). Students were given four broad topic ideas in my initial film camp, but I encouraged students early in the camp to choose their own theme if they wanted. This helped boost creativity because students are less limited by the teacher's ideas and imagination than if they have been told to choose only prescribed topics. I asked students to commit to a genre early on, but one group ended up changing their genre and topic on the second day when they saw the topic was not developing satisfactorily in the storyboard stage. Giving ideas to students can help them, but consider saving specific topic ideas for when students have spent too much time in indecision. This decision-making opportunity allows students to gain a deeper sense of ownership and control over the direction of their creative efforts. When thinking about vital pre-production steps, it is also important to ponder the technology used in short filmmaking.

Digital filmmaking obviously requires technology, and working with tech often brings complications and the need for troubleshooting. This is one reason that teachers shy away from giving students a filmmaking project: teachers' inexperience working with technology. A project like a summer film camp requires the teacher to have basic PowerPoint competence, general understanding of how to use a digital camera, a little familiarity with file types, and access to and willingness to spend a few minutes learning a free PC-based movie editing program (iMovie for Apple products and Windows Live Movie Maker for Windows operating systems). If a teacher is not an expert in all these areas, they should not dismiss the project idea completely though.

One method for overcoming nervousness about the technical side of overseeing a film course is to practice with the camera's video function and with video editing software. Instructors can create a sample movie, including storyboarding, script writing, filming, editing and production to acquaint them with the basics and have a better frame of reference when explaining to their students. The students will enjoy the teacher's finished work, and some will appreciate that the teachers underwent the process themselves. YouTube has numerous tutorials on how to use the intuitive editing software. Windows XP Movie Maker, the program on many Korean schools' computers, has features that netizens review more highly than the Windows 7 version of the software. Regardless of the version one has, Windows Movie Maker is a powerful, free, and user-friendly program.

Adding another layer of worry onto teachers who are already unsure about the technology is the looming concern about how to explain these details to students who seemingly have trouble responding to a simple imperative to raise their hands. How does a teacher communicate all of the instructions to students and still have time for them to make their movies? Having a film pack or camp workbook helps significantly improve student understanding and efficiency. It also helps to have groups of mixed or higher level proficiency students, but this isn't always in our control. Teachers do not have to know how to explain directions to every student; they only have to communicate the instructions to the highest level students and give them the responsibility of helping the others understand. This gives students some control and it also empowers them to help others learn and gain understanding of the materials.

While exploring these technologies, avoid getting so caught up in the bells and whistles that pedagogy is sacrificed. Hofer and Swan (2005) write in their "Digital Moviemaking and Pedagogy" article, "The danger starting with the technology, however, is that the use of technology can be separate from, and often incongruent with, typical classroom practice and lead to forced or contrived use in the classroom" (102). This danger they mention is a real concern in the English camp environment. Additionally, Heitink, Fisser, and McKenney (2012) quoted EFL teachers as saying, "Video recording gave so many extra points of attention that [we] tended to forget the content and language part of the activities" (1368). One teacher in their study overcame the problem by watching the students' videos as a class and asking critical questions to get students thinking about the films in new ways (Heitink, et al., 2012, 1368). In my particular camp, students did not have time to critically analyze their films, but students may be given more time for thinking about their finished work in future film camps.

Timeframes for camp length can vary widely. Teachers on the website Waygook.org talk about running film camps over the course of 3-15 days (Shhowse and Arsalan, 2012). Some NETs teach a semester-long course on short filmmaking, though the feverishly paced momentum present in camp seasons helps move the project along efficiently and keeps student interest fresh. An instructor might sacrifice a little finesse and polish by having a briefer camp, but that simply produces a different final look, not necessarily a worse one. Further teacher experimentation might be helpful for observing how the quality and depth of short films can change if the students have more time to bring the project into existence.

Typically, native English teachers do not contribute to the camp or after school schedule, but ideally each day can be a separate module rather than combining two modules. McKinney and Voogt (2011) ran a filmmaking course for elementary students, and according to their findings:

> It was more difficult for teachers to organize double-lessons than had been anticipated. And the start-up time and effort were deemed too great for lessons that picked up where a previous session had ended more than a day before. Single-lesson-sized chunks of 45 minutes worked best (713).

This 'one module per day' schedule may be hard for NETs to carry out, but it is something to consider if one is given scheduling leeway.

This high school's film camp schedule was broken down into seven daily units (Appendix C). Students spent the first day on introductions, chose groups, reviewed movie genres, and watched a few "viral videos," including a Korean student-made film. The second day was for studying storyboards, choosing a film topic, establishing group roles, and creating storyboards. The third day was a focused script-writing session that built on plotlines from the storyboards written a day earlier. Students needed far more teacher interaction this day while they were checking script dialogue and grammar. Changing the pace a little, the fourth day was a venture into basic filming techniques, camera angles, shot composition, plus sound and lighting tutorials. The fifth and sixth days (straddling a weekend) focused on primary filming and preliminary editing, and the seventh day was final editing and the film presentation event.

On paper, the film camp lasted a total of fourteen in-class hours, including time for explanations, ice breakers, English games, and warm-ups, but the number is slightly misleading. The time spent creating daily lesson materials added hours to the total. The time needed for completion may also vary per specific film. It was necessary to spend time outside of class toward the end of the camp to help one film crew edit their movie, since they had problems with file formats and compatibility. These particular students also spent an additional six to ten hours editing and filming bonus footage, or filming darkness-based scenes for their horror film. The investment paid off by the end of the camp. Lessons flowed more smoothly, final edits were cleaner, the award show worked well, and the students could focus on the joy of their creations instead of being distracted by problems caused by laziness.

This project was simplified logistically because high school students were the ones working and managing their time, as opposed to younger students. Leading such an activity with younger groups is possible, but it would be a different experience for teachers to step back and let students at those age levels explore their independence more. Having some prior awareness of the students' personalities and degree of responsibility helps too, though it is not necessarily a prerequisite. For the particular group of students with whom I was working, I had no qualms about sending them into the school grounds to film in an outdoor location while others went to a different floor of the school to film their interior shots. Other students might need more careful monitoring and supervision. These students knew how to operate their own cameras, had probably made short films on their own or in other classes, and could work responsibly within a time frame. Despite the students' responsible work habits, some aspects of collaboration added difficult variables to manage.

Unless the scheduling works out exactly according to plan, some groups will finish their assigned tasks sooner than other groups. When this happens in a sequential project, it can be difficult to keep the quicker students occupied productively. Keep some extra games planned on the side. Also, they might have to share cameras; some students will be filming while others will be waiting for their turn, or be unable to work with their movie data. Depending on the production stage, students can revise scripts, play English games, practice lines, experiment with camera techniques and filming angles, make bonus films that relate to their other interests, or talk about editing strategies. Whether or not students are sharing cameras, they should hold up a sign between takes identifying the movie project, scene number, and take number. My students used a laminated piece of paper as a low-cost whiteboard for keeping track of takes. This added task helps students stay organized and saves time at the editing stage.

Timing conflicts are not the only factors, since sound, lighting, and other technical problems may also arise. For example, some of the scenes in the finished films had poor audio, and the students did not find the problem in time to re-shoot. This issue was a limitation with the technology hardware, and maybe if camp had been longer or if I had been more experienced, the students could have worked with voice-overs, re-shoots, and other tools to improve the end result. The students realized this audio error before the movie screening day, and they were resourceful enough to include subtitles throughout their movie. Subtitles were so well received that I uploaded subtitles for the other two films. Is it the end of the world if the students' final film is not suitable for an art film festival? By no means. But depending on one's goals for the course, details like how well audiences can understand the dialogue could be part of a grading rubric.

Careful script review should also be done mid-project, including having the teacher check the progress students are making and comparing that progress to the camp goals; not enough time went into this aspect in this English film camp. Grammar errors in the students' dialogue were acceptable since the goal was emphasizing student-driven learning and creativity over perfection; however, one film had significantly less dialogue than the others, and was mostly special effects shots aside from two isolated scenes of dialogue and some 'silent film-esque' typed titles spliced between action scenes. The students had a successful learning experience though, and as researchers of EFL short film projects found, "A bad script didn't mean the students didn't learn anything [...]" (Heitink, et al, 2012, 1368). The students under observation went on to revise their script and re-shoot. It might be wise for NETs to set a minimum number of spoken lines. While this might feel limiting, it helps students develop a fleshed-out narrative more effectively.

Scheduling is important, but one must also consider the bottom line as a factor in planning a film camp. If you make some equipment and supply concessions, it is possible to offer a film camp at an extremely low cost. My school had no summer camp budget that year, so I decided to spend my own funds on camp supplies. Some schools do provide a budget for camps—others do not. In the latter case, one must decide if or how much to spend from one's own resources (Appendix D). Since students provided their own props and cameras, costs were minimal, only requiring a few large purchases like a tripod. Camera enthusiasts might already have this, though teachers should consider whether or not to let students borrow their camera equipment. Most students wore their school uniforms during filming, though some groups added costumes as needed. Having an extra spotlight was helpful, but the students survived poorly lit shots without it after it disappeared from the classroom (be sure to secure your film making supplies). Food on the last day of class is optional; having popcorn is a cheap option that lends a cultural aspect and movie theater feel to the event.

Considering the present digital age, it's not necessary to make DVD copies of the movies for students to access the finished content. Even so, I felt that students should have something tangible to take away from the project. If camps or classes allow for more time, and if the instructor has access to a DVD burner at the school, students could potentially be part of the DVD making process as well. I did not set aside enough time for this during camp, so the physical DVD of collected short films the students received several weeks later was more of a memento gift than a product they had crafted themselves. When making the final edit, I added a bonus movie encouraging them and praising their creative accomplishment.

A cautionary word: if instructors decide to teach this project to minors, they ought to be mindful of privacy. Some students asked that their films not be made public for all of YouTube, so I set the video uploads to "private"; they are accessible only with a URL. If students have no nametags on their uniforms, anonymity is slightly easier, though the students should have some sort of identification in their film credits. Should one decide to use a short film project, it's immensely helpful to have existing content to show students so they gain a general concept of project possibilities. It is helpful to have sample movies from other teachers when teaching a film project for the first time, and I'm grateful that NETs on Waygook.org openly shared their classes' films.

Review and pre-screen the student films apart from the group before debuting them at the awards show or another public venue, in the unlikely scenario that something problematic slipped through the editing cracks. It may be an obvious tip, but this scrutiny is particularly important if some of the filming takes place away from the teacher's supervision. One never knows what may have made it to the final cut, and it is better to spend the extra few minutes ahead of time and avoid problems or student embarrassment later. Whether the problem is a mispronounced line, a distracting noise or person in the background, bad lighting in a shot, or a wardrobe malfunction, it makes a huge difference to invest a few extra minutes of review.

While it's necessary to mention problems, highlighting the positive side of giving EFL students a chance to shine through short film making also merits some attention. Educational and personal benefits to EFL students participating in a film camp can be numerous. Among those benefits, students overcame their initial shyness, and several students mentioned their increased confidence on camp feedback sheets that they wrote after finishing their projects. Others may enjoy the discovery that they can collaborate and make friends with younger classmates; considering the Korean hierarchical system of social distance between grade levels, that is no minor discovery. Students will likely exhibit tremendous perseverance with the project, remaining excited about completing their projects and avoiding getting discouraged with small bumps in the road. In this 2011 camp, all three film crews overcame scheduling problems, technology failures, bouts of the giggles, and complications with trying to pronounce a second language clearly in front of a camera. With the exception of one group's last-minute editing, students all finished their projects in a timely way.

Relying on students' creativity led to successful results. All three groups completed films that had recognizable narrative elements. Each project had different strengths: one focused primarily on the main star's character development, one had clever special effects and suspense (for a horror parody, it is acceptable to omit character development), and the third had a good narrative structure, story framing, and witty interactions. If an instructor wanted to use a short film project in the context of graded work, it would be important to hold to certain criteria and develop an evaluative rubric, but for an inter-session camp, the variety in the projects and the different strengths they displayed far exceeded expectations. While all of their short films are imitative in nature (i.e., parodies), the students worked hard to let their own creative ideas permeate the scripts and final productions.

When students get the opportunity to create something, and the assignment catches their interest, one may be pleasantly surprised by the amount of time and energy the students are willing to invest in the project. Not only did these students subtitle and edit the films over the weekend without being prompted to do so, two of the three groups filmed bonus content or a bloopers reel to include in the final awards show. This proved to me that the ELLs were excited to use their talents, and they produced greater quality and quantity results by being more engaged in their schoolwork than they might have with a standard format language production assignment. Hofer and Swan (2005) report similar findings, saying:

> [One teacher] described a video in which his classroom of English language learners produced their own video tour of their school campus. He reported that the students were highly motivated and that the project spurred the students to further develop their language skills following the project (105).

Many students in this camp competed in a speech contest later in the year. Whether the seven days of movie camp contributed to that display of confidence cannot be measured, but some students mentioned increased confidence after attending film camp.

Remember the importance of taking a background role as a resource, producer, and facilitator; the people to empower are the students. As Anderson (2002) writes, "The teacher must give up control; it's hard, but needed for student success and experimentation" (19). The experiences above offer suggestions, but when the rubber meets the road, the students should be the ones in the driver's seat, not the teacher. It is of paramount importance for students to take responsibility and feel ownership of their projects. One way to help students apply the intangible lessons they learned to other subjects and areas of learning is to give them ample opportunities for reflection. Reflection helps reinforce the lessons, and teachers ought to emphasize reflective thinking during and after the process for students and for ourselves.

When I watch the short films and reflect on my students' responses, I am convinced that the benefits of this project outweigh the costs involved. The more NETs who engage students in these projects and inspire other teachers, the more instructors can give these students positive opportunities for growing as creative learners. Watching student-made videos is what led me to try the camp initially, but the creative joy and enthusiasm I saw in my own students is what prompted my interest in improving my methods and repeating the project in the future. Students can get lost in the commerce of education, but by teaching short film making camps in a second language, we can empower our students to pursue creative freedom and take over the wheel as they accelerate toward new learning opportunities.

Acknowledgements

Having access to tested classroom resources allows a teacher to step more confidently into unfamiliar territory. This was the case when I decided to embark on an English summer filmmaking camp for Korean public high school students. Several teachers collaborated to make and share resources, and much of the structure for the camp plus many of the materials in this presentation had their beginnings in teachers' collaborative dialogue.

I am indebted to whitespider (Kate Daivson), Brit_1 (Tim Eustace), and other contributors on Waygook.org for resources and lesson ideas that motivated me to carry out a filmmaking camp. My lessons and my students' final projects might not have come to pass if not for these teachers' generosity with their materials, expertise and EFL camp experiences. I hope my resources will aid readers who seek to help Korean EFL students be creative through film.

References

Anderson, M. A. (2002). The evolution of a curriculum: Yes, you can manage iMovies with 170 kids! *Multimedia Schools. 9*(4), 17-19.

Heitink, M., Fisser, P., & McKenney, S. (2012). Learning Literacy and Content Through Video Activities in Primary Education. In P. Resta (Ed.), Proceedings of Society for Information Technology & Teacher Education International Conference 2012, 1363-1369.

Hofer, M., & Owings Swan, K. (2005). Digital moviemaking— The harmonization of technology, pedagogy, and content. International Journal of Technology in Teaching and Learning. 1(2), 102-110.

McKenney, S., & Voogt, J. (2011). Facilitating digital video production in the language arts curriculum. Australian Journal of Educational Technology. 27(4), 709-726.

Shhowse & Arsalan. (2012, May 14). "Make a Movie Camp." Waygook.org. Messages posted to http://waygook.org/index.php/topic,2318

Appendix A – Film Pack Contents

One film pack (placed in folders by the teacher) was distributed to each group of students on the second day of film camp, and these packs contained the following project planning items.

    Camp cover page
- lists school name, camp theme, and dates of the camp

    Group roles sign-up sheet
- includes director, camera operator, assistant, and actors, with Korean translations

    Filming themes page
- gives students an idea of some topic or genre options

    Equipment checklist
- lists name tags, completed film pack, camera, battery, memory card, tripod, scripts, costumes, props, with Korean translations

    Costume and prop list
- for both categories, students write what they already have and what they still need

    Filming location sample
- consists of a map of school grounds in English

    Editing form
- includes students' directions for how to edit (if the teacher has to complete the editing)

Appendix B – Short Films/Clips Used in Film Camp

Since many of these clips are accessed through YouTube, and some may disappear from time to time, I created a playlist of EFL-friendly resource videos that were used in the 2011 Sorae High School English Camp. The playlist can be accessed at the following URL:
http://www.youtube.com/playlist?list=PL01DFB67B768176D1

Appendix C – Camp Schedule and Syllabus/Outline
Day 1: Orientation, and Introductions
Warm-ups, English games, Activities
- Introductions and make name tags.
- Icebreaker game.
- Daily 'silly songs'.
- Introduce theme.
- Review supplies.
- Learn film vocab.

Practice, and Production
- Learn film genres.
- Watch short films for ideas.
- Films: TBA.
- Brainstorm what students saw.

Follow up, Review, and Application
- Play a genre ID game.
- Decide team members.
- Design a team name and logo.

Key Terms
- Go viral.
- Make a movie.
- Popular culture.
- Our favorite.

Materials List
- Name tags. Videos.
- A4 paper.
- PPT Markers.
- Et cetera.

Day2: Storyboards

Warm-ups, English games, Activities
- Play '2 Truths and a Lie' icebreaker.
- Learn about storyboard-ing through video, and PPT.
- Film *For the Birds*.

Practice, and Production
- Explain boards.
- Groups make story-boards.
- Vote on best story-boards.
- Complete forms in film packs.

Follow up, Review, and Application
- Determine film roles for students.
- Submit decided roles to teacher.
- Reflect on the day's activities.

Key Terms
- Writer, actor. -Scene, enter,
- exit, screenplay.
- Director.
- Filmmaker.
- Cameraman.

Materials List
- Name Tags.
- Film packs.
- Game supplies/items.
- PPT. Pens/Pencils.

Day3: Script Writing, and Character Development
Warm-ups, English games, Activities
- Play 'chutes and marbles' game to build teamwork.
- Write a 'silly story', contrast with a real story.

Practice, and Production
- Work in teams to write screenplay.
- Discuss ideas or grammar.
- Watch short film samples.

Follow up, Review, and Application
- Play group English game or outdoor activity.
- Revise, and practice with film scripts.
- Compare scripts.

Key Terms
- We plan to…
- We will…
- INT(erior).
- EXT(erior).

Materials List
- Name Tags.
- Film packs.
- PPT.
- Pens/Pencils.
- Sample script(s).
- Game supplies.

Day 4: Light, Sound, Costumes, and Angles

Warm-ups, English games, Activities
- Play 'All my neighbors' to get students speaking.
- Work on scripts again to check grammar & vocab.

Practice, and Production
- Learn, and practice film methods by watching videos and PPT shows.
- Practice with actual cameras.
- Film rehearsal.

Follow up, Review, and Application
- Play quiz game to review filming angles.
- Plan costumes.
- Reflect on current progress.

Key Terms
- Panoramic sweep.
- Close up/widen.
- Point of view.
- Transition.
- Fade in/out.
- Emotion words.

Materials List
- Name Tags.
- Film packs.
- Game supplies/items.
- Laptop Cameras (for practicing).

Day 5: Filming
Warm-ups, English games, Activities
- Play 'Would you Rather' to practice speaking.
- Check equipment and review roles.

Practice, and Production
- Begin filming movie.
- Have 1 camera per student team.
- Play games during down time.

Follow up, Review, and Application
- Get next day's instructions.
- Write reflection of filming status if time allows.

Key Terms
- Lights, Camera.
- Action.
- Cut.
- That's a wrap!
- Take it from
- the top.

Materials List
- Name Tags.
- Film Packs.
- Cameras.
- Tripod(s).
- Memory Cards.
- Editing forms

Day 6: Filming, and Editing

Warm-ups, English games, Activities
- Play 'This Is a Fork' for focus.
- Practice speaking with warm-ups.
- Talk about PiFan (Bucheon film fest).

Practice, and Production
- Finish filming, reshoot takes as needed.
- Act in, film, and direct the movie.
- Watch Korean EFL short films.

Follow up, Review, and Application
- Edit films at school or give files to teacher.
- Groups submit editing form.
- Take group photo for DVD.

Key Terms
- Roll the credits.
- Flash cut.
- Inter cut.
- Back to
- Review earlier terms.

Materials List
- Name Tags.
- Laptop (demo).
- Cameras.
- Tripod(s).
- Group photos
- for DVD cover.

Day 7: Movie Scripting

Warm-ups, English games, Activities
- Sing 'silly songs'.
- Review key terms, and watch a warm- up video.

Practice, and Production
- Watch finished movies together.
- Have a party, and awards ceremony.

Follow up, Review, and Application
- Reflect on movies: what worked, what to change, give camp feedback.

Key Terms
- I enjoyed…
- I did not enjoy…
- I would change…

Materials List
- Completed films.
- Party food. (DVDs to be given out later).

Appendix D – Budget and Cost Details

Material	Description/Notes	Number Used	Cost (KRW)
Camera	Point and shoot digital cameras. Teacher brought one and a student from each group brought one.	4	Previously owned, no added expense
Tripod	Expensive, but an extremely helpful tool, and able to be used after completion of camp.	1	35,000
Lighting Aids	A purchased, battery-powered LED-lamp to overcome lighting problems.	1	15,000
Paper goods	Name tags, colored paper, copies, workbook folders and film packs.	School provided copies. Teacher bought colored paper, folders, and name tags.	25,000
Props	Costumes, items relevant to narrative, brought by students.	Varied by group, but all students used props.	Costs not borne by teacher
Snacks	Teacher bought snacks for a party.	Adjust to class size.	30,000
Student Rewards	Stickers, candy, U.S. coins, pencils, small writing tablets, foreign postage stamps, miscellaneous items.	Several awarded to each student daily.	30,000
DVDs	Blank DVDs for recording movies.	20	25,000
		Total Expenses	**160,000**

Appendix E – Movie Theme Ideas
Theme One: About School
Description
- A promotional film about school.

It Could Include
- Reasons to attend our school.
- Student or teacher interviews.
- Music, sports, classes, lunch.

It MUST Include
- [Our School Name] on location, speaking notes.

Length
- 5-10 minutes

Theme Two: Famous Story
Description
- Recreate a famous event from history.

It Could Include
Music (soundtrack), costumes, and historical settings.

It MUST Include
- Dialogue, character interactions, drama.

Length
- 5-10 minutes

Theme Three: K-Drama
Description
- Create a scene or story like a Korean Drama.

It Could Include
- Music (soundtrack), costumes or props, and a sad or funny theme.

It MUST Include
- Dialogue, character interactions, drama, storyline.

Length
- 5-10 minutes

Theme Four: Music Video
Description
- Make a music video.

It Could Include
- Lip syncing, dancing, or singing.
- Action relating to the story.
- Storytelling through music.

It MUST Include
- Scripted dialogue (This can fit in with the song's theme).

Length
- 3-6 minutes

Theme Five: Mystery/Suspense

Description
- Make a scary movie, but take it seriously.

It Could Include
- Special effects, fake blood, costumes, or a mystery.
- Detectives, supernatural creatures, or political people.

It MUST Include
- Dialogue, character interactions, sound effects, props.

Length
- 5-10 minutes

Theme Six: News Show

Description
- Weather report, or world or local news

It Could Include
- Business costumes and appropriate set.
- Serious or funny tone.

It MUST Include
- Dialogue, speaking roles, character interaction, news.

Length
- 5-10 minutes

Theme Seven: Parody

Description
- A short film to make fun of a famous movie or genre type.

It Could Include
- Scary movie concept.
- Sitcom concept.
- Action movie concept.
- Reality TV concept.

It MUST Include
- Dialogue, character interactions or voice-overs, subtitles, costumes, and props.

Length
- 5-10 minutes

Appendix F – Storyboard Sample

41. Getting Started with TESOL Research: Searching the Literature

Eric D. Reynolds

This paper is part of a larger series of articles that seeks to break the process of conducting research into manageable parts. Within this article some of the foundations of how a variety of processes are at play in research, and how they mirror some of the processes associated with writing. Looking specifically at the literature search process, distinction between the Korean environment and the environment from which many of have come, looking specifically at what 'can' be done with free, nearly free and available resources to create the best research that we can.

Introduction

One of the most important and pressing responsibilities both in my work with the graduate students in our MATESOL program and in my role as research special interest group facilitator for Korea TESOL is figuring out how to set novice researchers up for success. This work is intended as part of a longer project that attempts to break the act of conducting TESOL research into manageable steps. Obviously, as Confucius said, a journey "begins under one's feet," and in the case of the journey of a research project what is under our feet is previous research on the topic. The intent of this paper then is *not* research in its own right, but to offer a 'how to' for conducting a literature search, as a first step in a literature review for a research project. While novice researchers will likely gain the most from this article, it's my hope that more seasoned researchers will find many useful ideas, tips, and hints for improving their literature search.

The Writing Process

The steps in the process of research mirror the steps in the writing process in many ways. My first introduction to process writing was as an undergraduate English major in the 1980s. In my teaching of composition class we read Peter Elbow's (1981) *Writing with Power*. For me, it was mind blowing. Like most in my generation, the standard teaching methodology for the process of composing essays I received had been to:

- construct an outline
- to match the specific genre (comparison and contrast, informative, persuasive, and so on)
- then write the paper and
- finally to turn it in.

However in actual practice, we only received limited instruction on creating outlines. Moreover, for the vast majority of papers I turned in, the only significant feedback I received was corrective feedback on the final draft. Of course, volume and quality of that feedback varied greatly between my individual English teachers. However, here is the 'kicker', I like many of my peers often tossed my returned papers in a folder (or the trash) after checking my grade without reviewing the detailed comments and edits from those teachers who did take the time and care to give extensive feedback.

The preceding anecdote well illustrates the most important thing that I learned in that undergraduate teaching of composition course: teaching through a process writing approach not only increases the students' writing abilities, but it also greatly increases the potential for the instructors feedback on writing to have direct and greater impact on both the students' writing process and their writing products (Paulus, 1999; Tuzi, 2004; Lee, 2011). That kernel of knowledge brings us back to the intent of this article. While the process of writing in general, me errors the process of conducting a research project, the research process is more complex–and often more chaotic! Obviously, this increasing complexity is due to the fact that in addition to 'just writing', researchers need to engage in a number of other activities/products, in roughly this order: search and survey the literature in the field, write the literature review and posit their research questions, design methodology and research instruments to study those research questions, collect and analyze the data generated, write the results and conclusions, and weave the entire research project into a coherent manuscript. A cursory glance over these activities/products reveals two major points of written composition–the literature review and the discussion section–however, each and every stage in the process of conducting a research project involves some level of writing, whether taking notes during a literature survey (Rempel, 2010; Crowley, 2007), designing, drafting, and finalizing research instruments (Creswell, 2008), or making scratchings and field notes while collecting data (Emerson, Fretz, & Shaw, 1995). Ultimately, just as writing is integral to each step of the research process, and understanding of process is integral to the successful completion of a research product.

What is a Literature Search?
Aside from the passion for a particular topic that provides the impetus for beginning, the first step in a research project is usually a survey of the literature in the field. The two specific activities in this step of the research project that are the focus of this paper are literature search and reference/citation management. While most academic writers are intimately familiar with the process of a literature review, it's important for me to pull out the notion of 'literature search' from the overall literature review process. The operational definition of literature search for this paper is the act of accessing the Internet, particularly Google search and library databases, which has

become the ubiquitous source of academic research in the 21st-century. For novice researchers and those who have been away from academic research for even a year or two, the most effective – and *cost*-efficient – tools for literature search may be thoroughly new and unfamiliar. Thus, the primary purpose of this article is to introduce tools available for novice researchers and those returning to research after a temporary hiatus, and to offer tips and how-to advice for the use and implementation of these software tools.

Literature Search 'How to'

One impetus to start this project is how little attention the topic of literature search received in the literature. While a research project as opposed to this how-to article, would have inspired me to a more thorough literature search, the fact is I was not able to come up with a single research article focused specifically on the literature search as an element of second language academic writing. Neither through a cursory Google scholar (GS) search, nor through a review of the extensive selected bibliographies of 'recent scholarship in L2 academic writing' Tony Silva and colleagues at the *Journal of Second Language Writing* (cf. Silva & McMartin-Miller, 2012; 2011; Silva & Paiz, 2012) was I able to find a single article focused on the issue. My goal in this section is to offer some practical advice on how to conduct your literature search in the Korean environment. If you're a Korean reader who grew up here and attended a Korean university, you may well know more about this process than I do and will explain in this paper, but perhaps you will find some useful tips. If however, your educational background is in a North American or European country, you may be quite surprised in the substantive differences in access as you begin your literature search. The section is broken into four parts: Welcome to Korea!, using Google, integrating Google with your database access, and leveraging community to improve your literature review.

Welcome to Korea!

While the phrase is a bit tongue in cheek, my purpose in "Welcoming" you to Korea is to point out some of the systemic difficulties and differences that I have faced–and you may face– in conducting a literature search in Korean. In relating my stories, I will also offer the ways that I have worked through the problems in hopes that my solutions may serve to address some of the issues that you will run into. Indeed, in terms of my ability to search through the literature in our field, the transition from being graduate student and a big American university, the University of Illinois at Urbana-Champaign (UIUC), to being at a much smaller Korean university, Woosong University in Daejeon, was more than a little disheartening. Admittedly, UIUC is one of the most wired universities in the United States , and indeed in the entire world (Rhey, 2006) and Woosong is "just" a regional institution, so the comparison is hardly fair. Simultaneously, my frustration in moving from a palace of technology to the backwoods of the academic connectivity was palpable. Let me review some differences that you might notice in your institutions.

While a PhD student, whenever I accessed an academic database or even GS, my web browser communicated directly the University of Illinois from wherever I was hooked up to the Internet. Then through an authentication process that calls itself 'Shibboleth' recognized me as an active student and entitled to access the databases that the university has purchased. The process was seamless, like hand in glove. That is how easy start a literature search when you are a member of the technological 'haves'. At Woosong, however, conducting literature searches for my projects requires
the navigation of a variety of obstacles, particularly language, limitations to access. The first one, language, is my fault. Unsurprisingly, most of the library's resources are for Korean

faculty and students and therefore are not in English. Similarly, while some of the faculty do access the international journals in English, our university is a regional school, not a national flagship university, so the pressure to publish the results of our research in internationally recognized, read 'English Language', journals is not as high as the pressure at the upper echelons of academia. Moreover, the staff at our university library is working primarily to serve their primary customers: Koreans. Consequently, no library staff have been selected for English proficiency, or assigned to assist the international faculty in English.

The second problem that threaten to stymie my efforts at literature search probably has less to do with the differences between Korea and the United States than it has to do with the difference between small programs at small, young universities and large programs at large, established universities: a general lack of resources. Our MATESOL program is very well known and established in Korea, so by local standards we are fairly well. Relative to international standards we are a step or two down the ladder from institutions with truly international reputations. Consequently, our faculty works hard to share what resources we have and build our own access. One big project over the years has been creating our own library and writing center. Unlike the US, Canadian, and Australian institutions our faculty members are familiar with, Woosong does not appear to have long term plans for the acquisition of such resources and renewal of them as their value depreciates–academic journals and reference works depreciate only slightly more slowly than our computers. Thus, our program took it upon ourselves to submit 'case-by-case' requests for funding for books for the library as well as computer hardware and software. While a long-term plan to manage our library is definitely needed, we created in-house a useful, albeit tiny, version of the sort of palace

I recall the UIUC library being. Moreover, the faculty placed in the library–and carefully marked as 'on loan' – their own resources including copies of the journals from the professional organizations to which they belong, textbooks they purchased with their own funds, and even photocopies of seminal articles from their own academic careers. In all of these materials have been catalogued into a library database, come and where possible within copyright restrictions, they have also been digitized.

Another issue connected to the lack of resources is again an issue of funding:
> In a world where subscriptions to some medical journals can cost more than $10,000 a year, and many colleges in developing countries cannot afford more than a handful of scholarly publications (Schmidt, 2010).

As you may well know, there is a major debate within academia regarding the profit motive associated with academic journals resulting in what John Willinsky of Stanford's Public Knowledge Project (2012). <http://pkp.sfu.ca/>. At the root of this "open" movement (open source/open access/open journal) is an issue that requires critical attention: the differential access to academic publishing available to people in "have nations" versus those in the "have not nations." While not the central point of this article, I can viscerally feel the handicaps associated with conducting research as a faculty and researcher at a globally middle level institution versus my previous status at a, globally-speaking, upper echelon university. Fortunately, our administration has supported efforts campus-wide to increase our faculty access to international databases. Moreover, in a completely coincidental stroke of good luck, one of the staff from campus' main library joined our MATESOL program as a student. Upon discovering her connections, we were able to work closely with her in making the most of what *was* available, as well as using her expertise to access online services and even received a bit of free faculty training. While these three obstacles–language barriers, lack of local resources, lack of access to international journals– have hampered our ability to do our research work in the program, we have done just about as well as we could with the available resources, and have found plenty of ways to expand our opportunities which will be addressed in the following sections.

Google: Something Everybody Learns How to Use, but *Not* at School

If you had not noticed, one of the harsh realities of academic research is money—the 'haves' versus the 'have nots'. Thank goodness for the anarchy of the Internet! Of course, Internet access is not entirely free, and I have worked at universities in the Third World that have no Internet access. The relative difference in cost for Internet access versus the cost of creating a physical rather than virtual library, or purchasing access to academic journals through individual memberships or academic databases, as to make the cost of Internet access nearly free. Google, too, is free to the user, because it is supported entirely by advertisements. While the youngest of the readers of this journal will have grown up in a Google world, we should note that Google arose from the Stanford Integrated Digital Library Project to "develop the enabling technologies for a single, integrated 'virtual' *library*" (Berry, 1996, 26; italic emphasis added). Moreover, Google is not yet 20 years old (Brin & Page, 1998). Indeed, the ubiquity of the explosion of Google into our lives means that we have lived with Google as a verb almost as long as we have with Google itself (McFedries, 2003).

However, any teacher that assigns writing tasks assignments knows that the original Google has severe limitations for academic writing and literature search--the most often noted weakness is the preference for popular rather than rigorous sources. Consequently, "specialist, in-depth information required by academic users" (Taylor, 2007, 4) was still relegated to traditional libraries and databases, that is, until GS came along in 2004. While I am not entirely certain what an algorithm is, Google assures us that the GS algorithms work to filter out much of the less rigorous research from commercial interests, non-academic groups and organizations, and dreaded bloggers. However, as many of my students have found, when your database has not purchased access to the article you want, you often meet a screen that allows you to purchase the article, but at prices few of us can afford–generally in the range of 30-50 US dollars per article. As a point of reference, my reference page for this article has about 20 references so far, which at the high-end rate would amount to $1000! [Don't worry! I have not paid a penny, yet.] GS provides a partial workaround, because it often returns multiple links for the individual documents it finds, some free and some not, whereas your library-based database searches can only provide access through their individual databases. Ultimately, I advise my students and colleagues to use GS first for four basic reasons: GS offers a more thorough review of all of the information available on the Internet, the filter out the 'rash' well enough, multiple links are often returned for each source and yes, GS is free.

Discovering Your Institution's Database Access

While GS is certainly my initial recommendation to students and colleagues, I always encourage students to use whatever traditional academic databases to which they have access. If you work in a public school or a private institution, then you may find have no paid database access whatsoever. If however, you work in a university, you may be pleasantly surprised at what has been hiding right under your nose. A number of reasons support this plan of action: Sources from traditional databases are more likely to meet the rigorous standards of academic research, some sources are only available through traditional databases, Korean language sources are often not accessible through GS, and in those cases where GS can provide free access, you may determine that your university has purchased access for that source.

While it may be a professional conceit among librarians, few would disagree that some truth lies in suggestion that Google, in particular, but GS as well, "might not, perhaps, be the best source of information in a particular field" (Taylor, 2007, 4). GS does return links to non-academic sources. Moreover, GS still relies on the popularity of the source as part of its search, instead of relying solely on the applicability to the search terms. Academic databases on the other hand rely heavily on keyword searches in particular terms that have been inserted by the authors and managers of the database. Consequently, we have good cause to believe that such databases will return superior results in terms of the quality of the sources. So, learning how to use the databases to which your university has access can be tremendously important. If, like me, your Korean is not very good at all, and, like Woosong University, your university does not or cannot provide much English language assistance it behooves you to call in some favors of your bilingual friends.

The first step is just to go to the library, and start asking questions. If you have not already found out the web address of your library's website, make sure you get it. Work with your bilingual friends to poke around on the site and try to find the page that links up to databases—one tip is that the letters 'DB' may be used to indicate the database in either the link address, or the linked text itself—a bit of Konglish. Our library separates the databases between internal, Korean databases (국내학술DB) and international databases (해외학술DB). Accessing both types of databases can actually be quite useful for you in your research, particularly if you were research is focusing on the Korean environment. When using Google scholar to find resources, Korean journals appear much less often in the list returned than Western journals. However, a great deal of the research conducted about ESL in Korea in submitting published in Korean journals. Some of that is published in Korean, but a good portion of the articles in Korean EFL journals are indeed written in English. Consequently, you may be missing out on some of the better research in our field by not looking in Korean databases. As far as the international databases are concerned, and again my experience is limited to Woosong, access to databases through our library link directly to the same databases you're familiar with when working at Western universities. One unfortunate reality of the database profit earning system became clear through the level of access we have at Woosong. Many databases are a not single monolithic service, rather they are broken up and sold as individual packages. This can be good or bad news for you. On the bad side, your University may not have access to the package that most closely matches your field of study. For example, we have a strong business program, so we have the business package from JSTOR, but not the linguistics package or the education package–so no TESOL Quarterly. On the good side, a smaller, and therefore cheaper, package specific to the research interests most closely related to TESOL may prove easier to acquire finding for. In spite of such disappointments, we often meet happy surprises. We do have access to the Web of Knowledge, Emerald, EBSCO, and Science Direct. That access lets us retrieve articles from several good journals from our field including *System*, *Teaching and Teacher Education*, the *Journal of English for Academic Purposes*, *World Englishes*, the *Journal of Second Language Writing*, and others;

however, as you can see, we do not have access to some of the biggest journals in the field.

Leveraging Community for Access

For the students and faculty in our program this final point has proven to be the most important. Simply put, we return to the money issue: Institutional support for academic research is substantially less than what is common in North American universities. So how do you fix that problem? The same way you did as a student: community. As mentioned above, we pooled our resources, so that each of us knew about the resources each of us had individually acquired, and added them to a web accessible database available on the university intranet. Also as mentioned above, we encouraged a student who worked in the library to arrange a tour of the resources available there. In classes students were encouraged to collaborate and share resources. Students who have friends enrolled in "big" western university with more complete Internet access have been able to use those contacts for access. I hope this sounds like normal "collegiality" to you: it should. Our goal was to take the community to another level, to leverage what we had. Using the programs Moodle we made great strides in building that community. In addition, students and faculty have been able to inter-connect our community with other communities, using their places of work and their external professional communities (like KOTESOL) as additional as resources. Social media like Facebook have proven useful access points for materials and information.

Most importantly, the use of community helps support the sorts of divergent thinking that only communities are capable of doing. In other words, technology generally does what we tell it too, it does what it is designed to do. Community however works to find the best solution to mutual problems. When we go to our friends and colleagues and explain what we are doing the problems we have and what we need to get, they are likely to say, 'Let's try this' and introduce you to something new as they are to stick with something that does not work well. This is how we become aware of new techniques and software advances. Because the landscape of online literature searches is changing so rapidly, normal academic publishing channels struggle and often fail to keep pace. Indeed, this article is likely to seem out of date by the time you are reading it. A virtuous cycle of community interaction seems the best medicine for keeping pace in this rapidly changing and highly competitive area.

Conclusion

If you are new to academic research, you will face a learning curve in doing your literature search. If are experienced at research but have stepped away for even a very short while, the tools available to you have improved and changed, and you will find some newer and better ones. Remember that this is a process, much like the writing process, but with more stages, different elements, ore complexity and often a touch of chaos. My first advice is the Google Scholar is a great tool for the price, making it your go-to starting point is not a bad choice. However, traditional databases and libraries offer advantages that Google cannot yet match. Integrating traditional (paid) library sources with brand new (free) sources is a great plan. Also, Korea has not caught up to the level of access that you may have found if you had the chance to work at one of the "palaces" in the western, but do not let that discourage you. By leveraging your community for the maximum access that is possibly available, you can conduct a world-class literature search that will meet the most rigorous standards.

References

Berry, J. W. (1996). Digital libraries: new initiatives with worldwide implications. *Collection Building*, 15(4), 21–33. doi:10.1108/01604959610150094

Brin, S., & Page, L. (1998). The anatomy of a large-scale hypertextual Web search engine. *Computer Networks and ISDN Systems* (107–117). Elsevier Science Publishers B. V.

Burns, A. (2009). *Doing Action Research in English Language Teaching: A Guide for Practitioners*. New York: Routledge.

Creswell, J. W. (2008). *Research Design: Qualitative, Quantitative, and Mixed Methods Approaches* (3rd ed.). Thousand Oaks, CA: Sage Publications, Inc.

Crowley, K. (2007). The literature review – Not sinking, writing. In C. Denholm and T. Evans, *Supervising Doctorates Downunder: Keys to Effective Supervision in Australia & N Z*. (208-214). Camberwell, Victoria: ACER Press.

Elbow, P. (1981). *Writing With Power: Techniques for Mastering the Writing Process*. New York: Oxford University Press.

Emerson, R. M., Fretz, R. I., & Shaw, L. L. (1995). *Writing Ethnographic Fieldnotes*. Chicago: University of Chicago Press.

Holland, M. (2012). Reference management software for students, researchers and academics. *Journal of Paramedic Practice*, 4(8), 484–487.

Kern, M. K., & Hensley, M. K. (2011). Citation management software. *Reference & User Services Quarterly*, 50(3), 204–208.

Lee, I. (2011). Working smarter, not working harder: Revisiting teacher feedback in the L2 writing classroom. *Canadian Modern Language Review/ La Revue canadienne des langues vivantes*, 67(3), 377–399. doi:10.3138/cmlr.67.3.377

Machi, L. A., & McEvoy, B. T. (2008). *The Literature Review: Six Steps to Success*. Thousand Oaks, CA: Corwin Press.

McFedries, P. (2003). Google this. *IEEE Spectrum*, 40(2), 68. doi:10.1109/MSPEC.2003.1176520

Paulus, T. M. (1999). The effect of peer and teacher feedback on student writing. *Journal of Second Language Writing, 8*(3), 265–289. doi:10.1016/S1060- 3743(99)80117-9

Rempel, H. G. (2010). A longitudinal assessment of graduate student research behavior and the impact of attending a library literature review workshop. *College & Research Libraries, 71*(6), 532–547.

Rhey, E. (2006). Top 20 wired colleges. *PCMAG*. Retrieved from http://www.pcmag.com/article2/0,2817,2073400,00.asp.

Ridley, D. (2012). *The Literature Review: A Step-by-Step Guide for Students* (2nd ed.). Thousand Oaks, CA: Sage Publications Ltd.

Schmidt, P. (2010, February 14). New journals, free online, let scholars speak out. *The Chronicle of Higher Education*. Retrieved from http://chronicle.com/article/Open-Access-Journals-Break-/64143

Silva, T., & McMartin-Miller, C. (2011). Selected bibliography of recent scholarship in second language writing, *20*, 306–311.

Silva, T., & McMartin-Miller, C. (2012). Selected bibliography of recent scholarship in second language writing, *21*, 76–80.

Silva, T., & Paiz, J. M. (2012). Selected bibliography of recent scholarship in second language writing, *21*, 181–186.

Taylor, S. (2007). Google Scholar – friend or foe? *Interlending & Document Supply, 35*(1), 4–6. doi:10.1108/02641610710728122

Tuzi, F. (2004). The impact of e-feedback on the revisions of L2 writers in an academic writing course. *Computers and Composition, 21*(2), 217–235. doi:10.1016/j.compcom.2004.02.003

About the Book

2017 marks the tenth anniversary of the first issue of *TESOL Interfaces*, the online journal of the graduate School of TESOL-MALL at Woosong University in the Republic of Korea. For this very special occasion, we are releasing a compendium of these journal articles in print form, covering selected articles from volumes 1 through 6 (years 2007 to 2012).

About the Editor

David Kent is an assistant professor at the graduate school of TESOL-MALL at Woosong University in the Republic of Korea. He has been working and teaching in Korea since 1995, and with a doctorate specializing in education from Curtin University in Australia, he is a specialist in computer assisted language learning (CALL) and the teaching of English to speakers of other languages (TESOL). He has presented at international conferences, as well as published a number of peer-reviewed journal articles, books, and book chapters in his areas of expertise.